LIFE SPACE
&
ECONOMIC SPACE

LIFE SPACE
&
ECONOMIC SPACE

Essays in Third World Planning

John Friedmann

Routledge
Taylor & Francis Group

LONDON AND NEW YORK

First published 1988 by Transaction Publishers

2 Park Square, Milton Park, Abingdon, Oxfordshire OX14 4RN
605 Third Avenue, New York, NY 10017

Routledge is an imprint of the Taylor & Francis Group, an informa business

First issued in paperback 2020

Library of Congress Catalog Number: 87-19443

Library of Congress Cataloging-in-Publication Data

Friedmann, John
    Life space and economic space.

    Includes index.
    ISBN 0-7658-0942-7 (alk. paper)
        1. Regional planning—Developing countries. 2. Space in economics.
3. Urbanization—Developing countries. 4. Rural development—Developing countries. I. Title.
HT395.D44F75   1987   338.9'009172'4   87-19443
ISBN 0-88738-201-0

ISBN 13: 978-0-7658-0942-1 (pbk)
ISBN 13: 978-0-88738-201-7 (hbk)

Contents

Acknowledgements

Chapter 1. Reprinted from Hedrick Folmer and Jan Oosterhaven, eds., *Spatial Inequalities and Regional Development*. Boston: Martin Nijhoff Publishing, 1979, 23–45. With permission of the publisher.

Chapter 2. Reprinted from *Development and Change*, 10, 1 (January 1979), 125–176. With permission of Sage Publications.

Chapter 3. Reprinted from *International Journal of Urban and Regional Research*, 6, 3 (September 1982), 309–344. With permission of Edward Arnold (Publishers) Limited.

Chapter 4. Reprinted from Dudley Seers and Kjell Öström, eds., *The Crisis of European Regions*. London: The Macmillian Press, Limited, 1983, 148–162. With permission of the publishers.

Chapter 5. Reprinted from *Comparative Urban and Community Research*, 1, 1 (1987). With permission of Transaction Publishers.

Chapter 6. Reprinted from *Development and Change*, 4, 3 (1972–3), 12–51. With permission of Sage Publications.

Chapter 7. Reprinted from R. P. Misra, ed., *Humanizing Development. Essays on People, Space, and Development in Honour of Masahiko Honjo*. Singapore: Maruzen Asia, 1981, pp. 143–160. With permission of the editor.

Chapter 8. Reprinted from *Economic Development and Cultural Change*, 29, 2 (January 1981), 235–262. With permission of the University of Chicago Press.

Chapter 9. Reprinted from *Environment and Planning D: Society and Space*, 3 (1985), 155–167. With permission of Pion Ltd.

Chapter 11. Reprinted from *Overland* (Sydney, New South Wales), 104 (September 1986), 5–11. With permission of the editor.

Preface

With a single exception, all essays in this volume were written within the last ten years; four date since 1985; and one is published here for the first time. Their subject is the planning of development in the Third World—the strategies that should be chosen to propel national economies from poverty to wealth, from dependency to autonomy, and from tyranny to open democracy.

In contrast to most writings on development, these essays are written from a spatial perspective. Sometimes the relevant space is global, as in the discussion of "world cities." At other times, the issue is a national space, as in the essay on strategies of crisis management, where I take a critical look at a proposed employment strategy for the Philippines. More often, the focus is on regional and even local space, for instance when I talk about contradictions between city and countryside, the barrio economy of Latin American cities, or agropolitan development in rural Asia. A spatial focus is fundamental for decision making at all levels. Private firms must locate production facilities at specific sites as well as organize area-specific markets, while governments must decide on territorial policies: whether to import or produce domestically, how to cope with what has been called the urban transition, how to promote development in rural areas, where to make public infrastructure investments, how to maintain some sort of regional balance in development, and how much autonomy to allow to subsidiary provincial and local governments in the areal division of powers. Space thus appears to be a basic variable for understanding development historically and for devising public policies.

Apart from the four hierarchical levels of spatial organization and decision making already mentioned—global, national, regional, and local—I draw a basic distinction between economic and territorial space. The tradition of economic spatial analysis extends back to Heinrich von Thünen, a nineteenth-century German agronomist who first discovered the mediating role of transport costs to markets as a key variable in the spatial patterning of agricultural production. Other scholars followed: location theorists like Alfred Weber, geographers like Walter Christaller and Brian Berry, economists like August Lösch, Walter Isard, and François Perroux. The space with which these scholars were concerned was a result of market forces—supply and demand relationships mediated by economic distance. In every case, their criterion for normative order was efficiency in both production and distribution from the perspective of the firm. The result was an unbounded, infinite (though structured) space. In fact, in the economics of space, boundaries exert an effect similar to distance; they are a means of artificially enhancing the friction of distance. The implication for public policy is that the task of governments is a residual one, concerned primarily with reducing the friction of space by lowering or abolishing tariffs, building transport links in support of private investments, and so forth.

In contradistinction to economic space is a politically organized or territorial space, bounded by customs or laws limiting the powers of political units from the nation-state on down to local governments and households. Territorial space is fundamental for the life of political communities. It has historical continuity and a name that for its inhabitants symbolizes both a landscape and a distinctive way of life. Territorial space is always particular.

The conflict-ridden intersection of these two spaces—the one driven by profits, the other by politics, and both driven by the need to survive—is a theme common to all of these essays. And because I see the conflict between them as essentially uneven—capital being mobile over increasingly vaster distances, while territorial units are rooted in place (though in imperialistic fashion they can sometimes extend their power across frontiers)—and because it is a conflict over autonomy of action, I tend to favor territorial approaches to development that will strengthen territorial relations and resistance to domination from without by capital.

The essays collected here have yet another characteristic in common. Except for chapter 6, all of them are written under the sign of crisis and impending dissolution. They reflect or respond to a widely held perception that the old order of things is crumbling all around us, so that answers derived from traditional models of the world are either irrelevant or, worse, counterproductive. This perception is not limited to this or that aspect of economics, politics, or system of belief. Though spatially differentiated, with different manifestations in different parts of the world, it is a total and pervasive crisis. A condition of crisis with these dimensions has no single cause; it is overdetermined. Because of the structural complexity of the crisis, we fail to see clearly how we might extricate ourselves and resume a course that represents at least a semblance of orderly movement toward solving some of the most urgent problems on the world agenda: fear of physical devastation, fear of hunger and destitution, and fear of the arbitrary power of the state to deprive citizens of their most elemental rights.

The present generation no longer holds faith with linear progress, nor with its twentieth-century counterpart, the marvellous "take-off" into cumulative growth and the rainbow of a consumer society conjured up for us by Professor Walt Rostow less than thirty years ago and now all but forgotten. Throughout much of the world, ordinary people have found the strength to resist within their own communities and households, in country villages as well as in the barrios of large cities, where they are struggling for survival with human dignity under their own forms of democratic governance. They have grown increasingly skeptical of grand solutions, and particularly of solutions promised by the state, which more often than not seem to abort in disaster. It is to this elementary politics of the barrio that I dedicate these essays in the hope—and I confess it is nothing more than hope—that from these rudimentary beginnings will in due course emerge a resourceful and energetic democratic movement with the political vision to construct a new order in which livelihood, the object of economics, will be subordinated to the broader and more encompassing values of life itself.

Notes

1. Territorial relations encompass class relations. To make territory the opposite of capital, as I have done here, emphasizes the need for political alliances across class, ethnicity, and gender differences and posits a common ground between them.

Part I
URBANIZATION IN THE GLOBAL ECONOMY

1

On the Contradictions Between City and Countryside

The bourgeoisie has subjected the country to the rule of towns. It has created enormous cities, has greatly increased the urban population as compared with the rural, and has thus rescued a considerable part of the population from the idiocy of rural life. Just as it has made the country dependent on the towns, so it has made barbarian and semi-barbarian countries dependent on the civilized ones, nations of peasants on nations of bourgeois, the East on the West (Karl Marx and Friedrich Engels, Manifesto of the Communist Party).

This essay was originally written and presented at a conference in 1977. The reference date is of some significance. For many of us, the mid-seventies were characterized by two intellectual events. The first was the rediscovery of the importance of agricultural, more particularly of rural, development in the field of Third World policy studies. Agriculture, of course, had always been the point of departure in the macro-economics of capitalist development, where it was identified with low-productivity labor and traditional cultural practices. An urban-based industrialization would put an end to all of that in due course. But even though the so-called newly industrializing countries were forging ahead at rates of 5 to 15 percent a year in the increased value of their industrial product, poverty was not being significantly diminished. Indeed, in many countries the evidence pointed in the other direction. Poverty was increasing not only in relative but in absolute terms. This called for remedial measures. It also shifted the rural economy back into the limelight of policy discussions.

The second event was the rediscovery of the Western Marxist tradition of scholarship. This process of rediscovery had actually begun in France a decade earlier, but by the early seventies it had spread to the United States and alert scholars proceeded to educate themselves in the new literature. I was part of a generation that came under the sway of these exciting new teachings that included such central terms as social class, class conflict, contradiction, mode of production, and dialectics. In particular, I was taken with the dialectical mode of thinking, which I found to be congenial.

In my version of dialectical thinking—and several versions are conceivable—opposite but conflicting social forces form a unity. Life is filled with these conflicts; indeed, I would argue, as have others, that when conflict ceases, life also ceases. Harmonious integration— the equilibrium state so dear to neoclassical economists—exists only as a limiting condition. Most Western social scientists find it difficult to work in this mode. When there is conflict, they argue, it must be "resolved." Indeed, conflict is seen as "dysfunctional" to the human enterprise. Unsurprisingly, they found my introduction of the dialectical mode a hard pill to swallow.

In the essay here reprinted, I talked about the conflict between "territory" and "function," or what I would later call (see chapter 4 below) life space and economic space. I tried carefully to spell out the meanings of these terms. Arguing for their universality, I called the conflict between them a "cosmic" conflict. A conflict or contradiction of this sort is one that, no matter how hard we try, refused to go away. During the nineteenth century, for instance, local and regional territorialism, as in pre-Bismarckian Germany, was shifted to the next level of spatial integration: the nation-state. Today, the struggle has shifted once again, this time to the global scale. Contrary to the dreams of some ideologues, however, the transnational corporation and the transnational bank will not become the new units of world integration. Indeed, in response to the drive for the totalization of the functional mode of integration, we are seeing the pendulum swing back to a renewed assertion of territorial power grounded in civil society and politics.

This theme—the continuing struggle for territorial identity and political autonomy—runs through this book. It is the thread that ties my arguments together. In the following essay, I use the imagery of city and countryside to illustrate my theme. But, as we shall see, there are other levels of analysis where this conflict is being enacted.

The *locus classicus* on the question of rural-urban relations is *The German Ideology* (Marx and Engels). Because it sets forth the essential themes to be developed here, it will be useful to quote the pertinent passage *in extenso:*

> The existence of the town implies, at the same time, the necessity of administration, police, taxes, etc.; in short, of the municipality, and thus of politics in general. Here first became manifest the division of the

population into two great classes, which is directly based on the division of labour and on the instruments of production. The town already is in actual fact the conception of the population, of the instruments of production, of capital, of pleasures, of needs, while the country demonstrates just the opposite fact, isolation and separation. The antagonism between town and country can only exist within the framework of private property. It is the most crass expression of the subjection of the individual under the division of labour, under a definite activity forced upon him—a subjection which makes one man into a restricted town-animal, the other into a restricted country-animal, and daily creates anew the conflict between their interests. Labour is here again the chief thing, power *over* individuals, and as long as the latter exists, private property must exist. The abolition of the antagonism between town and country is one of the first conditions of communal life, a condition which again depends on a mass of material premises and which cannot be fulfilled by the mere will, as anyone can see at first glance . . . The separation of town and country can also be understood as the separation of capital and landed property, as the beginning of the existence and development of capital independent of landed property—the beginning of property having its basis only in labour and exchange (Marx and Engels 1970, p. 69).

In this famous passage, Marx and Engels refer to the 'antagonism' between town and countryside, tracing the conflict to the spatial division of labor. But only a year or two later, in the *Communist Manifesto,* they wrote about the 'gradual abolition of the distinction between town and country'. And to confuse matters still further, a footnote in the English translation of this work reminds us that 'in the German edition of 1848, the word "distinction" reads "antithesis" ' (Marx and Engels 1975, p. 60).

Now antagonism, distinction, antithesis, and contradiction—this last term being currently in vogue—are clearly not synonymous; each conveys a different theoretical meaning. Because clarification of this central concept is essential to my task, 'contradiction' is made the subject of an extended theoretical inquiry in Section 1. This is followed, in Section 2, by an examination of the nature of the contradiction between the functional and territorial bases of social integration. A final component of the theoretical framework is added in Section 3, where the related concepts of city and countryside are discussed in terms that will be useful to the further development of my topic. The remaining two sections are devoted to an extended analysis of the clash between rural and urban-centered interests. Section 4 concerns the pseudo-resolution of this clash within the core countries of western capitalism, while section 5 projects the argument into a global context. The question is: if rural-urban contradictions were 'successfully' resolved within the advanced capitalist nations, could not this process be replicated with a view to the ultimate integration of the world economy into a single, homogeneous system of functional relationships?

1
Contradictions: Cosmic and Historical

Contradictions are everywhere in the world. Without contradictions there would be no world (Mao Tse-tung, On the Ten Great Relationships).

In ordinary usage, the notion of contradiction suffers from a certain imprecision of meaning. Some of this, no doubt, must be attributed to history. Originally a term in logic ('statement A "contradicts" statement B' in the sense that A and B cannot be logically maintained at the same time), it came to be applied, in the hands of German idealist philosophers (Kant, Hegel), to relations in reality (Williams 1976, 91–93). Subsequently, it played a key role in the formalization of dialectical materialism.[1] In Marxist thought, contradiction acquired specific, if sometimes elusive, historical and existential meanings; it became simultaneously a condition and principal method of revolutionary practice.

In this paper, I shall use contradiction to refer to *a standing in mutual opposition of two social forces which, though interpenetrating and clashing, are complementary to one another, comprising a unity, a whole.*[2] The broad scope of this definition can be rendered more precise by distinguishing its several moments. Contradictions that are constitutive of the human condition, I propose to call *cosmic* contradictions. An example would be the contradictions that exist between the individual self and the matrix of social relations that sustains us and through which we become human. A cosmic contradiction also exists between the two opposing bases of social integration: functional and territorial. I shall return to this contradiction in the next section. For the present, let it suffice to note that cosmic contradictions can change in only two respects; in their external appearance (or form) and in the balance of opposing forces. They can never be resolved in any final way.

All other (non-cosmic) contradictions, I call *historical*. Historical contradictions are non-permanent. When their resolution can be accomplished without destroying the unity they comprise, they are *non-antagonistic*. But the resolution of *antagonistic* contradictions will constantly bring forth *new* unities. Antagonistic contradictions are the major generative force in history.[3]

Non-antagonistic contradictions arise within the context of antagonistic struggle. Capitalist competition for market dominance, for example, is non-antagonistic: the market areas in contention may be divided by mutual agreement, leaving each firm in monopolistic control over a portion of the whole. Similarly, in the lexicon of Maoist ideology, some contradictions are said to arise 'among the people'. But again, their resolution—through communal education, for example—will not violate the essential unity of the people which is defined by their continuing antagonistic struggle against the hostile forces of capitalism. What determines the nature of a contradiction is the correct method of its resolution. Non-antagonistic contradictions will yield to peaceful methods; antagonistic contradictions will not.

This taxonomy is helpful in clarifying the theoretical use of the concept. Equally important, however, are the forms contradictions take in the general movement of history. According to the well-known Hegelian schema, contradictions are resolved through specific actions that 'surpass' them, leading to a new and higher unity, a movement which suggests the image of a forward-surging spiral.[4] In the process, although the formerly opposing forces are destroyed and vanish from earth, some of the 'positive' and usually secondary elements are rescued into the next ('higher') stage of the historical process, where they are retained.[5] But every new unity, in turn, will generate new forces in opposition to itself, and so the process continues without let-up, destroying, surpassing, retaining, in a continuing upward spiral of historical progress.[6]

In this ontology, there are no 'cosmic' contradictions. Instead, the outward appearance of historical phenomena in Hegel veils the unity of spirit that pervades all things. All contradictions strain towards an expression of this unity. And only when the 'final' contradiction has been overcome will humankind embark upon the true course of history. This mystical vision animates such fundamentally divergent thinkers as Karl Marx (the 'higher phase of communist society') and Pierre Teilhard de Chardin ('Omega').[7] Hegel 'stood on his head', one must conclude, is still indubitably Hegel (Althusser 1969).

Just as Hegel's philosophy, together with its materialist inversion, is, in the final analysis, monistic (i.e. reducible to a single, indivisible unity), so traditional Chinese, including present-day Maoist, thought is fundamentally dualistic (i.e. ultimate reality is two, not one). The idea of an ontogenetic unity ('world spirit') is utterly alien to this thought; all existing unities are made up of the opposing forces of *yin* and *yang*.

Thus, in the earliest of Chinese classics, the *Book of Changes*, we may read: 'The two principles in opposition are united in a relation based on homogeneity; they do not combat but complement each other. The difference in level creates a potential, as it were, by virtue of which movement and living expression of energy became possible' (Wilhelm 1968, 281–282). Here the emphasis is on the complementarity of opposites, to the point where the ancient commentator even questions whether or not the two opposing forces express a dualistic point of view ('A relation based on homogeneity'). Several thousand years later, Mao Tse-tung would emphasize the aspect of struggle between them, as each elemental force presses against its opposite (and opposing) force, attempting to maintain, to increase, to reduce, or to invert the relative imbalance between them, changing one thing into another in an infinite sequence of historical transformations. For Mao: 'the unity of opposites is the most basic law . . . There is no such thing as the negation of the negation. Affirmation, negation, affirmation, negation . . . in the development of things, every link in the chain of events is both affirmation and negation . . . The life of dialectics is the continuous movement towards opposites. . . . Engels spoke of moving from the realm of necessity to the realm of freedom, and said that freedom is the understanding of necessity. This sentence is not complete . . . Does merely understanding make you free? Freedom is the understanding of necessity *and* the transformation of necessity—one has some work to do, too . . . Thus it is that only by transformation can freedom be obtained' (Schramm 1974, 226–230).

In this dualistic view, contradictions may change their specific, historical form, but inherently they remain the same, merely alternating in their position of relative strength or weakness. It follows that the flux of history is cyclical rather than progressive. All apparent unities are constitutive of forces in contradiction and struggle.

Throughout the remainder of this essay, I intend to follow this (non-Hegelian) dualistic interpretation of the concept of contradiction.

2
Functional and Territorial Bases of Social Transformation

Every social formation, by definition, must be conformed or 'integrated'. That is the essential condition of its continued stability and growth. The meaning of integration, however, is an elusive one (Seymour 1976, 3–10). It is not identical with homogenization, alignment, equilibrium. These terms signify an absence of life, the *punto muerto* of maximum entropy. The integration of a social formation is rather the form of its struggle to become. Integration is, therefore, akin to differentiation, opposition, and tension; it is the result of forces locked in perpetual struggle.

In any social formation, there exist two principal bases of social integration, functional and territorial. Together, they constitute a 'cosmic' unity of opposites—apart, yet together. The first term refers to linkages among entities organized into hierarchical networks on a basis of self-interest. Where a relationship between two entities is functional, one is using the other as an instrument to accomplish a purpose of its own. With respect to power, such relationships are symmetrical only in the limit. By contrast, territorial integration refers to those ties of history and sentiment that bind the members of a geographically bounded community to one another.[8] Territorial communities are communities informed by a deep attachment to their territorial base. Their consciousness curves back upon itself and comes to rest in its history. Transcending interests of class—a functional concept—such a community defines itself collectively in struggle against the outside world.[9]

As territorial entities expand through either conquest or peaceful annexation, they must increasingly resort to corporate and bureaucratic power for the control and management of their domain. Concurrently, their internal or normative power is weakened, until it is no longer able to make an adequate response to the impacts—mostly disintegrative—of increased functional power. But territorial power is similarly threatened by an expansion of corporate power (resulting, for example, from the efficient extraction of monopoly profits). Corporate power will seek to impose its own principle of social organization, the pursuit of private gain, on territorial forms of organization.

Some of the major distinctions between functional and territorial organizations are shown schematically in Table 1.1.

3
Concepts of City and Countryside

The theoretical framework for an analysis of rural-urban relations will be completed with the distillation of analytically useful concepts of city and countryside. In line with the distinction between functional and territorial organization, two very different concepts of the city, together with their corresponding concepts of countryside, may be distinguished.

To begin with the functional concept, cities appear as *spatially organized subsystems of society that are characterized by a high*

TABLE 1.1

	Functional Organization	Territorial Organization
TIME	rate of change (dy/dt)	history (concrete succession of events)
SPACE	cost of overcoming distance (e.g. 'gravity models')	regional geography
SYSTEM	unbounded, but global in the limit ('spaceship earth')	physically bounded (partial closure) at neighborhood, local, regional, national, and imperial levels
SOCIAL RELATIONS	hierarchical, instrumental	hierarchical, ascriptive
FORM OF ORGANIZATION	contractual, associational	reciprocal, communal
POWER BASE	utilitarian and coercive	normative and coercive
INTEGERS	individual, interest group, social class, corporation	folk, tribe, nation, people

relative density of population and a predominance of non-primary (specifically non-agricultural) activities. In this perspective, the designation of 'city' serves as a metaphor for a functional, primarily economic clustering of human activities which creates its own topological (abstract) space. Such 'cities' have obviously no history; their temporal dimension is best expressed as a rate of change, and their performance is assessed from primarily an economic point of view. At issue is their efficiency as centers of production, distribution, and capital accumulation, as formulated by Lucien Romier:

> . . . large cities are formed by national and international connections and movements; their future is bound up in a network of vaster activities; and their destiny crosses administrative and even territorial borders to follow the general trade routes (in Mariátegui 1971, p. 174).

José Carlos Mariátegui gave succinct expression to this functional concept. 'A great city,' he wrote in 1931, 'is basically a market and a factory' (Mariátegui 1971, p. 178). The functional mentality is also at work in such doubtlessly useful but vapid concepts as Standard Metropolitan Statistical Area (SMSA) and Functional Economic Area

(FEA) (Berry 1969). These 'areas'—no longer even nominally cities—are linked into a system, the so-called space-economy, whose structure is mediated through a measure of generalized access (Isard 1956). Although the economic space of a nation can be mapped, showing a differentiated profile of appropriate index values (which themselves are chosen to express an urban bias), only that space will be drawn which is to some extent already integrated with the market economy (Berry 1975). In this perspective, rural areas will show up as economic areas whose low 'profile' is different in quantity but not in quality from so-called cities, or they remain virtually blank, much as uncharted areas of the Antarctic used to be portrayed on ancient maps.[11]

This perception is reflected in the practice of corporate interests that reside at the principal nodes of the space economy. Rural areas are scanned by them for their potential instrumental value in expanding corporate production and for accumulating wealth. To the extent that they may have such value, rural 'peripheries' will be organized to supply a steady stream of resources to a growing market economy whose ultimate extent is global.

In the contrasting language of territorial organization, *the city appears as a bounded, territorial unit, part of a specific social formation that is characterized by the relatively high density of its population, a predominance of non-primary (non-agricultural) activities, and a degree of political autonomy whose theoretical value my range from virtually zero to 100 percent.*[12] A territorial city is therefore an historical and political entity, that is interconnected with other, similarly constituted units in a variety of ways. It is a place, with a physiognomy of its own, and it always has a name.[13] Walls are symbolic of territorial cities, but they are not a defining characteristic.[14]

Against the background of such cities, rural areas—the countryside—are also territorially defined, and rural populations are seen as being grouped and bound together by a remembered past, a certain pattern of relations between man and land, a common dialect or language, a set of religious beliefs, familiar customs. Under territorial rule, rural regions are typically subdued and politically dominated by the city. Their appearance in history as politically autonomous areas is as brief as it is infrequent.

Howard Spodek provides us with one of the best images of the territorial city and its reciprocally dependent countryside. His objects are the headquarters towns in Saurashtra, India, up to the advent of British rule in 1863:

> Two elements in the structure of headquarters towns impeded regional and market integration. First, within the headquarters town, the military

ruler and the professional and business classes—particularly those with wide-ranging contacts—often battled with one another. The goal of the ruler, which was usually to maximize political control over his subjects, conflicted with the goals of the merchants and professionals, which were to make profits and to exercise skills and talents. The ruler usually did not want the town market and court to be independent entities. He wanted them subject to his will . . .

Towns in India impeded political and economic integration in a second way. The towns, which may have served as hinges vertically linking higher and lower levels of the polity, nevertheless served as military headquarters for antagonistic relations with neighboring towns, so to speak, horizontally. Frequently, towns were militantly hostile to one another. This hostility could have led to creative competition, but at least as often it resulted in warfare. Persistent warfare and the threat of war inhibited political and market integration.

These two tensions frequently marked the urban system in pre-Independence India: tension between the land-holding town rulers and the non-landed merchant and professional classes; and tensions between neighboring towns which served as headquarters for local, often militarily antagonistic rajas . . .

When the British began to dominate the Saurashtra region politically, they found 162 fortified settlements in its 25,000 square miles . . . Trade between kingdoms was minimal . . . The politically and culturally fragmented peninsula had no unifying urban hierarchy.

Struggles within the town walls between military rulers, usually Rajputs, and the merchants and professionals are copiously documented both in Indian and British sources . . . The rulers were tied to the land and capital city, for these were the bases of their power. The merchants and professionals, however, saw geographical mobility as their main lever of power. They bargained with the prince, threatening to desert and take their capital and skills with them if their demands were not met. Often they did leave, either by choice or forced out by coercion. Loyalty to the state did not often develop (Spodek 1973, 254–256).

To describe the territorial city, Spodek had to set it off against the functional city. And, indeed, both forms of description are jointly necessary for a complete account: the city is a node in a global network of economic relations; it is also a place, possessing a political life of its own, a history, a unique appearance, a mode of life, a sense of being.[15] After four centuries of steady attrition, this second, psycho-historical dimension is only vestigially present.[16] Both corporate and bureaucratic power have become consolidated at the national level, extending cities into an intricate network of functional relations. Symbolized in the literature as 'megalopolis' (e.g. Gottman 1961; Soja 1968a), this network is more accurately described as a fabric of invisible relations (financial, communications, freight and people movements). As a result, the city has become a staging ground of conflicting national and international forces. Whether it will re-emerge as an organic element in a revitalized cultural region, as in Lewis Mumford's vision of a 'regional city', remains to be seen. It may be noted, however, that regionalism is beginning to re-emerge as a potent *political* force in many countries, especially in Europe.[17]

The *cosmic* contradiction between city and countryside is therefore between the functional organization of bureaucratic and corporate power, on the one hand, and territorially organized power—at all the relevant scales—on the other. It is between two contradictory yet complementary modes of social existence. Other, *historical* contradictions are similarly present, for instance, in Howard Spodek's account of territorial warfare in Saurashtra, or in the competition among corporate powers for resources and markets in the periphery of major economic regions. Whereas these historical contradictions are amenable to some form of resolution, the cosmic contradiction is, ultimately, not.

4
The Pseudo-Resolution of Contradictions in the Core Countries of Capitalism

Coincident with the spectacular rise of capitalist forms of organization, the industrial revolution unleashed a series of violent forces that, in the end, brought on the nearly total collapse of local forms of territorial governance. Among these forces were relentless economic growth, the continuous technological transformation of both commodities and their methods of production, explosive demographic expansion, vast interregional migration, the settlement of new continents, and the consequent de-population of the older rural areas.

As cities expanded, they also burst their traditional 'containers', spilling out into the surrounding countryside. Where they were still surrounded by a wall, the wall, in a fateful and symbolic gesture, was torn down. The old unity of territory and governance was beginning to crack. In the more densely populated regions, cities actually fused as physical entities, forming vast sheets of urbanism, Patrick Geddes' 'conurbations'.

Cities were becoming *unbounded* spatial structures. It was therefore only a matter of time before a new 'science' would spring up to measure the dimensions of this new formation, trace its topography, and discover the sources of its 'lawful' behavior. The Regional Science

Association was founded in 1954. The flavor of its dominant interest is captured in the following introduction to a major paper delivered at the Association's first annual meeting. According to the author:

> This article suggests a method for describing the magnitude of a city's influence on its surrounding hinterland. And a method is proposed for partitioning an entire terrain into metropolitan regions or even urban trade areas (Carroll 1955, p. D-2).

The functional reductionism of this approach is unmistakable. About the same time, Don Martindale and Gertrud Neuwirth wrote their laconic epitaph commemorating the passing of the territorial city:

> The modern city is losing its external and formal structure. Internally it is in a state of decay while the new community represented by the nation everywhere grows at its expense. The age of the city seems to be at an end (Weber 1958, p. 62).

The new urban scale, coincident with the appearance of a national hierarchy of cities and a nationally integrated economy, was ultimately justified by referring to the immense gains in economic efficiency that were supposed to be realized (Borts and Stein 1964; Mera 1975). The immediate evidence for this was the seemingly irresistible growth of national production and the resulting affluence of the population at large. These gains were dearly bought, however. Bourgeois complacency was profoundly shaken by the accumulation of misery and squalor in cities, by cyclical instability, by massive structural unemployment, by life-destroying pollution, by the rapid exhaustion of natural resources, by increasingly devastating and senseless wars, by widespread social alienation. All the same, many 'costs' were thought to be the unavoidable byproducts of a modern industrial economy:

> . . . rapid economic progress is impossible without painful readjustments. Ancient philosophies have to be scrapped; old social institutions have to disintegrate; bonds of caste, creed, and race have to be burst; and large numbers of persons who cannot keep up with progress have to have their expectations of a comfortable life frustrated. Very few communities are willing to pay the full price of economic progress (United Nations 1951, p. 15).

That, as it happened, was the collective wisdom of a group of international experts which had been asked to advise the United Nations on measures of full employment in the underdeveloped countries of the world. It brings to mind Joseph Schumpeter's exultation in the process of 'creative destruction', whose break with the past he understood to be radical and complete (Schumpeter 1947, Chapter 7). This conscious turning away from the past, this virulent anti-historicism, found its ultimate expression in the celebrated phrase of Henry Ford: History is bunk! It might have been more accurate to say that history had been reduced to a bundle of growth rates.

This dismissal of history as a source of relevant knowledge pointed to a more general phenomenon: the loss of territoriality and the corresponding loss of social bonds that were not based exclusively on calculation. Gains had become privatized, and this made it easier to ignore the social costs of corporate expansion which accrued primarily to territorial entities.[18]

As local territorial organizations disintegrated under the impact of fundmental rationalization, class conflict replaced the rivalry of towns and regions. This new conflict—appropriate to the newly dominant mode of functional organization—was chiefly an urban phenomenon, but it was present as well in those rural areas where agricultural production was organized along corporate lines, as in California. For all practical purposes, such areas were rural in only external appearance. In every other respect, they had become a part of the unbounded city.

Territorial power had not altogether vanished, however; it had merely been displaced to the national level. Although its reintegration around the nucleus of the state occurred slowly and unevenly—it had begun much earlier in France, for instance, than in Germany or Italy—it was chiefly during the 19th and 20th centuries that local power was rendered all but impotent (Holborn 1954).

Just as territorial power re-emerged at the national level, so corporate power was re-organized on a predominantly national basis. Colonial empires were not yet part of an internationalized network of relations, they merely extended the national economy into the backyard of distant regions overseas. On the other hand, the hierarchy of corporate command was by no means identical with that of territory. Economic locations, for instance, were almost completely independent of the power of the state. Although *raison d'état* might suggest a greater degree of regional balance, policy and incentive measures were largely impotent to guide entrepreneurial investments into the more backward regions of the country (Stöhr and Tödtling, see Chapter 6). Not only were the instruments too weak to affect the private calculus significantly, but the political will was often lacking for subordinating corporate to territorial power. So long as it was possible to privatize gains while socializing losses, one did not have to try too hard to equalize the benefits of economic growth across all regions. As economists were eager to point out, 'people prosperity' should always be preferred to 'place prosperity'. If areas were bypassed by economic progress (which is to say that they were unattractive as potential locations for private businesses), it would be irrational, they argued, to direct social resources from their most efficient employments to economically unattractive regions. The obvious solution is to facilitate the movement of people from the backward areas to major nodes of opportunity—the growth poles of the national (an international) economy. Alternatively, backward areas could be made accessible to metropolitan consumers for second homes and outdoor recreation. They would thus be brought integrally into the urban field (Friedmann and Miller 1965). The argument was more than theoretical; it was based on observable trends. As urban infrastructure spread across the continent in Western Europe and North America, homogeneous economic spaces were created that made it possible to locate production facilities almost anywhere and still be within overnight trucking distance from major markets.

Within the core countries of western capitalism, functional patterns of social integration were winning out over divided territorial powers almost everywhere. Local powers were dissolved and reintegrated at the national level. And as the contradictions between city and countryside were slowly overcome, the class struggle was left as the major and unchallenged conflict within the national domain.

With the substantial victory of corporate power, older social distinctions between rural and urban areas all but vanished. Left was a set of spatially continuous indicators which failed to reveal any fundamental differences in the spatial structure of activities (Berry 1975).[19]

The annihilation of significant territorial units at subnational levels did not, however, succeed in destroying their reality in the consciousness of people. Reacting to the threat of social disintegration before the relentless advance of corporate power, the advocates of the new regionalism in western Europe are beginning to demand greater political autonomy, the subordination of corporate to territorial interests, a reduction in the spatial division of labor, and the creation of economically more self-reliant regions (Gaviria 1976; Friedmann and Weaver 1978, Chapter 8).

5

The Globalization of the Conflict

The parallel and, indeed interdependent growth of corporate and national power, extending over a period of two centuries, made it seem natural to assume a virtual identity of interests. Evidently, there was more than a grain of truth in Marx's and Engel's sarcastic reference to existing governments in Western Europe as the Executive Committee of the Bourgeoisie. This presumptive identity of interests occasioned a theory of imperialism in which the wealth of metropolitan countries in the North was gained by subduing and exploiting colonial peoples in the southern hemisphere. Neo-imperialism, it was argued, continued this policy, but chiefly in the guise of unequal exchange relations (Lenin 1970; Frank 1967; Amin 1974).

What may have been true of the 19th and early 20th century, however, when colonies were little more than distant national peripheries, is certainly no longer true in the era of communication satellites and transnational corporations. A partial interdependence of interests obscures the fundamental difference between the functional, non-territorial nature of the corporation and the historical sense of unity which constitutes the basis of national territorial power.[20]

Until fairly recently, corporate enterprise was typically restricted to operate within national boundaries. The costs of overcoming distance had laid down a graded pattern of spatial efficiencies, yielding the hierarchical system of nodal areas through which economic space is organized. But the pattern of spatial efficiencies which in the course of two centuries had expanded to the size of national boundaries, drastically changed as economic growth came to be based on science, and as transport and communication technologies improved, shrinking first national and then global distances to the size of a village.

This change, manifested in a radical reduction of transport and communication costs, was reinforced by an equally dramatic shift in relative emphasis from fixed plant and equipment to finance capital. This dematerialization of the forces of production facilitated the merging of financial resources from different points of origin ('money doesn't smell') and, in a quick progression, led to the *de-nationalization* of corporate power.

The real power of finance capital resides in its global mobility. When profits on investment are as high as 40 percent a year, as in many Third World countries, investments can be written off in less than half a decade without loss, and the recovered capital transferred to any part of the globe that happens to be temporarily more attractive.[21] Cheap, almost instantaneous communication, and now even supersonic jet travel, have made finance capital virtually independent of location. As a result, very large cities — Tokyo, Los Angeles, São Paulo, New York, London — have become primary centers within a global inter-locking system of banking and communication. But as financial centers, their world-wide dominance has been 'etheralized'; it is no longer territorial.

The occasional alliance between finance capital and territorial power is not a necessary but an historical relation. To a very large extent, finance capital has become independent of territorial power.[22] This is true for even leading capitalist countries, a development which is only now beginning to be noted. A functionally integrated world economy no longer requires a well-defined geographic center as an element of its structure.[23] Or, as Melvin Webber (1964) put it in a celebrated phrase, it has become a 'non-place urban realm'. The lodestone of this realm, its constant North, is corporate profits, a criterion that includes as well the safeguarding of essential raw materials and the expansion and protection of markets. It is not geared to any national or local interest.[24]

The global division of labor is organized through a system of point locations and connecting flows of commodities, information, and financial instruments. This spatial dimension of corporate expansion is accomplished with the assistance of quasi-territorial institutions, such as the European Economic Community and non-territorial organizations, incuding the International Monetary Fund, the World Bank, and the Organization for Economic Cooperation and Development. Major world capitals play a coordinative role, but their choice as a location for corporate staff is largely a matter of historical accident and convenience (Heenan 1977). London is a major finanical market; it also happens to have the cheapest secretarial labor force in Westen Europe. A step or two further down the financial hierarchy, is Beirut. But when Beirut was engulfed in civil war, much of the financial capital moved to Amman. And if Amman should capsize, then there is Kuwait or some other principality along the Arab Gulf. Let it be noted: the first route of British supersonic jets was to Bahrain!

What is happening today is clearly the attempt by corporations to replicate their earlier national phase on the scale of the whole globe. As a consequence, national territories in the world periphery are penetrated at suitable points, and these points are gradually incorporated and absorbed into the whole global network of economic relations (Michalet 1975). The earlier effort had successfully wiped out most local territorial entities as effective political actors. It had reconcentrated power at the national level, and it had realigned people's lives according to functional principles. Today, the denationalized corporation seeks to achieve the same purpose by weakening the integrity of nation states, undermining their power and authority to act. Its long-term project is to totalize the principle of functional integration and to resolve all social questions by the calculus of profit. As Citicorp's Walter B. Wriston said: 'Far too many of the world's people have now seen what the global shopping center holds in store for them. They will not easily accept having the doors slammed shut by nationalism'.[25]

Or will they? That is indeed the fateful question of our time. Will territorial power, after all, succumb to corporate and bureaucratic power, history to economic growth? Should we imagine the globalization of the economy to the exclusion of the territorial principle? Or, more precisely, should we imagine a world in which the principle of territorial integration has become the pliant tool of corporate power?

The latter course in conceivable, even though it may not be desirable, but the former, involving the *totalization* of the principle of functional organization, is not. In a unity of opposites, one aspect cannot be 'totalized' without destroying the very unity which allows it to exist: to be integrated implies to be perpetually engaged in struggle.

The real question is rather the terms of that struggle. Which force is to be dominant? Up to now, functional forces have been nearly everywhere victorious. Yet, the territorial principle is far from being down and out: its maintenance has proved to be essential to the hegemonic rise of corporate power. It was needed for the general maintenance of economic and political stability; for the provision of economic services not profitable on private account; for the mobilization of investment capital over and above the capacity of the private sector; for the management of the 'social costs' of private enterprise, including pollution, resource degradation, unemployment, inflation, and income inequality; for the reproduction of the labor force through the provision of minimum essential housing, health, and education; and for the penetration and control of peripheral economies.

The managers of the global system are quite aware of their continued need for some degree of territorial integration at the level of the nation-state (Peccei, 1969). But in accepting this need, they are also obliged to accept the basic contradictions that accompany territorial integration: its potential conflict with all functionally integrated structures.

The danger is real and ever-present: that functional forces will undermine their own stability and power by dissolving territorial integrity. With rapidly mounting social costs, and tensions within national social formations rising to nearly intolerable levels of intensity, this danger has never been so great as now. It is the threatened breakdown of the world economy that foreshadows a possible reconstruction of the social order along communalist lines and a concomitant recovery and strengthening of territorial values.

Notes

The research for this essay was done while the author was on a Guggenheim Foundation fellowship at the Centre for Environmental Studies in London, England. Earlier drafts received very helpful comments from Peter Marris, Edward Soja, Clyde Weaver, and the editors of the present volume.

1. It was Engels, rather than Marx, who formalized the dialectic as a way of viewing the world and so transformed the loose notion of contradiction-in-reality into a more rigorous concept (Engels 1976; Ollman 1971, Chapter 5).

2. The unity (the whole, the entity) arises from the contradictory relation; it is not pre-existing to it. Thus there are no ultimate entities in the universe, only forces-in-relation. According to Colletti (1975), this is the only true dialectical form of opposition, but it exists exclusively in logic. Relations of opposition in reality, on the other hand, are instances of contrariety *(Realrepugnanz)*, and are without logical contradiction.

   This distinction is made in order to save Marxism for science, or possibly the other way round. The argument is that, in a unity of opposites, neither of the two component forces has ontological reality by itself; it is a mere shadow, whose existence requires the constant presence of the other. Adopting Colletti's position, both proletarians and bourgeois would, in themselves alone, be merely fictions (epiphenomena).

   Colletti's argument is not convincing. To reach it, he has to dip into idealist philosophy. From an historical materialist point of view, the proletariat exists not for itself alone, but only as the dialectical opposite of capitalist social forces. Eliminate capitalism, and the proletariat, in its specific historical appearance and mission, is eliminated as well. Within capitalism, however, the proletariat is 'real' enough and not, as Colletti seems to think, an instance of the metaphysical imagination. For a non-dialectical 'systems' view of this same problem, see Edgar S. Dunn, Jr. (1971, Chapter VI).

3. The distinction between antagonistic and non-antagonistic contradictions is taken from Mao Tse-tung (1968, 70–71): "Contradiction and struggle are universal and absolute, but the methods of resolving contradictions, that is, the forms of the struggle, differ according to the differences in the nature of the contradiction. Some contradictions are characterized by open antagonism, others are not. In accordance with the concrete development of things, some contradictions which were originally non-antagonistic develop into antagonistic ones, while others which were originally antagonistic develop into non-antagonistic ones . . . Economically, the contradiction between town and country is an extremely antagonistic one both in capitalist society . . . and in the Kuomintang areas in China . . . But in a socialist country and in our revolutionary base areas, this antagonistic contradiction has changed into one that is non-antagonistic; and when communist society is reached, it will be abolished." Lenin said, 'Antagonism and contradiction are not at all one and the same. Under socialism the first will disappear, the second will remain.' That is to say, antagonism is one form, but not the only form of the struggle of opposites; the formula of antagonism cannot be arbitrarily applied everywhere.

4. According to Friedrich Engels, the most important dialectical laws are the

'transformation of quantity to quality—mutual penetration of polar opposites and the transformation of each other when carried to extremes — development through contradiction or negation — spiral form of development' (cited in Ollman 1971, p. 55).

5. The German equivalent of 'surpassing' — *aufheben* — means both a 'raising up' and a 'preserving' and thus contains the notions of progressive change as well as continuity.

6. Hegelian dilectics, with its dual moment of destruction and preservation in historical processes, appeals to a romantic streak in the German imagination. The Valhallian rhetoric of destruction (which also appears in Joseph Schumpeter's celebrated phrase, 'gales of creative destruction', referring to economic innovations under capitalism) accounts for much of the romantic appeal of Marxist writings.

7. With the achievement of a classless society from which all coercive (political) power is absent, antagonistic contradictions will also have been overcome. At this point, pre-history comes to an end, and humankind's true history begins to unfold. Marx's profound intuition of this history is perhaps best expressed in a short paragraph of the *Critique of the Gotha Program* (Marx 1972, p. 17). In all fairness, it should be noted that what is historical transformation in Marx becomes transfiguration with Teilhard de Chardin. All the same, de Chardin's 'hyper-personal' at the Omega-point of History is still this side of Heaven (de Chardin 1965, Book IV, Chapter 2).

8. This description of the two bases of social integration bears a certain family resemblance to such well-worn sociological distinctions as organic and mechanical solidarity (Durkheim) and society and community (Tönnies). These earlier concepts, however, were modelled, not as a 'unity of opposites' but as 'ideal types' of two contrasting (and mutually exclusive) forms of social organization which might subsequently be applied to the study of social history (from the primary relations of *Gemeinschaft* to the secondary, associative relations of *Gesellschaft*, from 'traditional' society to 'modern'). By contrast, functional and territorial bases of social integration are complementary forces that stand in contradiction to each other; they are complex social forms which arise from this double interaction.

9. All social integration above the level of the small, face-to-face group occurs on the basis of either territory or function. This is true of even nomadic tribes whose migrations are fixed within a given territorial range or of Jews in the *diaspora* whose common history is comprehensible only with reference to their expulsion from their ancestral home in Judea. (Cf. Porteous 1976).

In territorially integrated societies, history and place are one. This is beautifully illustrated in the following description, based on the *Chinese Book of Rites (sheking)*, on the founding of a new city:
'There is a settled order in which one must proceed. The ramparts are first raised: they are the most sacred part of the town. Afterwards the temple of the ancestors *[Miao]* is built. Care is taken to plant trees meanwhile (hazels and chestnuts) whose fruits and berries will be offered to the ancestors, and those trees which are used to make coffins and sonorous drums. ''In ancient times when the plan of the capital was traced, they did not fail to choose the most important rising ground in the kingdom and

constitute the ancestral temple, nor to select trees of the finest growth to make the sacred forest.'' When the walls, the altars and the plantations which are to give sanctity to the town are finished, the palace and houses are built' (Granet 1958).

The symbolic quality of this historical action reveals the reverence with which human beings approach the task of staking out a territorial core for their lives.

Yet territory is merely the ground for human history. It is collective experience which creates the essential bond between human beings. Thus Duchacek (1970, p. 20): 'It should be recognized that men identify not only with a territory as such but also (if not primarily) with its political and economic system, its methods and goals, *and with its history and its destiny'*(emphasis added).

10. This distinction is also recognized by Miguel Morales (1976, p. 83): ''A third tendency, finally has been shown to exist in the formal and a-historical use of the term region. This has contributed to an asymmetrical relation: on one hand, the evident descriptive power of the term, and on the other, its inability to explain. In these cases, two aspects have dominated the scene: in the first, space is conceived mathematically, in abstract form, which allows one to know areas based on topological considerations; in the second, which is identified with empirical systems analysis, *the historical meaning of the process of regionalization as a specific social process has been practically dissolved in its phenomenological appearance.* Regions, in that case, are converted into mere study areas or areas for action *without significant historical contents;* eventually, they become formalized planning areas which in their practical aspects are manifestly efficient'' (translated from the Spanish; emphasis added).

11. Such a map is produced by Edward W. Soja (1968b, fig. 47) for post-independence Kenya. This map (together with the accompanying text) distinguishes between the political (national) boundaries of Kenya and the 'effective national territory' which occupied no more than a fifth of the former. The only data shown for the 'empty' four-fifths are 'Shifta attacks and ethnic conflicts'.

12. Political autonomy was virtually absent in the Islamic city of the Middle ages (Lapidus 1967). The Greek *polis*, on the other hand, enjoyed complete autonomy in principle (Finley 1973). In practice, of course, many *poleis* were joined in ''leagues'' with their neighbors; others were in a permanent condition of subjection to the more powerful' (Pounds 1969, p. 136).

13. A magnificent 'territorial' portrayal of a city is found in Kollek and Pearlman (1968). Territorial thinking is beginning as well to enter contemporary planning practice (see Lynch 1976).

14. Max Weber (1958) made its protective walls one of the defining characteristics of the western city. The symbolic value of walls in defining a place leans on the following paragraph from Lewis Mumford's *The City in History* (1961, p. 52): ''Now all organic phenomena have limits of growth and extension, which are set by their very need to remain self-sustaining and self-directing: they can grow at the expense of their neighbors only by losing the very facilities that their neighbors' activities contribute to their

own life. Small primitive communities accept these limitations and thus dynamic balance, just as natural ecological communities register them." The walls are drawn 'protectively' around a particular uniqueness; they define the 'placeness' of a place (see also note 9).

15. Historically, there has been a gradual evolution of the city from place to node. This evolution is beautifully traced and recorded in Mumford (1938). A more dialectical urban history in which the fate of the city as a place becomes intertwined with the fate of the national economy is found in Conot (1974). The 'great city' of Conot's saga is Detroit.

16. According to Charles Tilly (1976, p. 374),' . . . the two centuries after 1700 produced an enormous concentration of resources and means of coercion under the control of national states, to the virtual exclusion of other levels of government. . . . A whole series of organizational changes closely linked to urbanization, industrialization and the expansion of capitalism greatly reduced the role of the communal group as a setting for mobilization and as a repository for power; the association of one kind or another came to be the characteristic vehicle for collective action. The rise of the joint-stock company, the political party, the labor union, the club all belong to the same general trend.'

17. Duchacek (1970) is undoubtedly the best general study on the subject. For Spain, see the extremely provocative *Asalto al Centralismo* (1976). For Great Britain: Hechter 1975. For France: Dulong 1975 and n.d.

18. Kenneth Arrow (1963) was awarded the Nobel Prize for demonstrating that a community welfare function, which is essentially a territorial concept, cannot be logically derived from the assumptions of the reigning economic paradigm which ascribed fundamental reality to individual utilities.

19. As a result, of this evening out of rural-urban differences, amenities are becoming increasingly decisive for industrial location. This shift in locational criteria from resources and transport costs to social amenities (Klaassen 1968) means that settlement patterns are becoming independent of economic location. Increasingly in the future, jobs will follow people, and not the other way around.

20. As is well known, when faced with the task of expelling foreign invaders of their own countries, both Stalin and Mao relied on nationalist sentiments to rally the population in defense of their soil. It may be that the belly is the ultimate task master; all the same, ideas and sentiments seem real enough when millions are prepared to lay down their lives in defense of them.

21. In a recent year, for example, employment in Mexico's border industries (i.e. American firms operating in Mexico under a special arrangment which permits them to take advantage of low-cost labor), fell from 80,000 to 30,000. The wages of Mexican workers had risen, and Haiti had once more become politically attractive. Thus, in the early 1970s, Haiti, where women work for 40 cents a day, experienced an enormous industrial boom whose conterpart was economic depression in northern Mexico! (See Dillman 1976; Biderman 1974).

22. According to Holland (1975, p. 368): 'The new imperialism is different. The parent country has given way to the parent company, which rarely has any interest in developing the infrastructure or strengthening the administration of the country in which its subsidiaries operate. It leaves the social costs of running some of the poorest countries in the world to

local governments while maximizing the private benefits of the multi-national corporation which it heads.

23. The following quotation from the Chairman of Citicorp demonstrates fairly clearly the thinking which stands behind my assertion of the loss of a geographic center for the emerging world economy: "As a last resort, all the multinational company can do in its relations with a sovereign state is to make an appeal to reason. If this fails, capital, both human and material, will leave for countries where it is more welcome. Whether or not there is a shortage of capital is the subject of debate, but no one asserts there is a surplus. Since men and money will in the long run go where they are wanted and stay where they are well treated, capital can be attracted but not driven.

In the long run, it all comes down to this: the figure of the global company in any one area will be determined by the degree to which a particular government is willing and able to sacrifice the material well-being of its citizens to non-economic factors. Everything we've discussed thus far will be resolved almost automatically when our nation-states make up their minds concerning this one basic question.

The reality of a global market place has been the driving force pushing us along the path of developing a rational world economy. Progress that has been made owes almost nothing to the political imagination. . . .   Far too many of the world's people have now seen what the global shopping center holds in store for them. They will not easily accept having the doors slammed shut by nationalism" (Wriston 1976).

These remarks were meant for British ears, and they were pointed at British policy! Now Citicorp is based in New York City, and it is possible to argue that what is true for the rest of the world is not true for the United States, where territorial and corporate interests are largely one and the same. I grant that there exists a certain historical coincidence between them, but it is not a structural phenomenon. Citicorp's location in New York is a matter of relative convenience. If New York should ever become incapable of being governed, Citicorp would pack its tapes and books and shift its headquarters to London or some other hospitable city where essential banking and communication services are available.

24. This statement does not preclude the possibility of a temporary conjunction of corporate and national (territorial) interests. It is these conjunctions that lend credence to expressions such as 'American imperialism' (see, e.g., Joint Economic Committee 1977). I wish to insist, however, that such conjunctions are not structural; they are ephemeral as the wind.

25. See Note 23. Methods of conducting business such as those revealed by the Lockheed scandals of recent memory and involving pay-offs to heads of state and other top-ranking government officials are only a tiny glimmering of what must be extremely widespread practices. The Vice-President of the United States had to resign for accepting bribes, and former Prime Minister Tanaka is standing trial in Japan on similar charges. As Quisling of Norway sold out to Nazi Germany, so Agnew and Tanaka have sold out to corporate interests. Is there a difference? (Quisling was shot after the war as a collaborator. Agnew has become a successful author-businessman. Tanaka went to jail.)

References

Althusser, L., *For Marx*. Pantheon, New York, 1969.

Amin, S., *Accumulation on a world scale: a critique of the theory of underdevelopment*. 2 vols. Monthly Review Press, New York, 1974.

Arrow, K., *Social choice and individual values*. 2nd ed. Wiley, New York 1963.

Asalto al centralismo: la reivindicación de la autonómia en las nacionalidades y regiones del estado Español. Avabce/Intervención, Madrid, 1976.

Berry, B. J. L., *Metropolitan area definition; a re-evaluation of concept and statistical practice*. Rev. ed. Bureau of the Census Working Paper no. 28, Washington, D.C. 1969.

Berry, B. J. L., 'The geography of the United States in the year 2000', in J. Friedmann and W. Alonso (eds.), *Regionl policy: readings in theory and applications*. MIT Press, Cambridge, Mass., 1975.

Biderman, J., *Enclave development: the case of multinational assembly industries on Mexico's northern border* Master's thesis, Department of City and Regional Planning, University of California, Berkeley, 1974.

Borts, G. H. and J. L. Stein, *Economic growth in a free market*. Columbia University Press, New York, 1964.

Carroll, J. D., Jr., 'Spatial interaction and the urban-metropolitan regional description'. *Papers and Proceedings, Regional Science Association*, vol. 1, D1–14, 1955.

Colletti, L., 'Marxism and the dialectic', *New Left Review*, no. 93, 3–30, 1975.

Conot, R., *American odyssey: a unique history of America told through the life of a great city*. William Morrow, New York, 1974.

de Chardin, P. T., *The phenomenon of man*. Harper and Row, New York, 1965.

Dillman, C. D., 'Maquiladoras in Mexico's northern border communities and the border industrialization program', *Tijdschrift voor Econ. en Soc. Geografie*, vol. 67, 138–50, 1976.

Duchacek, I.D., *Comparative federalism: the territorial dimension of politics*. Holt, Rinehart and Winston, New York, 1970.

Dulong, R., *La question Bretonne*. Presses de la Fondation Nationale des Sciences Politiques, Paris, 1975.

Dulong, R., *La question regionale en France*. 1 Monographies, Ecole des Hautes Etudes en Sciences Sociales, Centre d'Ettudes des Mouvement Sociaux, Paris, n.d.

Dunn, E. S., Jr., *Economic and social development: a process of social learning*. The Johns Hopkins Press, Baltimore, 1971.

Engels, F., *Anti-Dühring*. Foreign Languages Press, Peking, 1976.

Finley, M. I., *Democracy ancient and modern*.Rutgers University Press, New Brunswick, N.J., 1973.

Frank, A. G., *Capitalism and underdevelopment in Latin America: historical studies of Chile and Brazil*. Monthly Review Press, New York, 1967.

Friedmann, J. and J. Miller, 'The urban field', *Journal of American Institute of Planners*, vol. 31, 312–320, 1965.

Friedmann, Jr. and C. Weaver, *Territory and function: the evolution of regional planning doctrine*. Edward Arnold, London, 1978.

Gottman, J., *Megapolis: the urbanized northeastern seaboard of the United States*. Twentieth Century Fund, New York, 1961.

Gaviria, M., *Ecologismo y ordenación del territorio en españa.* Cuadernos para el Diagolo, Madrid, 1976.

Granet, M., *Chinese civilization.*Meridian Books, New York, 1958.

Hechter, M., *Internal colonialism: the Celtic fringe in British national development, 1536–1966.* Routledge and Kegan Paul, London, 1975.

Heenan, D. A., 'Global cities of tomorrow', *Harvard Business Review,* vol. 5, 79–92, 1977.

Holborn, H., *The political collapse of Europe.* Knopf, New York, 1954.

Holland, S., *The socialist challenge.* Quartet Books, London, 1975.

Isard, W., *Location and space economy: a general theory relating to industrial areas, land use, trade, and urban structure.* Wiley, New York, 1956.

Joint Economic Committee, Congress of the United States, *The United States response to the new international order: the econmic implications for Latin America and the United States.* U.S. Government Printing Office, Washington, D.C. 1977.

Klassen, L. H., *Social amenities in area economic growth: an analysis of methods for defining needs.* OECD, Paris, 1968.

Kollek, T. and M. Pearlman, *Jerusalem: sacred city of mankind: a history of forty centuries.* Weidenfeld and Nicholson, London, 1968.

Lapidus, I. M., *Muslin cities in the later middle ages.* Harvard University Press, Cmbridge, Mass., 1967.

Lenin, V. I., *Imperialism: the highest stage of capitalism.* Foreign Languages Press, Peking, 1970.

Lynch, K., *Managing the sense of a region.* MIT Press, Cambridge, Mass., 1976.

Mao Tse-tung, *Four essays on philosophy.* Foreign Languages Press, Peking, 1968.

Mariátegui, J. C., *Seven interpretive essays on Peruvian Reality.*University of Texas Press, Austin, 1971.

Marx, K., *Critique of the Gotha Program.* Foreign Languages Press, Peking, 1972.

Marx, K. and F. Engels, *Manifesto of the communist party.* Foreign Languages Press, Peking, 1975.

Mark, K. and F. Engels, *The German Ideology.* Part One. C.J. Arthur (ed.), International Publishers, New York 1970.

Mera, K., *Income distribution and regional development.* University of Tokyo Press, Tokyo, 1975.

Michalet, C. A., *Les firmes multinationales et la nouvelle division internationale du travail.* International Labour Office, Geneva, 1975.

Morales, A. M., 'Consideraciones generales sobre la planificación urbano-regional en América Latina', *Revista Interamericana de Planificacion,* vol. 10, 78–91, 1976.

Mumford, L., *The city in history: its origins, its transformations, and its prospects.* Harcourt, Brace and World, New York, 1961.

Mumford, L., *The culture of cities.* Harcourt, Brance, New York, 1938.

Ollman, B., *Alienation: Marx's concept of man in capitalist society.* University Press, Cambridge, 1971.

Peccei, A., *The chasm ahead.* Collier-Macmillan, London, 1969.

Poteous, J. D., 'Home: the territorial core', *The Geographical review,* vol. 66, 383–390, 1976.

Pounds, N. J. G., 'The urbanization on the classical world', *Annals of the Association of American Geographers*, vol. 59, no. 1, 1969.

Schramm (ed.), *Mao Tse-tung unrehearsed: talks and letters, 1956–71*. Penguin, London, 1974.

Schumpeter, J. A., *Capitalism, socialism and democracy*. 2nd ed. Harper and Bros., New York, 1947.

Seymour, J. D., *China: the politics of revolutionary reintegration*. Crowell, New York, 1976.

Soja, E. W., 'Communication and territorial integration in East Africa: an introduction to transaction flow analysis', *East Lake Geographer*, vol. 4, 39–57, 1968a.

Soja, E. W., *the geography of modernization in Kenya*. Syracuse University Press, Syracuse, N.Y., 1968b.

Spodek, H., 'Urban politics in the local kingdoms of India: a view from the princely capitals of Saurashtra under British rule', *Modern Asian Studies*, vol. 7, 253–275, 1973.

Tilly, C., 'Major forms of collective action in Western Europe, 1500–1975', *Theory and Society*, vol. 3, 365–376, 1976.

United Nations, *Measures for the economic development of underdeveloped countries*. Report by a group of experts. Department of Economic Affairs, New York, 1951.

Weber, M., *The city*. Free Press, Glencoe, Ill., 1958.

Webber, M. M., 'The urban place and the nonplace urban realm', in M.M. Webber et al., *Explorations into urban structure*. University of Pennsylvania Press, Philadelphia, 1964.

Wilhelm. R., (ed.), *The I Ching, or book of changes*. 3rd ed. Routledge and Kegan Paul, London, 1968.

Williams, R., *Keywords: a vocabulary of culture and society*. Fontana, London, 1976.

Wriston, W. B., *People, politics and productivity: the world corporation in the 1980s*. Citicorp, London, 1976.

2
The Crisis of Transition:
A Critique of Strategies of Crisis
Management

This paper attacks two versions of economic-development doctrine, both rooted in the language of neoclassical economics: export substitution (more properly called export promotion) and redistribution-with-growth. Both these theories are of Anglo-American origin, and they all but preempted professional discourse during the second half of the 1970s. In the following decade, export promotion actually became the conventional wisdom of the day. A central issue was the degree to which a national government should encourage integration with the emerging global economy. In world-economic terms, a poor and technically backward country can compete in world markets for industrial products only on the basis of cheap labor. The policy problem, then, is first, how to keep the price of labor down, and second, how to attract transnational firms to a given country (e.g., through capital subsidies, the maintenance of law and order, etc.). A related policy dimension, though less frequently discussed, is the question of how to achieve technology transfers and employment multipliers linked to industrial growth points in export enclaves on the coast.

Proponents of the export-promotion model like to cite the cases of successful economic growth in the Four Little Tigers—Hongkong, Taiwan, Singapore, and South Korea. What these countries, with their law-and-order regimes, could accomplish might be replicated elsewhere in Southeast Asia and, by implication, in other parts of the world. Redistribution-with-growth theorists also favored export promotion (though in somewehat more tempered form than the advocates of export promotion pure and simple), if only to help pay off the massive debt incurred by many poor countries after the 1973 oil shock. On the other hand, they insisted that some part of the new growth increments should be channelled toward certain target groups of the poor. Once again, the Four Little Tigers were called upon to perform. They seemed to have managed the transition to a prosperous market economy even while taking care of their poor.

28

My critique, which cast doubt on many of the claims of both of these policy cures, also took exception to the uniform neglect of politics in the usual presentations of the two doctrines. It insisted that all development policy is based on extra-economic ideologies that favor some social groups over others. It also noted how neoclassical theory tends to treat politics by assumption.

In writing this paper, I stepped onto a hornets' nest, and the hornets flew up angrily and struck back. The orginal publishers had sought comments from Martin Bronfenbrenner, Gustav Ranis, and Hans W. Singer, three beacon lights in the field. All of them thought my reading of the evidence either tendentious or overly pessimistic. Bronfenbrenner called me to task for believing in Murphy's Law: "If anything can go wrong it will." I replied to my critics at length. (Our exchange is reprinted in the Appendix, page 295.)

A decade after the drafting of this text, I find that it retains much of its relevance. Global restructuring continues, and the Pacific Rim has become the new world trading zone, outpacing the more staid Atlantic Community. The arguments raised in our debate of ten years ago are far from having been resolved. Three of the Four Little Tigers have gotten fatter, and the fourth—Hongkong—is sitting on the fence, waiting to see which way the wind will blow after 1997 when the colony will be reabsorbed into China. The Philippine economy has slid downhill despite having heeded the export-promotion strategists; or perhaps it declined just because her policy makers heeded the foreign advice. With the possible exception of Malaysia, other countries in Southeast Asia are not faring much better, though neither Thailand nor Indonesia has yet suffered political collapse. (Both countries are oil exporters.)

Today we can perhaps see more clearly how the debate of the seventies concerned the contradictions between life space and economic space. For neo-classical economists, territorial values are seen as an obstacle to an efficient growth transition. For territorially based politicians, reality seems fraught with difficult choices. To what extent should they promote and encourage their countries' integration with the global system? What price are they prepared to pay? Both the Shah of Iran and President Marcos of the Philippines were to contemplate the disastrous outcomes of their neoclassical policies in exile.

Most current theories of economic growth and development are to a very considerable extent the handiwork of economists raised in the neo-classical tradition of their discipline. This essentially Anglo-Saxon heritage stresses the logical and practical separation of questions of efficiency in production from those of equity in distribution (Schultz 1949; Lewis 1955; Streeten 1955). Welfare economists have unsuccessfully tried to formulate an objective and universally valid principle of distribution (Arrow 1963). Failing in this, they concluded that questions of welfare fall outside their purview and are, strictly speaking, the business of politicians. Economists might advise the latter on how best to achieve a given distribution, but as professionals they have nothing to say about the desirability of the distribution itself.

This, at least, has been the official posture of most neo-classical economists, and especially of those who see their discipline as a positive science. The matter, however, is not quite so simple. Typically, economists' advice to politicians is based on a special model of production and distribution, in which efficiency is portrayed as a continuous variable that declines monotonically with increases in equity (Alonso 1968; Mera 1975). Gains in social justice, it is argued, can be obtained only at the expense of production. But the reverse also holds true: high rates of growth are achievable only with major inequalities in distribution.[1] This way of putting the matter places politicians in a difficult position. For if we assume that poor countries want to get rich, what politician would dare to sacrifice even an ounce of future affluence for a pound of present justice?

By declaring distributional equity 'out-of-bounds' so far as their own science was concerned, economists voted, in effect, for inequality. Social justice would come at some future date, they seemed to say, either as the 'natural' working-out of market forces and the result of continued increases in productivity, or from political choice.

This benign view of one of the most hotly debated social issues of our time was the easier to maintain because equality itself was a rather vague idea around which buzzed a swarm of possible meanings and interpretations. Moreover, most economists insisted that, regardless of what people thought should be the case, high-growth economies required substantial inequality in the distribution of both productive wealth and income.[2]

To build an argument around this last contention, they reached back to Joseph Schumpeter's early work on entrepreneurship and innovation (Schumpeter 1934; orig. 1926). In every society, Schumpeter had claimed, only a few individuals were by nature endowed to act in entrepreneurial capacities and to employ resources in ways that would maximize returns both for themselves and for society. If followed that resources had to be channelled towards those who were best equipped to make allocative decisions. Because private entrepreneurs were geared to a relatively short investment horizon and some investments (such as infrastructure) would take rather long to mature, a secondary stream of resources would have to be directed to the State, which would act in a supportive capacity. In addition, however, capitalists needed incentives that would get them to save and invest a larger proportion of their income than they might normally care to do. Thus, they had to be assured not only of control over a large portion of society's wealth but also of continued high returns from their investments.

Given this ideology masquerading as positive science, the initial disclaimer of economists that they were purely objective in their judgments, advising politicians solely with regard to the costs and benefits of alternative courses of action, turned out to be merely a case of false consciousness.

The modern theory of economic growth and development was invented in the late 1940s and early 1950s. It came about as a direct result of the prior invention of national product accounts by Colin Clark (1938) and Simon Kuznets (1941). For the first time, it became possible to reduce all exchange values produced in the economy to the global figures of gross national product. It was logical, therefore, that economic growth would come to be defined as a steady increase in that single, magical number. However, because it was difficult completely to exclude considerations of welfare from policy discussions of economic growth, a simple measure was invented to describe 'development' as a socially desirable form of growth: population was divided into the total product of the economy, yielding the now notorious quotient of GNP per capita. This was not, of course, a measure of distribution or, for that matter, even a meaningful indicator of social welfare, though it was often used in this sense. It was, quite simply, an indicator that would show how much each man, woman and child would receive if income were to be equally apportioned among them. Development theory could then be reduced to a statement of the efficient conditions that would raise the gross production value of a nation at a rate faster than that of its population.[3]

In this way, development theory succeeded in avoiding all explicit reference to distribution. Instead, the problem was solved by assumption. Theorists simply *assumed* that people would be better off with high rates of economic growth than without them. Initially, the achievement of high growth would indeed require a substantial inequality of wealth and income. But trickle-down effects would eventually channel income in the direction of the poor, while increases in productivity would ensure that employed labour (remunerated at the rate of its marginal contribution to the value of production) would receive its proper reward in the form of higher wages. If politicians desired a more equal distribution, this was, of course, their privilege; it could be achieved, however, only by sacrificing an appreciable amount of growth. The redistribution of productive wealth was, as a rule, not seriously considered.

Most early economic development theory stressed the role of capital to the virtual exclusion of every other factor. This gave rise to the widespread use of the capital-output ratio as a planning device. In time, other considerations were emphasized, and variables continue to be added to this day. An economy had to become a 12-percent saver, ran one argument (Lewis 1955). Efficiently invested, this quantum of capital would yield a growth rate sufficient to overcome the increases in population. Eventually, this ratio was raised to twice and even more the original estimate. But the argument that priority had to be given to the accumulation of capital remained.

As far as specific investment policies were concerned, economists were nearly unanimous in advocating urban industrialization. Colin Clark (1940) had classified productive activities into three mutually exclusive sectors: primary (or extractive), secondary (or manufacturing), and tertiary (or services). With scarcely a dissenting voice, economists proclaimed the secondary sector as the truly productive and dynamic one in the economy. Agriculture (which constituted the bulk of the primary sector) would become more productive in the measure that investment took place, rural population was syphoned-off to cities, and production was reorganized along capitalist, high-technology lines. Services (including trades) would, in turn, expand as a function of gains in manufacturing production but would be incapable of generating growth independently.

This was all more or less in accord with eighteenth and nineteenth century British economic history (Polanyi 1944). The so-called developing countries, seeking to become even more like the West, would have to retrace roughly the same evolutionary sequence. The only difference, it was believed, was the speed at which they would accomplish this feat. Current performance showed that annual economic growth rates of between 5 and 10 per cent could be sustained, and this proved to be well above the rates which had been experienced by Western countries, including Britain, during the heyday of their own industrialization. Because of the separation of problems of efficiency from those of equity, and because of the de facto insistence on the requirements of inequality in the distribution of wealth and income as a condition of economic growth, I shall call the policies derived from the doctrine, *policies of unequal development*.

Inevitably, unequal development came to be constructed as a success model. Its first complete formulation was W. W. Rostow's stages of economic growth theory (1961). Accordingly to its author, a capitalist economy typically moves through a series of 'stages' that includes the now famous 'take-off' into sustained growth which terminates in what Rostow called the age of high mass consumption.

Rostow's stage model of economic growth was sharply criticized both by liberal and left-wing critics during the 1960s, in part, perhaps, because of its provocative presentations as a self-styled 'non-Communist manifesto'. Recently, however, a major study has been published under the prestigious sponsorship of the World Bank, which largely recapitulates Rostovian theory but substitutes for its historical, quasi-intuitive speculations the hard evidence of statistical science. I shall quote:

> In describing the processes of development, we have tried to replace the notion of dichotomy between less developed and developed countries with the concept of a transition from one state to another. This transition is defined by a set of structural changes that have almost always accompanied the growth of per capita income in recent decades. Most of these features have already been identified in the history of industrial countries, which Kuznets describes as 'modern economic growth'.
>
> The present study compares the recent experience of developing countries with the earlier development and present structure of the advanced countries. In this comparison the hypothesis that continuous structural change is related to the growth of income is better supported by our statistical evidence than is the alternative hypothesis that different structural relations characterize developed and developing countries, however defined. We have therefore focused our attention on the nature of the processes that are fundamental to the transition. (Chenery and Syrquin 1975: 135).

Although this study is of fairly recent origin, the basic model of unequal development continues to be used. As with Rostow, the key indicator is income per head, and all countries appear to be headed towards a stage of universal development of which the currently high-income countries are the forerunners. Traditional and modern societies are linked by a process of structural transition. The authors go on to describe the shape of this transition:

> Most of the ten processes analyzed here [employment by sectors, urbanization, demographic transition, income distribution, etc.] can be

> described by a logistic or other form of S-shaped curve having asymptotes at low and high levels of income. The upper asymptote has an obvious interpretation for such structural characteristics as the rate of saving or investment, the share of industry, the proportion of the population receiving higher education, or the birth rate. These asymptotes provide a set of measures of the direction in which most economies are moving in any historical period . . . The estimates for developing countries also suggest that change accelerates in certain periods of a country's development. (Ibidem: 135–136).

It is during the transition that profound structural dislocations are expected to occur: the countryside becomes depopulated, cities expand at a tremendous rate, the economy becomes integrated into the international system, new industries spring up everywhere, manufacturing replaces agriculture as the principal sector, the automobile takes over from older forms of transportation. This vast transformation is projected as necessary to achieving high incomes per head. An early United Nations report put the requirement in stark, dramatic language:

> . . . rapid economic progress is impossible without painful readjustments. Ancient philosophies have to be scrapped; old social institutions have to disintegrate; bonds of caste, creed, and race have to be burst; and large numbers of persons who cannot keep up with progress have to have their expectations of a comfortable life frustrated. Very few communities are willing to pay the full price of economic progress (United Nations 1951: 15).

As told by Chenery and Syrquin, however, the story sounds more reassuring. Yes, they say, there will be dislocations, and especially during the transition, our indicators will show a pattern of increasingly severe disequilibria in the relevant variables. But with proper management, disequilibria can be corrected. The thing to remember is the ultimate object of development, or the achievement of high per capita incomes, and the specific structural correlates of this state. In other words, a condition of social turbulence can be successfully managed so long as governments maintain an even-handed course, continuing to employ resources efficiently. But if a country should be poorly governed, the transition will be delayed; indeed, it might never be completed. The economy would be caught in what is picturesquely called a low-level equilibrium trap. 'Very few communities are willing to pay the full price of economic progress', said the UN experts in 1951.

Strategies of Crisis Management

By the end of the 1960s, it was obvious to nearly everyone that the first UN Development Decade had sadly failed in meeting its ambitions. Precise measures might not always be available, but clouds of crisis were gathering in the Third World: endemic hunger, decline in the real incomes of peasants and workers, widespread underemployment, increasing population pressure, exploding cities, widening regional inequalities, mounting political tensions, growing military repression. The 'crisis of transition' was in full swing. The question was whether this crisis would be surmounted by continuing policy applications of the doctrine of unequal development, or whether major modifications of the doctrine were in order, and finally, whether a wholly new approach to development might prevent the crisis from degenerating into even greater chaos.

The call to action was sounded by Dudley Seers who at the time was Director of the prestigious Institute of Development Studies at Sussex University. In a speech to the Society for International Development, Seers challenged the view that development could be measured by the customary indicator of income per head. He chided economists and policy administrators for their failure to take distribution and related criteria into account:

> The questions to ask about a country's development are therefore: What has been happening to poverty? What has been happening to unemployment? What has been happening to inequality? If all three of these have declined from high levels, then beyond doubt this has been a period of development for all concerned. If one or two of these central problems have been growing worse, especially if all three have, it would be strange to call the result 'development', even if per capita income doubled (Seers 1969, 3).

That same year, the International Labour Office initiated the World Employment Program (ILO 1971). Its purpose was to place an objective of full, productive employment alongside traditional income objectives in national planning.

My purpose in this essay is to investigate whether and to what extent these strategies of crisis management represent significant departures from the doctrine of unequal development, which is what they claim to be, and whether they are at all likely to succeed in coping with the crisis of transition, returning the economy to a condition of equilibrium at relatively high levels of per capita income.

Because of their forceful exposition, two strategies of crisis management have arrived at a position of prominence. I shall call them, respectively, the strategies of export substitution and of redistribution with growth.[4]

Export Substitution is largely American in inspiration Its *locus classicus* is Paauw and Fei's *The Transition in Open Dualistic Economies* (1973), where the underlying theory is explained. It was this theory which informed the ILO Report, *Sharing in Development: A Programme of Employment, Equity and Growth for the Philippines* (1974), prepared under the guidance of Gustav Ranis, director of the Yale Economic Growth Center. This Center has done important policy work not only for the ILO, but also for the US Agency for International Development. Furthermore, Fei and Ranis had collaborated on an earlier work, *Development of a Labor Surplus Economy: Survey and Critique* (1964), which stands as a landmark in American development studies. The Paauw-Fei volume may be read as an updating of that earlier book.

The alternative strategy of Redistribution with Growth (RwG) follows the title of a collection of papers written by Chenery, Ahluwalia, Bell, Duloy, and Jolly (1974). Hollis Chenery is Vice President for Research of the World Bank and one of the leading specialists in development economics. Both Ahluwalia and Duloy are associated with Chenery's Development Research Center at the Bank, and the two remaining authors—Jolly and Bell—are both with Sussex University's Institute of Development Studies (IDS), of which Richard Jolly is Director.

The origin of the RwG strategy can be traced to Hans Singer's seminal essay, 'A Model of Redistribution from Growth', which served as the basic policies framework for an ILO-sponsored mission to Kenya (ILO 1972: 365–370). Singer is a distinguished development economist who, in co-directorship with Richard Jolly, had directed the Kenya mission. Their report, *Employment, Incomes and Equality: A Strategy for Increasing Productive Employment in Kenya* (1972) may be regarded as the policy counterpart of the more theoretical statement embodied in the Chenery et al volume referred to above.

Just as the strategy of Export Substitution may be characterized as essentially American in spirit, so the RwG strategy clearly reveals its British origin. It reflects the institutions of the British welfare state, with its idea of 'fair shares' and 'balanced growth'. In a larger sense, it also reflects the grand political tradition of the Fabians and the British Labour Party (social democracy) and is a perfect instance of the pragmatic philosophy of 'muddling through'.

The Export Substitution Strategy

The Export Substitution strategy is proposed for what its authors call 'open dualistic economies' of medium size. The countries to which they have specific reference are all located in East and Southeast Asia:

the Philippines, Malaysia, Thailand, Singapore, Taiwan, Hong Kong and the Republic of Korea. One gets the impression that they would want to include Indonesia and possibly Sri Lanka as well, but not the countries of the Indian sub-continent.

The Export Substitution strategy is identified as appropriate to a specific phase in a general model of the modern transition. The crisis of transition, argue its authors, is due to the fact that the stage of import substitution which necessarily precedes it has not been overcome. As a result, the overall economic growth rate has declined, which is causing labour to become surplus at a rapidly growing rate and income differences to be exacerbated. Import substitution has exhausted itself, because domestic markets are limited, and all that can be produced and marketed domestically is already being produced. The next 'big push' must therefore come from the export of manufactured commodities which will increasingly 'substitute' for the traditional primary exports of minerals and specialized food products. To conquer foreign markets, however, the country's economy must become more tightly integrated with the world economic system. It must be able to out-compete its competitors. Basically, this means (a) increasing efficiency in production, (b) keeping wages low, (c) investing heavily in export industries. By rapidly industrializing, with a view to export markets, surplus labour will be readily 'mopped up' and put to work in industry. When all the surplus has been so employed, wages will begin to rise, and income differences will start to diminish. Meanwhile, emergency 'welfare' programmes can help to tide over the poorer segments of the population until their situation gradually improves. *The time for this to happen is about a decade.*

Fortunately, this theory is concisely summarized on pages 115–117 of Paauw and Fei (1973). I shall therefore quote directly from this summary, adding, where appropriate, critical comments to illustrate the meaning of the passage cited. Following this, I shall make a few additional comments based on the Philippine Report which, though it follows the general logic of the theory quite closely, does have additional features which are important to note.

> (1) The emergence of the ES (export substitution) phase signifies that the industrial entrepreneur, having achieved maturity, is able to utilize surplus labour released from the agricultural sector to exploit innumerable trade opportunities.

Comment: The authors seem to imply that the industrial entrepreneur, as they call him, is indigenous to the country, that he has 'grown up' out of youthful beginnings and has 'matured'. This was during the preceding import-substitution phase. But from other evidence we know that the bulk of 'modern' industry is owned and operated by foreign capitalists. The ILO Philippine Report, for instance, says: 'United States investors held 76 per cent of the total direct equity investment in 1970' (p. 283), and '33.5 per cent of total assets of industry was controlled by foreigners' (Ibidem). The ratios were even higher for banking (59 per cent) and for mining (48 per cent). We are therefore not dealing with entrepeneurs who 'mature' from experience, but with large international corporations that establish branches of their operation in a developing country if the circumstances there are favourable for making money.

Reference is made to 'surplus labour' which is a favourite expression and leaves one wondering what this labour is 'surplus' to. The implication is that workers have become redundant in the countryside and have moved to the city, where they remain as 'surplus', only now in relation to the corporate sector which holds them, as it were, 'in reserve'. Being held in reserve means that wages can be held down as well, *and this is what the strategy is all about*.

Observe how the language cited subtly suggests that 'labour' (i.e. working people) is (are) a tool in the hands of capitalist entrepreneurs to 'exploit . . . trade opportunities'. The profits from this exploitation, of course, accrue to the capitalist. For only because labour is 'surplus' and 'in reserve' can wages be held down to a minimum of subsistence (and even less than subsistence, as we shall see). The Philippine Report, addressing, among others, labour union leaders, admonishes them to practice 'wage restraint'. Here the matter is put more bluntly:

(2) Central to this process are the expansion of labour supply through population growth and the reallocation of labour from a agriculture to the industrial sector.

Comment: The basic theme is emphasized. One gets the impression that the authors welcome rapid population growth because in this way an 'unlimited' supply of labour made redundant in agriculture becomes available for industry . . . at subsistence and below-subsistence wages. The individual and family enterprise sector must hold labour in readiness until, by and by, it is needed in, and can advance into the corporate sector.

(3) As explained in the familiar model of the closed labour-surplus economy, analysis of this process must emphasize labour absorption by the industrial sector, and labour release by the agricultural sector. The

case of the open dualistic model may be analyzed by a slight modification of the closed model, which we briefly sketch.

For analysis of labour absorption by industry, the real wage in terms of industrial goods, w_i, is assumed to be relatively constant because of the labour surplus conditions ('unlimited supply of labour').

Comment: To assume a constant real wage in this context implies that the wages of the great mass of urban workers are set equal to subsistence, or to the minimum required to reproduce the labour power of the worker. Since the labour supply is regarded as 'unlimited', however, the real wage w_i, may in practice be allowed to fall *below* subsistence needs since labour can be worn out and replaced at no cost to the entrepreneur-capitalist. Labour is therefore treated as virtually a 'free good'; it is disposable. Even with this amendment, however, the assumption of a constant real wage turns out to be a fiction, since inflation—which typically is a condition accompanying capitalist development—*erodes* the real incomes of unprotected and unorganized workers (that workers shall remain unprotected and unorganized is a further assumption of this model).[5]

(4) Rapidity of labour absorption then depends upon the rate of increase in the demand for labour, MPP_L (Marginal Physical Productivity of Labour). Labour is absorbed rapidly when (1) labour-using innovation raises MPP_L, (2) the real wage, w_i, remains at a constant level causing income distribution to favour industrial profits and leading to (3) a high rate of industrial capital accumulation (again raising MPP_L).

Comment: This is the nineteenth century model of industrialization which resulted in Marx's *Capital*, Vol. 1 and Friedrich Engels's *Condition of the Working Classes in England*. The case for exploitation has rarely been presented in more pristine form. A further assumption is introduced here: entrepreneurs will save and invest at a high rate, because they are motivated by a high rate of profits which they can extract from the 'unlimited' supply of labour at their disposal. In other words, the 'Asian' entrepreneur is expected to behave like the nineteenth century model mill owner in Manchester. Actually, as we have seen, the principal beneficiaries of this policy will be foreign investors (and, therefore, the consumers of imported products in the core countries of the world economic system).

Because the object is to maximize profits, and labour-intensive innovations are to be used rather than complex machinery, increasing productivity of labour becomes a key issue in organizing production. So long as labour is virtually costless, there are two principal ways of increasing productivity: by lengthening the time worked and by speed-up. Both are classical forms of worker exploitation.

> (5) In the analysis of labour releases from agriculture, expansion of agricultural productivity assures an increasing supply of labour as well as agricultural goods to the industrial sector. This, in turn, leads to internal terms of trade favourable to industry and, hence, to the relative 'cheapness' of labour supply, i.e. a low real wage, w_i. Industrial profits are thus enhanced and capital accumulation is promoted.

Comment: The points already made are emphasized, in case we did not get the message the first time around: industrial wages must be kept *low*. Earlier, the authors told us that population increase will help to replenish the supply of surplus labour; now they want to make sure the entrepreneur will not run short of his supply and recommend mechanization in agriculture (expansion of agricultural productivity means productivity of labour primarily, for else there would be no labour release from this sector) as well as increasing production (to lower food costs in cities). Both policies imply something like the Green Revolution which, as is known from a variety of sources, tends to favour the larger, more well-situated farmers, at the expense of those living on the margins of subsistence (Griffin 1974).

Turning the internal terms of trade against agriculture may be a counter-productive strategy (if the intention is to encourage farmers to invest in their business), unless it is assumed that farmers are also industrial entrepreneurs (or at least businessmen with an urban out-look) and so are able to profit in both ways: what they 'save' through adverse terms of trade they can 'invest' in the city (most probably in real estate, but possibly in transport or some other sort of business). Thus, the model implies absentee landlords and commercial farming operations, and therefore greater income inequality (and growing ine-quality of landed wealth) in rural areas. The peasant population is to be squeezed off the land and proletarianized in the interest of rapid capital accumulation in the city.

> (6) The traditional agricultural sector, T, now replaced the agricultural export sector, X, as the major source of intersectoral finance for indus-trial capital accumulation.

Comment: By traditional agricultural sector the authors obviously mean the food-producing sector, whether 'traditional' or not. They do *not* mean the export or cash-crop sector, which is already part of the corporate econom . The base for financin industrial development has been broadened. You cannot extract a surplus until production has been increased above subsistence needs, So, agricultural development is promoted with this objective in view. The Green Revolution is the counterpart of the 'enclosure movement' in Great Britain. Agriculture finances industrial development in four ways: through its export earnings (chiefly corporate farming); through migration out of rural areas (investment in skills); through indirect monetary transfers via adverse and declining internal terms of trade; and through plentiful and cheap supplies of food and industrial raw materials which permit industrialists to hold their costs to a minimum.

(7) The opportunity of trade offers the open economy advantages not available to the closed economy. First, labour reallocation to the industrial sector can occur at a more rapid pace. This is true because the industrial sector in an open economy has the option of acquiring needed food and raw materials from abroad by concentrating on labour-intensive exports. Second, this permits a more rapid rate of capital accumulation than in the closed economy.

Comment: It takes exploited labour to exploit labour. A clever strategy, indeed. Export earnings from manufacturing—which in the first place are made possible by hiring workers at starvation wages—are then used, in part, to import food and raw materials from abroad at prices which, especially for food, may fall below the price at home. This practice will force domestic farmers to sell at lower cost, perhaps even below their costs of production. It is a way of squeezing the last penny out of the farmers, of ensuring a dualism in the organization of the agriculural sector that is identical in function to the dualism created in the urban-industrial sector. Only relentless cost-reduction in farming permits survival of the business. Note the veil of language that is used to mask who gains from these prescriptions and who loses. An 'open economy' does not actually have 'opportunity of trade', but people do, traders do, and more specifically merchant traders connected with overseas markets. Nor does the 'industrial sector' acquire needed food and raw materials from abroad, but the industrial-commercial elite of the country, in collaboration with high government officials. And the reason? Their personal gain or profit, which is hidden in the phrase 'permits a more rapid rate of capital accumulation . . .'

(8)The closed economy model implies a turning point thesis for the development of the labour-surplus economy. As population expands, continued expansion of the industrial employment and labour reallocation will eventually lead to a turning point at which the economy's surplus is exhausted. At this point, the real wage in the industrial sector will begin to rise sharply. The implication of this phenomenon for the open economy is that the economy will lose its cheap labour advantage after the turning point. This will necessitate that the industrial sector find a new comparative advantage in international trade (e.g. skilled labour, technology, or capital). Note: this implies that the export substitution phase is primarily based upon utilization of unskilled labour. Skilled labour become more relevant as the surplus of unskilled labour becomes exhausted.

Comment: The moral authority of the authors' prescriptive model depends entirely upon the validity of this paragraph. Up to now, the authors have sketched a path of rising inequality; now, however, a 'turning point' appears: wages rise sharply, the income distribution improves; the economy is headed for equilibrium again. Up to now, the economy was almost entirely export-oriented: the size of its domestic market was minimal (i.e. since the mass of the workers would remain at or below subsistence, domestic per capita consumption would not exceed by very much the level that had been previously attained during the import substitution period). With the coming of the turning point, however, and the dramatic improvement in real wages, the beginnings of a mass market appear that will permit the gradual increase of production for domestic use.

A crucial question is when the 'turning point' can be expected to arrive. Given the relentless increase in population—of which the authors of the model approve—and a continuing exodus from agriculture — which is the result of the authors' policies—the increase of industrial employment in the corporate sector—which is the only sector that is dynamic in the economy and which is producing for export — must be on a scale that is immense and accumulating relentlessly in order to 'absorb' the 'surplus' labour to the threshold of the 'turning point'. (A few years of sluggish expansion can wreak havoc with this model.) The authors imply that the time period for reaching the turning-point is very short (counting from the initiation of the export-substitution strategy). They suggest a period lasting for at most a decade or two. This may be optimistic. Particular skills may soon become in short supply, but the premise of the policy is that production will be based on *unskilled* labour. And thus, the mass of the labouring population, will continue to be much longer 'in surplus.' (More skilled workers may, indeed, fare somewhat better.)

But let us join in the authors' optimism, and now the turning point is here; it has arrived. What happens then? Well, it seems that when this fateful moment comes, 'the economy will lose its cheap labour advantage' and the corporate sector industries that have been sustaining the export-drive will pick up their plants and leave for other countries where there is still surplus labour to be exploited. Remember that the export industries are, for the most part, branch plants of multinational corporations, that their only reason for being is to make money for their owners, and that their local investment has long been written off, so that even physically abandoning plant and equipment (rather than selling it off, or re-exporting what may be left of it and movable) would not leave them any poorer. These enterprises have no interest at all in finding 'a new comparative advantage in international trade'. Quite simply, when it is no longer economic for them to operate their plant, they will leave to go elsewhere. And a major domestic economic crisis will be produced.

This crisis can be overcome, according to the authors, by 'switching' to more dynamic modern industries that require higher capitalization and skills. But what has prepared the country for this shift? Why should it be possible for a country like the Philippines, for instance, to suddenly become like Switzerland? (The suddenness of the transition is quite deliberately part of the model.) In an 'open' world economy in which the poor countries produce labour-intensively, and controls are exercised through multinational channels that guide the flow of finance, information, and technical knowledge, the entire science-technology-skills complex is concentrated in the West. Now that the labour advantage has disappeared, *and no other advantage exists*, why should industrial capital pour in to establish more skill-intensive production lines? And if the reference is to private domestic capital resources, what should motivate them to undertake independent industrial ventures, when the only markets are abroad and access to these markets is barred by international cartel arrangements? According to this line of reasoning, the mythical turning point referred to in the quoted paragraph may never arrive.

But even if it does—and the cases of Korea and Taiwan are constantly referred to by the authors as their historical models—*there is no guarantee whatever that there will be a decisive redistribution of income towards the working class*. For throughout their book, the authors appear to assume that the level of wage income is exclusively determined by market realtions between a corporate employment *giver* and an individual employment *taker*. And so, only *merited* increases in wages are allowed and these only after labour shortages begin to appear. Until then, workers must demonstrate an attitude of 'wage restraint' ($w_i = k$) which, in practice, means the absence of collective bargaining and the absence also of effective instruments of collective bargaining, or unions. The employment giver will only pay for labour that is required by the market; no more, no less. To expect, from this interaction, a sharp closing of the income distribution gap, the binomial distribution between workers' income and capitalists' income being transformed into a single distribution with steadily narrowing polarities, is to expect the impossible.

Yet, this is precisely what the authors ask us to do. Behind their model lies a belief—if that is what it is—in the universal harmony of interests. This is made explicit in the ILO Report on the Philippine economy (1974), a report that closely reflects the policy model which has been commended. The pertinent paragraph comes at the very end of the report where we find the following language: 'The interest of no single group need be sacrified if that group is capable of flexible response to the real opportunities now facing the Philippines. With a sharing of effort, as well as of restraint and responsibility, there can come a sharing in the fruits of rapid development' (p. 384).

This closing benediction addresses groups that, as such, do not exist. The only *organized* group capable of independent and coherent action is the national oligarchy. The restraint and responsibility exhortations are addressed to the peasants and workers who do not constitute a 'group' at all but a heap of atomized individuals and, what is more, are not supposed to form as a group acting in its own interests. How then is effort to be shared? It is the sharing between 'unlimited supplies of labour' and 'mature entrepreneurs', with the full force of governmental power standing behind and supporting the latter. Sharing implies a voluntary, cooperative effort. But how can one speak of voluntary cooperation when workers are *forced* into industry at starvation wages, or alternatively, into a holding sector (the reserve army of labour) where they can eke out a pitiful living until such a time as their bodies are needed in the foreign-owned corporate sector?

The universal harmony of interests is a pure myth.

The ILO report on the Philippines is essentially a detailed application of this policy model. The discrepancies are relatively few, the coincidences many. The goal is to raise and maintain the growth of GNP to 8 or 9 per cent per annum and even more, and to reach the 'turning point' where labour becomes relatively scarce within six to eight years. This objective, with GNP remaining enthroned and the entire strategy a purified version of the doctrine of unequal development, is to be achieved in two complementary ways: though rural 'mobilization' and through industrial export promotion.

But the rural strategy is weak. It covers five points: a decentralized programme of infrastructure investments at the *barrio* (district) level, equivalent to $1,000 per barrio or 2 per cent of the national budget;

support for existing land reform programmes (covering exactly 15 lines in a text of 16 pages of recommendations); a programme of credit and technical assistance to medium and small-scale industry for the production of wage goods to be sold to the rural population (but no programme to protect these industries against competition from the corporate sector); the propagation of Green Revolution technologies with what will surely be an empty warning against mechanization; and a programme of rural electrification and other measures intended to assist in the regional decentralization of industries.

Here are all the right words, but the real intention is mentioned only in passing, *which is to move people off the farm as quickly as possible and into the cities, where they will join the lumpenproletariat in the street economy, constituting a reserve army of labour whose function is to hold wages down.*

Fully two pages are devoted to wages policy in the summary recommendations. The text is specifically devised to give an incorrect impression of what are the real intentions of the Mission's recommendations. So, we may read here for example that:

> the basic and fundamental purpose of the mission is to ensure that the past 20 years of unbalanced growth make way for a balanced development pattern in which the hitherto disadvantaged parties share more fully.

Sounds great! Redress social injustice. The 'disadvantaged parties' in the case are the peasants and the majority of urban workers. But the authors continue:

> In practical terms, this means that our basic strategy must be directed towards a sustained increase in the incomes of the working families of the Philippines, an objective which can be accomplished only by mopping up, as quickly as possible, the unemployed and under-employed labour force.

Mopping up? Sounds like an easy job. Most people are already fully employed, so there is only a small remainder that needs to be taken care of. As quickly as possible.

> In other words, we fully agree with those who have called unemployment the worst exploitation of the working man.

Amen. Go on.

> The attempt to facilitate and support the proposed investment and export boom in new labour-intensive industries which we have outlined will

make it possible for the urban-industrial sector not only to absorb rapidly the increments to the urban labour force resulting from continuing population growth and existing surpluses in the urban sector but also to be able effectively to absorb the residual migration from the rural areas (inevitably even under conditions of successful application of the rural mobilization prong of our strategy).

An investment and export boom? In new labour-intensive industries? How is that to be accomplished? The answer is put in the negative:

The most dependable method of reversing the trend of *deteriorating real wages and incomes* of the working man and the *worsening distribution of income generally* in the Philippines resides in the successful implementation of the strategy outlined. This will enable the *period of continued pressure on wages* to be curtailed sharply so that the income of working families can benefit almost immediately and be assured of dramatic and sustained increases *within a decade. Any policies which deflect the Philippine Government from this objective, no matter how well intentioned, must be viewed as inimical to the very purposes of guaranteeing fuller employment, a higher wage bill and a better distribution of income.* (Emphasis added)

Immediate benefits? Dramatic and sustained increases in income now? Well no, not quite. Perhaps within a decade. Meanwhile, the Philippine Government is told to follow a policy of holding wages low, as low as possible, and constant over the period of transition. What is, in practice, exploitation must be presented as a positive incomes policy:

wage policies must try to protect the working class against further erosion of their real incomes, so that the consumption levels of the lower income groups are protected . . . To the extent that legal minimum wages have by now, in fact, come to approach a true minimum, we suggest that no further erosion in the real wage be permitted. (All of the above quotations are from ILO 1974, 45–46.)

Of course. You do not want to have bodies on your conscience. The 'true minimum' is starvation. Only when actual wage levels have eroded to subsistence should government act to level off the trend. Things could not be expressed more graphically.

But, to be fair, the working class is not the only one whose livelihood is to be treatened now for the sake of a long-term benefit (hence the phrase wage *restraint*). For Philippine industry to become more efficient and to compete in international markets, it must be exposed to external competition. Import duties should be liberalized; the economy should be 'opened' to the world (i.e. the West and Japan). Specifically, it is proposed to lower import tariffs to 30 per cent across the board for all products, including luxuries. Philippine industry will either have to spruce up or go under. (If it goes under, the capitalist may lose his factory but keep his bank account; the worker loses his or her job.) The following quotation tells the story:

> The only hope that the Philippine industrial sector as a whole has of remaining flexibly competitive in the future rests on the admission of increased competitive pressure over time (p. 43).

This pressure may come from lower tariffs, but also from higher interest rates, and an undervalued exchange rate. In addition, it will come from the encouragement of foreign corporations to invest directly in the Philippines economy. Or, as the mission puts it: 'foreign private capital should be given access and welcome' (p. 50). In addition to competitively low wages, private capital will be motivated to come to the Philippines if the Government creates a sufficient number of Export Processing Zones. These are industrial estates (another subsidy to capital!) for firms specializing in the processing and assembly of imported materials for re-export. In both importing and exporting activities, the firms established in such zones are exempted from any duties they might otherwise have had to pay. Their contribution to the domestic economy lies exclusively in their wage bill though, in principle, such industries may develop backward linkages with domestic 'feeder' industries.

The lengths to which the authors of the ILO-sponsored Philippine study will go to accommodate multinational corporations may be gleaned from the following excerpt:

> More Export Processing Zones would enable the Philippine Government to take full advantage of the services of foreigners, i.e. their capital, their technology, and their sales relations in the foreign markets, *while allowing the Philippines to exploit its own exportable resources—namely abundant labour* . . . If it were politically feasible, even the requirement of domestic minimum wages legislation might be waived if the Export Processing Zone can be viewed as 'foreign territory' analogous to the export of labour to Guam. (Emphasis added; p. 291)

Earlier, the mission had recommended letting wages 'erode' to a 'true minimum' and levelling off at that point. Now, the suggestion is to lop off EPZs as 'foreign territory' from the Philippines; in other words, to permit foreign firms to exploit Philippine workers without having to pay attention to Philippine law, without, in fact, having to pay attention to any law other than their own.

Yet in all, the mission is concerned with the poorest part of the population and solicitous of their well-being. So, a picturesquely titled and modestly-scaled 'low-end poverty redressal programme' is proposed. Outlined on pp. 271-276, the language and the mentality it reflects defies easy summary. Let it be noted, though, that what the mission regards here as appropriate expenditures is for such purposes as urban sewage, milk for school children, and an increase in the Department of Social Welfare's small entrepreneurship support programme.

One specific example will have to do duty for the text as a whole which, in itself, is a classical demonstration of the unequal development doctrine at work:

> It is a well known fact that improved nutrition, for instance in the form of free or subsidized school or pre-school lunches, can have a major impact on the intellectual and physical growth of the individual *and thus prove to be a very profitable investment in the long run also.* In recent years a project supported by the Agency for International Development has been providing over 1 million children with a *mixture of milk, flour, and local sugar;* local nutritionists . . . now suggest a mixture of *mongo* flour, rice flour, coconut flour and fish concentrate. This is claimed to be an acceptable food stuff which can be produced entirely from local materials, at a cost of 5 or 6 centavos per helping. With a target group of children aged 7–9 from the poorest 50 per cent of the families, the national cost of the programme would be approximately 25 million pesos. This should not be an unacceptable burden, and we recommend that serious attention be given to it. (p. 275; emphasis added).

Seeing that, once the turning point is passed, the Philippines will have to find their position in the international economy on the basis of skilled labour, maybe the Government ought to act now to invest in the labour force of the future at least to the extent of permitting the full biological development of their brain and not allow it to be stunted by endemic hunger. A very profitable investment, indeed. Even so, one should observe the careful tone adopted by the mission. They recommend that 'serious attention' be given to their proposal to feed fishmeal to Philippine school children to avoid mass starvation among them. Nothing like as much attention, though, as making sure that wages do not rise. To help the poor become less poor is called a 'misguided intention'. Nothing can be done until the 'turning point' has been reached. *Everything depends on that mystical vision.*

The Redistribution with Growth Strategy

It is difficult to critique the Strategy of Redistribution with Growth (RwG) (Chénery et al. 1974) because, unlike Export Substitution, no explicit theory supports it. What underlies it is a moral tone; principles of social justice demand that attention be given to the problems of distribution that arise in economic growth and development. Sheer growth will not resolve the problems of massive poverty. On the contrary; there is evidence that the situation of the poor may be deteriorating in some countries. What should be done?

The answer is a pragmatic one. The proponents of RwG might have said that what is done is to foment a social revolution. But academics and high bank officials are unlikely to speak out for revolution. A RwG strategy that does not look to revolution might then engage in some reform-mongering: accelerating GNP growth through raising savings, and allocating resources more efficiently, with benefits to all groups in the society; redistribution of existing assets; asset redistribution by redirecting new investment into the creation of assets generating income for the poorest; and transfer of income in support of consumption of the poorest. This is the full range of policy options, and the authors of the RwG strategy assert that, to some extent, all of them must be used, but the actual mix of policy will, of course, vary from situation to situation. On the whole, however, the emphasis is on (a) efficient growth and (b) redistribution of the increments from growth to the poor (broken down into specific 'target groups') in the form of tailor-made income-producing investment programmes. In other words, the idea is to build up the productive capacity of 'the poor' *without reducing the present income of 'the rich'*. To put this another way, the strategy aims at accelerating the growth of the informal and peasant sectors of the economy by slightly reducing the overall potential growth of the corporate sector.[6]

The use of the term 'target group', which is quite central to the policy analysis of RwG, suggests two things: first, that it constitutes a subgroup of the society and second, that there exists a 'marksman' that is taking aim; the target group is regarded as an object of public policy (international agencies, the state), *not as a codeterminer of its own future*. Its role is to receive, not give.

The overall target group is called 'the poor'. Now the poor may be variously defined; in the report by Chenery et al they are defined as the lowest 40 per cent of population in income distribution. In most parts of the world, this means that population group which, in the aggregate, has an estimated annual income of less than $75 per capita.

The definition of the poor is thus an economic one. This circumscribes the area of possible solutions. To make the poor less poor is seen as an economic problem. Had 'the poor' been identified in terms of their lack of access to political power, for example, a political solution might have been considered appropriate. But then, perhaps, the designation 'target group' would have had to disappear as being inappropriate.

The target group is defined as the lower end of an income distribution. Their poverty is, therefore, defined not merely in economic terms but specifically in terms of individual monetary income rather than in services or *social income*. Had the emphasis been on services, a basic needs approach might have been proposed with far-reaching implications for change. But it was not.

Let us look at this lower end. Table 2.2 in the Chenery et al volume (1974) provides some of the relevant data. Two columns are critical. One is labelled Population below $50, the other Population below $75. The figures aggregated for the three main continents are given in Table 2.1 (data are for 1969).

The 'insignificant' difference between these two estimates of 'only' $25 per capita encompasses nearly one-fifth of the population on these three continents. Although the 'insignificant' difference may, in fact, spell the difference between living and dying, it can be agreed that, by American or European standards, $25 per capita per year is not a very great sum of money, and that even $75 means little more than bare survival. What would have happened, then, if Chenery et al. had taken, say, $100 per capita as their threshold of absolute poverty? A majority of the world's population would then have been covered, including the vast majority of people living in Africa and Asia.

Obviously, this is a numbers game, and it is ultimately to no purpose except for this: had Chenery et al. taken a higher figure—$100 will do to illustrate the point, but why not, say, $250?—*the whole notion of target groups and the poor, of some subcategory of the population for whom it is legitimate to show some concern, would have evaporated, as the affected population would, with each higher threshold limit,*

TABLE 2.1

| | Per cent of Population | |
	Below $50	Below $75
Latin America	10.8	17.4
Asia	36.1	56.4
Africa	28.4	43.6
Total	30.5	47.9

gradually approach 100 per cent of national population. At that point, 'reform-mongering' would have to cease and more fundamental questions would have to be addressed. For the target group approach is only convenient so long as it allows you to hold everything else constant while diverting 2 or 3 per cent of GNP towards investment in the informal (urban) sector and in small-scale farming (Chenery et al. 1974).

So much for the 'logic' of target groups and the whole approach to RwG. On the more practical side, it might be pointed out that experience in the past has shown that, even in Western countries with a commitment to the ideals of social democracy, social programmes which are intended to benefit 'the poor' generally end up by benefiting the not-so-poor, that is, the upper income strata of the designated target population. There is no evidence at all to suggest that the fate of a general policy of RwG in poor, agrarian societies would be any different, unless there were a radical and thorough-going redistribution of assets, especially of land, towards the lower income strata (including landless labour) and a major rearrangement of access to social power in favour of 'the poor'. Neither of these strategies, however, is regarded as politically 'feasible' by the authors of RwG. This being so, one can predict with reasonable certainty that the specific policies recommended both in the Chenery et al. volume and in the ILO Kenya Mission Report—even if they were carried out to the letter, which is unlikely in itself—would end up by benefiting primarily those families and individuals who are already better situated with respect to power than the majority of the poor.

It is difficult to disagree with the noble intentions of the RwG advocates. Indeed, it is difficult to criticize any flexible, pragmatic, and realistic policy with regard to income distribution and social justice.[7] On the other hand, the very resilience of this stance—its slippery quality, as I might also call it—is its greatest weakness. Slipperiness or robustness—whatever word is used—results from the fact that structural issues are not faced in all their seriousness. So we find attention being given to the problems of 'small producers' in the informal sector, *but no mention of inflation which erodes their earnings;* small farming is discussed at length, *but not internal terms of trade.* Yet both inflation and the internal terms of trade reduce the incomes of the poor but not the rich (because the rich know how to defend themselves; they have access to social power, and they are protected by the state). Or yet again, with attention being focussed on the individual and family enterprise sector, there is no recognition of the need to protect this sector against competition from corporate business. Yet without this protection, informal sector production can survive only in the interstices of the economy.

The reason for this neglect is not merely an unwillingness to face up to questions of structural change. Rather, it is the tacit belief that, somehow, the problem of growth has been solved so that the only problem that remains is how to redistribute from this growth. This is quite clear, for example, in the Kenya Report.

Now it happens that Kenya is an outstanding example of a country that is practicing policies of unequal development. And that means, among other things, giving absolute priority to growth and growth-efficiency. The ILO recommends that some of this efficiently realized growth be diverted to investments in the poor. It does not challenge the structure that is producing the growth in the first place. *It merely presumes its continued existence.*[8] Given this situation, redistribution becomes a marginal rather than a central objective of development policy and will only be pursued to the extent that it suits the needs of the ruling class in the society, *that is, to the extent that it is not cheaper and more expedient to employ repressive methods against the poor.* In addition, where the structural conditions of growth remain untouched, redistribution policies will be contradicted by the continuous generation of countervailing pressures in the economy, such as high inflation and terms of trade that are adverse to the informal sector generally in both urban and rural areas.

Another example may help to make this clear. Within the logic of unequal development, the export-substitution model is no doubt the strongest candidate for implementation. Once import-substitution policies have been exhausted, there is little a country can do to maintain a high rate of growth except to adopt a policy of export substitution. This holds for Kenya as much as it does for the Philippines. But we have seen that one of the requirements of an export-substitution policy is what is euphemistically called wage restraint ($w_i = k$). And we have also seen that this means, in practice, a wage that is held at minimum survival levels.

Here, then, is a potential contradiction. If, on the one hand, wages must be held to survival levels so as to ensure continued rapid economic growth and, on the other, raised to achieve a fairer distribution of the product, which of the two policies is likely to win out? The answer is: the policy of wage restraint in every case, *because economic growth is taken as the primary objective.* The problem of poverty in agrarian, newly industrializing societies does not reside primarily in the 'informal' sector; *it is not a problem of the poor.* A solution must be found in the corporate sector by transforming that sector. Where growth is primary, and export-substitution is accepted as the only viable strategy, workers cannot be allowed to organize themselves in order extract the best possible conditions from their employers and the legislature. Labour unions and political movements of the 'left' that represent the interests of the working class and poor peasantry must be suppressed; they are inimical to growth. And given this situation, what is the likely result of policies that aim at RwG?

Reform-mongering, to use Albert Hirschman's celebrated phrase, must fail because it refuses to countenance the necessity of major structural change in the economy whose purpose is to achieve an organization of production that will guarantee the equal development of the economy. In the political climate existing in the Third World today, all attempts to take from the rich to give to the poor are bound to fail. Only policies that *place growth incentives where the people are* and are capable of producing a true merger of growth with distribution, efficiency with equity, have any hopes for long-term success. But this approach would require a definition of 'the poor' in terms of their relative lack of access to social power (and not their level of consumption).[9] When this is done, labour unions, political parties of the left, and agrarian transformation would become central issues of development policy. An explicit conflict model would replace the model of universal harmony of interests which is the ideological smokescreen for actual police repression. The central question would then be: how should a country organize itself for economic growth to satisfy criteria of equity *at the same time?* How can an equal development be achieved?

Conclusions

On close examination, the two strategies of crisis management turn out to be only different versions of the doctrine of unequal development. The Export Substitution model is a purified version of this doctrine, adapted to policy use; it depends heavily on the assumption that maximizing economic growth must be the first objective and hence, on criteria of efficiency and on the integration of enclave economies in poor countries with the global economy of world capitalism on the basis of an international division of labour. Because of this, the strategy implies continued domination of the domestic economy by foreign interests and the use of domestic political power to hold wages and peasant incomes to subsistence levels. Specifically, this policy has been proposed for the Philippines, and it is actually being carried out in countries such as Brazil and Mexico.

The RwG Strategy is basically the same as Export Substitution, but is liberalized and sweetened by a humanistic concern with social justice and the 'downtrodden poor'. The strategy allows for redistribution *from* growth by investing in the formal sector and by sponsoring comprehensive rural development programmes that are complementary to the rapid expansion of the corporate sector in agriculture. It is presented as a strategy that is limited in time and supplementary to strategies for maintaining a high growth rate. It is referred to as a strategy that would not cost very much to carry out but would still have a big effect on the well-being and satisfaction of people.

But RwG gets caught up in its own, internal contradictions, because (a) it assumes the existence of an adequate growth rate (and hence implicitly affirms a policy of export-substitution)[10] and (b) it does not contemplate political action by people acting on their own behalf but assumes a liberal government that is motivated by the same humanistic and benign concerns as are the authors of the model.

(Comments on this essay from Martin Bronfenbrenner, Gustav Ranis, and Hans Singer, and my reply, are reprinted in the Appendix.)

Notes

1. Richardson (1977), arguing within the general framework of neo-classical economics, nevertheless maintains that there are significant areas where solutions may satisfy both criteria, achieving higher levels of allocative efficiency as well as greater equity in the results.
2. This belief is not inconsistent with a positivistic ideology which insists that the business of science is not to make value judgements but merely to report on 'how things really are'.
3. For one of the first official uses of this indicator, see United Nations (1951).
4. A third, 'basic needs' strategy is currently being debated. Its precise contours, however, are by no means clear. For an attempted authoritative definition, see Streeten (1977).
5. The assumption of constant real wages in industry is contradicted by the evidence. In Pakistan, for example, real wages in industry declined about 11 per cent between 1954 and 1966–67 (Griffin and Khan 1972: ch. 9). There is also evidence of growing malnutrition in parts of rural Asia (ILO 1977: 140) and of precipitously declining agricultural wages (ibidem: 246).
6. The following critique has some points in common with Leys (1975). It is, however, different in slant and emphasis, and the points are therefore still worth making. In view of the continued popularity of RwG, they have lost none of their edge.
7. This quality of resilience/slipperiness is characteristic of the ILO Kenya Report (1972). Quite correctly, in my view, the Report addresses three main contradictions or imbalances in Kenya's economic development: the contradiction between population growth and the nature of technology

applied (capital intensity); the contradiction between the centre and the periphery (urban primacy); and the contradiction between the formal and informal sectors (distribution of economic benefits). But no main strategy other than the slogan of redistribution from growth is presented. Instead there are 94 specific recommendations made in the summary text and probably there are many more in the main body of the report, a veritable smorgasbord of policies from which the Government presumably is at liberty to choose what it likes and how much it likes. To criticize any single one of these policies will get you nowhere. It is the form of presentation that is vulnerable.

8. 'If high priority is given to [the employment] objective, this automatically *means that the resources made available by economic growth* should benefit those now lacking income-earning opportunities' (ILO 1972: 109; emphasis added). How growth is to be achieved is not discussed; it is merely assumed to happen.

9. Social power is multifaceted. It comprises at least the following: productive wealth in land and tools; information and knowledge; education for adaptive action and for further learning; financial resources and contact networks.

10. As a result, RwG does not face up to the question of how growth is to be reconciled with equity. The trick is performed through Chenery's econometric model which, of course, by-passes the political question. The problem is solved through assumption.

References

Alonso, W. (1968). 'Equity and its Relation to Efficiency in Urbanization' (Berkeley: University of California, Centre for Planning and Development Research, WP 78)

Arrow, K. (1963). Social Choice and Individual Values (2nd edn. London: John Wiley & Sons)

Chenery, H. et al (1974). Redistribution with Growth (London: Oxford University Press)

Chenery, H. and M. Syrquin (1975). Patterns of Development: 1950–1970 (London: Oxford University Press)

Clark, C. (1938). National Income and Outlay (London: Macmillan)

———. (1940). The Conditions of Economic Progress (London: Macmillan)

Fei, J. and G. Ranis (1964). Development of a Labor Surplus Economy: Survey and Critique (Homewood, Ill.: Irwin)

Friedmann, J. and M. Douglass (1975). 'Agropolitan Development: Towards a New Strategy for Regional Development in Asia', in Growth Pole Strategy and Regional Development in Asia (Nagoya: UNCRD)

Griffin, K. (1974). The Political Economy of Agrarian Change: an Essay on the Green Revolution (London: Macmillan)

Griffin, K. and A. R. Khan (eds.) (1972). Growth and Inequality in Pakistan (London: Macmillan)

Hirschman, A. (1963). Journeys Toward Progress: Studies of Economic Policy Making in Latin America (New York: The Twentieth Century Fund)

ILO (1971). The World Employment Programme. Report IV. International Labour Conference, 56th Session (Geneva: ILO)

————. (1972). Employment, Incomes and Equality: A Strategy for Increasing Productive Employment in Kenya (Geneva: ILO)

————. (1974). Sharing in Development: A Programme of Employment, Equity and Growth for the Philippines (Geneva: ILO)

————. (1976). Employment Growth and Basic Needs: A One-World Problem (Geneva: ILO)

————. (1977). Poverty and Landlessness in Rural Asia (Geneva: ILO)

Kuzents, S. (1941). National Income and Its Composition, 1919–1938 (New York: National Bureau of Economic Research)

Lewis, W. A. (1955). Theory of Economic Growth (London: George Allen & Unwin)

Leys, C. (1975). 'The Politics of Redistribution with Growth' IDS Bulletin, Vol. 7 (2), 4–8. With reply by R. Jolly

Mera, K. (1975). Income Distribution and Regional Development (Tokyo: Tokyo University Press)

Paauw, D. and J. Fei (1975). The Transition in Open Dualistic Economies: Theory and Southeast Asian Experience (New Haven: Yale University Press)

Polanyi, K. (1944). The Great Transformation (New York: Rinehart & Co.)

Richardson, H. W. (1977). 'Aggregate Efficiency and Interregional Equity' (Paper presented at the Regional Science Symposium, University of Groningen, Holland, September 20–23)

Rostow, W. W. (1961). The Stages of Economic Growth: A Non-Communist Manifesto (Cambridge, Mass.: Harvard University Press)

Schultz, T. W. (1949). Production and Welfare of Agriculture (New York: The Macmillan Co.)

Schumpeter, J. (1934; orig. 1926). The Theory of Economic Development (Cambridge, Mass.: Harvard University Press)

Seers, D. (1969). 'The Meaning of Development' (Paper presented at the 11th World Conference of the Society for International Development, New Delhi, 14–17 November). International Development Review, December, 2–6.

Streeten, P. (1955). 'Appendix: Recent Controversies', in G. Myrdal, The Political Element in the Development of Economic Theory (Cambridge, Mass.: Harvard University Press)

Streeten, P. (1977). 'The Distinctive Features of a Basic Needs Approach to Development', International Development Review, Vol. 19 (3), 8–16

United Nations (1951). Measures for the Economic Development of Underdeveloped Countries (Report by a Group of Experts. New York: Department of Economic Affairs)

3
World City Formation

As someone deeply interested in the spatial dimensions of economic growth—my doctoral dissertation had probed the subject using the Tennessee Valley as my experimental field—it was only natural that I should be attracted to the possibility of linking the new economic globalism to phenomena of urbanization. Out of my reading and thinking emerged the notion of a world city hierarchy through which, I believed, the global system was being organized in space. Goetz Wolff (at the time a graduate student at UCLA) and I defined world cities as centers of global capital accumulation; alternatively, we viewed them as nodes of control through which the global economic system was being managed.

World cities exist in both core and semi-peripheral countries of the global system, and there is a spatial division of functions among them. But whatever their place in the hierarchy, world cities help to articulate with the global economy the regional or national economies they dominate. From this role arise a number of contradictions *that may be considered among the moving forces of contemporary history:*

a. In core countries
   1. Free-trade advocacy (expansion of economic space) vs. protectionism and anti-immigration sentiment (protection of territorial space).
   2. The large and growing ethnic underclass of immigrants and the relatively small national overclass in high-immigrant societies such as the United States.
   3. The increasing wealth of the overclass and its growing fear of ultimate disaster, giving rise to private police forces, an obsession with security, and escapism into the fantasyland of postmodern culture.
b. In semi-peripheral countries (also known as Newly Industrializing Countries)
   1. Export-orientation vs. endogenous development (similar to a.1 above).
   2. Contradictions arising from urban growth due to a massive outflow of rural migrants. This rural exodus is an attempt in part

57

to resolve contradictions resulting from export-promotion strategies. It leads to joblessness, a bulging informal sector, severe housing shortages, insufficient infrastructure, and other well-known maladies of Third World urbanization. Spatial polarization (urban primacy) is yet another outcome.

3. *Cultural nationalism vs. cosmopolitanism. In China, this has given rise to the current controversy over "spiritual pollution." Elsewhere, countries attempt to program at least some hours of national material over television. The Iranian revolution was successful in part because of the disaffection of large numbers from the Shah's "modernization" policies, which conformed to a Western cosmopolitan model.*

4. *Authoritarianism vs. democracy. The foregoing contradictions tend to lead to social turmoil and unrest (class war, regional wars). But global capital requires, above all, political stability and a favorable investment climate. Authoritarian regimes and military dictatorships are consequently common occurrences in the semi-periphery of the global economy, despite the historical connection (in the West) between the rise of capitalism and political liberalism. A good deal of the political struggle in countries such as Korea and Chile is over the introduction of liberal democratic practices.*

Written in 1981, the following paper was one of the first to link urbanizational processes to worldwide economic forces. I followed this up with a shorter essay in 1986 that introduced several case studies of world-cities-in-formation, including New York, Tokyo, and São Paulo ("The World City Hypothesis," Development and Change, *17, 1 [January 1986], 69–84). More such empirically grounded studies are needed. But even the limited evidence to date suggests that the "world city hypothesis" is essentially correct and points in the direction of fruitful inquiry.*

Our paper concerns the spatial articulation of the emerging world system of production and markets through a global network of cities.[1] Specifically, it is about the principal urban regions in this network, dominant in the hierarchy, in which most of the world's active capital is concentrated. As cities go, they are large in size, typically ranging from five to fifteen million inhabitants, and they are expanding rapidly. In space, they may extend outward by as much as 60 miles from an original centre. These vast, highly urbanized—and urbanizing—regions play a vital part in the great capitalist undertaking to organize the world for the efficient extraction of surplus. Our basic argument is that the character of the urbanizing processes—economic, social, and spatial—which define life in these 'cities' reflect, to a considerable extent, the mode of their integration into the world economy.

We propose, then, a new look at cities from the perspective of the world economic system-in-formation. The processes we will describe lead to new problem configurations. The central issue is the control of urban life. Whose interests will be served: those of the resident populations or of transnational corporations, or of the nation states that provide the political setting for world urbanization? Planners are directly engaged on this contested terrain. They are called upon to clarify the issues and to help in searching for solutions. Obviously, they will have to gain a solid, comprehensive understanding of the forces at work. And they will have to rethink their basic practices, since what is happening in world cities is in large measure brought about by forces that lie beyond the normal range of political—and policy—control. How can planners and, indeed, how can the people themselves, living in world cities, gain ascendancy over these forces? That is the basic question. Towards the end of this paper we shall venture a few observations about the tasks we face and their implications for planning.

This paper, then, serves a triple purpose. First, it is meant to provide a heuristic for the study of cities and correlative processes or urban change. This is the world city perspective, and it is capable, we contend, of accounting for much that we observe in contemporary urbanization. Second, we propose to identify major areas of ignorance concerning the related economic, technical, and urban transitions through which we are passing. Finally, we hope to lay the groundwork for a new approach to public intervention into the urbanization processes of at least those cities that are becoming closely linked into the world economy.

I

Our argument is a relatively simple one. Since the second world war, the processes by which capitalist institutions have freed themselves from national constraints and have proceeded to organize global production and markets for their own intrinsic purposes have greatly accelerated. The actors principally responsible for reorganizing the economic map of the world are the transnational corporations, themselves in bitter and cannibalistic conflict for the control of economic space. The emerging global system of economic relations assumes its material form in particular, typically urban, localities that are enmeshed with the global system in a variety of ways.

The specific mode of their integration with this system gives rise to an urban hierarchy of influence and control. At the apex of this hierarchy are found a small number of massive urban regions that we shall call world cities. Tightly interconnected with each other through decision-making and finance, they constitute a worldwide system of control over production and market expansion. Examples of world-cities-in-the-making include such metropolises as Tokyo, Los Angeles, San Francisco, Miami, New York, London, Paris, Randstadt, Holland, Frankfurt, Zurich, Singapore, Hong Kong and São Paulo.[2]

To label them world cities is a matter of convenience. In each and every instance, their specific role must be determined through empirical research. Only this much we can say: their determining characteristic is not their size of population. This is more properly regarded as a consequence of their economic and political role. A more fundamental question is in what specific ways these urban regions are becoming integrated with the global system of economic relations. Two aspects need to be considered:

1. the form and strength of the city's integration (e.g. to what extent it serves as a headquarters location for transnational corporations; the extent to which it has become a safe place for the investment of 'surplus' capital, as in real estate; its importance as a producer of commodities for the world market; its role as an ideological centre; or its relative strength as a world market);

2. the spatial dominance assigned by capital to the city (e.g. whether its financial and/or market control is primarily global in scope, or whether it is less than global, extending over a multinational region of the world, or articulating a national economy with the world system).

These criteria of world system integration must be viewed in a dynamic, historical perspective. Urban roles in the world system are not permanently fixed. Functions change; the strength of the relationship changes; spatial dominance changes. Indeed, the very concept of a world economy articulated through urban structures is as old as the ancient empires. Rome was perhaps the first great imperial city. One may think of Venice in its Golden Age, or of nineteenth-century London. While recognizing this historical continuity, we would still argue that the present situation is substantially different. What then is new?

First, we must consider the truly global nature of the world economy. Even imperial London, ruling over an empire 'where the sun never sets', controlled only portions of the world. The present trans-national system of space economy, on the other hand, is in principle unlimited. It is best understood as a spatial system which has its own internal structure of dominance/subdominance. Following Immanuel Wallerstein, we may label its three major regional components as core, semi-periphery, and periphery. *Core areas* include those older, already industrialized and possibly 'postindustrial' regions that contain the vast majority of corporate headquarters and continue to be the major markets for world production (northwest Europe, North America, Australia, Japan). The *semi-periphery* includes rapidly industrializing areas whose economies are still dependent on core-region capital and technical knowledge. They play a significant role in extending markets into the world periphery. Mexico, Brazil, Spain, Egypt, Singapore, Taiwan, and the Republic of Korea would be examples of semi-peripheral regions. And the *world periphery* comprises what is left of market economies. Predominantly agrarian, the people of the world periphery are poor, technologically backward, and politically weak.

This analytical scheme must be deftly handled. It is a first approximation to a deeper understanding of world city structure. Above all, it is an historical classification. Over the span of one or two generations, a country may change its position as it moves from periphery to semi-peripheral status (ROK, Spain, Brazil), from semi-periphery to core (Japan), and even perhaps back from core region status to the semi-periphery (Great Britain), or the ultimate decline into peripheral obscurity (Lebanon, Iran). What makes this typology attractive is the assumption that cities situated in any of the three world regions will tend to have significant features in common. As the movement of particular countries through the three-level hierarchy suggest, these features do not in any sense determine economic and other outcomes. They do, however, point to conditions that significantly influence city growth and the quality of urban life.

The world economy is thus no longer defined by the imperial reach of a Rome, a Venice, or even a London, but by a linked set of markets and production units organized and controlled by transnational capital. World cities are a material manifestation of this control, and they occur exclusively in core and semi-peripheral regions where they serve as banking and financial centres, administrative headquaters, centres of ideological control, and so forth. Without them, the world-spanning system of economic relations would be unthinkable.

This conception of the world city as an instrument for the control of production and market organization implies that the world economy, spatially articulated through world cities, is dialectically related to the national economies of the countries in which these cities are situated. *It posits an inherent contradiction between the interests of transnational capital and those of particular nation states that have their own historical trajectory.* World cities are asked to play a dual role. Essential to making the world safe for capital, they also articulate given national economies with the world system. As such, they have considerable salience for national policy makers who must respond to political imperatives that are only coincidentally convergent with the interests of the transnationals. World cities lie at the junction between the world economy and the territorial nation state.

Finally, the global economy is superimposed upon an international system of states. Nation states have their own political fears and ambitions. They form alliances, and they exact tribute. They must protect their frontiers against actual and potential enemies. Wishing to ensure their continuing power in the assembly of nations, or even to enlarge their power, they must provide for a continuing flow of raw materials and food supplies.

And so, an international politics comes into being, independent of transnational capital. In the course of events, it may be convenient for the state to align itself with international capital. In the recent case of Chile, where the fall of Allende was engineered by the CIA, the tie-in between Anaconda, ITT, and American imperial power is common knowledge. But, as the case of the OPEC countries goes to show, neoimperialism is not the only option.

On the other hand, although transnational capital desires maximum freedom from state intervention in the movements of finance capital, information, and commodities, it is vitally interested in having the state assume as large a part as possible of the costs of production, including the reproduction of the labour force and the maintenance of 'law and order'. It is clear, therefore, that they would benefit from a strategy to prevent a possible collusion among nation states directed against themsleves. Being essential to both transnational capital and national political interests, world cities may become bargaining counters in the ensuing struggles.[3]

They are therefore also major arenas for political conflict. How these conflicts are resolved will shape the future of the world economy. Because many diverging interests are involved, it is a multifaceted struggle. There is, of course, the classical instance of the struggle between transnational capital and the national bourgeoisie; between politically organized nation states and transnational capital; and between the people of a given city and the national polity, though this may be the weakest part.[4]

There is, then, nothing inevitable about either the world economy or its concrete materialization in world cities. Capital is in conflict with itself and with the political-territorial entities where it must come to rest. There is no manifest destiny. Yet the emerging world economy is an historical event and this allows us to formulate our central hypothesis: *the mode of world system integration (form and strength of integration; spatial dominance) will affect in determinate ways the economic, social, spatial and political structure of world cities and the urbanizing processes to which they are subject.*

Why this should be, and the specific mechanisms through which these relationships are mediated will be elaborated in the following pages. We should like to make it clear that what we describe is not a Weberian 'ideal type' of a fully formed 'world city'. All that we intend is to point to certain structural tendencies in the formation of those cities that appear to play a major role in the organization of world markets and production. We have in mind a heuristic for the empirical study of world city formation.

II

In making the internationalization of capital central to our analysis, we focus upon a combination of complex processes that are indeterminate, contradictory, and irregular. There is little dispute about the fact of the worldwide expansion of market relations. But the cause—the driving force—of the internationalization of capital is debated: Is internationalization merely a working out of the internal logic of capitalism? Or has labour in the industrialized countries created a situation where capital now finds it more profitable to locate in the periphery?

We proceed under the assumption that both 'windows'—to use David Harvey's felicitous image—contribute to the needed understanding of the global order. The contradictions inherent in the capitalist economy and the basic struggle which results from the domination of labour by capital are the major forces which account for both the spatial and temporal irregularities of the world economy. A city's mode of integration with the global economy cannot simply be understood by identifying its functional role in the articulation of the system. Rather, we suggest that the driving forces of competition, the need for accumulation, and the challenges posed by political struggle make the intersection of world economy/world city a point of intense conflict and dynamic change. World city integration is not a mechanical process; it involves many interconnected changes that leave few aspects of its life untouched and create the arenas for concerted action.

In the following pages, we will address these changes, first for the economic system viewed as a totality and then for particular cities and urban regions under-going a change-over to world-city status. Because we are still too close to them, and their complexity is a formidable obstacle to understanding, we can as yet make few positive assertions about these changes. A more modest intention at this stage is to raise some significant questions about them and to suggest the general direction that research should take as it seeks to model the tectonics of history.

1. *Expansion of the world economic system: an agenda of ignorance*

a. *The corporate structure of capital accumulation:* The transnational corporation is the chief instrument for the globalization of the economy. There is evidence that effective, worldwide competition is taking place increasingly among a shrinking number of firms, each of which commands a wide array of diverse and often non-complementary production facilities. Production, with its built-in concern with quality, counts for less with many of these firms than their financial profit sheet. Decision-making is increasingly abstract and far removed from the line of production. Indeed, production units will be readily sacrificed in the interest of the overall financial strategy. Thus, there is a marked tendency for the concentration of capital in corporations whose total sales rival the gross national product of all but the largest national economies.[5]

These corporate giants, virtually immune from bankruptcy, can divest themselves of resources as readily as they acquire them. Much of their strategic bookkeeping is internal to the firm, and involves fictitious transfer prices. Their gains (or losses) are produced by 'creative' accountants. They pay few taxes and are well on the way to becoming independent of national controls. Their leverage in bargaining is virtually unchecked.

But our knowledge of the transnational corporation is both superficial and largely anecdotal. Are they truly devoid of any national interest, as they are sometimes said to be? Does their national origin have no bearing on their ultimate performance? What is the internal structure of their decision-making? Where transnational corporations enter into partnership with national capital, are decisions different from what they would be in the absence of shared control? What are the evolving relations between transnational capital and international institutions, such as the United Nations and its affiliated agencies or the IMF and the World Bank? What is the specific role of the banking sector in the worldwide expansion of capital? Are the banks themselves becoming transnationalized? To what extent do they become direct investors? And what are the linkages between the banks, international organizations, and corporate capital? Are hierarchies maintained in the emerging power structure or is the situation a more fluid one, with frequent unpredictable shifts in the distribution of effective power?

b. The changing technological bases of the global expansion of capital: The world economic system is emerging in parallel with a series of profound technological breakthroughs whose ultimate consequences for life are at present only dimly perceived. Some of these innovations have made the worldwide organization of economic activities possible (computers, communication satellites, wide-bodied jets); others suggest an incipient revolution in production (microelectronics, robotization). Still other innovations promise to restructure the bases of energy production (nuclear power, coal liquification, synfuels, photovoltaic cells). Beyond these technological wonders, some of which have already been assimilated and become part of our everyday environment, loom still further revolutionary changes: genetic engineering, nuclear fusion, widespread new applications of laser technology. Fundamental questions need to be raised concerning the long-term social and economic effects of these technologies, particularly as they bear on the spatial division of labour and the possibilities of full-time employment.

To take only one example, microelectronics. It is essentially an information technology. Because of large expected gains in productivity, microelectronics are being introduced to virtually all industrial processes. How will the spread of this technology affect work in manufacturing, offices, and the provision of services? In what ways will occupational requirements change as a result? Will jobs become more technical (as they appear to be in the defence establishment), or will robotization lead to a 'deskilling' of labour? How will effects on the labour process be reflected in labour relations and the formation of working-class consciousness? With a reduction of direct labour costs, will manufacturing activities remain in the advanced or core countries of the world economy, reversing the recent trend to the dispersal of manufacturing to the countries of the periphery? What political strategies will these countries adopt as they struggle for survival in a technological world that is beyond their ability to control?

These questions exceed our present ability to answer them, but there is little doubt that any major technology—and microelectronics is only one of a growing number that are transforming life towards the end of the twentieth century—will give rise to contradictions and societal responses. It is not beyond human control. Technology is rather a direct response to the needs of capital and its relentless drive for innovation; the constant competitive pressure for greater cost effectiveness; and the development of a market in which technology is sold like any other commodity. Technology, then, must be regarded as a social product. It is not 'autonomous', as Langdon Winner (1977) would have us believe, but an object of political choice.

c. Changes in production—upward shifts in capital intensity and occupational structure; the critical role of R & D: Sociologists such as Daniel Bell have been predicting for some time the coming of a 'postindustrial society'. Other social analysts speak of an 'information' society. These discussions all point to one important development not only in the American economy but, to a degree, in the economies of all the leading countries of industrial capitalism: the simple transformation of raw materials into final products is more and more left to robotized labour and to assembly operations depending on unskilled labour of young women and minorities. As technology is becoming more refined at all stages of production, distribution, and investment, the proportion which information processing represents of value-added appears to be rising. Thus it may well be the case that the postindustrial society is a reality, or will soon become so, but it will be limited to only a few sectors of the global economy, while the rest of the world confines its contribution to direct production through manual labour. The core countries of capitalism are thus assigned the role of research lab, control room, and financier, while the periphery produces. Thus a new class of structure of the world economy comes into being.

These are the broad-stroke understandings that we have. But there is much more that we need to know both concerning technical questions and the wider political implications of the observed trends. For instance, what are the long-term trends in the requirements for capital in specific production sectors? What is the rate of capital obsolescence in specific industries? What changes in the character of their employment can be projected? There is also the competitive requirement of basing product development on research. What percentage of corporate net income is reinvested in R & D work by different sectors? How critical to economic survival are these expenditures? How closely related to production does R & D work need to be? And what are the overall implications for the international division of labour of the resulting rise in capital intensity, the technification of the labour force, the increasingly rapid depreciation of capital stock, and the rising percentage of R & D expenditures? Finally, does the growing technification of production lead to tighter control by management of labour in the work-place? Will it make national economies more vulnerable to both external and internal disruptions? And is it likely to make the world more democratic or more authoritarian? If the work of Richard Falk (1981) is any indication, the prospects for democracy around the world are poor and rapidly diminishing.

d. Sectoral employment shifts, the international division of labour, and informal employment: What are the implications of the opening up of world markets and of global production for the structure of world employment? Capital locations follow a product cycle pattern, different criteria bring applied to headquarters and R & D facilities, production requiring skilled labour, and mass production. Given computerized, electronic communications, it is now possible to spatially separate investments that were formerly joined. Capital can take full advantage of differentials in labour costs while retaining essential control over the entire production process. As a result, in the industrial countries, a general levelling of employment in manufacturing may be observed, while professionalized services are expanding. Agricultural employment, on the other hand, seems to have shrunk to an irreducible minimum. The situation is quite different in the periphery. There, with only few exceptions, agriculturally dependent employment continues to grow at about 1% a year, while manufacturing is slowly gaining though, in relation to the total labour force, it rarely rises above 20%.

Overall, physical labour is becoming more automated, and that is true even for office work which is otherwise a rapidly expanding sector. As a result, and especially when measured against a growing labour force in both periphery and core (because of population growth, extended working age, and the increased participation of women in remunerated labour), insufficient jobs are available in the 'formal' sector to provide for anything like full employment as we now know it (the 40-hour week). In core countries, these trends are aggravated by the shift of some direct production jobs to the periphery (or semi-periphery), encouraged in this move by the clear expectation (on the part of capital) of lower labour costs and a more compliant work force. The resulting surplus of labour may be absorbed into low-wage 'informal' employment and the increased home production of services. But in the long term, we can look forward to an overall reduction in working hours, new work-sharing practices, and perhaps even increased employment in labour-intensive public works (public job creation).

The extent to which the forgoing generalizations are valid must be tested in research. What are the employment prospects in specific countries, and what implications follow for educational and training programmes? What are the likely consequences of massive labour redundancy, and the growing differences in income and life chances between the technostructure on the one hand and directly productive workers and the 'informal' sector on the other, both within individual countries and among the hierarchy of world regions?

e. *The differential mobility of capital, labour, and land:* Capital has become almost instantaneously mobile over the entire globe. Even fixed capital costs can often be recovered within the span of only a few years. Although other factors of production are less mobile, the critical long-distance mobility of technical elites approximates that of fixed capital (in some instances, electronic communications may be a substitute for physical relocation). Other workers, both blue and white collar, are more dependent in their lives upon community support and consequently far less mobile. (The personal needs of techno-elites are often provided by the organizations for which they work). Differences of race, religion, culture, and language impose further constraints on the long-distance movement of labour. Land, finally, is completely immobile. Even so, with appropriate investments, land can be prepared to meet the specific needs of capital almost anywhere in the world. Except for agriculture, its importance as a factor of production may be considered minimal.

The differential mobilities of capital, land, and labour lead to profound problems for territorially organized and therefore relatively immobile societies. What are the possibilities of transnational capital holding such societies 'ransom' in order to extract from them concessions that go against the national interest? What grounds, if any, exist for negotiations between them? What social and political consequences ensue from the flow of core region elites to semi-peripheral world cities and the reverse flow of production labour from periphery to the core? Is organized labour capable of becoming truly international so as to bargain effectively with transnational corporations on a global basis? Will effective power to deal with the consequences of an expanding world economic system perhaps devolve upon a new level of regional government, encouraging the fragmentation of the political world under the protective umbrella of an ailing nation state, transnational enterprise, and world bureaucracies?

f. Formation of transnational elites and their ideology: A 'new class' of technocrats is managing the current transition of the world economic order. They are found in business, government, and international organizations. They are highly educated, possessing specialized professional skills, and some are paid extremely well. Many are economists, accountants, lawyers, engineers, architects, and information specialists. Their chief characteristic, however, is a willingness to serve the interests of transnational capital in its global expansion, putting national interests second. They are a highly mobile, polyglot group capable of working under pressure in fluid situations. We know as yet little about them.

It is sometimes claimed that, as a result of their common educational experience, transnational elites will share a similar outlook. Evidence of their thinking is found in writings sponsored by such organizations as the Club of Rome, the Club de Genève, and the Trilateral Commission. What are their specifically political ideas and agendas? What biases typically inform their judgements? Can one speak of a transnational ethos?

Technical elites must be distinguished from the transnational directive structures (capitalists) who employ them. What are the relations of power between them? To what extent is capital dependent on the servants it employs? And how does it maintain its dominance over them? Or is the master-servant relationship reversed, with transnational elites prevailing in the decisions of capital?

And finally, how large are the new elites? What is their occupational composition? And what proportion of their time do even presumptively national bureaucracies spend on specifically global affairs, rendering their *de jure* national status transnational in fact? Is there a general trend towards an increase in their number?

g. The long-run prospect: limits to system-wide growth: The Club of Rome, which is an organization composed of the new transnational elites, was the first dramatically to propound the view that the economic growth of the past generations cannot be indefinitely sustained without meeting with major catastrophes. Although the organization of the economy on a global basis and the development of related technology may be a possible means to overcome the constraints imposed by nature on production and the satisfaction of 'insatiable' human wants, it may well be merely a postponement of the eventual limits. At the same time, the hierarchy of world regions may be a convenient way for the dominant powers to shift the incidence of the constraints to those who are weaker than they.

One 'limit to growth' which is likely to come into play within less than two generations is the finite physical supply of traditional sources of energy, especially petroleum and natural gas. Most projections place the virtual exhaustion of these resources sometime into the twenty-first century. How will the gradual exhaustion of these vital energy supplies affect the balance of power among nations? There are, of course, alternative sources of power in the wings, nuclear fusion, along with solar energy. Is their development likely to speed the transnationalization of capital? What happens to countries that have no ready supply of energy within their own boundaries? Must they become vassal states of those that have? Will the struggle to maintain the flow of energy ultimately shift the balance of world power?

There are those who argue that the new awareness of 'spaceship earth' will come to replace traditional tribal ethics. Or is the ethics of one world merely a clever ploy to shift the cost of resources shortages onto the backs of weaker nations under the pious phases of 'global resource management'.

2. The formation of world cities

In the foregoing paragraphs, current changes in the formation of the world economic system were identified by looking at the system as a whole. At a certain level of abstraction, this procedure has validity. But processes of change assume a concrete, historical form at precisely those points where the globe-girdling economy is drawn together and intensified.

The world city today is in transition, which is to say it is in movement. Perhaps it has always been like this. Equilibrium is not part of the experience of large cities. Structural instability manifests itself in a variety of ways: dramatic changes in the distribution of employment, the polarization of class divisions, physical expansion and decaying older areas, political conflict. We shall have a quick look at all of these to render more specific how the formation of the world cities is affecting the quality of life within them.

World cities are the control centres of the global economy. Their status, of course, is evolving in the measure that given regions are integrated in a dominant role with the world system. And like the golden cities of ancient empires, they draw unto themselves the wealth of the world that is ruled by them. They become the major points for the accumulation of capital and 'all that money can buy'. They are luxurious, splendid cities whose very splendour obscures the poverty on which their wealth is based. The juxtaposition is not merely spatial; it is a functional relation: rich and poor define each other.

It is not a new story, and yet its particular features are new. As we attempt to describe the changes that occur as urban regions strive for world city status, several things must be borne in mind. The characteristics we are describing are merely tendencies, not final destinations. Particular cities will exhibit particular features. Still, the account we give of conditions prevailing in urban regions as they become world cities may be regarded as the best current hypothesis. In every instance, we have tried to relate it back to specific aspects of integration with global economy. Not only are world cities in themselves not uniform, there is no definite cut-off point with other cities that belong to the same system but are not so tightly integrated with the global economy, have only a national/subnational span of control, or are integrated primarily on a basis of dependency. In a way, the world economy is everywhere, and many of the features we will describe may be found in cities other than those we are discussing here.

The world city 'approach' is, in the first instance, a methodology, a point of departure, an initial hypothesis. It is a way of asking questions and of bringing footloose facts into relation. We do not have an all-embracing theory of world city formation.

a. Economic restructuring: A primary fact about emerging world cities is the impact which the incipient shifts in the structure of their employment will have on the economy and on the social composition of their population. The dynamism of the world city economy results chiefly from the growth of a primary cluster of high-level business services which employs a large number of professionals—the transnational elite—and ancillary staffs of clerical personnel. The activities are those which are coming to define the chief economic functions of the world city: *management, banking and finance, legal services, accounting, technical consulting, telecommunications and computing, international transportation, research, and higher education.*

A secondary cluster of employment, also in rapid ascendancy, may be defined as essentially serving the first. Its demand is largely derived, and it employs proportionately a much smaller number of professionals: *real estate, construction activities, hotel services, restaurants, luxury shopping, entertainment, private police and domestic services.* A more varied mix than the primary cluster, its fortunes are closely tied to it. Although most jobs in this cluster are permanent and reasonably well-paid, this is not true for domestic services which is the most vulnerable employment sector and the most exploited.

A tertiary cluster of service employment centres on *international tourism.* To a considerable extent, this overlaps with the secondary cluster (hotels, restaurants, luxury shopping, entertainment), and like that cluster, it is tied to the performance of the world economy.

The growth of the first three clusters is taking place at the expense of *manufacturing employment*. Although a large cluster, its numbers are gradually declining as a proportion of all employment. Some industry serves the specialized needs of local markets, while other sectors—in Los Angeles, for example, electronics and garment industries—are choosing world city locations because of the large influx of cheap labour which helps to keep the average cost of wages down. The future of manufacturing employment in the world city is not bright, however. The next two decades will see the rapid automation and robotization of many jobs. While factories will still be producing and earning large and perhaps even rising profits, they will be largely devoid of working people.

Government services constitute a fifth cluster. They are concerned with the maintenance and reproduction of the world city, as well as the provision of certain items of collective consumption: the planning and regulation of urban land use and expansion; the provision of public housing, basic utilities, and transportaion services; the maintenance of public order; education; business regulation; urban parks; sanitation; and public welfare for the destitute.

Because of the uniqueness and scale of world cities, and because they are often considered national showcases, the government sector tends to be larger here than elsewhere. And because it is a political and, for the most part, technically backward sector, with uncertain criteria of adequate performance, it tends to be bloated, employing large numbers of people at relatively low levels of productivity and wages. Moreover, because the world city extends over many political jurisdictions that are contiguous with each other, there is much overlap and redundancy in employment. During periods of depression, government will often be the employer of the last resort. Its internal rhythm tends to be counter-cyclical.

A sixth and, at least in some cities, numerically the largest cluster, embraces the *'informal'*, *'floating'*, or *'street' economy* which ranges from the casual services of day labourers and shoeshine boys to fruit vendors, glaziers, rug dealers, and modest artisans. Frequently an extension of the household economy, most informal activities require little or no overhead (though they do require start-up capital). They demand long hours, and the returns are low and uncertain. They offer no security to those who work in them. New arrivals to the city often find their first job in the informal sector, and many of them stay there. When times are bad, some makeshift income-earning opportunities can always be found in the informal sector for people who are temporarily unemployed. Although informal sector work may be a choice between independence and security for some, for many more it is the only way to survive in the city. The cluster of informal activities takes up the slack in the 'formal' economy, and thus despite its marginal character, it tends to be tolerated by the state.

Some informal activities are not as 'unorganized' or 'casual' as they might appear. Perhaps increasingly, small businesses are subcontracted by large, frequently multinational corporations who in this way are able to lower their costs of operation. Informal businesses are usually beyond the reach of government regulation. They don't pay minimum wages and their labour is often self-exploited. Much of it is done by women and children.

But essentially the informal sector exists because of the large influx of people into the world city from other cities and from the countryside, people who are attracted to the world city as to a honey pot. They don't all find legitimate employment. A significant number drift into *illicit occupations* which perhaps more than elsewhere appear to thrive in the large city: thieves, pickpockets, swindlers, pimps, prostitutes, drug peddlers, black marketeers . . . the list can be extended with endless refinements.

Finally, there is the undefined category of those without a steady income: the full-time unemployed, who depend on family and public charity for support. Excepting women, who manage their households but are not paid for this, and therefore do not appear in the official statistics, their numbers are surprisingly small—in the order of 5–10% of the labour force.[6]

b. Social restructuring: The primary social fact about world city formation is the polarization of its social class divisions.

Transnational elites are the dominant class in the world city, and the city is arranged to cater to their life styles and occupational necessities. It is a cosmopolitan world that surrounds them, corresponding to their own high energy, rootlessness, and affluence. Members of this class are predominantly males between the ages of 30 and 50. Because of their importance to the city, they are a class well served.[7]

The contrast with the third (or so) of the population who make up the permanent underclass of the world city could scarcely be more striking. The underclass are the victims of a system that holds out little hope to them in the periphery from which they came but also fails them in the very nerve centres of the world economy where they are queueing for a job. They crowd along the edges of the primary economy—the 'formal' sector—or settle in its interstices, barely tolerated, yet providing personal services to the ruling class, doing the dirty work of the city. The ruling class and its dependent middle sectors enjoy permement employment, a steady income, and complete legality; they do not have to justify their existence. For all practical purposes they *are* the city. The underclass lives at its sufferance.[8]

Many, though not all, of the underclass are of different ethnic origin than the ruling strata; often, they have a different skin colour as well, or speak a different dialect or language. These immigrant workers give to many world cities a distinctly 'third world' aspect: Puerto Ricans and Haitians in New York, Mexicans in Los Angeles and San Francisco, barefoot Indians in Mexico City, 'nordestinos' in São Paulo, Jamaicans in London, Algerians in Paris, Turks in Frankfurt, Malays in Singapore.

There is a city that serves this underclass, as suited to their own condition if not their preferences and needs, as is the city of the 'upper circuit'. Physically separated from and many times larger than the citadel of the ruling class, it is the ghetto of the poor. Both cities live under the constant threat of violence: the upper city is guarded by private security forces, while the lower city is the double victim of its own incipient violence and of police repression. The typical world city situation is thus for *both* the crime rate and police expenditures to rise.

Racism reinforces class contradictions, and a good deal of ethnic and racial hostility is found within the working class itself. Under conditions of tight labour markets, 'foreign' workers, whether undocumented or not, frequently occasion racist outbursts, as 'national' workers (particularly among the underclass) struggle to preserve their limited terrain for livelihood. Street gangs of different ethnic origin, and the pitched battles between them, especially in the United States, are a major manifestation of this violence.

Yet racial conflict is only one facet of the general increase in violence that is brought on by class polarization. Terrorism, kidnapping, street demonstrations, and rioting are other common forms. There is an undeniable fascination with violence among residents in the world city which is picked up and amplified by the popular media. Yet for all the turmoil, world city conflicts are not a sign of an impending revolution. A good deal of the violence occurs within the working class itself and is measure of its internal divisions. The world city is in any event immune to revolutionary action. Lacking a political centre, it can only be rendered impotent—at the present time a rather unlikely occurrence.

Confronted with violence, the nation state responds in coin. Given the severity of its fiscal constraints in the face of constantly rising costs, it resorts to the simplest, least imaginative alternative: the application of brute force. The response is acceptable to the new ruling class who generally prefer administrative to political solutions. But police repression can at best contain class violence; it cannot eliminate or significantly reduce it. Violence is here to stay.

c. Physical restructuring: Over the next generation, world cities can be expected to grow to unprecedented size. By the end of the century, the typical world city will have ten million people or more. Much of the increase will have come from migration.

Obviously, a population that rivals that of a medium-sized country by today's standards can no longer be considered a city in the traditional sense. It is an urbanized region or, as Friedmann and Miller (1965) called it nearly two decades ago, an 'urban field'. In the case of Los Angeles, for example, the pertinent economic region has been defined as having a radius of about 60 miles (roughly 80 minutes commuting at normal speeds); it represents the life space for more than half the population of California!

The urban field is essentially an economic concept. Although it does not correspond to the traditional political concept of the city as *civitas,* it imposes its own logic on the vestiges of the political city which struggles to survive in this highly charged, volatile materialization of capitalist energy. The urban field is expanding, more rapidly in most cases than even the increase in population, but it is expanding unequally, regardless of whether one applies functional, social, or economic criteria. Underlying its kaleidoscopic spatial form is the ever-shifting topography of land values which quickly and efficiently excludes all potential users who are unable to meet the price of a given parcel of land. Of course, this method does not at all correspond to any social need, least of all to the need of what Joan Nelson (1979) has called 'access to power'.

The effects of the unequal internal growth of urban fields is illustrated by some data for Los Angeles County. Within this county of seven million people are found 47 cities of metropolitan size. During the past decade, population change among these cities varied from −7 to +233%, with 9 cities showing gains of over 30%, compared to an overall, region-wide rate of growth of only 13%. These simple figures hide the actual drama of economic and political adjustment, which was a veritable saga of boom and busts. And yet, there was virtually no compensatory action, *because the political mechanism for such action did not exist.* Quite the contrary, the 47 metropolitan-sized cities of

Los Angeles were engaged in competitive feuding among themselves—a struggle that was barely alleviated by symbolic gestures towards 'regional' planning. On the other hand, a whole set of new administrative agencies has come into being which manage, using purely technical criteria, the essential services that hold the region of Los Angeles together: authorities that are only vaguely accountable to political bodies and are largely independent of annual budgetary allocations, such as port and rapid transit authorities—municipal 'departments' that are in every sense like public corporations.

The concentration of activities and wealth on a world city scale imposes extraordinary strains on the natural resources on which the continued viability of the world city depends. To feed its voracious appetite for water and energy (which tends to grow at multiples of the increases in population), the city must reach further and further afield, sometimes for hundreds of miles, across mountains and deserts and even national boundaries. As it does so, it comes inevitably into conflict with competing interests and jurisdictions.

At the same time, and considering sheer volume alone, the world city faces enormous problems of waste mangement. Pollution at levels of concentration dangerous to human health pose a constant and growing threat. Huge areas must be set aside for low-intensity uses of the land, such as airports, water treatment facilities, solid waste disposal, agriculture and dairying, and urban mass recreation.

This enormously varied complex of activities must be knitted together through high-speed transport devices and linked to the outside world through a system of international transport terminals and telecommunications capable of serving the entire region. And of course it must have a basic infrastructure of utilities that serves the housing and industrial needs of the city. At a scale of ten or twenty million people each, and an area of several hundred square miles, these common basic needs of the world city can be satisfied only with the considered application of high technology. But high technology renders the city more vulnerable: the growing reliance on ever more sophisticated methods may be counterproductive in the end. Its costs will escalate even as the quality of its services deteriorates.

Examples of this are currently best documented—as in James Fallows's (1981) work—for the American defence establishment, but appearance of similar phenomena in the world city can only be a matter of time.

In its internal spatial structure, the world city may be divided, as we suggested in the preceding section, into the 'citadel' and the 'ghetto'. Its geography is typically one of inequality and class domination. The citadel serves the specific needs of the transnational elites and their immediate retinues who rule the city's economic life, the ghetto is adapted to the circumstances of the permanent underclass.

With its towers of steel and glass and its fanciful shopping malls, the citadel is the city's most vulnerable symbol. Its smooth surfaces suggest the sleek impersonality of money power. Its interior spaces are ample, elegant, and plush. In appropriately secluded spaces, the transnational elites have built their residences and playgrounds: country clubs and bridle paths and private beaches.

The overcrowded ghettos exist in the far shadows of the citadel, where it is further divided into racial and ethnic enclaves. Some areas are shanty towns. None are well provided with public services: garbage does not get collected, only the police in their squad cars are visibly in evidence. In many places, ghetto residents are allowed outside their zones only during working hours: their appearance in the citadel after dark creates a small panic. With its dozens of apartheid Sowetos, South Africa is perhaps the extreme case of a country whose elites are gripped in fear of their underclass, but political manifestations of this fear are found to a degree in nearly all world cities. Not long ago, the papers in Los Angeles were filled with horror stories of 'marauders' sallying forth from the black ghetto to the citadel on the West Side to rob, rape and kill. They called it 'predatory crime'. The implication was clear: at night, ghetto residents belong to the ghettos. There, isolated like a virus, they can harm only each other.

d. Political conflict: Every restructuring implies conflict. And when conflict occurs in the public domain, it concerns the distribution of costs and benefits, and who shall gain advantage for the next round of the struggle. Focused on the world city, political conflict is multidimensional; it is also at the heart of the matter, as if all the world's lines of force came together here, and the contradictions in the self-expansion of capital are magnified on a scale commensurate with that of the world city itself. In the absence of counter-forces, complex feedback loops tend to destabilize the system, and localized conflicts may suddenly erupt into a worldwide crisis.

The emergence of world cities sets into motion processes that restructure people's life spaces and the economic space that intersects with them. Economic space obeys the logic of capital: it is profit-motivated and individualized. Life spaces are territorial: they are the areas that people occupy, in which their dreams are made, their lives unfold. They are thus the areas they really care about. For the dominant actors in economic space, life space is nothing but a hindrance, an irrational residue of a more primitive existence. Yet it can neither be denied nor circumvented. Every economic space overlaps with an existing life space, and without this, economic enterprise would perish. On the other hand, for people who are collectively the sovereign in their respective life spaces, the space of economic logic is the basis for their physical survival.

It is thus very clear that a restructuring of these two kinds of space is bound to generate deep conflicts. In practice, because so many cross currents bear down on them, the reasons for conflicts are often hard to isolate. Conflicts persist, they have a history and a future, they interconnect in place, and the system of world cities ensures their transmittal from continent to continent. Though it may not be very enlightening, it might be more accurate to speak of them as a form of social turbulence.

There are the conflicts over livelihood, as the restructuring of economic space draws jobs away from one place to resurrect them in another, or as entirely new kinds of job are suddenly ascendant for which older workers are not qualified. There are racial and ethnic conflicts, as workers battle over access to the few good jobs there are, and even over jobs that are less desirable but relatively more abundant. There are struggles between world city and the national periphery over the political autonomy of peripheral regions, as the periphery sees its collective life chances systematically denied by the imperial interests of world city cores. There are conflicts over the spaces within the city, as people seek access to housing they can afford, defend their neighbourhoods from the intrusion of capitalist logic, or merely struggle for turf to enjoy the freedom of following lifeways of their own. There are the political campaigns launched by concerned citizens to protect and enhance the quality of their lives as they perceive it: in struggles for the environment, against nuclear power, for child care centres, for the access of handicapped workers in public facilities . . . struggles and campaigns which are incapable of being separated from the peculiar setting of world cities. Or there are the bitter and tenacious struggles of poor people, workers who belong to one class fraction or another, for greater access to the conditions for social power: the right to organize, to demonstrate, to call to account, to gain control over the conditions of their work, to keep their bodies healthy, to educate their children and themselves, to higher incomes, to sources of the means for livelihood.

All these struggles are occurring simultaneously. They are centred on the restructuring process and in the contradictions that arise from the interfacing of economic and life spaces. As such, they reveal to the astute observer the true forces at work in the world city and the actual distribution of power. Also, of course, they determine the ultimate outcomes we observe . . . not only the outcomes of the particular struggles being waged, but of the form and direction which world city development will take. For outcomes are *not* predetermined. Broad tendencies may be irreversible in the medium term, such as the integration of the world economic system under the aegis of transnational capital. But within that historical tendency, there are always opportunities for action. It is precisely at the searing points of political conflict that opportunities arise for a concerted effort to change the course of history.

Territorial planners must grasp the essential nature of these conflicts and the contradictions which underlie them. It is here that they must make their interventions, furthering progressive forces in their attempt to withstand the dissolution of life spaces into a vast economic space controlled by capital. Because we cannot survive without life spaces of our own, capital's unmitigated success would be disastrous. For people cannot be treated as commodities without losing some of their essential humanity.

Conflict between life space and economic space poses new questions for the state. More than ever, the state is faced with multiple contradictions and difficult choices. Some would say that the state itself is threatened by the dramatic appearance of transnational power. On the world periphery, the choice may be the relatively simple one between complete dependency (with all that this implies in terms of uneven development) and stone age survival. In the semiperiphery, which has already chosen a dependent development path, the problems of choice are more complex. More highly articulated than in the periphery, the state reflects within its own structure many of the conflicts within civil society and the economy. As class fraction is pitted against class fraction, territory against class, working class against capital, and citizens against the state, and as all these conflicts come together in successive waves of 'turbulence' in the world city, the state is merely one more actor, trying to safeguard its own specific interests.

One such interest is the political integration of its territory. Semiperipheral states are especially concerned with regional inequalities, focal points of regional revolt, regional resources development, and rural land reform. In countries such as Mexico and Brazil, regional issues have been major concerns of state action, and civil wars have been fought over them.

Regional questions recede in the territorially more integrated countries of the world core area. Here, the more important conflicts tend to be between national and transnational fractions of capital, and the state becomes a major 'arena' for the conduct of this struggle. Much of it is over specific legislation and the budget allocation.

In all this turmoil, a major loser is the local state. Small, isolated, without financial power, and encapsulated within the world economy, it is barely able to provide for even the minimal services its population needs. And yet, instead of seeking alliances with neighboring cities and organized labour, it leaves the real decisons to the higher powers on which it is itself dependent, or to the quasi-independent authorities created by state charter that manage the infrastructure of global capital-system-wide facilities such as ports, airports, rapid transit, water supply, communications, and electric power.

III

A reasonable question might be asked: what does a world city perspective contribute to the study of urbanization, particularly of large cities? Does it add significantly to our theoretical understanding of urbanization? Will it enhance the state's abilty to cope with the multifaceted problems of large and rapidly growing cities? In these regards, what is distinctive about the world city perspective?

We can move closer to an answer by briefly recounting the inadequacies of existing approaches to the study of contemporary urbanization. The most prevalent practice is that of the traditional social sciences. When one reviews the thousands of urban studies by social scientists, one is struck by the extreme fragmentation of their knowledge (see, e.g., Friedmann and Wulff, 1976). There are individual city studies, and there are studies from within the specialized perspectives of the major disciplines. But the studies do not add up: they leave one suspended in a void of meaning. The lack of comprehensive theories of urbanization is perhaps not surprising. Less excusable is our failure to articulate a common framework that would enable us to relate individual city studies to the larger vision of process and structure in the formation of human settlements.

The major alternative to traditional social science studies is the neomarxist tradition. Here we find two separate strands of analysis: the world systems approach of Wallerstein, Amin, and Frank and urban studies influenced by Henri Lefebvre, Manuel Castells, and David Harvey. For some strange reason, these two lines of study have not been synthesized. Recent collections of Marxist writings on the city still treat the city as an isolated phenomenon whose internal structure is somehow 'determined' by abstract capitalist forces. No attempt has been made to bring observed facts about large cities into relation with the emerging world economy (Harloe, 1977; Tabb and Sawers, 1978; Dear and Scott, 1981, excepting the chapter contributed by R. B. Cohen).

The one major exception to this generalization is the new book by Alejandro Portes and John Walton (1981). The authors are explicit about their world system perspective and carry through with it in the study of such important world city phenomena as international migration (guest workers, undocumented workers), the urban informal sector, and social class formation. It is indeed an exemplary study of what we have in mind, though the urban focus is not as sharp as it might be, and individual cities are not analyzed.

The perspective we propose here builds on the work of Portes and Walton (1981). It attempts to bring together the relatively abstract formulations of the world systems approach by grounding them at the key points of articulation between the world economic system and its spatial expression, the world city. We believe that this perspective provides us with a comprehensive framework for understanding distinctive processes of urban change. By focusing on the world city, we are led to ask new questions about urbanization and to formulate new theoretical understandings. At the same time, the perspective provides us with a new basis for intervention by the state and guides planners' attention to some of the fundamental causes of economic, social and spatial dislocation in the world city.

1. Methodological considerations

As we had occasion to remark at the start of this essay, the world city perspective is a framework for the study of urbanization; it is not a theory. From a methodological standpoint it may be characterized as follows:

1. its *systematic* nature which puts in first place of importance as an explanatory variable, an expanding world capitalist economy;
2. an emphasis on the crucial role in the formation and articulation of the world system of very large urban regions which constitute its *spatial system*. The critical variable in the study of particular world city regions is their *mode of integration* with the world economy;
3. the use of a *dialectical model* of interpretation in which the territorial interests of particular world cities and the nation states within which they are situated are seen as being both united with and opposed to the interests of transnational corporations that are the principal actors in the world economy. This formulation is captured

by saying that every world city, being integrated along both functional and territorial lines, has a dual but contradictory aspect;
4. an explicitly *historical approach* that focuses on the transition of particular cities to world city status in the context of the evolution of the capitalist system as a whole.

Given these initial commitments, what can we say about the phrasing of particular studies? We have little to go on by way of actual experience. At least one recent study stands out by coming very close to the methodology that we would urge; Harley L. Browning's and Bryan Roberts's 'Urbanization, sectoral transformation, and the utilization of labour in Latin America' (1980). This innovative essay is both historical and comparative, introducing the emerging world economy as a means for interpreting the changing character of Latin American urbanization.

In general, we should like to see both empirical and historical studies of particular world cities. The specific mode of their integration into the global economy has to be brought into the study, and the spatio-temporal structure of core and periphery within which they are located should be made explicit. The problem focus of these studies would be the *restructuring of economic, social, and spatial relations, and the ensuing political conflicts in world city formation.* It would be the dynamic processes of the evolving system, and on the contradictions which arise from the dialectical encounter between territorial and economic interests. Although not a theory in itself, the world city perspective is likely to give rise to specific theories that link the expansion of the global economy to particular features of world city formation.

2. *Planning for world city growth*

Concern with urbanization is ultimately a very practical interest: the wish to avoid problems and to make things better. This interest we believe to be almost universally shared. It implies that planners should fasten their attention on the contradictions that generally arise in the course of change, that they should heed the resulting conflicts and struggles among contending powers, and that they should pay particular attention to the role of the state. They themselves, of course, do not stand apart from these processes, but are swept up in them as yet another group of actors. This fact has profound implications for their practice.

What does a world city perspective contribute to planning interventions, affected chiefly through the agency of the state, though they may involve many other actors, as solutions are hammered out in the heat of contending interests?

a. The world city perspective permits planners to deal more realistically with urban contradictions. It provides them with a heuristic that leads them to identify the major structural causes of specific problems. It will suggest to them that many *local problems can ultimately have only global solutions*. These two levels of analysis and action are intertwined, often antagonistically. If planners remain parochial, they cannot serve the larger public interest, but neither can they be very effective clerks of capital. Planners' attention must become increasingly system-wide. But, a world perspective in itself is not enough. Somehow, this perspective must be joined to local initiative and political accountability. Purely technical solutions ultimately serve only the interests of the powerful.

b. The world city perspective is not meant to suggest that the expansion and penetration of international capital is the 'only game in town'. It would be wrong to resign ourselves to a presumptive 'sweep of history' in which outcomes are predetermined. A corollary to the first point above is that *local actions may have global consequences*. It is precisely because of the reciprocal relationship between the international economic system and the world city that struggles in the urban arena may have profound ramifications for the global order. The contradictions of capitalism, as well as territorial and environmental constraints, create the necessary space for actions whose aim is capital's subordination to a political purpose. Thus, what appear to be localized battles—about freeway expansion, social service cut-backs, plant closings, airport noise abatement, or housing demolition—must be seen as extracting a price from capital which inevitabley needs space for its activities. In some cases, capital may respond by 'fleeing' to more suitable locations. But it cannot escape the world city. The world city is essential for the management of global capital which has little choice but to settle there and come to terms with local populations. Unless the functional importance of the world city for capital is recognized by planners, the opportunity for exercising political leverage may be lost. For capital is not invulnerable, nor are politically organized territories always impotent.

c. Planning for world city growth must be *partisan planning* that asserts not only territorial interests over those of transnational capital but, *within the territorial context,* the interests of the working class both as a whole and decomposed into its several fractions, including the large 'underclass' of workers who, having been pushed to the margins of the social order, are the most exploited and oppressed. The reason for this partisanship is that conflicting interests cannot be harmonized merely through technocratic goodwill. Planners are enjoined to take sides in the struggle. Acting in the public domain, they are empowered to speak for political communities. And a political community cannot be founded on injustice.

d. Partisan planners necessarily adopt a political perspective in their work. Their primary audience is the political community from which their authority derives. But the urbanized region of a given world city extends far beyond the boundaries of particular communities. Planners must therefore work to enlarge the scope of political action by building *coalitions* and *networks* among both organized communities and interest groups that are shaped by common class position, ethnicity, gender, and specifically functional concerns. In particular, they must try to mirror the ability of transnationals to mobilize resources on a global scale by organizing community and labour groups, wherever they may be, so that they might act in concert. Initially, these efforts may be limited only to monitoring and the exchange of information, but the long-term goal would be to coordinate policies and actions that would contain the drive of capital to dominate the life spaces that we inhabit.

Only further work will tell whether the framework we propose is valid intellectually and useful in practice. Its adoption requires a major shift in orientation and emphasis from our usual ways of dealing with cities—pragmatic, fragmented, more interested in cosmetics than in basic change. For the first time, we can begin to see linkages across the different worlds—first, second and third; north and south; core and periphery—with learning and knowledge gained from experience travelling in all directions, none able to claim superiority by the mere fact of having arrived first in time at some particular way station of history.

Notes

1. This essay was written jointly with Goetz Wolff. We are greatly indebted to John Walton for his insightful critique of an earlier version of this paper and to our students in the Colloquium on the Future of the City whose skepticism and relentless questioning forced us in a number of instances to reconsider our argument and to sharpen its formulation. Special thanks are due to Suha Ulgen, Marco Cenzatti, Iraj Iman, Trevor Campbell, Bish Sanyal, Ramon Sevilla, Dan Meyer, Subhash Gupta, Christian Lefevre, Carlos Gonzalez, and Don Parson.
2. A problem is posed by cities in the actually existing socialist countries, particularly China and the Soviet Union. The question is an empirical one: how and to what extent are their major cities tied into the international

capitalist economy and therefore subject to its influence? Only further research can provide answers to this question.

3. Examples would be China's willingness to accept Hongkong's 'colonial' status in return for having a 'window to the west' or the imposition of a 'user tax' on transnational corporate capital for the privilege of doing business in a given world city.

4. This is not true, of course, of city states such as Singapore. But the fact remains that as urban regions, most world cities extend over multiple political jurisdictions which see their respective interests rather differently. Typically, world cities are managed by administrative bodies ('authorities') which have only the most tenuous of accountability requirements. World city is an economic, not a political concept. Many of its problems derive from this lack of political definition.

5. For example, gross sales for Exxon and General Motors in 1978 ranked between the GNP of Czechoslovakia and Austria, or 23rd and 24th in a ranking of all countries. See Todaro, 1981, 401.

6. The following employment estimates are of the roughest sort, particularly as they fail to distinguish between world cities in core and semi-periphery. But they may help to put things in perspective:

Cluster	% of Urban Labour Force
1 High-level business services	10–20
2 Derived demand sectors	15–30
3 Tourism	**
4 Manufacturing	15–20
5 Government services	10–15
6 Informal economy	10–40
7 Unemployed	5–10

**Included in Cluster 2.

7. There is no question in whose interests the city is arranged. The case of New York is a recent example. New York politics had been traditionally populist. Massive income transfers took place from property owners to the working-class poor. But the costs mounted until the city suffered virtual bankruptcy. Its final recovery (essential to its continuing role as a leading world city) was professionally managed for a committee of bankers who helped to bail the city out. The cure was drastic. Countless services which the poor had previously enjoyed and which had rendered their condition, if not hopeful, at least tolerable, were abandoned. Only services which were absolutely essential for social reproduction were retained, albeit at greatly reduced levels. But the operation of the city as a world centre was scarcely affected by these cut-backs. On the contrary, within a few years, the authorities spoke enthusiastically of a New York City renaissance. It was not a renaissance of the ghetto, however, but of Wall Street and Fifth Avenue.

8. This formulation begs the question of class formation. It appears to leave out the traditional blue collar working class altogether. But the traditional blue collar is gradually disappearing from the world city. Its place is being taken by a working class with mimetic propensities: its members aspire to a life of glamorous affluence. Although in the case of the armies of clerical workers, this aspiration remains largely a dream, union struggles and

worker solidarity are not part of their daily life experience. Politically inarticulate, they tend to identify with the interests of the transnational elites. If this reading is correct, the major lines of class conflict are drawn, in the first instance, between the 'upper' and 'lower' circuits of the world city economy or between the so-called underclass and all the rest.

Bibliography

References to works used in the preparation of this essay. A bibliographical essay prepared by Goetz Wolff and originally an appendix to the paper, has been excluded here.

American Assembly 1975: *Global companies: the political economy of world business.* Englewood Cliffs, NJ: Prentice-Hall.

Amin, S. 1974: *Accumulation on a world scale: a critique of the theory of underdevelopment.* New York: Monthly Review Press.

Aronowitz, S. 1981: A metatheoretical critique of Immanuel Wallerstein's *The modern world system. Theory and Society* 10 (July), 503–20.

Baird, P. and McCaughan, E. 1979: *Beyond the border: Mexico and the US today.* New York: North American Congress on Latin America.

Barnet, R. J. and Müller, R. E. 1974: *Global reach: the power of multinational corporations.* New York: Simon and Schuster.

Bell, D. 1973: *The coming of postindustrial society: a venture towards social forecasting.* New York: Basic Books.

Blanpain, R. and Morgan, A. 1977: *The industrial relations and employment impacts of multinational enterprises: an inquiry into the issues.* Paris: OECD.

Bluestone, B. and Harrison, B. 1980: *Capital and communities: the causes and consequences of private disinvestment.* Washington, DC: The Progressive Alliance.

Böhning, W. R. 1976: Migration from developing to high income areas. In ILO, Tripartite World Conference on Employment, Income Distribution and Social Progress and the International Division of Labour, Background papers, volume II: International strategies for employment, Geneva: ILO, 119–38.

Bromley, R. editor, 1979: *The urban informal sector: critical perspectives.* Oxford: Pergamon Press.

Brooke, M. Z. 1978: *The strategy of multinational enterprise: organization and finance.* London: Pitman.

Brooke, M. Z. and van Beusekom, M. 1979: *International corporate planning.* London: Pitman.

Browning, H. L. and Roberts, B. R. 1980: Urbanization, sectoral transformation, and the utilization of labour in Latin America. *Comparative Urban Research* 8, 86–104.

Bruce-Biggs, B. editor, 1979: *The new class?* New Brunswick, NJ: Transaction Books.

Carney, J., Hudson, R. and Lewis, J. editors, 1980: *Regional crisis: new perspectives on European regional theory.* London: Croom Helm.

Castells, M. 1976: The wild city. *Kapitalistate* 4/5.

————. 1978: *City, class, and power*. London: Macmillan.

————. 1979: *Multinational capital, national states and local communities*. A report on urbanization and social change in the third world, based on field work research in Latin American squatter settlements. Berkeley: Institute of Urban and Regional Research.

Chase-Dunn, K. forthcoming: The system of world cities, 800–1975. In Timberlake, M., editor, *Urbanization and the world system*.

Cockburn, C. 1977: *The local state: management of cities and people*. London: Pluto Press.

Cohen, R. B. 1981: The new international division of labour, multinational corporations and urban hierachy. In Dear, M. and Scott, A. J., editors, *Urbanization and urban planning in capitalist society*, New York: Methuen, 287–315.

CSE Microelectronics Group 1980: *Microelectronics: capitalist technology and the working class*. London: CSE Books.

Daly, H. E. 1977: *Steady-state economics: the economics of biophysical equilibrium and moral growth*. San Francisco: W. H. Freeman.

————. 1980: *Economics, ecology, ethics: essays toward a steady-state economy*. San Francisco: W. H. Freeman.

Dear, M. and Scott, A. J. editors, 1981: *Urbanization and urban planning in capitalist society*. New York: Methuen.

Drucker, P. 1980: *Managing in turbulent times*. New York: Harper and Row.

Dunning, J. H. 1970: *Studies in international investment*. London: Allen and Unwin. editor, 1971: *The Multinational enterprise*. New York: Praeger.

Edwards, R. 1979: *Contested terrain: the transformation of the workplace in the twentieth century*. New York: Basic Books.

Ellul, J. 1964: *The technological society*. New York: Vintage Books.

Falk, R. 1981: *Human rights and state sovereignty*. New York: Holmes and Meier.

Fallows, J. 1981: *National defense*. New York: Random House.

Ford, D. and Chris Ryan, C. 1981: Taking technology to market. *Harvard Business Review* (March–April), 117–26.

Frank, A. G. 1970: The development of underdevelopment. In *Latin America: underdevelopment or revolution*, New York: Monthly Review Press, 3–94.

Freedman, D. H. editor, 1979: *Employment: outlook and insights. A collection of essays on industrialized market-economy countries*. Geneva: International Labour Office.

Friedland, R. forthcoming: *Power and crisis in the central city*. London: Macmillan.

Friedman, J. 1978: The political economy of urban renewal. Urban Planning, UCLA, Masters thesis.

Friedmann, J. 1972: A generalized theory of polarized development. In Hansen, N., editor, *Growth centres in regional economic development*, New York, Free Press.

————. 1979: On the contradictions between city and countryside. In Former, H. and Oosterhaven, J., editors, *Spatial inequalities and regional development*, Boston: Martinus Nijhoff Publishers.

Friedmann, J. and Miller, J. 1965: The urban field. *American Institute of Planners Journal* 31 (November), 312–20.

Friedmann, J. and Sullivan, F. 1974: Labour absorption in the urban economy: the case of developing countries. *Economic Development and Cultural Change* 22, 385–413.

Friedmann, J. and Weaver, C. 1979: *Territory and function: the evolution of regional planning*. Berkeley and Los Angeles: University of California Press.

Friedmann, J. and Wulff, R. 1976: *The urban transition: comparative studies of newly industrializing societies*. London: Edward Arnold.

Fröbel, F., Heinrichs, J. and Kreye, O. 1980: *The new international division of labour: structural unemployment in industrialized countries and industrialization in developing countries*. Cambridge: Cambridge University Press.

Georgescu-Roegen, N. 1971: The entropy law and the economic process. Cambridge, Massachusetts: Harvard University Press.

Gladwin, T. N. and Walter, J. 1980: *Multinationals under fire*. New York: Wiley.

Goodman, R. 1979: *The last entrepreneurs: America's regional wars for jobs and dollars*. New York: Simon and Schuster.

Gouldner, A. W. 1979: *The future of intellectuals and the rise of the new class*. New York: Seabury.

Hall, P. 1979: *The world cities*, second edition. New York: McGraw-Hill. (Originally, 1966.)

Harloe, M. editor, 1977: *Captive cities: studies in the political economy of cities and regions*. Chichester: John Wiley.

Harrison, B. 1981: *Rationalization, restructuring, and industrial reorganization in older regions: the economic transformation of New England since world war II*. Cambridge, Massachusetts: Joint Centre for Urban Studies of MIT and Harvard University.

Harvey, D. 1973: *Social justice and the city*. London: Edward Arnold.

———. 1975: The geography of capitalist accumulation: a reconstruction of marxian theory. *Antipode* (September), 9–21.

———. 1978: The urban process under capitalism: a framework for analysis. *International Journal of Urban and Regional Research* 2, 101–32.

de la Haye, Y. 1979: *Marx and Engels on the means of communication*. New York: International General.

Heenan, D. A. 1977: Global cities of tomorrow. *Harvard Business Review* 55 (May–June), 79–92.

Hicks, U. K. W. 1974: *The large city: a world problem*. London: Macmillan.

Hill, R. C. 1977: Capital accumulation and urbanization in the United States. *Comparative Urban Research* 4 (2 and 3), 39–60.

Hirsch, F. 1976: *Social limits to growth*. Cambridge, Massachusetts: Harvard University Press.

Ho, Kwon Ping 1980: Bargaining on the free trade zones. *New Internationalist* (April), 12–14.

Hopkins, T. K. 1979: The study of capitalist world-economy: some introductory considerations. In Goldfrank, W. L., editor, *The world-system of capitalism: past and present:* volume 2 Political economy of the world system annuals, Beverly Hills: Sage, 21–52.

Hymer, H. 1976: *The international operation of national firms*. Cambridge, Massachusetts: MIT Press.

————. 1979: *The multinational corporation: a radical approach:* Edited by R. B. Cohen, New York: Cambridge University Press.

ILO 1979: *Growth, structural change and manpower policy*. Geneva: International Labour Office.

Idris-Soven, A. Idris-Soven, E. and Vaughn, M. K. editors, 1978: *The world as company town: multinational corporations and social change*. The Hague: Mouton.

Interfutures 1979: *Facing the future: mastering the probable and managing the unpredictable*. Paris: OECD.

Kantrow, A. M. 1980: The strategy-technology connection. *Harvard business review* (July–August), 6–21.

Kaplan, B. editor, 1978: *Social change in the capitalist world economy*. Volume 1 Political economy of the world-system annuals. Beverly Hills: Sage.

Kearney: Management Consultants 1977: *A study of trade and employment in the electronics industry*. Prepared for the US Department of Labor, Office of Foreign Economic Research, Bureau of International Labor Affairs, Contact ILAB 75–10.

Kindleberger, C. 1969: *American business abroad*. New Haven, Connecticut: Yale University Press.

Kujawa, E. editor, 1973: *American labour and the multinational corporation*. New York: Praeger.

Kumar, K. editor, 1980: *Transnational enterprises: their impact on third world societies and cultures*. Boulder, Colorado: Westview Press.

Lefebvre, H. 1968: *Le droit a la ville*. Paris: Editions Anthropos.

Lenin, V. I. edn 1970: *Imperialism: the highest stage of capitalism*. Peking: Foreign Language Press.

McGee, T. G. and Yeung, Y. M. 1977: *Hawkers in southeast asian cities: planning for the bazaar economy*. Ottawa: International Development Research Center.

Malecki, E. J. 1980: Corporate organization of R and D and the location of technological activities. *Regional studies* 14, 219–34.

Mandel, E. 1971: *Marxist economic theory*, volume 1. New York: Monthly Review Press.

————. 1798: *Late capitalism*. London: Verso.

————. 1980: *Long waves of capitalist development: the marxist interpretation*. New York: Cambridge University Press.

Marx, K. and Engels, F. 1848: *The communist manifesto*. Reprinted in McLellan, D., editor, *Kark Marx: selected writings*, Oxford: Oxford University Press, 1977.

Mass, J. and Senge, P. M. 1981: Reindustrilization: aiming for the right targets. *Technology review* 83 (August–September), 56–65.

Massey, D. 1978: Capital and locational change: the UK electrical engineering and electronics industries. *The review of radical political economics* 10 (Fall), 39–54.

————. 1979: In what sense a regional problem? *Regional Studies* 13, 233–43.

Mattelart, A. 1979: *Multinational corporations and the control of culture: the ideological apparatuses of imperialism*. New Jersey: Humanities Press.

————. 1980: *Mass media, ideologies, and the revolutionary movement*. Sussex: Harvester Press.

Meadows, H., Meadows, D, Randers J. and Behrens, W. W. III 1972: *The limits to growth: a report for the Club of Rome's project on the predicament of mankind.* New York: Universe Books.

Merrington, J. 1975: Town and country in the transition to capitalism. *New left review* 93 (September–October), 71–92.

Mollenkopf, H. 1978: The postwar politics of urban development. In Tabb, W. R. and Sawers, L., editors. *Marxism and the metropolis: New Perspectives in urban political economy,* New York: Oxford University Press, 117–52.

Morris, D. and Hess, K. 1975: *Neighborhood power.* Boston: Beacon Press.

Murray, R. 1971: The internationalization of capital and the nation state. *New Left Review* 67 (May–June), 84–109.

———. 1972: Underdevelopment, international firms and the international division of labour. In *Towards a new world economy,* compiled by the Society for International Development, Rotterdam: University of Rotterdam Press.

Nelson, J. M. 1979: *Access to power: politics and the urban poor in developing countries.* Princeton, New Jersey: Princeton University Press.

Norton, R. D. and Rees, J. 1979: The product cycle and the spatial decentralization of American manufacturing. *Regional studies* 13, 141–51.

Ophuls, W. 1977: *Ecology and the politics of scarcity.* San Francisco: W. H. Freeman

Palloix, C. 1977: The self-expansion of capital on a world scale. *Review of Radical Political Economics* 9 (Summer), 1–28.

Palma, G. 1978: Dependency: a formal theory of underdevelopment or a methodology for the analysis of concrete situations of underdevelopment? *World Development* 6, (July/August), 925–36.

Peattie, L. R. 1980: Anthropological perspectives on the concepts of dualism, the informal sector and marginality in the development urban economies. *International Regional Science Review* 5,1 (Fall), 1–32.

Perlman, E. 1978: *Myth of marginality: urban poverty politics in Rio de Janeiro.* Berkeley: University of California Press.

Perry, D. C. and Watkins, A. editors, 1977: *The rise of the sunbelt cities.* Volume 14 Urban Affairs Annual Reviews. Beverly Hills: Sage.

Piven, F. F. and Cloweard, R. A. 1979: *Poor people's movements: why they succeed, how they fail.* New York: Vintage.

Portes, A. and Walton J. 1981: *Labour, class and the international system.* New York: Academic Press.

Power, L. in collaboration with Garling M. and Hardman, A. 1979: *Migrant workers in western Europe and the United States.* Elmsford, NY: Pergamon Press.

Pred, A. 1977: *City-systems in advanced economics: past growth, present processes and future development options.* New York: Wiley.

Rada, J. 1980: *The impact of microelectronics: a tentative appraisal of information technology.* Geneva: ILO

Radice, H. editor, 1975: *International firms and modern imperialism.* Harmondsworth: Penguin Books.

Resources for the Future 1979: *Scarcity and growth reconsidered.* Baltimore: John Hopkins University Press.

Rifkin, J. and Howard T. 1980: *Entropy: a new world view.* New York: Viking Press.

Roberts, B. R. 1978: *Cities of peasants: the political economy of urbanization in the third world*. London: Edward Arnold.

Ross, R., Shakow, D. M. and Susman, P. 1980: Local planners—global constraints. *Policy Sciences* 12 (June), 1–25.

Rothschild, E. 1981: Reagan and the real America. *New York Review of Books* 28 (February), 12–18.

Santos, M. 1975: *The shared space: the two circuits of urban economy in the underdeveloped countries and their spatial repercussions*. London: Methuen.

Saxenian, A. L. 1980: Silicon chips and spatial structure: the industrial basis of urbanization in Santa Clara County, California. University of California, Berkeley, MCP thesis.

Schiller, H. I. 1976: *Communication and cultural domination*. White Plains, New York: M. E. Sharpe.

Security Pacific National Bank 1981: *The sixty mile circle: the economy of the greater Los Angeles area*. Los Angeles: Public Affairs Research Department, Security Pacific National Bank.

Shoup, L. H. and Minter, W. 1977: *Imperial brain trust: the council on foreign relations and United States foreign policy*. New York: Monthly Review Press.

Sklar, H. editor, 1980: *Trilateralism: the trilateral commission and elite planning for world management*. Boston: South End Press.

Smith, V. K. editor, 1979: *Scarcity and growth reconsidered*. Baltimore: John Hopkins University Press for Resources for the Future.

Soja, E. W. 1980: The sociospatial dialectic. *Annals of the Association of American Geographers* 70 (June), 207–25.

Sterling Hobe Corporation 1978: *International transfer of semi-conductor technology*. Prepared for the US Department of Labour, Bureau of International Labour Affairs, Contact J9K700B (October).

Storper, M. and Walker, R. 1979: *Systems and marxist theories of industrial location: a review*. Berkeley: Institute of Urban and Regional Development, Working Paper 312.

Tabb, W. K. and Sawers, L. editors, 1978: *Marxism and the metropolis: new perspectives in world political economy*. New York: Oxford University Press.

Todaro, M. 1981: *Economic development in the third world*, second edition. New York: Longman.

United Nations 1973: *Multinational corporations in world development*. New York: United Nations Department of Economic and Social Affairs.

———. 1978: *Transnational corporations in world development: a reexamination*. New York: United Nations.

Vernon, R. 1971: *Sovereignty at bay: the multinational spread of US enterprises*. New York: Basic Books.

———. 1977: *Storm over the multinationals: the real issue*: Cambridge, Massachusetts: Harvard University Press.

Walker, P. editor, 1979: *Between labour and capital*. Boston: South End Press.

Wallerstein, I. 1974a: The rise and future demise of the world capitalist system. *Comparative studies in society and history* 16, 387–415.

———. 1974b: *The modern world system*. New York: Academic Press.

———. 1979: *The capitalist world economy*. New York: Cambridge University Press.

Walton, J. 1976: Political economy of world systems: directions for comparative research. In Walton J. and Massoti, L. H., editors, *The city in comparative perspective: cross-national research and new directions in theory*, Beverly Hills: Sage-Halstead Press.

Weinstein, B. L. and Firestine, R. E. 1978: *Regional growth and decline in the United States: the rise of the sunbelt and the decline of the northeast*. New York: Praeger.

Winner, L. 1977: *Autonomous technology: technics-out-of-control as a theme in political thought*. Cambridge, Massachusetts: MIT Press.

Wolff, G. 1981: Capital and labour in the central city. Manuscript, Graduate Programme in Urban Planning, UCLA.

Zimbalist, A. editor, 1979: *Case studies on the labour process*. New York: Monthly Review Press.

4
Life Space and Economic Space: Contradictions in Regional Development

This paper was presented at a European conference on regional planning organized by Dudley Seers and Kjell Öström in February 1981. The meeting took place at Luleå University in the heart of a famous coal-mining district in northern Sweden. The frozen ground beneath our feet was hollowed out with miles upon miles of mining shafts and subterranean corridors. It was a bleak setting in which to take stock of our knowledge of the development of regions.

The conference itself was of note. The third in a series, it represented a quixotic effort on the part of scholars like Seers to resist the headlong rush to embrace the new globalism, signifying the erasure of all boundaries and the ultimate triumph of economics over politics. In the background of the conference hovered an idea that was rarely addressed head-on: a Europe of regions, where each region's historical character might be allowed full scope to develop according to its own traditions. To be sure, there was a good deal of the usual talk about regional disparities, but also a growing acknowledgement of political action made evident by social movements asserting regional autonomy "from within."

My own paper took up a theme I had touched upon some years earlier: the contradictions between territory and function, life space and economic space (see chapter 1). Only now the language was less contorted and oblique. By 1981 I was fairly clear about my theoretical position. Politics, as I saw it, was primary. The actors who produced what we call the economy—firms and corporations—should be subordinated to the political will of the community. Only in this way would the trend toward the increasing social costs of enterprise be checked, and a halt be called to the unlimited expansion of production. In the United States, we were at the beginning of the Reagan era, where National Growth Days would be proclaimed, where decontrolling the economy was becoming an article of faith, where private enrichment at the expense of the community was hailed as an American virtue, and where expansion of the state's security apparatus helped to finance economic recovery. As a nation, we were swept up into the violence of industrial restructuring, marked by thousands of plant closings throughout the country and growing joblessness. Official unemployment stood at 12 percent. For the first time ever, local coalitions of labor and community sprang up in a desperate and usually unsuccessful effort to fight back against the systematic destruction of viable communities, as corporate capital moved to offshore sites in the Third World (and occasionally to more hospitable regions within the United States), where labor was found to be more pliant, and labor costs were only a fraction of what they were at the original location.

My paper grew out of this particular experience, offering a vocabulary and set of concepts with which to mount a powerful critique of the "logic" of capital restructuring. The paper ended rather lamely, with a series of exhortations about the primacy of a democratic politics, a democratic socialism in the face of Reagan and Thatcher. Despite the absence of a political echo, I continue to think that my vision of a revitalized political community designed to fit a human scale is the only genuine power capable of resisting the growing arrogance of transnational capital.

Regional theory relies to a large extent on the core-periphery model and its related concepts of dependency, unequal development, and geographical transfer of value. Despite its simplifications, it is, in many respects, a convenient model: used with circumspection, it can lead to significant results, both for analysis and practice.

In its original formulation, the model of core-periphery relations goes back to the early work of François Perroux (1950) and the classic two-region models of Gunnar Myrdal (1957) and Albert O. Hirschman (1958). Of the three, only Perroux's version is couched in the pure language of economics; it is the only one which strenuously avoids a geographic reference. Perroux eventually came to work with a regional construct, but his initial concept of 'growth pole' referred to 'leading industrial complexes' that were highly interconnected with other industrial sectors through input-output linkages and thus could send out growth 'impulses' to the rest of the economy—wherever this might be. In striking contrast, both Myrdal and Hirschman introduced political variables into their analyses. With this, they perforce introduced a territorial dimension, because the conduct of politics requires a space within which authority relations are legitimized.

Myrdal's version of 'cumulative causation' suggested an upwardly spiralling accumulation of power within a region the growth of which, on balance, generated 'back-wash' effects in weaker, colonised economies. Though more optimistic in outlook, Hirschman's model was even more explicitly political. He insisted that uneven regional development would eventually generate political pressures to persuade central authorities of the desirability of transferring resources from rich lands to poor, reestablishing—albeit only approximately, and for short periods—an ever-elusive spatial equilibrium.

In a series of studies, I developed this model of core-periphery relations still further, with a view to undergirding the practice of regional planning with appropriate theory. In a work published in 1972, I brought together economic, geographic, and political variables into a set of interconnected hypotheses. 'A general theory of polarized development' proved too unwieldly, however, to gain much popularity. In any event, it was soon overtaken by Marxist approaches to regional analysis which, though they made extensive use of the core-periphery imagery, did so essentially to illuminate the mechanisms of uneven development on a world scale (Frank, 1967; Hymer, 1972; Amin, 1974; Wallerstein, 1974; Lipietz, 1977; Hadjimichalis, 1981).[1]

Marxist scholarship has made four major contributions to regional analysis. Its theoretical point of departure is the *world system of market relations*. Its models increasingly incorporate a *theory of the state* as an integral element. Its focus is on specific mechanisms for the *geographical transfer of value*. And its political emphasis is on *regional social movements* and their struggles as an instrument of change.

Particularly in its Marxist incarnation, there is much that can be learned from the core-periphery model. It is primarily in this version that political variables are clearly distinguished from economic ones. But, because Marxists are generally disinterested in policy prescription, they have failed to articulate the practical implications of their work, which thus remains at such a high level of abstraction that conceptual ambiguities are not resolved. Granted that the relation between core and periphery involves conflicting interests, what is the nature of this conflict? Should it be understood as between region and region (Goodman, 1979), or between capital and the regions as Stuart Holland (1976) claims? Or is the conflict rather within capital itself, though fought out on the terrain of regions, with multinationals pitted against national and regional fractions of the bourgeoisie (Palloix, 1977; Markusen, 1978)?

In the following pages, I propose to take a closer look at these questions. I shall do so by treating political and economic variables within a dialectical framework which attempts to transcend the core-periphery model in its several versions.[2]

Life Space and Economic Space

Two geographies together constitute a 'unity of opposites'; I shall call them *life space* and *economic space*. Although both are necessary for the sustenance of modern societies, they are inherently in conflict with each other. Over the last two centuries, economic space has been subverting, invading and fragmenting the life spaces of individuals and communities.

Life space is, at once, the theatre of life, understood as a convivial life, and an expression of it. Economic space corresponds more narrowly to the conditions of livelihood, or the maintenance of life.

Life spaces exist on different scales. In their narrowest conception, they refer to neighborly spaces that contain the vast majority of people's daily round of activities. In the United States, they are defined by a radius of about four miles (Friedmann, 1980). From this immediate area shared with others, we rise to more encompassing life spaces: city, province, and finally the nation.

Life spaces are typically bounded, territorial spaces. Especially evident at the national level, where boundaries have legal force, boundedness is a characteristic that, to some extent, is true of life spaces on any scale. They are the ground on which the history of a people is enacted. For this reason they represent a distinctive value to people who will often refer to themselves as coming from a particular place, with its own history and politics . . . a space that matters.

Places have names. They constitute political communities, especially on the national scale, but often on lower scales as well, even down to neighborhoods (Oakerson, 1981). What do I mean by a political community? Is it the Rousseauvian idea of a people organised for a life in common; it is the Sovereign to which the State is held accountable; it is the democratic myth of a social compact.

In talking about development in the language of life spaces, I have in mind an *integral* development which seeks to achieve particular individual and collective *needs* of a community. It is a development defined *from within*, and its specific meaning will vary among places.

Needs may be understood as reciprocal and moral claims, in the sense that individuals can make claims upon their communities for the satisfaction of their 'needs', even as the community, in turn, lays claims to part of the individual's labour contribution for collective needs. Characteristically, needs are finite in nature, and they can be legitimately established only in a political discourse where contending claims are weighed in balance and measured against available resources.

In contrast, economic space is abstract and discontinuous, consisting primarily of locations (nodes) and linkages (flows of commodities, capital, labour and information). As an abstract space, it undergoes continuous change and transformation, but basically it is an a-historical space, the transformations of which are expressed in the language of differential calculus.

The principal actors which constitute and, indeed, produce this abstract economic space are firms and corporations. Their purpose is the pursuit of profit, and they operate according to a central principle: *that the amassing of surplus from production should be private, while social costs should be absorbed on public account.* The formal choice criterion for actions productive of economic space is, thus, efficiency in the accumulation of a surplus.

Economic space is open and unlimited; it can expand in all directions. Indeed, its continuous expansion is vital to the reproduction of capitalist relations as a whole. Expansion occurs ruthlessly, through the destruction of inefficient producers and their replacement by firms that are more viable.

Economic space is superposed over the life spaces of individuals and communities. This creates the illusion of national, regional, and even urban economies. If, however, we were careful in our use of words, we should have to speak of a world economy that *impacts upon* the life space of nations, regions, and cities, reserving the concept of a national (regional, etc.) economy for those countries where the major economic variables are substantially determined *from within*. But this is increasingly rare.

We are suffering from a confusion of values, where livelihood, instead of being subordinated to life, is ascendant over life, reducing life to a function of economic calculation. In the ideology of capital, life is set equal to consumption, so that increases in income (and, therefore, of consumption) are presumed to lead to gains in human satisfactions or in happiness (Scitovsky, 1976). This is the felicity calculus of utilitarian fame. Throughout the capitalist world, development policy is based on it.[3]

I do not wish to be misunderstood. For individual households, the linear relation of income to happiness may well apply, but only to a point which is itself socially determined, where the household's basic needs are satisfied. Beyond this, the simple linear relationship ceases to hold. Though aggregate income may continue to rise, the sum of happiness in society need not increase (Easterlin, 1974). As people are thrown out of work, as their relative income position worsens, as they consume more 'positional' goods or are more anxious about the future, their combined happiness may actually decline (Scitovsky, 1976; Hirsch, 1976). Most Western countries (and, I should think, especially the United States) appear already to have passed the point where the basic needs of everyone can be met out of present production, although this fact is masked by the greatly unequal distribution of income and wealth.[4]

In what follows, then, my concern is with a situation where the felicity calculus is no longer tenable, and where happiness depends primarily on things other than further increases in income. Whereas the all-absorbing primacy of livelihood is justified so long as basic needs are not yet being met substantially, the continued assimilation of life values to the value of livelihood beyond the threshold of basic needs has led to severe disruptions which, overall, have diminished the quality of our lives. What is the evidence for this?

Firstly, we can see the result in the dissolution of life spaces and their progressive assimilation to economic space. The capitalist city has no reverence for life: it bulldozes neighbourhoods to make way for business; it abandons entire regions, because profits are greater somewhere else. Deprived of their life spaces, people's lives are reduced to a purely economic dimension as workers and consumers—at least so long as there is work. For many, there is no prospect of any work in the economy, and such work as is available is often destructive of the human spirit. Just as the South Bronx is the symbol of the city laid waste by capitalism, so the television tube is the ultimate symbol of consumer idiocy: complete passivity, a catatonic frenzy.

But the dissolution of life space goes on each day in the countryside as well. It is made visible in the systematic destruction of the land— deforestation, erosion, desertification; the gouging of the earth by voracious strip mining; the silent death of acid rain; the accumulation of nuclear wastes in remote regions; the poisoning of lakes, streams and underground reservoirs by industrial residuals.

Secondly, under the hegemony of economics over life, development has come to be understood primarily as the expansion and growth of production measured over the territory of nations, regions or cities in strictly market terms, i.e., without subtracting the social costs of production. The point has often been made, but it needs to be made again and again, more than ever at a time when the social costs of production appear to be rising at dizzying speed.

Exhibit 1: Each time there is a motor vehicle accident, the GNP goes up. The police, the garage, the hospital, the insurance company and the lawyers must be paid. Absurdly, the more severe the accident, the greater the increase in GNP. We can speak of the economic productivity of accidents.

Exhibit 2: Each time a crime is committed, the GNP goes up. The logic is the same as in the preceding case. In addition, there are the expenditures of the rich to protect themselves against break-ins: electric fences, motorized guards, closed-circuit television, steel doors, double locks. A whole industry feeds on crime insecurity and fear.

Exhibit 3: As air and water pollution increases, so does the GNP. Consulting firms specialize in 'environmental impact' statements. There are expensive law suits to force/escape compliance with anti-pollution legislation. There is a new technology of pollution control which employs tens of thousands of workers. All this shows up as increases in production—as 'development'.

Exhibit 4: Because of high labour costs, a factory shuts down in Region A, throwing hundreds of workers out of a job, and undercutting the livelihood of thousands more as the ripple effects of unemployment and uncertainty spread throughout the community. The factory opens up an identical operation in Region B, where it escapes union labour and can hire a docile labour force for only a fraction of what it used to pay. Because of new machinery, and in the absence of other constraints on labour exploitation, productivity goes up. So does GNP, by the amount of the new production in Region B, by the public expenditures in infrastructure meant to entice the facility to the new area, by the costs entailed by the move itself, by the increase in the welfare bureaucracy in Region A, etc.

It is quite possible and, indeed, given the low overall growth rates currently prevailing in Western economies, quite probable, that any reasonable attempt to measure the changes in product *net* of social costs—in short, to count only net social benefits—would show actual long-term *declines* of real income in most countries. Subjectively, we experience these declines as a diminishing quality of life.[5] Where livelihood triumphs over life, the relentless pursuit of growth for its own sake will ultimately lead to the destruction of life.[6]

Thirdly, economic growth and the associated social changes are carried by global capital into the life spaces of individuals and the community. As an outside force, it impacts upon the lives of people, creating new dependencies. A specific form of dependency is the subordination of the local work force to the logic of capital. Because capital is extremely mobile, it can blackmail political communities into accepting wage levels and other working conditions that are competitive on the world market. The terms of this bargain inevitably favour capital; they have to do with livelihood, not life. Wages are pushed down from $10 to $3 per hour; overtime work is paid at the regular scale; and union organisations are broken.

The outstanding example of what is happening is the imminent establishment of 'enterprise zones' in the older industrial regions of the United States, and especially in the 'inner city' where the normal rules of territorial life would be suspended. (Under the name of 'export platforms', such zones are already proliferating in Third World countries.) In enterprise zones, trade unions would be off-limits; taxes nonexistent or very low; tariffs waived; the cost of utilities subsidized; and the basic infrastructure provided by the local community, whose principal tangible benefit would be the wages and salaries paid out by firms. Yet even the total wage bill would be relatively low. At the first stirrings of worker discontent, capital will threaten to pack up and move to some other, more compliant place. With millions of hungry workers waiting for jobs—any sort of job—from Kenya to the Philippines, from Haiti to China—and with the physical constraints on the mobility of capital virtually zero, such gains as organised labour has scored, in over a century of struggle, may be lost within the blinking of an eye. Although the world market for labour is not yet homogeneous, and perhaps never will be, the overall tendency is clear. Life space is being colonized by capital, to be absorbed into the economic space of the world system.

Fourthly, the snowballing social costs of production which must be assumed by the community have led to what James O'Connor (1973) has called the fiscal crisis of the State. These costs include inflation, unemployment, chronic poverty, pollution, rural abandonment, the destruction of old industrial centres, and criminal behaviour. Ultimately, they cannot be ignored by the State, because the State can maintain itself only through a balance of voluntary citizen allegiance and repression. As mass allegiance to the State declines, repression automatically goes up, and the terms are set for an all-out struggle over the principal levers of State power.

But the problems persist. Continuously generated by a process that is blind to the needs of life, money can alleviate some of their effects; it cannot destroy them at the source.

The fiscal crisis of the State is an expression of the deepest contradictions of the system. As the multiple economic crises grow in severity, and the need for intervention by the State increases, the ability and, indeed, the willingness of citizens to fund the interventions of the State declines. Moreover, such intervention as the State does manage to effect tend to reduce citizens to objects of bureaucratic solicitude, a condition they instinctively resent. The result is a profound and spreading sense of alienation.

In the United States, the election in 1980 of an arch-conservative administration such as Reagan's, with its promises of reviving the ancient virtues of hard work, thrift and enterprise, may be viewed as a quixotic attempt to break out of these multiple contradictions. Yet this same administration, dedicated to the shrinking of the State, proceeds to build up the State's repressive apparatus under the guise of fighting communism abroad and criminals at home.

And still the problems do not go away; in fact, they are bound to get worse. Not only are the conditions which generate them virtually unchanged, but now the State has washed its hands of them. The State has abandoned the people to the forces of an unregulated market.

In the past, regional planning (as an activity of the State) made desultory attempts to lessen some of the problems engendered by the violent invasion by economic space of the life spaces of historically constituted communities. It did so, primarily, by adopting the model of economic space: its expressed concern was with spatial income inequalities, unemployment, and the adoption of a locational framework for the analysis of regional underdevelopment. Derived from the same framework, regional policy dealt with location incentives, calculating income and employment 'multipliers' as well as 'leakages' from new investments. As the spatial setting for accelerated industrialisation, growth centres were identified and linked into networks whose structure was hierarchically arranged.[7]

This forthright embrace of economic forces and their 'space', gathering momentum in the early 1950s, would last unchallenged for two decades (Friedmann and Weaver, 1979). Where regional policies succeeded, they managed to implement the growth centre doctrine on which they were based: facilitating the importation of economic growth into people's life spaces, integrating regions and localities into the global network of economic relations on a basis of inequality, and intensifying the exploitation of the work force by paying wages that were barely competitive on the world market. In other respects, they failed. Despite persistent efforts, the periphery remained periphery; in more cases than one, the famous income gap increased (Stöhr and Tödtling, 1979).

The Reordering of Values

If there is a solution to this complex, contradictory situation, the path to it will not be easy. It will call for changes, the political practicality of which may be questioned. Yet the more probable alternative is not attractive. If it were merely a question of having to put up with stubborn regional inequalities, one might manage to live with that. The threatening collapse of the existing State system is quite another matter. The specific form of this collapse is not incipient social chaos, though it is also that. It is, rather, the attempt to shore up by force the State's dwindling authority. Fascism has been the historical answer to the failures of bourgeois democracy in managing the multiple crises of the capitalist world (Gross, 1980).

Chaos, fascism, and the possibility of bloody struggle can be avoided only if we recognise that we are, indeed, suffering from a troubling confusion of values. Accepting that, a reordering of values becomes the initial and most important step: *life must come first, then livelihood*.[8] Speaking practically, this means subordinating economic space to the political authority of the State. It means protecting the historical life space of cities, regions, and the nation from the blind incursions of capital. To extend this protection, the State must have control over the basic conditions of livelihood within a given territory, and exercise this power in the interests of the people as a whole.[9]

A State so inclined would have to rest on a very different base of power than at present. It would have to rest directly on the power of the people mobilised for a life in common in both their life space and place of work. This may be stated more succinctly. If the State is to respond effectively to their needs, people must first reclaim their sovereign power by revitalising the political communities in which they live. Implied is a restructuring of institutions in the direction of self-management and greater local autonomy. One solution would be to form a structure of territorial assemblies in which the life spaces of individuals would be joined to economic space, and the principle of delegation would replace traditional forms of interest representation (Pitkin, 1967; Friedmann, 1980). Through the agency of such a system, and building on the experience of Yugoslavia, a genuine public discourse about the goals of territorial development viewed in relation to the means available could be sustained (Tyson, 1980).

To recover the political community and the life spaces which it at once expresses and protects, two conditions must be met. The first is to make steady and continuous progess towards an *equalisation among households of access to the bases of social power*. Reference is to such bases as knowledge and pertinent skills, social and political organisation, instruments of production (including access to good health), relevant information, social networks, and financial means. Improving a household's access to them will enhance its ability to pursue its own objectives in cooperation with others. In this view, poverty is not simply a condition of low income. It is substantial inequality in access to the means for an autonomous life within the community (Friedmann, 1979). The gradual attrition of poverty in this sense, a result of popular struggles, will be experienced as a liberating movement from dependent passivity to autonomous political action.

The second condition for a genuine political discourse—a true development 'from within'—is the creation of opportunities for what Jürgen Habermas (1979) calls *a process of 'undistorted communication' about questions in the public domain.* Concretely, Habermas means that differences in social power should not weigh excessively in the exchange of symbolic meanings as they bear on public action.

Communication in democratic politics must be open and multidirectional, reflecting as accurately as possible the totality of contending meanings (Forester, 1980; Kemp, forthcoming). But the full exchange and exploration of meanings is a time-consuming business, as the exchange gives rise to new understandings, and these may lead to actions that, in turn, occasion further insights into process and situation (Marris, 1981). Because of its time-consuming character, open communication can be expected to slow down the responses of public bodies, and it may put a brake on the frenetic pace of technologically driven change (Tyson, 1980). But this, of course, is precisely what the reassertion of the dominance of life space over livelihood and its 'autonomous' technology intends (Winner, 1977).[10]

Within a restructured political community, regional planning would again find a legitimate mission. It would assist political bodies in articulating their needs and possibilities for development, provide information that is pertinent, project images of possible futures, and carry out specific technical studies for its client, which is the political community at large and not merely the central State. The desire for comprehensive coordination will give way to the articulation of needs and the negotiations of appropriate programmes and relationships among political bodies. Conflict based on both territory and class will, of course, continue. But in a restructured situation, it will be understood less as a striving for power than as a way of raising people's consciousness and improving the information bases of planning. The ultimate resolution of conflict will remain political, as it is now.

Notes

1. Though standing frankly in the Marxist tradition, none of the named authors uses class analysis as a starting point for their arguments. Their

emphasis is on only one of the two poles of what Edward Soja (1980) has aptly called the socio-spatial dialectic.

2. The dialectic here is not Hegelian, in which contradictory *logical* categories are superseded in a grand synthesis, as history moves ever forward towards a final resolution of all conflict, which is its *telos*. Rather, I have in mind a traditional Eastern concept in which two opposing forces meet and clash without ever resolving the contradictions between them. In such a Taoist dialectic, the victory of one force over the other would imply the destruction of the particular system of order they comprise, a system which sustains itself only through conflict (Freiberg, 1977).

3. On 15 April 1981, President Ronald Reagan declared Growth Day. His proclamation included the following paragraph: 'As we look to the future, we know that it is only through growth that we can continue our American way of life and hope to enjoy increased prosperity. For a growing economy sustains our democracy and the partnership between workers and business and industry. Only with economic growth and free enterprise can we ensure the expansion of economic and social opportunities which will benefit all Americans' *(Los Angeles Times, 14 April 1981)*.

4. The critical point would be the value of production that would, in principle, allow for the satisfaction of the basic material needs of the political community. Given existing inequalities, with glut and deprivation existing side by side, a massive redistribution of national product to meet everyone's material basic needs would require a restructuring of economic activities that now produce an excess of 'un-needed' commodities. It would, in fact, require the building of a socialist economy.

5. The profound sense that the 'quality of life' is deteriorating is not pervasive only throughout the cosmopolitan West. It is also the experience of a large part of the world's rural population whose conditions of livelihood are being destroyed (ILO, 1977).

6. The particular shortcoming of the social accounting framework which I have highlighted is only one of its many problems. Its practical importance is this: the failure to deduct the social costs of production leads to wrong-headed decisions. For an excellent and full discussion, see Seers (1976).

7. Growth centres are a metaphysical concept in urban geography, and were made to have a meaning virtually identical to 'city'. The current favourite which has replaced it, *enterprise zones* or *export platforms,* is clearly more useful as a descriptive concept in policy analysis.

8. I am speaking of those situations where people's basic needs can be satisfied, in principle, out of present production. Where this is not, as yet, the case, as in most countries of the world periphery, the production of a decent livelihood *is* the relevant basic need, and has priority.

Although I do not intend to introduce the 'idealistic' argument that, somehow, values must change before the world can be set aright, one's value position must, in some sense, become clear. I can be outraged at exploitation, or I can overlook its existence. I can do battle for equality of treatment in the market-place, or I can believe in the superior claims of male white professionals. I can advocate a fundamental democracy and people's right to self-determination, or I can defend elitism. In short, we must all take positions that ultimately relate our practice to fundamental questions of value. Marxists, though not Marx himself, have tended to put the matter of livelihood first. In this, they have merely mirrored the capitalist ethos. The alternative, obviously, is to subordinate the question of livelihood to life itself. That was Marx's view, and it leaves room for a political perspective, which is what I wish to emphasise in this chapter.

9. As a practical matter, what can the state do to assert its new authority? It can limit its participation in the world economy through 'selective closure', encouraging a more autonomous development based on domestic resources and skills, and on a concept of social efficiency; it can directly participate in the financing and mangement of key economic sectors that would otherwise be controlled by trans-national capital, ensuring their conformity with social purposes and using this power as a lever for negotiating with global capital; and it can undertake research to revise the system of social accounts so that it comes more closely to reflect the true costs of production, factor scarcities (such as energy) and non-market activities. A revised set of social accounts is perhaps the most important step of all. Until we have an accurate measure of what we produce as a nation, in terms that are appropriate, public policy will continue to be based on ignorance and, even worse, misinformation.

10. Critics will argue that what I am proposing here will only increase one of the major social problems we face, the growing measure of labour redundancy. But, contrary to common expectations such as President Reagan's (see Note 3 above), the recovery of high rates of economic growth—even if it were possible, which is doubtful—will not yield substantial increases in full-time jobs. The impact on labour of rapidly rising costs of capital cannot be overcome by merely stepping up the rate of GNP by a couple of percentage points. On the contrary, if my surmises are correct, increasing the rate of economic growth will only speed us on the road to national disaster.

A socially responsive state would have considerable control over technological choices. It could, for instance, opt for more labour-intensive methods of production. It could redirect human energies towards the provision of collective needs and the improvement of people's life spaces. And it could facilitate political participation, by helping to restructure the political community on which its own future depends. In various ways, then, social redundancy can be curbed. In a 'good society', no one would be socially redundant.

References

Amin, S. (1974) *Accumulation on a World Scale: A Critique of the Theory of Underdevelopment* (New York: Monthly Review Press) 2 vols.

Easterlin, R. A. (1974) 'Does economic growth improve the human lot?', in P. A. Davis and M. W. Reder (eds), *Nations and Households in Economic Growth: Essays in Honor of Moses Abramovitz* (New York: Academic Press).

Forester, J. (1980) 'Critical theory and planning practice', *Journal of the American Planning Association*, vol. 46, pp. 275–86.

Frank, A. G. (1967) *Capitalism and Underdevelopment in Latin America* (New York: Monthly Review Press).

Freiberg, J. W. (1977) 'The dialectic in China: Maoist and Daoist', *Bulletin of Concerned Asian Scholars*, vol. 9, no. 12 (January–March) pp. 2–19.

Friedmann, J. (1972) 'A general theory of polarized development', in N. M. Hansen (ed.) *Growth Centers in Regional Development* (New York: The Free Press; London: Collier-Macmillan).

Friedmann, J. (1979) 'Urban poverty in Latin America', *Development Dialogue*, vol. 1, pp. 98–114.

Friedmann, J. (1980) 'Urban communes, self management, and the reconstruction of the local state', UCLA, School of Architecture and Urban Planning, Working Paper.

Friedmann, J. and C. Weaver (1979) *Territory and Function: The Evolution of Regional Planning* (Berkeley: University of California Press; London: Edward Arnold).

Goodman, R. (1979) *The Last Entrepreneurs: America's Regional Wars for Jobs and Dollars* (New York: Simon & Schuster).

Gross, B. M. (1980) *Friendly Fascism: The New Face of Power in America* (New York: M. Evans).

Habermas, J. (1979) *Communication and the Evolution of Society* (Boston, Mass.: Beacon Press) ch. 1.

Hadjimichalis, C. (1981) 'Regional crisis: the State and regional social movements in southern Europe', in this volume.

Hirsch, F. (1976) *Social Limits to Growth* (Cambridge, Mass.: Harvard University Press).

Hirschman, A. O. (1958) *The Strategy of Economic Growth* (New Haven: Yale University Press).

Holland, S. (1976) *Capital Versus the Regions* (London: Macmillan).

Hymer, S. (1972) 'The internationalisation of capital', *Journal of Economic Issues*, vol. 6, pp. 91–111.

International Labour Office (1977) *Poverty and Landlessness in Rural Asia* (Geneva: ILO).

Kemp, R. (forthcoming) 'Critical planning theory—review and critiques', in P. Healey *et al.* (eds). *Planning Theory into the 1980s* (Oxford: Pergamon).

Lipietz, A. (1977) *Le Capital et son Espace* (Paris: Maspèro).

Markusen, A. R. (1978) 'Regionalism and the capitalist State: the case of the United States', *Kapitalstate*, vol. 7, pp. 39–62.

Marris, P. (1981) 'Meaning and action' (unpublished manuscript).

Myrdal, G. (1957) *Economic Theory and Underdeveloped Regions* (London: Duckworth).

Oakerson, R. J. (1981) 'Neighborhood incorporation: a constitutional approach to neighborhood scale political development', NORG Bulletin (Indiana University), March.

O'Connor, J. (1973) *The Fiscal Crisis of the State* (New York: St. Martin's Press).

Palloix, C. (1977) 'The self-expansion of capital on a world scale', *Review of Radical Political Economics*, vol. 9, pp. 1–29.

Perroux, F. (1950) 'Economic space: theory and applications', *Quarterly Review of Economics*, vol. 64, pp.89–104.

Pitkin, H. F. (1967) *The Concept of Representation* (Berkeley: University of California Press).

Scitovsky, T. (1976) *The Joyless Economy* (New York: Oxford University Press).

Seers, D. (1976) 'The political economy of national accounting', in A. Cairncross and M. Puri (eds), *Employment, Income Distribution and Devel-
opment Theory: Problems of the Developing Countries: Essays in Hon-
our of H. W. Singer* (London: Macmillan).
Soja, E. (1980) 'The socio-spatial dialectic', Annals of the Association of
American Geographers, vol. 70, no. 2 (June) pp. 207–25.
Stöhr, W. and F. Tödtling (1979) 'Spatial equity: some antitheses to current
regional development doctrine', in H. Folmer and J. Oosterhaven (eds),
Spatial Inequalities and Regional Development (Boston, The Hague,
London: M. Nijhoff).
Tyson, L. d'A. (1980) *The Yogoslav Economic System and Its Performance in
the 1970s* (Berkeley: University of California, Institute of International
Relations) Research Series 44.
Wallerstein, I. (1974) 'The rise and future demise of the capitalist world
system', *Comparative Studies in Society and History*, vol. 16, no. 4
(September) pp. 387–415.
Winner, L. (1977) *Autonomous Technology: Technics-out-of-Control as a
Theme in Political Thought* (Cambridge, Mass.: MIT Press).

5
The Barrio Economy and Collective Self-Empowerment in Latin America

The dilemmas of capital restructuring are much greater for Third World economies than for the major industrial powers. The territorial integrity of entire nations has been seriously violated in the strenuous effort to maintain the worldwide hegemony of capital. The classical case in recent memory is that of Chile, which until 1973 was widely regarded as one of the outstanding instances of social democracy in Latin America. When the popular-unity coalition of Salvador Allende was toppled in a violent coup d'etat in 1973, it was replaced, with full U.S. support, by a military junta. Soon, American dollars and advisors flowed to this distant Andean nation of ten million people and the generals were happy to cooperate: Chile was opened up to international capital without restriction. The export-production model of development, involving the elimination of tariffs and the privatization and decontrol of the economy, was given its critical test.

The euphoria which followed was short-lived. Chile's foreign debt doubled and then doubled again. Luxury imports skyrocketed. Chilean industry, unable to meet international competition on this scale and in so short a time, shut down, throwing hundreds of thousands of workers out of jobs. By the time of the second oil shock in the late seventies, official unemployment for this highly urbanized economy reached an unprecedented thirty percent. Inflation eroded such wages as were still being paid. As the world price of tin, Chile's principal export, reached new lows, creditors called in their short-term loans. The only production sectors continuing to flourish were a nascent armaments industry supplying South Africa and governments in the Middle East and a wine industry exporting chiefly to the United States. Despite growing civil unrest and cooling U.S. passion because of continuing human-rights violations, the government of General Pinochet remained firmly in control.

But the systematic impoverishment of the mass of the working people eventually reaches its own limits. People will organize themselves to defend their livelihood. And so, throughout the working class barrios of Santiago and other major Chilean cities, spontaneous action groups initiated self-help efforts of survival. Democratic in conception, and in many cases with a strong spiritual foundation (the Catholic church being one of the major institutional sponsors of these self-help movements), these efforts, beyond the reach of the state, are also encountered in other Latin American countries. Important instances have been documented for Brazil, Argentina, Peru, and Colombia. After the recent earthquake that rendered hundreds of thousands of individuals homeless, the capacity for self-organization of the popular sectors of civil society in Mexico City was thought by many to be a "miracle." The importance of this phenomenon can only be grasped if we recall that in the Latin American tradition, people look primarily to the state to resolve their problems. That people are no longer exclusively pressing the state with their claims for a redress of grievances but are beginning to act for themselves must be regarded as a major turning point in the history of the continent, with long-term implications for the future of politics.

The following paper, written with Mauricio Salguero, reviews the literature on the emergence of popular action for livelihood and survival in South America and proposes as a guide to further study the model of a barrio economy, that is, of a humanly scaled territorial economy in which production for use compliments production for the market under the control of the people residing in the barrio. What appeared as a utopia when I wrote the preceding essay on the dialectics of life space and economic space here finds its historical incarnation. The new movement for a development "from within" is by no means as yet firmly established, and it came about not because anyone "planned" it as such, but because it responded to the grim necessities of survival. What it portends for the future remains in the realm of speculation. But already it demonstrates, at least for Latin America, the possibilities of a development on a basis other than the subsumption of national economies to the logic of global capital.

Introduction

In many ways, the most hopeful sign in a Latin America widely perceived to be a continent "without a future," where the traditional development models have been all but exhausted, and the word "crisis" is used so pervasively that it has acquired an everyday meaning no longer capable of arousing consternation, is the new activism of civil society that we have come to know as social movements.[1] The phenomenon is not unique to the region but is part of a worldwide reawakening of social forces that are neither of the state nor of the corporate economy but are rooted in household formations and their immediate organizations. In Latin America, this resurgence of civil society in the public domain has had specific proximate causes: the utter inability of the modern production sectors to provide a sufficient livelihood for any but a minor fraction of the working population, and a state whose repeated attempts at countervailing policies have proved ineffectual even as it has, in country after country, applied the stern old principle of *mano dura* to shore up its crumbling authority (Singer and Brandt 1982).[2]

There is a good deal of uncertainty about what these new grassroots movements really mean. In a highly original interpretation, colored by the European politics of the New Left, Tilman Evers proposes an essentially utopian view. He sees the movements as the carriers of a new collective identity:

> In a way, the new socio-cultural patterns of everyday sociability that germinate within the new social movements are part of [the bitter need for a founding project to reconstruct hegemony]. They are the embryos of a popular counter-foundation, in response to the ill-fated efforts from above. The dissolution of established socio-economic structures and socio-cultural orientations has had the effect, coupled with a devastating social disintegration, of "setting free" what remained of a constructive potential to find new, self-determined orientations and openings (Evers 1985, 63).

A Latin American voice, Ruth Cardoso, argues just as persuasively that the "new" social movements are neither new nor radical; that, by their very nature, they are easily co-opted by the state, and that neither in their intentions nor in their effects are they transformative of existing relations of power (Cardoso cited in Vink 1985). The fact is that urban social movements have indeed been around for quite some time, responsible for uncounted *invasiones* and *reivindicaciones* for at least thrity years (Goldrich et al. 1967–68; Castells 1976). But as sociologists have been quick to point out, their very success tends to weaken and exhaust these movements. Once land has been successfully claimed, once a particular demand for public services has been met, they dissolve as a social force, leaving material accomplishments as the only trace of their former existence. Some of the grassroots movements in Latin America are admittedly new, such as the movement for human rights in Chile or the Ecclesiastical Base Communities (EBCs) in Brazil. But they, too, must be seen as a response to a specific historical situation—conjunctural in the Marxist phrase—that will pass into oblivion once the conditions that gave rise to them are rectified. The return to democracy in Argentina all but terminated the human rights movement in that country, and the recent economic upsurge in Brazil, coinciding with a return to civilian rule and the persistent efforts of the conservative factions of the Catholic Church to regain lost terrain, have sharply curtailed the political significance of the EBCs (Mainwaring 1986). More fundamentally, not a few have argued that, in the absence of formal political organization, civil society lacks the capacity for sustained mobilization and transformative action.[3]

If this apparently realistic appraisal is at all near the truth, the study of the new civil activism would be at most of historical interest. We propose to go by a different road, however. The perspective of the past is valid and has in its favor that the past is, in any event, dead; its record is complete. With equal justification, however, we can claim a perspective from the unique vantage point of a possible future. Here the future speaks to our actions in the present: the record has still to be made. We are dealing, then, with possibilities that are invested with hope. Although it is unlikely that the possible future we imagine will emerge just as we think, to envision it at all does light a beacon in whose direction we can set forth.

The possible future that we propose to bring into relation with current grassroots movements in Latin America has both economic and political dimensions. We shall discuss each one in turn.

Global Crisis and the Political Economy of Survival

What is happening now in Latin American cities must be seen in historical perspective. Figure 5.1 is an attempt to sketch some salient dimensions of Latin America urban history since the early 1950s. By not differentiating among specific national histories, our account inevitably distorts reality. National experiences are by no means uniform throughout, nor does the timing of change necessarily coincide with our periodization. But there are sufficient similarities in the separate stories of cities in the region to attempt some provisional generalizations.

The table illustrates cycles of successive doctrine.[4] The first of these cycles spans the two decades after World War II. In Latin America, this is the period of the Keynesian state and is associated with the rise of national planning and the Alliance for Progress during the Kennedy administration. The reigning development doctrines are promulgated by Raúl Prebisch and W. W. Rostow: industrialization through import substitution and the "stages of growth" leading to the material utopia

Figure 5.1
The Urban Domain and the State, 1950–2000

Years	State	Development Model	The Urban Domain
1950s–1960s	liberal (Keynesian) welfare economic and social planning Social Policy: reforms redistributive policies (e.g. low-cost housing) directed popular participation	economic growth and development the consumer society (passive) industrialization through import substitution (foreign capital), restricted predominantly to elite markets capitalist transformation of rural areas: agribusiness massive expulsion from rural areas	high rates of urban growth the phenomenon of "marginality" (approximately 20 to 30% of urban population) stepped-up demand making (*reivindicaciones*) for items of collective consumption exceeds capacity of the state deterioration of living conditions
1960s–1980s	military and civil dictatorship neoliberal Social Policy: violent repression income redistribution towards the more affluent sectors	**Breakdown of Model I: Violence** GNP cult free market rapid accumulation privatization increased reliance on transnational capital industrialization for export (new international division of labor) increased indebtedness	explosion of informal-sector employment; unemployment 30–50% massive impoverishment, including middle strata hyperinflation social polarization

Breakdown of Model II: Global Crisis and New Beginnings

1980s–1990s	re-democratization (return of civilians to power), but the forms of democratization are not yet clearly defined (postliberal model)	walking on two legs: integration into the global economy *and a* politics of basic needs at the level of the local community	resurgence of civil society; self-organization, self-reliance, self-governance (empowerment)
	Social Policy:	expansion of internal markets through support of cooperatives and small enterprise	liberation of territorial space for autonomous action
	support of self-reliant practices		mobilization of nonconventional resources (e.g., mutual aid, dialogue, donation of labor time)
	decentralization of services and of planning		structural change from below toward new forms of the local state
	deconcentration of power to local actors		claim making for expanded civil and economic rights

of a mass-consumption society. With the massive transfer of rural population to the city, urbanization is accelerated, with growth rates of more than double the natural increase in the population. The inability of the "modern sector" to productively absorb the influx of rural migrants gives rise to the phenomeneon of "marginality" (for a critical review, see Sabatini 1986). Marginality is broadly defined as non-participation in the emerging consumer society. With some 20 to 30 percent of urban population living in shantytowns and *tugurios* (inner-city slums), the state launches major programs of redistribution, especially in housing. But these expenditures seem only to augment the flood tide of political demands on a state increasingly unable to respond to them with available resources. This concatenation of events, marked by the progressive deterioration of living standards among an already impoverished population—made doubly burdensome by runaway inflation—leads to a breakdown of this model and rising urban violence.

With the tacit support and sometimes active connivance of the U.S., military-civilian dictatorships are established in Brazil, Argentina, Uruguay, Chile, Bolivia, Ecuador, and Peru. While dissident elements are repressed, official terror is spreading (Linz and Stepan 1986).[5] On the economic front, the development model of Period I is replaced by a frank accumulation regime in which the growth of GNP is the overriding objective. State policies to bring hyperinflation under control are used to bring about an upward redistribution of income. Admidst an orgy of deregulation, free-trade euphoria, and reliance on monetary controls for maintaining essential macroeconomic equilibria, the neoliberal model of the state enjoys momentary popularity. With the massive influx of foreign private capital, indebtedness rises, the state acting as the ultimate guarantor of foreign loans. Although industrialization continues to be the first priority, the emphasis is not on the promotion of production for export. For a few years, economic "miracles" make newspaper headlines, adding fuel to the ideological debate, but after the oil shock of 1973 and especially after 1978, with the dramatic slowdown of the international economy "miracles" gradually yield to a sense of panic. The first, almost automatic response is to meet rising economic problems at home by going overseas to borrow more money from willing creditors of petrodollars. But by the early eighties, the major borrowers—Brazil, Mexico, Argentina, Chile, Peru—are in no condition to meet even the interest payments on their loans. The notorious debt crisis has arrived.

Meanwhile, in the urban sphere, unemployment reaches unprecedented levels, with 30 to 50 percent of the population living at close to subsistence levels (rising incidence of hunger, infant mortality, etc.) This situation crests in 1982/3, but, except for Brazil, whose economy rebounds in 1984, fails to show significant improvements thereafter. In some countries, such as Mexico, the deterioration of living standards continues. As states adopt IMF-imposed austerity regimes, impoverishment begins to spread even to the urban middle sectors. Social polarization increases. Large-scale capital flight, huge interest payments, and the drying up of foreign investments lead to actual disinvestment in many cases and to absolute declines in the real value of production. All this takes place in a context of global economic "restructuring," with new technologies coming on line, rising levels of unemployment even in the core countries of world capitalism, and increasingly loud demands in these same countries for protecting employment in the declining older industries and regions.

By the mid 1980s, the neoliberal model of the state has collapsed. Military regimes are once again replaced with civilian governments in a process hailed as democratization, and official terror gives way to a resumption of party politics and periodic elections. Only Chile and Paraguay hold on to the discredited model, while Central American states are gripped in the turmoil of civil war and U.S.-sponsored aggression. Another cycle is beginning.

In Fig. 5.1, we have attempted to link the mobilization of civil society, and more specifically its popular sector, with a new bifurcated development model that promotes both the integration of national economies with the global economic system and a politics of self-empowerment at the level of the local community (see Bitar 1985; Friedmann 1986; Geisse 1986; Max-Neef et al., 1986). This model has not yet been widely discussed, but in some countries, such as Peru, it appears on the verge of becoming reality. Beyond question is the surge of new activities in the barrios of large Latin American cities: a growing capacity for self-organization, self-reliance, and self-governance in a process of collective self-empowerment. In the course of this historical evolution, some barrios, such as in Chile, have even become a kind of "liberated" zone where nonconventional resources based on mutual aid, dialogue, and donation of labor time are mobilized (Max-Neef 1985). As the community becomes progressively empowered, the local state, inevitably implicated in this self-generated form of barrio development, is itself subject to transformation: its structures are being adapted to the demands of a participatory process. At the same time, the demand making so prominent during Period I is escalating to the claim making of Period III (Singer 1982). Underwritten with moral passion, claims are being staked out for expanded civil rights (local autonomy, participatory democracy) and economic rights (a decent livelihood and the collective provision of basic needs).

The preceding paragraph is written in a spirit of hope for a way out of the present impasse. It presupposes a structural reading of the economic crisis that points to a situation in which upwards of 50 percent of the urban population live a marginalized existence (Sunkel 1985; Aguilar 1985). The familiar models of industrialization and "modernization"—tied as they are to an emerging world economic order—are viewed as incapable of providing a satisfactory livelihood for all but a shrinking minority. We would argue that this is true even for Brazil, which is currently enjoying an economic boom (Reicher Madeira 1986). Faced with the likelihood of permanent crisis, household adaptations must be regarded as more than makeshift arrangements. For many households, the road to survival will lead them into a complex system of "informal" activities, where every last peso must be carefully weighed in balance with the effort (calories) necessary to produce it (Fass forthcoming). The rationality here conforms to the individual model of neoclassical economic theory; the system itself is not being challenged. For many others, however, the road will lead to new forms of cooperative activity with neighbors, the primary participants often being women, in which a new sociability is recovered in the teeth of continual assaults on one's identity as social failure, a *marginado* (Hardy 1984; 1985).

The vital connection of these responses to the political dimension remains to be considered. The first point we wish to make relates to the process by which poor people gain greater access to the bases for social—not yet political—power, primarily by joining in collective, community-based efforts of struggling for survival in difficult times. Empowerment is one aspect of larger social processes in which the future is foreshadowed; more precisely, with their emphasis on reciprocity, mutual aid, solidarity, social learning, participation, and egalitarianism, they are counterhegemonic processes in the specific Gramscian sense (Gramsci 1971; Evers 1985).

The prime example of this new politics at the level of the barrio is found in the Ecclesiastical Base Communities of Brazil, Mexico, and elsewhere (Betto 1984; Gómez-Hermosillo 1986). The intellectual leadership of the EBCs is particularly conscious of the break with hegemonic practices and relations within the sphere of the EBCs themselves. Beginning with a transformation of self through direct involvement with community work (including, importantly, festivities and celebrations), EBCs go on from there to collective tasks that deal directly with the survival problems of their members, but radiate outward to the rest of the local community, none of whom are, in principle, excluded from the benefits of collective action. It is at this point also that contact is necessarily made with the agents of the state—the local state in particular—and this, in turn, creates pressures for the transformation of (local) state structures toward greater independence from the center and more participatory practices of governance (Jacobi 1985; Pease Garcia 1986). Beyond this realm of possibilities lie still further transformative actions on the national plane that will require the formation of political parties with roots sunk deep into the popular barrio movement and other people's organizations, not least the labor movement and the mobilized peasantry. Such parties have yet to appear in Latin America, though the Partido dos Trabalhadores in Brazil may turn out to be the first example of its kind.[6]

We have said that our vantage point is the possible future—a future embodying hope. There are, of course, other possibilities less pleasant to contemplate. Latin American social formations can degenerate (once again) into the chaos of anarchy, civil war, death squads, galloping inflation, and massive immiseration. Or civil society can return to a state of passive acquiescence, punctuated with periodic and essentially senseless outbursts of popular anger *(quebra-quebras)*, in which authoritarian accumulation regimes function in an essentially depoliticized environment for the benefit of privileged elites. Given these options, we frankly opt for a future promising a genuine social and political renewal from below. It is not a great hope we nourish, but it is a hope grounded in some (admittedly selective) realities of the present day.

Our objective in writing this paper, then, is to propose a conceptual framework for research that will lead us to a deeper understanding of the transformative forces that are coming together in the popular barrios of Latin American cities as they confront the double challenge of survival (necessity) and political practice (freedom).[7]

Households and the Barrio Economy

Central to our conception of civil society is the household and, more specifically from a point of view of the production of life, the household economy (Borsotti 1978; Razeto 1984; Schmink 1984). In this conception, households, to be defined more precisely below, are viewed as *pro-active* units, achieving their goals in free association with other households similar to themselves. Households engage in the production of goods and services for both use and exchange. Both kinds of effort bring satisfactions in return. How households use available resources—the time, energy, and skills of their members—will depend on how they perceive their environment, the goals to which they aspire, and their expectations about the benefits they will receive for their effort. The objective conditions of their environment—the more intimate environment of the barrio and the wider spheres of the market economy—are also a relevant consideration.

Households, then, will be treated as fundamental units in the political economy of survival. Despite increasing reference to "household survival strategies", the definition of households for purposes of research has become quite problematic (Schmink 1984). As an irreducible social unit, households would nevertheless appear to be preferable as a unit of study than the atomized individual. For the purpose at hand, we shall therefore define households as *any group of related and/or unrelated individuals who, while living under the same roof and "eating from the same pot," constitute an economic decision-making unit.* By this definition, a single woman, living in the same dwelling and sharing meals with her three children, a distant cousin, and her lover, would be considered a household, whereas a lodging house would not. In general terms, the objective of any household is (1) to ensure its own reproduction as a unit within a given sociocultural context and (2) to improve its material condition. Households will thus devise "strategies" of both simple and extended social reproduction (Fass forthcoming).

Households are not homogeneous entities, however. They are composed of *individuals* whose objectives may or may not be identical with those of the household taken as a whole and who may or may not be willing to subordinate themselves to a common strategy. Moreover, they will enter into social relations with other households, forming *proximate networks* of reciprocity with neighbors and kin (Lomnitz 1977). They may also join in *cooperative types of enterprise and mutual-aid associations* (Hardy 1984). Finally, households are physically located in and part of an encompassing territorial community (the neighborhood, or barrio) whose objectives are evolved through more or less democratic procedures, but whose interests are not necessarily identical with those of any of its component units: individuals, households, and community organizations. The entire complex forms an articulated social whole that interacts with its environment in ways that give rise to multiple conflicts and contradictions (Capecchi and Pesce 1984).

Household resources can be invested in a number of sectors:

- the *household economy* itself (housing construction, food preparation, child care, care for sick or disabled, small livestock, etc.);

- the *territorial community*, or *barrio* (participation in social networks and mutual-aid efforts, participation in community-based organizations and Church activities, sportive events, community celebrations, etc.);
- the *political community* as the counterpart of civil society in the political sphere (demonstrations, civil strikes, membership in political parties, labor unions, and politically oriented social movements);
- the *cooperative economy*, typically located within the barrio and, though selling in external markets, organized very differently from either the informal sector or the private corporate sector, providing benefits to member households—and to the barrio as a whole—that, beyond monetary returns, are based on solidarity relations;
- the *informal economy* (sometimes also referred to as the unenumerated economy), frequently linked into the formal/official economy at the end of a long production chain, ranging from individual piecework production—home industry—to small-business enterprise, but also including domestic work, street vending, the underground economy, etc.;[8]
- the *formal (or enumerated) economy*, including both corporations and the state as employer;
- the *state* (e.g., primary and secondary education, jail, obligatory military service).

Of the seven domains of action identified, only the last two are *not* under the immediate control of the household economy, though the degree to which households actually control these domains will tend to vary a good deal.

In a household perspective, the barrio constitutes the space for the production and reproduction of its life, because it is here, in the immediacy of its everyday social relations, that households are able to increase their capacity for action by gaining improved access to social power (Friedmann 1987, ch. 9). As the habitat for the vast majority of the popular sectors, barrios typically have a name, a sense of their own identity, a history still fresh in the memory of their older inhabitants, dense social networks, a formal or informal structure of governance, and other attributes of a spatially defined political community. Although households may remain in their respective barrios for many years, the barrio's salience as a life space for its households will fluctuate with the relative attractiveness of the market economy. Accordingly, we shall hypothesize that, *as employment in the exchange economy declines and/or becomes less productive, households will tend to favor strategies that lead to an increased investment of their resources in the territorial community of the barrio and its component organizations.* The reverse of this hypothesis is also expected to hold true.

The relations between the household economy, its territorial base, and the market economy are shown schematically in Figure 5.2. The configuration here is one of several possible ones, and the pattern shown is greatly simplified. Nevertheless, Fig. 5.2 helps us to identify some critical dimensions of the problem.

The first thing we note about the model is that it shows households in four kinds of relation: among themselves (social networks), with the market economy in both formal and informal arrangements, with multiple-household or cooperative enterprises located within the barrio, and with community (self-help) organizations. Any given household will accordingly display a certain pattern of resource allocation among these areas of household investment, but the pattern itself— i.e., the relative allocation of household resources—will be subject to frequent modification and adjustment.[9] In making their decisions, households will generally be aware that they are dealing with two very different modes of production: inside the barrio, expected returns are measured primarily in terms of the direct *use value* of particular goods and services, feelings of good will, and social recognition; in the market economy, where relations are commodified, returns are counted exclusively in terms of money. This distinction is drawn in Fig. 5.2 by separately identifying solidarity and market exchange relations (a,b).

Related to this distinction is still another that draws a line between the barrio viewed as a moral economy (Polanyi 1977; Scott 1976), and consequently as a *community of limited needs*, and the *economy of infinite wants*, the market economy with which it is continuously in interaction. Within the community of limited need of the barrio, households tend to be focussed on the tasks of simple reproduction, or economic survival. The structure of this community (and thus of the barrio as a whole) is cellular, being articulated through networks of solidarity relations (Lomnitz 1977). In the form of its governance it is participatory and egalitarian. But as linkages to the market economy increase in importance, and differences in household incomes become more pronounced, solidarity relations tend to weaken.

Relations between the community of limited needs and the market are therefore central to our analysis. Within the barrio economy of Fig. 5.2, we have shown several multiple-household (cooperative) enterprises that maintain a dual relation to households based on both reciprocities and market exchange. These enterprises contain within themselves one of the major contradictions of the model. At the same

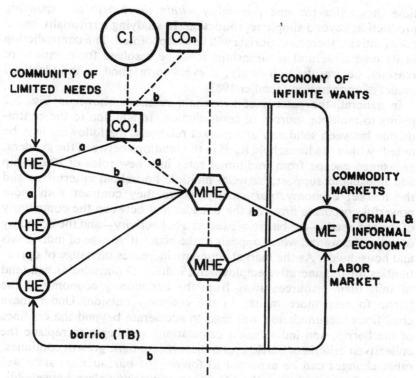

HE   household economy (including home industry)

MHE multiple household enterprise (cooperative)

CO   community (self-help) organization

ME   market economy

CI   civil institutions (church, political parties, foundations, etc.)

a   reciprocity (solidarity) relations (use values predominate)

b   market exchange relations (commodified)

TB   territorial base or life space

Figure 5.2
A Schematic Model of Household Relations

time they offer the one possibility *within the barrio* of expanding production beyond simple reproduction. In studying territorially based cooperatives, therefore, purists will be disappointed. The contradiction in its own structural relationships must be resolved for a variety of reasons, but results will rarely, if ever, correspond to the idealized model of cooperation (Tendler 1983).

In general, the pattern of household relations shown in Fig. 5.2 points to multiple sources of contradiction. In addition to the contradiction between solidarity and market relations, the following may be noted: within the household itself in the relations between the genders, as women escape from traditional roles into new roles of leadership and household support; between multiple household enterprises and the market economy, particularly where they contract with more powerful corporate firms on the outside; and between the community of limited needs—the barrio viewed as a collectivity—and the economy of unlimited wants, which appeals to the acquisitive urge of individuals and households. As the market economy increases the range of opportunities for remunerative employment, individual households will tend to shift their resources away from the community economy of the barrio to earn more money in the economy outside. Under these conditions, accumulation will tend to accelerate beyond the confines of the barrio, and individualist calculations will begin to replace the collectivist criteria of barrio economics. If economic growth continues, other changes can be expected to follow: the bureaucratic state will reassert its control over the life space of working-class households, economic exploitation of workers will increase, wealth will be progressively transferred out of the barrio, hierarchical relations will become more pronounced even within it, and participatory processes will atrophy.

The community of limited needs is thus an exceedingly vulnerable construction. At the personal level, participation in it can be highly satisfying experience, but households will tend to see it as a community of "last resort." As their own material situation improves, they will tend to reduce their involvement in community-based organizations, because these organizations do not promise to lead them out of poverty, according to the hegemonic definition of poverty as life at or below a certain subsistence income. This somewhat cynical conclusion must be tempered by two additional observations. First, along with many other observers, we do not expect a dramatic reversal in the conditions of Latin American urban economies. Although there may be local upsurges in formal employment possibilities, the prospects for a general resumption of high rates of economic growth on a long-term, secular basis, generating large numbers of new jobs, appear unlikely. For most countries, the existing economic crisis is likely to become the normal situation. This prospect, regarded as dismal by some, is nevertheless encouraging for the emergence of a new type of development from within the barrio communities themselves. Second, a great deal will depend on the success of multiple-household enterprises, such as worker-controlled cooperatives, because they alone, and not the micro enterprises of the informal sector, harbor the possibility of a genuine counterhegemonic praxis. For this reason, we propose to focus our work on production activities within the barrio. It is through these activities and their linkages into the community that we hope to capture the elusive phenomenon of collective self-empowerment that is at the heart of our research.

Specification of the Model and Questions for Research

In studying multiple-household enterprises and *micro-empresas* inside the barrio, we must continuously be aware of the contradictory nature of their external relations: their *forward linkages* (primarily marketing and purchasing arrangements in the larger economy), and their *backward linkages* into the community (strengthening solidarity relations, the convivial society, the role of women). In addition, we will want to look at *lateral linkups* among multiple-household enterprises with a given barrio, such as barrio cooperative associations, as well as between two or more barrios with the same city. Finally, we are interested in studying the broad social and political implications of the new forms of production within barrio communities. What can present initiatives tell us about the future of an "alternative" development engendered by conditions of prolonged structural crisis? Very little information is available on any of these questions. In the remainder of this paper, our purpose is to specify the many questions for research in more detail, based on the still quite limited knowledge we now possess.

1. The Barrio Economy: Households, Cooperatives, and the Informal Sector

Much of what we shall refer to as the *barrio economy*—the territorial base of household activities sustaining life and livelihood—remains invisible to the observer because of the imprecise use of the informal sector as an umbrella term to cover the great variety of officially unenumerated income-generating activities. Among the activities often lumped together in this sector, we find home-based industries (artisan production, textiles, knitware, electronics assembly), personal and repair services, small-scale manufacturing (micro enterprises), casual labor, domestic work, prostitution, and many other diverse trades. Some informal-sector workers produce directly for the final consumer, while others, possibly the majority, are situated at the end of long production chains, working for capitalist firms that control important shares of the consumer market (Portes 1984). As has frequently been observed, formal and informal sectors are linked to each other not only through relations of production but also in a more general, functional sense. Informal production, for example, tends to lower overall wage costs, offer flexibility to corporate management in weathering fluctuations in demand, and, by absorbing large quantities of labor at subsistence and below-subsistence levels, serves as a kind of buffer for the corporate economy.

This role of the informal sector leads to a curious result. During periods of economic recession the number of informal workers may actually increase, while the income earned per worker declines (Murillo and Lanzetta 1984; Hardy 1985). In this way, open unemployment tends to be less than it would otherwise be, even though the material condition of workers deteriorates to a point where households may be driven to adopt a new strategy in order to eke out an existence (Ross and Usher 1986).

Unable to earn a living in the informal economy—supplemented by such formal-sector income as may still come their way—many households turn for support to the *cooperative household sector,* or *sector asociativo,* within working-class barrios (Hardy 1984; Edy Chonchol 1984; Razeto et al. 1983; Razeto 1984; Hirschman 1985; Hardy and Razeto 1986; Guimāraes 1986). In this bifurcated sector, some services are produced cooperatively for the common benefit of its associated members (e.g., through community self-help organizations such as housing cooperatives and *ollas comunes,* or soup kitchens), while other organized-labor processes are producing chiefly for sale in outside markets (Hardy 1986; Molina and Henao 1986). Although both are fundamentally organized on the basis of *solidarity relations,* production for outside markets imposes special conditions that lead to the formation of *multiple-household enterprises* (MHEs). Neither cooperatives in the traditional sense nor micro enterprises organized according to proto-capitalist principles, they represent a category of production sui generis. The Chilean term for them is *organizaciones económicas populares* (OEP) (Razeto 1985).[10] They occupy a special place in the barrio economy. The typical multiple-household enterprise:

- is based within the social and physical space of the barrio, displaying strong "backward" linkages into individual households and community (self-help) organizations (solidarity linkages);
- is typically small-scale (less than fifty workers) but may be linked into larger, barrio-wide associations of similar enterprises;
- practices a form of collective decison making in which hierarchical relations are minimized;
- abides by the principle of equal pay for equal work;
- is not primarily devoted to profit maximization but to meeting the basic economic necessities of its members (i.e., does not extract surplus value and therefore accumulates very little, if at all);
- tends to attract a predominantly female labor force;
- practices mutual aid among its members;
- tends to be relatively short-lived, but easily regroups and reestablishes itself.

Although not all MHEs will be alike in their specific particularity, they stand in sharp contrast to the so-called micro enterprises of the informal sector, which are not territorially but individually organized and lack the close solidarity relations of the former (Strassmann 1986).[11]

This relatively simple typology of barrio economic activities may be summed up in Chart 5.1 (for comparison, see Fig. 5.2):

Individual households must devise a survival strategy appropriate for their specific situation that will optimize their time, labor, and skill resources over the array of potentially productive activities, with their specific rates of return in money and/or kind. These resource allocations are not likely to remain stable, as households endeavor to

Chart 5.1
The Barrio Economy

---

a. Formal (capitalist)-sector activities: for the most part, income earned outside the barrio. Accumulation is concentrated in this sector. Income may be spent inside the barrio.
b. Informal (proto-capitalist) sector:
   (1) micro-enterprises, producing both inside and outside the barrio but selling primarily outside the barrio.
   (2) other, such as domestic work, prostitution, ambulant trading, etc., for the most part carried out outside the barrio. May be further subdivided into semi-legal and illegal activities, including those customarily defined as "criminal."
c. Cooperative household (noncapitalist) sector
   (1) community (self-help) organizations
   (2) multiple-household enterprises (MHE)

---

optimize their economic situation in a series of adaptive moves among the three sectors and their respective subsectors. For our purposes, however, it is the cooperative household sector, and especially the multiple-household enterprise, which is of interest. Economically, it is the weakest of the three sectors and the one that brings the lowest monetary return. From a political and counterhegemonic perspective, on the other hand, it is also the sector that holds the greatest prospects for the future.

The best way to study MHEs in the context of the barrio economy is to investigate how they are articulated, in a *forward direction*, with capitalist markets and, in a *backward direction*, with the network of reciprocal relations within the barrio. As we have argued earlier, forward (market) linkages may have a disintegrating effect on solidarity relations, undermining the incipient counterhegemonic practices of households. These two sets of linkages and their interrelations therefore require the closest possible attention.

2. Forward Linkages: Marketing Relations

Like the informal economy, the cooperative household sector produces for markets. Although the question of how these markets are organized is of the utmost importance, very little information exists on the subject. Hardy (1984) reports how women's cooperatives in the Santiago suburb of Conchalí were initially assisted by the Church, acting through a beneficent foundation, in marketing their products in Santiago and exporting them abroad. When, after a number of years, responsibility for marketing was shifted to the cooperative itself, a crisis ensued, and many members dropped out. We have no information about subsequent events, but the changeover had undoubtedly far-reaching effects on the incipient cooperative movement.

More pertinent information is available on the informal sector. For example, whether formally organized or not, small-scale production is frequently tied into larger production ensembles through subcontracting arrangements (Portes 1984; Murillo and Lanzetta 1984; Holmes 1986). The resulting marketing relations tend to impose a harsh discipline on small producers and are inherently exploitative. A monopolistic buyer may set up one or more micro-enterprises with working capital and a supply of raw materials, while retaining key operational control. In this way, he arranges his supply network as an informally organized, dispersed "factory" (Piore and Sabel 1984). It is the buyer, then, who decides on the appropriate division of labor, imposes design and quality standards, sets delivery schedules convenient for himself, and establishes piecework rates. Unless multiple-household enterprises organize their own marketing, they will sooner or later be forced into similar arrangements, losing their autonomy and, indeed, much of their cooperative character as well. Within a very short time, they will turn into micro enterprises of the proto-capitalist type.

To retain their integrity as part of the cooperative household economy, MHEs must associate into larger entities and, in this new form, struggle to establish themselves in the market (Egana n.d.).[12] Associations may be required at both barrio and citywide levels. Through a system of cooperative stores, for example, or through cooperatively organized production ensembles, some of the essential features of the cooperative household sector can be preserved.[13] Even a change of scale, however, will tend to alter the relations of production from nonhierarchical solidarity at the base to relations articulated through the nexus of the market. Still and all, it is only by associating among themselves that MHEs can hope to preserve the essentials of cooperations, creating possibilities beyond the horizon of mere survival. We have no knowledge of the extent of associative relations in Latin American barrios, and the subject calls for thorough investigation.

3. Backward Linkages: Solidarity Relations and Social Mobilization

The new barrio movements represent a collective response to the deepening economic crisis in Latin America. A coalescence of diverse household strategies, they represent a new form of collective action. This much was already evident in the early 1980s. Writing of the Ecclesiastical Base Communities (Comunidades Eclesiais de Base, or CEBs) that were then beginning to be active in São Paulo and elsewhere in Brazil, Paul Singer found them to be "rooted in an ideological position completely different from that which inspired the movements of the previous decade" (1982, 290). He went on to explain:

> Instead of assuming that the needs of the peripheral *barrios* and impoverished populations stem from the negligence of the authorities, and that this might be overcome by an adequate mobilization of interested parties, privation is attributed to the very social organization inherent in capitalism. This, according to the CEBs, tends to trap individuals within the narrow circle of their personal interests and to prevent the development of a mutual solidarity which might unify the population and enable it to divide the fruits of its common efforts in a more equitable manner.

> The point of departure places an extremely high value on the participation of all members in the life of the Community as also on the protest movements which it comes to inspire. The exchange of votes for concessions on the part of the authorities—which is the essence of the so-called

> *politica de clientela* or clientelist politics—is from the point of view of
> this ideology, immoral at best. Access to public services is seen as a
> right to which all the city's inhabitants are entitled; exchanging votes for
> these services can only reinforce a system which is responsible for the
> injustices in the first place *(ibid.)*.

As this passage suggests, the Latin American barrio movement may
represent a good deal more than an act of sheer desperation in the face
of economic decline and massive unemployment. It is making a larger
claim—Singer calls it "unity in self-help"—that demands a new relationship between the local state and a self-organized citizenry. At the
same time, the new movements, building on traditional reciprocity
networks, display an extended sociability. Ivan Illich spoke of it as the
convivial society and imagined it as a utopian alternative to capitalist
relations (Illich 1975). What is novel about the extended sociability
that we encounter in actual fact is that it grows out of working people's
experience with active intervention in their own environments to
ensure the collective provision of basic survival needs. Some form of
social learning is evidently taking place, and the experience of autonomous community-based action is having positive effects on its participants, changing their very perceptions of the world and the possibilities
it holds for them.

Nevertheless, organized citizen movements do not, as a rule, occur
spontaneously, but require the catalytic action of an outside agency.
In some instances, the agent may be a political party. In the case of
Brazil's Ecclesiastical Base Communities, it is the radical wing of the
Catholic Church (Mainwaring 1986). The same has been true of barrio
movements in Chile, where the Church has played a key role in
organizing local communities, strengthening their capacity to resist.

Though the Church has been the most visible, it has not been the
only or even the principal agent of social mobilization. In Colombia,
for example, it is the state itself, through its recently formed Institute
of Natural Resources and the Environment (INDERENA), that is
promoting new forms of self-reliant community action.[14] Elsewhere,
research collectives have taken a leading role. In Bogotá, for example,
the Center for Research and Popular Education (CINEP) declares its
purpose to be "to contribute to changing the country's social, political,
and economic structures through action research and popular education" (personal communication, Manuel Uribe Ramón, April 1986).
Within the last ten years, research institutes similar to CINEP have
proliferated throughout the continent.

Outside intervention of whatever origin raises fundamental questions concerning leadership, financial support, and the long-term goals of intervention. Very little systematic information exists on any of these topics. We can therefore do no more than specify some of the questions that need to be asked.

a. *Leadership*

(1) Is it the objective of the intervention to encourage the development of an "organic" leadership from within the community itself, or to exert control indirectly through accommodationist community leaders? In other words, does the mobilizing agent aspire to lead the community himself or to plan to withdraw from the effort as an effective local leadership emerges?

(2) Is the leadership style personalistic in the traditional manner or broadly democratic, participatory, and inclusive?

(3) Are women encouraged to take a leading part in the mobilization effort? Is their presence in leadership councils in proportion to their numbers in the community?

(4) What methods of community organization are being used? Are practical problems being addressed as a matter of priority? Is due attention being given to the question of collective self-empowerment and therefore to a dynamic process of change involving social learning, or is the emphasis instead on traditional demand making (*reivindicaciones*)?

b. *Financial Support*

(1) How much outside support is made available to community-action groups, from what sources, and for what purposes?

(2) Are counterpart resources being generated, and in what proportion to outside assistance?

(3) Is aid made available in the form of grants, loans, or payments in kind, such as services, materials, etc.? How much accountability is required in the use of external resources?

(4) Does external financial assistance lead to new forms of patronage and dependency?

(5) Is there an expectation that local projects will ultimately become self-supporting and, if so, how? Over what period of time?

c. *Ultimate Objectives of the Intervention*

No external intervention is ever "naive" in the sense of being completely disinterested in the outcome. Objectives may be simple or complex and are, at any rate, always difficult to ascertain. Often they have to be imputed, since self-declarations may be designed to mislead.

An objective of social pacification, for example, might never be publicly declared, though it may well be the major motivation behind a specific external intervention. Other possible objectives include providing for the basic survival needs of the population, progressing toward a convivial society with a great deal of autonomy vis-a-vis the state, or creating new social relations of production with a view toward a future democratic socialism in a productive economy beyond the limits of simple reproduction.

The limited evidence we now have, chiefly from Brazil, Chile, Peru, and Colombia, is that a great deal of effort is expended to create new relations of solidarity within the cooperative-household sector of the barrio economy. Solidarity, mutual aid, conviviality: these are the incentive goods the community offers, in addition to the primary material benefits households can expect if they take part in the cooperative production of housing, local services, and commodities for sale.

Women are likely to be very active in community affairs and bring to them an organizational experience based on nonhierarchical relations, small groups, networks, dialogue, and mutual support. An intriguing question is whether this typically feminist style of social mobilization (Jagger 1983) carries over into the larger associative behavior required and the management of external market relations. It appears not to be the case, as men are likely to assume control whenever formal organizations emerge. Even so, important new roles for women and their newly won self-confidence and independence are having notable effects on gender relations within the household. In the longer term, they may well lead to a more assertive voice for women in the transformation of society and the local state.

4. Lateral Linkages and Political Practice: Transforming the Local State

Outside relations of the barrio economy are articulated in two ways: through market linkages and political articulations. The former we have already discussed. It now remains to look at the second.

Political articulations have typically been studied under the general category of urban social movements. The material interests defended by these movements have tended to be narrowly defined, in the trade-union manner, as housing, social infrastructure, and subsidies for transport and staple foods. When, responding to popular pressure, the state would meet these demands, the movements soon subsided. In the specialized literature, "urban social movements" was merely a fashionable name for traditional interest politics.

In contrast to this a-spatial approach, we propose to make political practice a dimension of a territorially-based barrio politics. We do so for three reasons: (1) because self-reliant development, self-management, and claims for greater community autonomy have traditionally been identified with territorial politics; (2) because we believe that the formation of barrio economies is the first essential step in moving the local state toward more decentralized, participatory structures; and (3) because a territorial politics of the popular sectors is likely to have more staying power and a greater potential for change than either the interest politics dear to pluralists or the working-class politics of the traditional Left. With regard to the latter, the relative numbers of blue-collar workers in modern factories and mining communities are so small that no significant action for structural change can be expected by organizing labor only at its place of work. Approximately half the workers in Latin America cities are now included in the informal and cooperative-household sectors. Working, if at all, in hundreds of thousands of small businesses, this near majority of the population cannot be effectively organized *except at their place of residence*, which is increasingly becoming a place of production as well. The new class politics must be territorially defined.[15]

The step from the barrio economy to a politics of change is neither simple nor straightforward. A myriad microscopic *organizaciones económicas populares*, no matter how effective they might be in solving people's survival problems, do not necessarily lead to a trans-formative political practice. *Lateral linkages* must first be established among them, both within a given barrio *(asociaciones de barrio)* and on a citywide scale in barrio confederations, before they can gain the clout necessary to make a difference on the political scene. They must also tie into progressive, politically organized forces—political parties of the sort that do not yet exist in Latin America, with strong popular roots—to gain a transformative vision beyond their own immediate interests and needs.[16] To translate economic interests into political practice, barrios need to raise their activism and political involvements to city, regional, and national levels.

The question of a territorially based progressive politics of this sort has received little attention so far (but see Bitar 1985). We shall therefore pose some of the more pertinent questions for future rsearch.

a. *Siege mentality vs. open democracy.*

It is sometimes said that the new barrio movement, for example, in Brazil, flourished as a protest movement during the period of dictator-ship, but with the return of democracy is now losing much of its earlier drive (see, for example, Mainwaring 1986, who is careful, however, to distinguish church-led base communities from the barrio movement in general). According to this account, barrio politics is particularly intense when the popular sectors are placed under siege by the state. Normal bourgeois politics tends not only to be more populist but allows individuals to seek satisfactions outside collective action—for example, through political parties or the traditional *política de clientela* mentioned by Paul Singer. If there were any truth in this, our arguments for a territorial politics would need to be sharply modified. But on the strength of admittedly limited evidence, we are inclined to doubt the hypothesis that strongly links barrio movements to a siege mentality. As one of the authors has argued elsewhere, to deal successfully with structural crisis, bourgeois politics in Latin America must yield to a participatory and open democratic style rooted in the politics of the barrio (Friedmann 1986). The simple reason for this is the demographics of the situation. From one-third to one-half the urban labor force subsists outside the state and corporate sectors and has no prospect of being incorporated into a national development program except on the strength of a revitalized barrio economy. The evidence from Brazil's Ecclesiastical Base Communities, corroborated in Peru, Colombia, and Chile, suggests that this hypothesis may have more validity than the first. Throughout the region, barrio movements are beginning to assert comprehensive claims for change in the name of economic, political, and human rights. Further research, however, is required to support or refute this hypothesis.

b. *The barrio economy: articulating modes of production and political culture.*

The barrio economy, as we have shown, is an expression of complex economic and social relations, involving formal, informal, and cooperative-household sectors. Contrary to neoclassical economics, which separates economic functions from residentiary functions, the political-economy approach sees them as interactive within the same territorial space. Production for exchange is directly related to household production for use and the solidarity relations of the barrio. To understand collective political responses at the level of the barrio, therefore, we must first gain a more adequate understanding of how, in particular barrios, the articulation of different modes of production (formal capitalist, informal capitalist, cooperative, and household) is effectuated, and how this articulation, in turn, is reflected in the political behavior of the barrio, its collective strength, leadership, activism, and so forth. In part, this has to do with the assessment of collective experience by individual households: are new ideologies coming to be accepted that reinforce a self-conscious political role? What new traits of political culture are coming to be part of the normal political behavior? How much social learning is going on and what, specifically, is being learned? These questions are fundamental to our claim that the new barrio movement has the potential to become a counterhegemonic force, prefiguring social relations that may become more generally accepted throughout civil society, a force that ultimately has the capacity not only to resist the state more effectively but to transform it.

c. *State control vs. collective self-empowerment*

The tendency to formalize the informal sector by extending state assistance to micro-enterprises, as in Colombia and Brazil, has already been noted. Moreover, the idea seems to be gaining in popularity. A bill currently before the U.S. Congress—the Micro Enterprise Promotion Act, H.R. 4894—directs the U.S. Agency for International Development to commit a portion of its development assistance to the promotion of micro enterprises owned by the urban and the rural poor. In the official view, assisting micro-enterprises may be seen as "encouraging individual entrepreneurs." In a more critical perspective, assistance to the informal sector may also be seen as the state seeking to extend its control over a large proto-capitalist sector, thus helping to ensure the reproduction of the system in dominance.

The question can now be raised whether a similar process of formalization, involving control and co-operation, is not also in store for the cooperative-household sector of the barrio economy. The answer is not immediately apparent. The barrio economy has considerable capacity for resistance, especially where it is closely linked to countervailing structures at the city level. The state, for its part, may see the cooperative-household sector as less of a threat than its alternatives and may therefore treat it rather gently. But even where the state comes in ostensibly to assist the cooperative sector, the resulting empowerment of barrio residents may outwiegh the state's ability to control its performance. The presence of the state is inevitably problematical. But it does not automatically spell the doom of counterhegemonic praxis. As Laclau and Mouffe (1985) point out, hegemony is itself a terrain of struggle.

d. *Organization vs. spontaneity in social movements.*

With this question, we reach the limits not only of barrio politics but also of the present research agenda. If planning for open democracy is indeed a necessary option for Latin America, as we believe it is, then it is likely that political parties will begin to compete for the favors of barrio voters, seeking to capture barrio movements and hitch them to their own purposes. They may, when in power, set up political bosses in the barrios, as the PRI has done in Mexico (Veliz 1978). Or they may try to establish a political base within the barrio, as the Chilean parties of the Center and Left did during the Frei government in the 1960s. If this were to happen again, would the result be to undermine community autonomy? Would it divide and fragment the popular sector? Or would it provide citizens with new channels for carrying their movement to the national scene? Opinions on these questions are divided, carrying forward an old argument within classical Marxism. On one side, there are those who, following Gramsci, come out strongly in favor of the politicization of urban social movements (Castells 1983; Laclau and Mouffe 1985). There are others who, like Piven and Cloward (1979), in a faint echo of Rosa Luxemburg, have asserted that only the spontaneous eruption of citizen anger will bring results benefitting the urban poor. For our part, we side with those who argue that social movements must be organized politically. But the question itself requires closer attention than it has received and lends itself particularly well to comparative research.

Toward an International Agenda for Collaborative Research

The conceptual framework we have sketched for understanding the movement for social and political empowerment in the barrios of large Latin American cities is a first attempt to make sense out of the welter of empirical information that has become available over the last half dozen or so years. As events continue to develop, and as we test the framework in specific settings, we shall almost certainly need to revise it. We have attempted to identify the many facets and dimensions of a phenomenon of historical proportions—the emergence in the region of the so-called popular sectors of civil society as an active force for social transformation. This social movement—if we may call it that— may be seen as a response on the part of working-class households to a persistent economic crisis whose most obvious characteristic is the lack of productive work for as much as 50 percent of the urban labor force. But the response has taken many forms and reflects, among other things, the severity of the economic crisis, the nature of the political regime in particular countries, political culture and traditions, and the specificity of the local situation. We are far from being able to systematically relate these structural conditions to particular forms of civil action; nevertheless their importance must be recognized. It is because of the variability in specific national and local conditions that a broadly comparative, international approach to the research is essential. A great deal of relevant research is already under way in Latin America, sponsored mostly by private research institutes such as the Academia de Humanismo Christiano in Chile, DESCO in Peru, CINEP in Colombia, CEDES in Argentina, and CEDAC along with other centers in Brazil.[17] Although studying the same broad phenomenon, researchers in different countries are not in close communication with each other or with scholars in Western Europe and North America. Yet it is obvious that it is only through the constant exchange of information and insight, and the persistent critical review of work in progress, that an adequate understanding of the urban survival economy and the progressive self-empowerment of the popular sectors can be gained in all of its rich diversity, and that its ultimate significance for political order and national development can be grasped. In the interest of such future collaboration, we propose to structure reseach around five focal concepts.

a. *The household economy.* Individual households may be viewed as social units engaged in the production of their life (see below) and thus as being both rational and political in the pursuit of their own objectives. As the smallest social unit having some stability over time, households can be studied in terms of their social, political, economic, cultural, and spatial relations, within the micro environment of the household itself and with other households and the world outside. In the context of household strategies for survival and material betterment, these five dimensions must each be separately taken into account. A key area for research is the relations of gender within the household and women's struggles against traditional relations of male dominance.

b. *The territorial economy of the barrio.* Household relations are initially constrained by distance. Household networks, therefore, are found primarily within an easy walking radius of one's home. This fact is decisive for the formation of the barrio economy as the first step up from the household economy itself. Within the barrio, the micro enterprises of the informal sector and the multiple-household enterprises of the cooperative sector are dominant. What distinguishes the barrio from all other territorially based economies, however, is the remarkable coexistence within it of market and nonmarket (reciprocity) relations. Though in many ways complementary, these two forms of relation stand in fundamental contradiction to each other. Success in the marketplace tends to undercut the more fragile relations of reciprocity and mutual trust. These relationships are best studied at two levels: that of the household itself, with a focus on its strategies of survival, and that of the cooperative sector, with emphasis on production linkages *forward* into markets *backward* into the community, and *laterally* to other production units in the formation of cooperative and other worker-controlled associations.

c. *The self-production of life.* This concept is introduced for three reasons: first, as a counterweight to the predominant perception of households as more or less passive consuming units engaged in the art of spending money; second, because it allows us to accept direct production for use (for the most part work performed by women) as regular work; and third, because it raises in dramatic form the question of collective self-empowerment. The self-production of life leads to household strategies for the allocation and use of its available resources of time, energy, skills, and knowledge. At the level of the barrio, it conduces to political claims for democratic self-governance, participatory decision making, and the formation of cooperative associations.

d. *Collective self-empowerment.* This concept focusses on the relative access of households, multiple-household enterprises, and other collective units within the barrio to the several bases of social power: time above survival needs; a secure activity space; social organization and networks; knowledge, skills and information; tools of production; and financial resources. In a household perspective, development is largely about empowerment, that is, about gaining greater access to these bases of social power in successive rounds of individual and/or collective struggle. The latter, however, requires social mobilization as a decisive step toward self-empowerment and raises a number of relevant questions for research, such as the role of external agents, contending ideologies, alternative leadership styles, and the choice of strategy.

e. *Political practice and the local state.* For individual working-class households, the room for successful manoeuvre tends to be restricted. More choice is possible when households engage in political practice. What seems to have been set alongside the old Latin American politics of *revindicaciones* is the assertion of fundamental citizen rights for basic necessities, empowerment, self-governance, political participation, and women's rights. Coinciding as it does with the current preoccupation of the national state with crisis management, this "politics of claims" (Peattie and Rein 1983) is beginning to have positive results, as the state is forced to take seriously old arguments for decentralization. Especially significant is the concurrent and increasingly insistent demand for an inclusive democratic order and the softening of hierarchical relations. This movement toward democratization requires a full-scale political analysis, particularly with a view toward a restructuring of the local state as it encounters an increasingly self-confident barrio movement pressing its claims for greater autonomy, state assistance, and civil rights.[18]

This brief summary makes evident that the study of the new civic (popular) activism in its territorial, economic, political, and cultural dimensions is no small assignment. Clearly, it cannot be done by one individual working alone or by a single research unit but requires long-term collaboration and comparative research over a period of years. We should therefore like to close our paper with a plea for such collaboration among research centers and individuals in countries where the movement appears to have progressed the furthest, among them Brazil, Argentina, Chile, Peru, Colombia, and Mexico.

Conclusion

The object of this essay has been to propose a conceptual frame for the study of civil society in Latin America, and more particularly its popular sector, from a perspective of self-renewal and emancipation. We have argued that the empirical focus of such a study must be the barrio economy as the center of possible counterhegemonic praxis, that is, as a potentially political praxis, neither colonized by capital nor subservient to the state. The transformative model we have in mind has as its main theoretical terms the *self-production of life*, taking the household as the smallest unit of production, and *collective self-empowerment*, by which we mean the process through which households gain greater access to the several bases of social power. The third term in our model, the *movement from social to political power*, remains, for the time being, little more than a possibility. The evidence for its existence is still very thin.

Why, of all possible objects for the study of civil society, have we settled on the barrio economy? The reasons are chiefly two. The first is empirical. The barrio economy internalizes a great deal of what we have called the self-production of life. If we want to study the articulation of market and nonmarket forces in the self-production of life, the barrio economy is preferable as an object of study to, say, the household economy or, worse still, the fate of isolated individuals. As a territorial economy, the barrio internalizes more articulations than the household sector and has the always present possibility of becoming a political subject, a self-conscious actor in the public domain. The second reason is praxis-related and pragmatic. In Latin America, factory labor in the large-scale, modern sector is a relatively small and, in some countries, declining fraction of the total work force. If civil society is to be mobilized for political ends, the factory cannot thus remain as the primary locus. As the home terrain for the self-production of life, the barrio economy is the more inclusive alternative. It brings in the long-term unemployed, the young first-time job seekers, women without steady remunerative work, workers active in the informal (unenumerated) sector, older folks, and even small children—in short, *the entire working-class sector of civil society* with their multiple needs and concerns, not only for "better wages and working conditions" but also for a better, more facilitative environment as the setting for the self-production of life. To be sure, the possibility of a counterhegemonic mobilization in the popular barrios of Latin American cities is only a latent possibility at this time, though there is growing evidence for it from a wide spread of cities, from Sao Paulo to Santiago to Lima and Medellín. The actual extent of mobilization is unknown. In a fluid struggle, the zone of battle is indeterminate and subject to rapid fluctuations. But at least we know that a struggle is under way. A unified struggle on many fronts, it will decide the future of the continent.

Notes

This essay was written jointly with Mauricio Salguero. We are especially grateful for the many thoughtful comments we received at a meeting convened at UCLA in October 1986, where an earlier draft was the focus for an extended critical discussion of the subject. Participants included Manuel Castells, Lisa Fuentes, Larissa Lomnitz, David Lopez, Lisa Peattie, Keith Pezzoli, Charles Reilly, Francisco Sabatini, John Walton, and Maurice Zeitlin. Additional extensive comments were received from José Luis Coraggio. To all of them our thanks. And of course the usual caveats apply; whatever faults remain are clearly our joint responsibility.

1. The term "civil society" frequently appears in discussions of social trends, especially by Latin American authors, and presumably refers, leaning on Gramsci's writings (1971), to a realm of action that is at least potentially autonomous of both the state and the corporate economy. With the urban household as its central institution, civil society can be further divided into sectors and classes. For the present, we shall use a simple division into "bourgeois" and "popular." This paper will be primarily concerned with the latter. By focussing on civil society, we place the emphasis on the domestic sphere of "reproduction" (which we here broaden by referring to it as the "production of life"), where it is the woman and not generally the male of the household who plays the privileged role. There are other implications of this choice of concepts—both theoretical and practical— that will become apparent in the course of this essay.

2. For the best and most recent treatment in English of Latin American social movements, see Slater 1985.

3. In their book on the poverty struggles of the 1960s, Piven and Cloward (1979) maintain just the opposite. Only the spontaneous uprisings of the poor, they argue, confronting bourgeois order with the spectre of anarchy, are able to produce gains for the poor. These gains, they would be the first to admit, are a far cry from the "structural transformation" proclaimed and hoped for by many Latin American intellectuals, but they are the only thing the poor can reasonably expect.

4. The term "development" is intended to cover normative dimensions that are broader than simple economic growth, or expansion in the volume of production. Specifically, it is meant to hint at an equitable distribution of income and positive gains in social indicators. In some of its meanings, however, it comes perilously close to the nineteenth-century idea of Progress—always capitalized—and may well be destined to suffer a similar fate. It might indeed be safer to speak exclusively of economic growth, conceived as the "engine" of development, but it is development that is the ideological coin of discourse. A related term is "modernization," but its meaning is even more slippery than that of development and seems ultimately to be derived from the cultural experience of advanced capitalist countries in Western Europe and North America.

5. The one exception to this statement is Peru, whose military regime for at least a number of years was social reformist without, however, destroying the power base of the traditional elites.

6. For an argument along this line, with specific reference to Nicaragua, see Coraggio 1985.

7. Although the focus of our research is urban, there is growing evidence that the phenomenon takes place in semi-rural and rural settings as well.

8. The concept of informal economy has become increasingly unpopular, and many scholars counsel against using it (see, for example, Breman 1985). Two reasons are usually given: first, dualistic formulations, of which the informal/formal dichotomy is one, can be grossly misleading by polarizing discussion around "ideal types"; and second, because the informal category is imprecise. We accept these criticisms. Still, the term "informal" (alternatively, unenumerated or unofficial) can be quite useful to distinguish a category of economic activities that is small-scale, market-oriented, and labor-intensive. For a recent summary of research, see Castells and Portes 1986.

9. Not shown here are investments in its own sphere of activities, in education, and in political action.

10. Hardy and Razeto define *organizaciones económicas populares as follows:*

> In general terms, we understand by "popular economic organizations" the different forms of association which are formed in order to confront the problem of subsistence or to satisfy specific economic needs among the popular sectors (especially among those having lower incomes) in order to develop specific economic activities or functions, such as the production and marketing of goods and services, the procurement, supply, or consumption of daily necessities for their associated membership, etc. In general, they consist of small groups of people who share the same situation and similar problems [of deprivation]: find

themselves linked by residing in the same barrio or settlement *(poblacion)*, by having worked in the same firm, by belonging to the same religious community, or by sharing the same ideological persuasion; and who decide to confront their immediate problems [of survival] jointly through an action which is meant to lead to a solution of these problems. (Hardy and Razeto 1986, 162; our translation.)

Among OEPs, Hardy and Razeto identify the following general types: workshops *(talleres laborales)*, organizations of the unemployed *(organizaciones de cesantes)*, organizations for the satisfaction of basic consumption needs, housing organizations, and other community-service organizations. About 20 percent of Santiago's working-class population participates in one or more of these self-help organizations.

11. Additional differences include hierarchial organization and individual decision making; patriarchy and bossism; the extensive use of family labor (self-exploitation); unequal pay for equal work; competitive behavior; and profit orientation.

12. Logically, there is a prior step to association. Before they can associate, MHEs must first consolidate and stabilize their business. This may require special training in the different tasks of self-management, stabilizing cash flow, securing regular market outlets, etc.

13. A famous example of cooperative production, which may be relevant to the Latin American case, is Mondragon in the Basque country of Spain. See Oakeshott (1978), Thomas and Logan (1982), and Jackall and Levin (1984).

14. In October 1985 INDERENA initiated a so-called Campaña Verde, or Green Campaign, with the aim to contribute to the development of a process of social participation. The objective of such a campaign is, in the long run, to go beyond the ecological issue: to promote self-help initiatives of the local community, develop mechanisms for local democracy, and consolidate the empowerment of citizens. The idea is to create the mechanisms that will allow the organized community to take responsibility for all the natural and social aspects that make up its environment (Ungar and Barrera 1986).

As of January 1986, 280 Green Councils ("Consejos Verdes") had been set up by different municipalities in Colombia. Although INDERENA is *initiating* the campaign, the project must be *undertaken* by civil society itself. INDERENA is prepared to give technical advice and share its modest resources, while local authorities constitute the bridge to help such resources reach their destination: civil society and the local community, which must take in their own hands, in an autonomous way, the control, organization, and management of the environment.

15. For a parallel argument relating to U.S. urban politics, see Katznelson (1981) and for Australia, Sandercock (1985). Because ethnic divisions are less of a factor in Latin American political life than in North America, the coalescence of barrio-based social movements in the major Latin American cities is conceivable, whereas in the U.S. it is not.

16. The need for a new form of political practice in Latin America should be fairly evident to those who follow the politics of the region. The majority of parties are elite-based and lack political organization at the grass roots.

17. Academía de Humanismo Cristiano, Catedral 1063, Piso 5, Santiago,

Chile; DESCO (Centro de Estudios y Promoción del Desarrollo), Av. Salaverry 1945, Lima 14, Peru; CINEP (Fundación Centro de Investigación y Educación Popular), Apartado Aereo 25916, Bogota, D.E., Colombia; CEDES (Centro de Estudios de Estado y Sociedad), Av. Pueyrredón 510, 7° Piso, 1032 Buenos Aires, Argentina; CEDAC (Centro de Estudos e Documentação Comunitaria), Rua dos Ingleses 325, Bela Vista, 01329 São Paulo, S.P., Brazil.

18. For a case study of barrio politics carried to the citywide level, where it claimed the right to participate in policies affecting *favelados*, see Rezende Afonso and Azevedo 1985.

Bibliography

Alonso M. Aguilar (1985). "Crisis and Development Strategies in Latin America," *Development and Peace*, Vol. 6, pp. 17–32.

Frei Betto (1984). *O Que é Comunidade Eclesial de Base*. 5th ed. São Paulo: Ed. Brasilienese.

Sergio Bitar (1985). "The Nature of the Latin American Crisis," *CEPAL Review*, No. 27 (December), 159–164.

Carlos A. Borsotti (1978). *Notas Sobre la Familia Como Unidad Socioeconomica. Cuadernos de la CEPAL*. Santiago (Chile): CEPAL/ILPES.

Jan Breman (1985). "A dualistic labour system? A critique of the "informal sector' concept," in Ray Bromley (ed.), *Planning for Small Enterprises in Third World Cities*. New York: Pergamon Press. (Orig. 1976).

Thomas C. Brunau (1982). *The Church in Brazil*. Austin: University of Texas Press.

V. Capecchi and A. Pesce (1984). "Reconsidering Diversity to Contend with Dualism," *Ecodevelopment News*. No. 31, Paris: International Research Center on Ecodevelopment and Development.

Manuel Castells (1976). *Movimientos sociales Urbanos en America Latina: Tendencias Historicas y Problemas Teoricas*. Lima: Pontífica Universidad Catolica.

Manuel Castells (1983). *The City and the Grassroots*. London: E. Arnold.

Manuel Castells and Alejandro Portes (1986). "World Underneath: The Origins, Dynamics, and Effects of the Informal Economy." Written for presentation at the Conference on the Study of the Informal Sector, Harpers Ferry, West Virginia, October 2–6.

Jose Luis Corragio (1985). "Social Movements and Revolution: The Case of Nicaragua," in Slater, ed. (1985), 203–232.

José Luis Corragio (1986a). *Nicaragua: Revolution and Democracy*. Boston: Allen & Unwin.

Jose Luis Corragio (1986b). "Economics and Politics in the Transition to Socialism: Reflections on the Nicaragua Experience," in Richard R. Fagen, Carmen Diana Deere, and José Luis Corragio, eds., *Transition and Development: Problems of Third World Socialism*. New York: Monthly Review Press.

Maria Edy Chonchol (1984). "Unofficial Sector and Social Creativity in Chile and Brazil," *Ecodevelopment News*, No. 31 (December) 25–30.

Rodrigo Egana (n.d.). *De Taller a Empresa de Trabajadores: La Experiencia de Servatec*. Santiago (Chile): Academía de Humanismo Cristiano.

Tilman Evers (1985). "Identity: The Hidden Side of New Social Movements in Latin America," in Slater, ed. (1985), 43–72.

Simon Fass (forthcoming). *The Political Economy of Survival*. Manuscript, Hubert Humphrey School of Public Affairs, University of Minnesota.

John Friedmann (1986). "Planning in Latin America: From Technocratic Illusion to Open Democracy," GSAUP Discussion Paper 204.

John Friedmann (1987). *Planning in the Public Domain: From Knowledge to Action*. Princeton, N.J.: Princeton University Press.

Guillermo Geisse (1986). "Desarrollo de ciudades medianas a traves del sector de sobreviviencia," *Revista Interamericana de Planificacion*, Vol. 20, No. 80 (December), 62–77.

D. Goldrich, R. B. Pratt, and C. R. Schuller (1967–68). "The Political Integration of Lower-Class Urban Settlements in Chile and Peru." *Studies in International Development*, 3, 1–22.

Rogelio Gómez-Hermosillo M. (1986). "La Iglesia del lado del pueblo?: CEB's y MUP en la Region Metropolitana," *El Cotidiano* (Cd. de Mexico), 2, 11, 54–61.

Antonio Gramsci (1971). *Selections from the Prison Notebooks*. Eds., Q. Hoare and G. Nowell Smith. London.

Roberto P. Guimarães (1986). "Cooperativismo y participacio popular: nuevas consideraciones respecto de un viejo tema," *Revista de la CEPAL #28*, (April), 181–194.

Clarisa Hardy (1984). *Los Talleres Artesanales de Conchali*. Santiago (Chile): Academía de Humanismo Cristiano. Colección de Experiencias Populares.

Clarisa Hardy (1985). "Estrategias Organizadas de Subsistencia: Los Sectores Populares Frente a Sus Necesidades en Chile." Documento de Trabajo 41. Santiago: Academía de Humanismo Cristiano, Programa de Economia del Trabajo.

Clarisa Hardy (1986). *Hambre & Dignidad = Ollas Comunes*. Santiago: Programa de Economiá de Trabajo (PET). Academía de Humanismo Cristiano. Colección de Experiencias Populares.

Clarisa Hardy and Luis Razeto (1986). "Sector informal y concertación social."

Albert O. Hirschman (1984). *Getting Ahead Collectively: Grassroots Experiences in Latin America*. New York: Pergamon Press.

John Holmes (1986). "The Organization and Location of Production Subcontracting," in Allen J. Scott and Michael Storper, eds., *Production, Work, Territory: The Geographical Anatomy of Industrial Capitalism*. Boston: Allen & Unwin.

Ivan Illich (1975). *Tools for Conviviality*. London: Fontana/Collins.

Robert Jackall and Henry M. Levin, eds. (1984). *Worker Cooperatives in America*. Berkeley: University of California Press.

Pedro Jacobi (1985). "Movimentos sociais urbanos e a crise: da explosao social a participacao popular," *Politica e Administração*, Vol. 1, No. 2 (July–Sept.), 223–238.

Allison M. Jaggar (1983). *Feminist Politics and Human Nature*. Totowa, N.J.: Rowan and Allanheld.

Ira Katznelson (1981). *City Trenches: Urban Politics and the Patterning of Class in the United States*. New York: Pantheon.

Ernesto Laclau and Chantal Mouffle (1985). *Hegemony and Socialist Strategy: Towards a Radical Democratic Politics*. London: Verso.

Juan J. Linz and Alfred Stepan, eds. (1978). *The Breakdown of Democratic Regimes: Latin America*. Baltimore, Md.: The Johns Hopkins Press.

Larissa Adler Lomnitz (1977). *Networks and Marginality: Life in a Mexican Shantytown*. New York: Academic Press.

Scott Mainwaring (1986). *The Catholic Church and Politics in Brazil, 1916–1985*. Stanford, Calif.: Stanford University Press.

Manfred Max-Neef (1985). "Another Development under Repressive Rule," *Development Dialogue* (Uppsala), No. 1, pp. 30–55.

Manfred Max-Neef et al. (1986). "Desarollo a Escala Humano: Una Opción Para el Futuro. *Development Dialogue* (Uppsala). Special number.

Humberto Molina G. and Carlos Arturo Henao R. (1986). *Censo Nacional de Proyectos Asociativos de Vivienda*. Bogotá: CPU—Universidad de los Andes.

Gabriel Murillo and Morica Lanzetta de Pardo (1984). "La articulación entre el sector informal y el sector formal de la economiá urbana: el caso de Bogota," in CLACSO, *Ciudades y Sistemas Urbanos Economia Informal y Desorden Espacial*. Buenos Aires: CLACSO.

Robert Oakeshott (1978). *The Case for Workers' Co-ops*. Boston: Routledge & Kegan Paul.

Henry Pease García (1986). "Experiencias para democratizar la gestion de la ciudad." Manuscript. Washington, D.C.: The Woodrow Wilson Center.

Lisa Peattie and Martin Rein (1983). *Women's Claims: A Study in Political Economy*. New York: Oxford University Press.

Michael Piore and Charles F. Sabel (1984). *The Second Industrial Divide: Possibilities for Prosperity*. New York: Basic Books.

Frances Fox Piven and Richard A. Cloward (1979). *Poor People's Movements: Why They Succeed, How They Fail*. New York: Vintage Books.

Karl Polanyi (1977). *The Livelihood of Man*. New York: Academic Press.

Alejandro Portes (1984). "El sector informal: definicion, controversias, relaciones con el desarrollo nacional," in CLACSO, *Ciudades Y Sistemas Urbanos: Economia Informal Y Desorden Espacial*. Buenos Aires: CLACSO.

Luis Razeto et al. (1983). *La Organizaciones Económicas Populares*. Santiago (Chile): Academía de Cristianismo Humano.

Luis Razeto (1984). *Economía de Solidaridad y Mercado Democrático*. Vol. I. Santiago (Chile): Academía de Humanismo Cristiano.

Luis Razeto (1985). *Las Empresas Alternativas*. Santiago (Chile): Academía de Humanismo Cristiano. Programa de Economia del Trabajo.

Felicia Reicher Madeira (1986). "Los jovenes en el Brasil: antiguos supestos y nuevos derroteros," *Revista de la CEPAL*, No. 29 (August), 57–80.

Mariza Rezende Alfonso and Sérgio de Azevedo (1985). "Cidade, poder público e movimento de favelados." Rio de Janeiro (UNU—Projeto Movimentos Sociais na América Latina).

David P. Ross and Peter J. Usher (1986). *From the Roots Up: Economic Development as if Community Mattered*. Croton-on-the-Hudson N.Y.: The Bootstrap Press.

Francisco Sabatini (1986). "Knowledge for Planning: Marginality Theories in Latin America." UCLA, Graduate School of Architecture and Urban Planning. Manuscript.

Abelardo Sanchez León (1986). "Lima y los hijos del desorden." Lima (Peru): DESCO. Manuscript. Washington, D.c.: The Woodrow Wilson Center.

Leonie Sandercock (1985). "The Importance of Place and a Politics of Place: From Wollongong to Bondi Beach," paper presented at the Conference on Place and Place-Making, Melbourne, Victoria, (Australia). Manuscript.

Marianne Schmink (1984). "Household Economic Strategies: Review and Research Agenda," *Latin American Research Review*, Vol. 19, No. 3, pp. 87–101.

James C. Scott (1976). *The Moral Economy of the Peasant: Rebellion and Subsistence in Southeast Asia*. New Haven, Conn.: Yale University Press.

Paul Singer (1982). "Neighborhood Movements in São Paulo," in Helen Safa, ed., *Towards a Political Economy of Urbanization in Third World Countries*. Delhi: Oxford University Press.

Paul Singer and Vinicius Caldeira Brandt, eds. (1982). *São Paulo: O Povo em Movimento*. 3rd ed. Petropolis: Vozes Ltda.

David Slater, ed. (1985). *New Social Movements and the State in Latin America*. Amsterdam: CEDLA (Center for Latin American Research and Documentation).

W. Paul Strassmann (1986). "Types of Neighbors and Home-Based Enterprises: Evidence from Lima, Peru," Manuscript. (To be published in *Urban Studies*).

Osvaldo Sunkel (1985). *America Latina Y la Crisis Economica Internacional; Ocho Tesis y Una Propuesta*. Buenos Aires: GEL. Coleccion Cuadernos del RIAL.

Judith Tendler (1983). *What to Think About Cooperatives: A Guide from Bolivia*. Rosslyn, Va.: The Inter-American Foundation.

Hank T. Thomas and Chris Logan (1982). *Mondragon: An Economic Analysis*. Boston: Allen and Unwin.

Elizabeth Ungar and Cristina Barrera (1986). "Participacion Popular y Ecología: La Campaña Verde." Bogota, Colombia: Universitad de Los Andes, Depto. de Ciencia Política.

Carlos G. Veliz-I. (1978). "Amigos Politicos o Amigos Sociales: The Politics of Putting Someone in Your Pocket," *Human Organization*, 37, 4: 368–377.

Nico Vink (1985). "Base Communities and Urban Social Movements: A Case Study of the Metalworkers' Strike 1980, Sao Bernardo, Brazil," in Slater, ed. (1985), 95–126.

Raymond Williams (1983). *The Year 2000*. New York: Pantheon.

Part II
Spatial Aspects of National Planning

6

The Spatial Organization of Power in the Development of Urban Systems

A problem that has escaped notice or at least public comment so far is that the prolonged longevity of university professors, extending over several cycles rapidly changing intellectual fashion, tends to render much of their earlier research either unfashionable, obsolete, or both. So I reprint the following essay with some degree of trepidation.

First published in 1973, it was on the frontier of the type of urban analysis then in vogue, with its belief in scientific explanation in the classical Weberian mode. But the printer's ink was scarcely dry when younger planners and geographers in Anglo-America would abruptly turn a cold shoulder on "bourgeois" social science, entranced by the new questions (and possibilities) put forward by scholars such as Manuel Castells and David Harvey who introduced a neo-Marxist paradigm to their respective disciplines. This exciting and novel approach to urban studies would eventually celebrate and alternately mourn its own triumphs and failures, but it did not necessarily invalidate the work that had preceded it.

Rereading my essay now in the light of what has passed during the intervening fifteen years—neo-Marxism itself has waned and been replaced by an eclectic "post modernism"—I find much in it that is still valid, not least the detailed account of spatial domination in Chile with which the essay closes. In the light of the earlier period, my objective was an innovative one: to suggest how relations of governmental and economic power in a national society may contribute to an understanding of the evolution of national urban systems. I was keen to introduce an explicit political dimension to the economic analysis of traditional relationships in the study of spatial organization and change. The fashion then current was to explain "growth poles" by reference to variables such as propulsive industries (F. Perroux) and economies of scale and agglomeration. My intention was not to replace this framework for analysis but to extend and deepen it by incorporating the dimension of power.

Because of the neo-Marxist "revolution" of the mid-seventies, my

147

essay failed to have the wider impact I expected. My own interests would also shift (see part I). Nevertheless, I believe that the essay retains much of its relevance today, even though this is now limited by the fact that it failed, as was common of all work done at the time, to take world economic integration into account as a key variable in spatial organization.

The study or urban systems in the context of national development is a relatively recent interest. Research has converged on two central questions: what variables account for the growth and development of urban systems? And, how is the growth and development of urban systems related to the more encompassing processes of national development? By 'development of urban systems' I mean the structural growth of urban settlements measured by population and the volume of economic activities. 'National development,' on the other hand, is used here as a shorthand expression for the structural transformation of a national economy to industrialism. Although these questions are clearly not the only ones deserving consideration, they have so far received most of the attention.

The linkages between urban and national development are still inadequately understood. It has nevertheless become clear that their study must employ an explicit spatial framework for analysis. The emergence of modern industrial enclaves within the matrix of an agrarian economy has given rise to dramatic shifts in population and employment and has accelerated urbanization. At the same time, urbanization seems to have been generating its own dynamics, in partial autonomy of the development of modern industry. These complex changes, occurring over the vastness of a national territory, have decisively affected the possibilities of national integration, by demanding new political loyalties, creating new patterns of transportation, giving birth to new social classes and elites, introducing new sets of 'modernizing' values, and differentially affecting the well-being and life chances of every member of the population according not only to who he was but also where he lived.

Regarded in this perspective, the study of urban systems has become the study of national development in its spatial dimension. A key question that may, therefore, be put is how the development of an urban system will affect the character and evolution of spatial integration measured by political institutions, transactions, and social justice.[1]

Students of urbanization have tended to explore economic explanations, such as the distribution of natural resources, the location of transport routes, the organization of markets, and economies of scale and agglomeration. With rare exceptions, they have neglected political explanations and, more specifically, explanations given in terms of the spatial distribution of power.[2] The purpose of this paper is to suggest how the analysis of power relations in a national society may contribute to our understanding of the ways in which urban systems evolve.

The concept of power is one of the most elusive in the social sciences. Here, it will refer to the ability of organizational and institutional actors, located in geographic space, to mobilize and allocate resources (manpower, capital, and information) and intentionally to structure the decision-field of others (i.e., to constrain the decisions of others by policies, rules, and commands). Both governmental and private economic power will be considered. Both kinds of power, I will assume, have the capacity to influence the location decisions of firms and households, the quantity, location, and application of resources, and the flow of innovations. By acting on these variables and, in turn, by being acted upon by them, the spatial distribution of power influences the growth and development of urban systems and, at a higher level of synthesis, also the spatial patterns of integration of a national society.

Like capital, power refers to a stock of resources rather than to a flow of these resources in use. It will consequently be distributed either *symmetrically* (referring to the capacities of actors that are roughly equal with respect to a common decision area) or *asymmetrically*. The uses of power, on the other hand, involve exchange relations or transactions which may be either *reciprocal* (regarded as bringing roughly equal net-benefits to the actors involved) or *non-reciprocal*. These distinctions allow us to construct a two-by-two matrix of power and exchange in urban systems (Fig. 6.1).[3] By shifting the argument to a consideration of urban systems, we are abstracting from the particular relations of power and exchange among actors distributed over the whole of a spatially integrated subsystem of society (a city) or an integrated system of cities.[4] The matrix, in fact, is intended to throw into relief the major forms of spatial integration across such systems.

According to this matrix, urban systems in Quadrants 1 and 2 are integrated on a basis of a rough equivalence of power; in Quadrants 3 and 4, they are integrated on a basis of inequality or dependence with respect to the urban system in Quadrant 1. Simple analogies may help to clarify these relationships.

Under 1 (symmetry *cum* reciprocity), relations are as those between friends: neither dominates the other, and the exchange between them will be in balance. Moreover, the rules governing their conduct with

Figure 6.1
A Model of Power and Exchange Relations in Urban Systems

Power Relations	Exchange Relations	
	Reciprocal	Non-Reciprocal
Symmetrical	1 fully integrated urban system: moral authority predominates	2 competitive urban system integrated on a basis of limited liability: utilitarian power predominates
Asymmetrical	3 active periphery of urban system integrated on a basis of protective dependency: utilitarian power predominates	4 passive periphery of urban system integrated on a basis of submissive dependency: coercive power predominates

respect to each other are accepted as morally right: the costs and benefits of transactions between them are not closely calculated. This relationship is typical of actors within core regions comprising one or several rapidly growing cities that display strong and complexly interwoven patterns of transaction. Where several cities are so related, the statistical form of the urban system will tend to be lognormal. Moreover, the laws and procedural rules under which transactions occur will not generally be open to challenge; their authority will be accepted as morally legitimate.

Under 2 (symmetry *cum* non-reciprocity), relations are as those between the owners of competing business firms: each transaction is separately negotiated in the hope of striking a bargain, so that commitments made in one period are not necessarily considered binding on decisions in subsequent periods. Although each separate transaction may end by being reciprocal, it will be so to only a limited extent; the ultimate intention of each actor is to gain superiority over his competitor. This would be the case of a loose federation of states each having its own integrated urban system, as in Yugoslavia, where the conditions of every inter-system transaction may themselves become the object of intensive bargaining among would-be equals, with the goods offered in exchange serving as the principal counters in negotiation.

Under 3 (asymmetry *cum* reciprocity), relations are as those between superiors and subordinates in bureaucratic organizations: each stands in need of the other, but for quite different reasons. The former require subordinates to accomplish their intentions, but also to rise in general esteem and power, while the latter need the protective benevolence of their superiors and the guarantee of a job. With respect to the organization controlled by their superiors, subordinates have a contractual relationship that may be renegotiated from time to time, but whose legitimacy is generally not at issue. This is the situation typical of many border provinces, such as Magallanes and Tarapaca in Chile which use their exposed position vis-à-vis Argentina, on the one hand, and Peru and Bolivia, on the other (an always threatened shift from 3 to 2), in bargaining for increased autonomy and economic benefits. (The relations of the Commonwealth of Puerto Rico to the United States is a similar instance; here the threat of national independence serves to strengthen the bargaining position of the Commonwealth.) Active peripheries are typically striving to build up one or more growth centers as core regions subordinate to the urban system in Quadrant 1. They do so in the hope—however much in the future—of ultimately being absorbed into the fully integrated core region itself.

Finally, under 4 (asymmetry *cum* non-reciprocity), relations are as those between master and slave: the master dominates his slave who, at least outwardly, gives evidence of properly submissive behavior but whose labors on behalf of his master are poorly rewarded. Occasional rebellion on the slave's part may invoke the full repressive power of the master. This is the case of economically backward regions under a regime of internal colonization (such as Bangladesh before independence) which have few cities, and whose domination by the core region in Quadrant 1 gives rise to an urban system having pronounced primacy characteristics. The latent capacity for rebellion by the passive periphery may induce the dominant interests in Quadrant 1 to invest heavily in the region and so to shift it eventually to Quadrant 3. Indeed, such measures may occasionally be taken for purely ideological reasons. On the other hand, the failure to invoke coercive power may result in little more than spreading anarchy without compensating economic benefit. This may be illustrated with reference to the recent economic collapse of the agricultural system in Chile's southern provinces or the continued agitation under Salvador Allende's Popular Unity Government of extreme left-wing revolutionary groups centered in the city of Concepción. Passive peripheries no longer fully dominated by the core in Quadrant 1 may eventually come within the area of influence of the competing system in 2. They have little strength of their own to resist such advances, and their original oppressor may be equally incapacitated.

In the following four sections, some of these relations of power and exchange in urban systems will be further analyzed. First, I shall try to show how the spatial distribution of governmental power influences the location decisions of entrepreneurs during the early phases of industrialization and how the growing interpenetration of governmental and private economic institutions channels the subsequent location decisions of individuals and households to locations of central power in excess of objective opportunities for productive employment. The resulting polarized pattern of urbanization tends to be self-perpetuating, whereas the eventual decentralization of productive activities into the passive periphery of major core regions tends to leave essential relations of power virtually unchanged.

The second example relates to the diffusion of innovations through the urban system. I will be concerned only with entrepreneurial innovations whose successful adoption translates into a relative increase in economic power to exploit specific resources in the environment. The diffusion of innovations will be considered in both space and time. The spatial diffusion of entrepreneurial innovations tends to be hierarchical, leading to a steadily increasing concentration of power in the largest cities of the urban hierarchy, while the rate of diffusion, at least initially, gives special advantage to early over late adopters. The resulting growth pattern of cities tends to be allometric, implying invariant ratios in the rates of growth among individual urban units. Passive peripheries are thus 'condemned' to a quasi-permanent condition of submissive dependency, though the active portions of the periphery may be able successfully to negotiate for growing autonomy in development decisions.

The third illustration concerns primarily the conflict patterns between competing economic and political elites, where the former are ethnically and/or culturally distinct from the latter and have primarily an urban base, while the latter's base of power tends to be in rural areas. Several options for resolving conflicting interests will be discussed, including cooptation, accommodation, open hostility, the creation of regional protectorates, and federative solutions, each of which will have different outcomes for the development of the relevant urban systems.

In the final section, a case study of dependency relations in Chile will be presented. Various forms of dependency will be discussed, together with their consequences for the development of urban systems in this small South American country.

No effort will be made to synthesize these four approaches to the study of power relations in urban systems. The paradigm presented in this section is intended to serve primarily as a source of hypotheses for testing in empirical settings. For this reason, too, I shall make no effort to append a section on policy options. At this stage in our knowledge, such an exercise would be gratuitous. The only firm conclusion we may draw is that the process of national development and spatial integration is an eminently political one, involving fundamental relations of power and exchange and the resolution of resulting conflicts. Planning which fails to recognize this basic truth and proceeds as though the spatial allocation of resources were merely an exercise in applied economic rationality is bound to be disappointing in its results.[5]

Economic Location and the Spatial Distribution of Power

Economic location theory has traditionally addressed the question of how the location decisions of individual firms are affected by spatial variations in the costs of production and distribution. This emphasis reflects in part the observations of location theorists in industrially mature economies. In countries of incipient or early industrialization, however, non-economic influences appear to weigh more heavily in location decisions than considerations of relative cost. In these countries, *the choice of a location tends to be strongly influenced by a desire of management to gain direct access to the relevant centers of governmental power.*

In the following, I shall assume an industrializing country of moderate size whose government is unitary and whose population is culturally homogeneous. Subsequently, I shall relax this assumption, but for now it will serve as a necessary constraint. In such a country, economic enterprise is exceedingly dependent on the central bureaucracy and the corridors of legislative power. Licenses to import machinery must be secured; special subsidies and other favors are sought; a complex system of legislation pertaining to the conduct of business must be learned; and contributions of public capital and credit are expected. At the same time, economic interrelationships are relatively weak: an inter-industry matrix would show many empty boxes.

In themselves, these conditions would not prescribe a central location. They are reinforced by additional considerations that make the creation or survival of new enterprise in provincial districts highly improbable. Among them are (a) a still rudimentary system of transport and communication, (b) the great importance attached to personal, face-to-face relations in the conduct of business, (c) a high degree of bureaucratic centralism, and (d) a superior infrastructure of economic and social facilities in the national capital, itself a reflection and symbol of accumulated (and steadily accumulating) power.

The resulting symbiosis between economic and governmental organizations creates a situation that consistently favors the nation's capital in subsequent business locations, though economic reasons, such as access to markets, undoubtedly contribute. Politicians, bureaucrats and businessmen mingle in exclusive social clubs and the city's top restaurants, send their children to private schools (or the national university), and form tight social networks of their own. From this central location, an essentially passive periphery is organized into administrative and market areas following the principal routes of transport. Capital resources and surplus agricultural labor are withdrawn from these areas at an accelerating pace, adding to the reservoir of economic power in the center. In consequence, the urban pattern changes from one of low-level equilibrium (many small, equally sized urban places) to one of growing primacy.[6]

With continuing development, however, certain changes in this spatial pattern may occur. Growing markets, the discovery of new natural resources, and a gradually improving system of transport and communications may render middlesized cities in the periphery increasingly attractive as possible business locations, a tendency that may be actively encouraged by explicit governmental policies for regional development. These changing circumstances, together with the growing organizational complexity of enterprise, make possible the physical separation of management from production units. With their vital decision functions thus removed, production units are released to locate according to economic criteria, while management components continue to be drawn to the center of governmental power. Even so, it is generally provincial administrative centers that are favored in the location of production units to facilitate the symbiotic decision process that governs the economic life of the nation.

Empirical evidence for this evolving pattern comes from a variety of country settings. For Latin America, the historian Richard M. Morse is quite emphatic. He writes:[7]

> In Latin America, it seems important that a city be a patrimonial center if it is to serve as a growth pole for economic development. Brasília is already the classic case for a modern frontier zone. Or, if a capital is not actually transferred to a frontier, the central power may spin off an outlying city under its direct support and tutelage, as in the case of Ciudad Guayana. Without denying the regional economic and ecological justifications for this city, it is probably accurate to say that its ultimate legitimation derives from a process of patrimonial schizogenesis. Or

again, if planners speak of decentralizing economic functions from a central corridor not to a frontier but to existing peripheral cities, it is usually implied that provincial capitals will be the beneficiaries. Thus it is no accident that the flourishing second-echelon growth centers (Monterrey, Guadalajara, Cali, Medellín, Córdoba, Pôrto Alegre, Curitiba) are so frequently regional political capitals. When this is not the case, as with Chimbote, Peru, the city may face enormous obstacles in developing urban infrastructure for economic activity because of its weak political leverage.

The second example refers to the Soviet Union and is reported by Chauncey Harris,[8]

> The importance of administrative and related functions is expressed in the relatively rapid growth of *oblast* centers. In about 60 percent of the *oblasts*, the center grew more rapidly than other urban units within their boundaries.

The third example comes from J. Barry Riddell's study of the spatial dynamics of modernization in Sierra Leone.[9]

> Thus it is evident that the process of modernization, as summarized by the component analysis, is dominated and directed by the network and the [urban-administrative] hierarchy, which together define the spatial fabric of the country.

The fourth example stems from Brazil, a country that has moved considerably beyond the first thresholds of industrialization. The concentration of modern business enterprise in Brazil was initially confined to the two principal centers of economic power: Rio de Janeiro and São Paulo. By the time the political capital of the nation was shifted to Brasília in the latter part of the 1960s, industrialization had already established a powerful base in these two cities and, to a much smaller extent, in several of the more important state capitals (Belo Horizonte, Pôrto Alegre). Because economic power had now become more important than political power, the physical move of governmental functions to Brasília did not entail a similarly massive shift of corporate headquarters to the planalto of Goias, though it did much to stimulate road building activity and cattle raising in the interior. By the same token, intensive government efforts to industrialize the traditionally backward regions in the North and Northeast of the country accomplished primarily the move of production units to these regions but failed to attract units of corporate management. With management remaining in the older centers, and attracting related business services, the 'decapitated' production units in the periphery found themselves dependent on extra-territorial decisions. Business profits, in particular, were transferred to the 'center' for reallocation.

The evidence for the pattern described is impressive. While political and economic decision-making power remain concentrated in the national capital, subsidiary growth centers spring up on the periphery, frequently paralleling the urban-administrative hierarchy. This process tends to induce a gradual filling out of the rank-size distribution of cities by encouraging the growth of intermediate urban centers. As a result, certain portions of the passive periphery may be activated sufficiently to bargain with central authorities for greater autonomy (e.g., the Northeast of Brazil). To the extent they are successful, the dependency relations of the remaining periphery may increasingly come to focus on these subsidiary, provincial centers.[10]

If we carry the analysis still further to include advanced industrial and post-industrial societies, the earlier pattern, though in a highly attenuated form, may still be discerned.[11] By this time, the extreme dependency of business on governmental power may have waned relative to the rapidly growing requirements for inter-industry contacts. Both market and supply areas will have become more diffused, and the transport and communications system will have made the relevant economic space more accessible from a larger number of central locations. Parts of the formerly active periphery may by now be effectively integrated into the principal core areas of the nation. Despite these new developments, however, certain nodal cities may still stand out as 'control centers', experiencing rapid growth, even though the initial close linkage between centers of governmental power and business location will have been lessened.[12] The urban system will now tend toward a lognormal form in the distribution of its centers and the passive periphery will be reduced to vestigial proportions.[13]

The foregoing description of the evolution of a spatial system is, of course, idealized to some extent. Small countries with only one or two major cities, very large countries such as the USSR, China, and India with a long-standing tradition of urbanism, countries with a federal structure of government, and countries with a culturally heterogeneous and regionalized population may follow a different sequence of events. In actively federal systems, for example, central power will, to some degree, be shared so that several governmental centers may simultaneously compete for industry (Yugoslavia). By the same token, regions having politically powerful minorities may gain certain privileges, such as greater decision autonomy, sooner than would be predicted by the model. In these situations, the 'idealized' spatial pattern may be distorted for the nation as a whole, though the pattern is likely to be replicated at the regional level.[14] Furthermore, once they are established, spatial patterns of urbanization tend to perpetuate themselves, casting a long shadow into the future.[15] The initial distribution of governmental power within a country will therefore tend to guide the subsequent evolution of the space economy.

The Spatial Diffusion of Innovations in the Development of Urban Systems

Studies of the spatial diffusion of innovations have only recently begun to turn from an exclusive concern with questions relating to geographic theory to broader issues of socio-economic development. These newer studies strongly suggest the possibility of interpreting the spatial dimensions of all facets of development, including urbanization, from a perspective of innovation diffusion. Although a parsimonious theory of the observed behavior is still some time away, its major contours are beginning to be seen.[16] An important link in such a theory is the relation of spatial diffusion to the distribution of economic power.

The basic thesis—to be elaborated in the following pages—may be briefly stated at the outset. The adoption of innovations, and particularly of entrepreneurial innovations (see below), *translates directly into an increase of effective power by the adopting unit over portions of its environment.* The firm adopting a corporate structure may push more traditionally organized competitors out of business; or the manufacturer introducing a piece of new machinery may improve the quality of his product (or lower his costs), capturing a larger share of the market. The cumulation of entrepreneurial innovations in a given city—the city being conceived as a spatially integrated subsystem of society—will therefore lead not only to its accelerated economic and demographic growth, but also to the consolidation of its hierarchical control over that portion of the urban system that has failed to adopt this particular set of innovations. Such a concentration of innovations in cities that have a high propensity for further innovation, produces the well known phenomenon of core regions that extend their control over the dependent peripheries of the country and, in some cases, beyond. The basic relations in the spatial distribution of economic power are thus seen to be an immediate outcome of the diffusion of innovations. Only a concerted governmental effort to establish conditions favorable to accelerated innovation at selected points in the periphery is likely to produce a marked reorganization of a growth pattern that, under normal conditions, displays remarkable stability. This stability, it turns out, is itself the result of innovation diffusion processes.

The extensive literature on innovation diffusion is generally deficient in that it fails to distinguish among broad categories of innovations. Basing a criterion of classification on structural form, for example, product, cultural, process, and organizational innovations may be distinguished. Alternatively, a classification based on salient characteristics of the adopting unit suggests a grouping into *consumer* and *entrepreneurial* innovations. These two systems of classification may be combined as follows:

   a. consumer innovations: product and cultural (related primarily to the *demand* side of economic transactions)
   b. entrepreneurial innovations: process and organizational (related primarily to the *supply* side of economic transactions)

This simplified system has the merit of facilitating the integration of spatial diffusion studies with economic theory. If, as seems probable, consumer innovations diffuse more rapidly and over wider areas than entrepreneurial innovations, a ready explanation for the spatial dynamics of the development process would seem to be at hand. Pressures for development arise from the side of demand (itself the result of prior diffusion processes) and occasion vast population migrations to the principal centers of entrepreneurial innovation where, it is hoped, these demands can be satisfied more expeditiously. This hope, of course, is usually disappointed. Only an explicit policy to contain the diffusion of consumer innovations (as in socialist economies) is able to reduce the level of demand sufficiently to permit the carrying out of a broader policy directed at a sustained and long-term increase in the supply bases of the economy.

In the remainder of this section, I shall refer exclusively to entrepreneurial innovations. Unfortunately, the empirical evidence for this type of innovation is slim compared to that available for consumer innovations. In the absence of sufficient studies, I am constrained to put forward a series of plausible but largely untested propositions that may hopefully serve as a basis for future comparative research.

Proposition 1

The spatial diffusion of entrepreneurial innovations follows the paths of exchange relations among cities. However, regardless of where in a system of cities an innovation enters, it will soon be captured by the largest city or cities in the system.

Evidence for this proposition, modified to include all growth-inducing innovations, has been brought together by Allan R. Pred who has also given this proposition an elegant mathematical formulation.[17] According to Pred, the strict hierarchial diffusion model, according to which innovations proceed in orderly progression down the urban size hierarchy of cities must be abandoned. This is true for the general case. In the ideal-typical developing country (moderate size, unitary government, culturally homogeneous population), however, the entry points for most innovations tend to be the largest, most cosmopolitan cities, such as the national capital or major port cities, and inter-urban contact networks tend to be hierarchial with respect to these cities; the number of non-hierarchial linkages are few. Where this is the case, the diffusion process will tend to be hierarchial even while obeying the general law governing spatial diffusion processes formulated by Pred. Moreover, some innovations, because of the intrinsic uniqueness or scale relative to the size of the national economy, never diffuse beyond the points of initial adoption and may, therefore, be regarded as *national* innovations, a stock exchange or oil refinery for example. For similar reasons, other innovations may be limited to only one per region (e.g., a hydro-electric installation) or one per city of a certain size (e.g., a municipal water works) and may thus be called *regional* and *urban* innovations respectively.

The accumulation of national innovations in only one city will give that city a preeminent role in directing the country's economic affairs. By analogy, the same will happen at lower hierarchical levels with cities that rapidly accumulate major regional and/or urban innovations. A hierarchy of urban centers exercising control over both national and regional economies is thus established. For reasons already stated, economic control centers will frequently coincide with centers of governmental power, so that the two hierarchies—economic and administrative—may eventually be joined.

Proposition II–A.

Especially during the starting-up phases of development, increased economic advantage accrues to the early adopters of innovations. To the extent that this 'initial advantage' is translated into vigorous urban growth, cities receiving the largest number of early innovations will tend to experience more rapid growth than cities adopting the same innovations later in time. With continuing development, however, the period required for a complete cycle of diffusion tends to diminish, so that smaller cities will increasingly come to share in exploiting the innovations in question, accelerating their own growth. The time sequence of innovation diffusion will nevertheless continue to be an important influence in the spatial distribution of economic power, since the rate at which innovations enter the urban system, relative to their downward diffusion, will tend to increase in the upper reaches of the hierarchy (see III below).

Proposition II–B.

Especially during the early phases of development, the rate of diffusion will tend to be faster for centers in proximity of the initial points of adoption than for centers of equivalent rank located at greater distance from these points.

Rogers distinguishes between *(a)* innovators, *(b)* early adopters, *(c)* early majority, *(d)* late majority, and *(e)* laggards whose distribution in time tends to follow the shape of an S-curve.[18] The slope of this curve will be different for each innovation, but will generally tend to rise over the period of development reflecting, among other things, improved transport and communication linkages, larger organizational scale, wider contact networks, and the accumulation of earlier innovations. Innovators and early adopters (counted as individual cities) will thus enjoy a quasi-monopolistic position in exploiting innovations before these innovations spread to other adopting units.

The diffusion process is governed by underlying patterns of information-exchange, especially of face-to-face communication. The spatial pattern of information exchange, however, is subject to declining intensity with distance, or distance decay. During the early period of a country's development, the distance decay curve tends to be rather steep (localism predominates), but eventually it tends to flatten out; communication processes become less constrained by distance, and other variables acquire greater salience. Centers located near points of initial adoption are therefore likely, *ceteris paribus*, to receive innovations earlier than centers of equivalent rank located at greater distance. This will tend to forge strong complementary links among adjacent centers, a process conducive to the formation of multi-centered core regions clustered around the largest, most innovative, and cosmopolitan cities of the country.

Proposition III

The probability of entrepreneurial innovations is an increasing function of city size. The larger the city in the size of its effective population, the greater will be the probability of innovation.[19]

This hypothesis, which underlies much of the preceding discussion, in turn depends on a number of intervening variables. In the following list, each variable is assumed to be an increasing function of city size.

1. *The demand for innovations.* Large cities have a greater need than small cities for innovations in helping solve new problems resulting from accelerated growth, growing population densities, increased specialization, and greater structural complexity. At the same time, organizations located in large cities tend to have a greater capacity for searching out potentially useful innovations than organizations in smaller centers.

2. *The financial, technical, and organizational resources for innovation.* Organizations in large cities tend to have greater access to and are able to mobilize resources for innovation more effectively than organizations in smaller cities.

3. *The propensity to innovate.* Innovative talent tends to move up the urban hierarchy within a country and down the hierarchy from external core regions to the largest, most cosmopolitan cities. The frequency of entrepreneurial skills in the population is therefore greater in large than in small cities.

4. *Cultural receptivity to innovations.* For many contemporary innovations, the requirements for receptivity—cultural, educational, linguistic, and technical—can be formidable. Persons having the skills which enable them to perceive the advantages of an innovation and also have the technical knowledge to carry them through tend to be more prevalent in large than in small cities.

5. *The stock of information available to potential innovators.* There is some evidence that the stock of available information to individuals and organizations increases exponentially with city size.[20] Large cities are information-saturated environments. The density of information is positively correlated with the probability of information.

6. *The range of contact networks.* The presence of information and a generalized receptivity are not in themselves sufficient for effective communication. Potential innovators must be tied into contact networks through which the relevant information is passed on. These networks tend to be more extensive, and there is probably greater redundancy of information, for organizations located in large than in small cities.

7. *Structural compatibility of innovations.* Before they can be implemented, many innovations require complementary innovations, such as supporting services. These are more likely to be present in large than in small cities. In addition, repeated innovation experience creates attitudes and expectations favorable to further innovation. Innovation in large cities tends to become an institutionalized process.

8. *Employment multipliers of innovation.* This relationship rests on

the idea that economic specialization, which tends to rise with increasing city size, implies higher employment multipliers from the adoption of an innovation. Multipliers are generated by the linkages of an innovation with supporting sectors. Large cities may also help support innovations in smaller cities, thus 'capturing' a part of the employment multiplier of such cities.

9. *Economic thresholds for innovation.* Innovations become economically feasible only at certain threshold sizes of total income and population. By definition, these thresholds increase with city size. In addition, there is some evidence that the threshold values for innovations have themselves been increasing over the period of industrialization.

Proposition IV

Over the course of development, the character of innovations changes in the direction of growing economic size, rising costs but also higher productivity, increasing specialization, and increasing technical complexity.

In the terminology adopted here, this proposition implies a relative increase in the number of national and regional innovations. Alternatively, we may say that the urban threshold sizes for innovation tend to rise with development. Entrepreneurial innovations will, therefore, tend to diffuse over progressively shorter hierarchical distances, assisting the growing polarization of development and leaving lower-order centers in a steadily worsening position, as both population and capital flow *up* the urban hierarchy in search of greater opportunity. These urban patterns will be reflected in growing regional differences in the levels of per capita income and other indices of socioeconomic development.

Proposition V

The adoption of an innovation in period I increases the probability of further innovation by the adopting unit in period II.

Innovation may be understood as part of a learning process in which prior success predisposes an actor to further innovation at an accelerating rate.[21] Clearly, there are upper limits to the rate of innovation, the capacity for continuous innovation rising progressively from individuals, to organizations, to society. But the existence of such limits does not deny the positive influence that learning has on the growth curve of innovation, as search behavior improves, and the entire process of introducing innovations into an existing system becomes routinized.

Rogers identifies the following characteristics of early adopters:[22]

Earlier adopters . . . have greater empathy, less dogmatism, greater ability to deal with abstractions, greater rationality, and more favorable attitudes toward change, risk, education, and science. They are less fatalistic and have higher achievement motivation scores and higher aspirations for their children. Earlier adopters have more social participation, are more highly integrated with the system, are more cosmopolite, have more change agent contact, have more exposure to both mass media and interpersonal channels, seek information more, have higher knowledge of innovations, and have more opinion leadership.

These characteristics are not inborn traits, however. They can be learned in the course of successful innovation. In the long run, an entire society may learn to be innovative, but initially the rapid learners will be found predominantly among the populations of large, cosmopolitan cities where innovations tend to be initially introduced. As a result, the rate of innovation in these cities is likely to be higher than the rate of diffusion of these innovations to other parts of the urban system, increasing the differences among centers in regular hierarchial sequence.

Concluding Comments

Except for Proposition 1, the innovation diffusion process described above follows closely the theoretical model evolved by J. R. Lasuén. His conclusions are worth quoting in full.[23] (In the following quotation the phrase 'urban system' may be substituted for 'system of regions'.)

> In our view, the system of regions grows and develops in a stable hierarchical order due to the factors maintaining the stability of the geographical diffusion patterns (stability in the functional diffusion patterns and rigidity in the firms' locations).
>
> Within each innovation set, the regions grow at differential rates (keeping the stable hierarchical order) due to the effect of the factors which control the feasibility of adoptions in the different regions (diffusion times, market sizes) in interaction with the values of the main characteristics of the innovation (scale of operations, adoption times).
>
> Over time, the values of the innovation set characteristics change (scales of operations increase; adoption time shortens). This causes further differentiation of regional growth rates.
>
> Consequently within every innovation set, regions grow stably hierarchized and allometrically. Over several innovation sets they also grow hierarchically stable and allometrically, but the allometries for every set have different values (normally of successively rising slopes).

In other words, the diffusion of innovations is such that size hierarchies of cities are maintained over successive cycles of diffusion, but the specific economic values captured over the entire system tend to rise in geometric progression from low-ranking to high-ranking cities. Top cities in the hierarchy will consequently adopt more innovations per unit of time than other cities in the system, spinning off older, less efficient innovations to the periphery. This process accounts for the frequently observed sliding scale of diminishing modernity and power as one descends the urban hierarchy. Towards the upper end of the hierarchy we find a preponderance of metropolitan types with far-flung contact networks while, lower down, narrowly circumscribed fields of interaction and limited horizons of aspiration, knowledge, and opportunity are more prevalent. This pattern corresponds to Allan Pred's large-city-focused model of urban systems growth in which a small but relatively stable set of large cities (or core regions) exerts decisive influence over the growth patterns of a larger set of lower-ranking peripheral regions. The resulting socio-economic indices have been carefully charted by Brian J. L. Berry.[24] The economic landscape of a country is cleft by huge troughs of economic backwardness that divide occasional peaks and ridges of high growth and material wellbeing.

This 'normal' patterning of urban growth can be altered only by changing the distribution of intervening variables and attracting production units into the periphery that are innovation-prone and likely to produce large employment as growth pole policies.[25] The selective activation of 'growth poles' in the periphery will, of course, merely replicate the national pattern of innovation diffusion on a regional scale. At this point the question remains unresolved over how many levels in the urban hierarchy this process of activating growth poles may be extended, and when the normal filtering processes of innovation must be allowed, for lack of suitable controls, to operate without policy intervention.

Interregional Patterns of Conflict and Accommodation

Innovative entrepreneurial elites in urban areas are frequently found among foreign or national ethnic (or cultural) minorities. Although the entrepreneurial role of foreign 'colonial' elites is generally recognized, national minorities which have gained control over significant portions of the modern economic sector are equally important. The Jews in Western Europe were an early instance of such an elite. In the newly industrializing countries, the Chinese in Malaysia and Indonesia,[26] the Ibo in Nigeria,[27] the Antioqueños in Colombia,[28] and the Arabs, Italians, Germans, and Jews in Latin American countries[29] are frequently cited examples of urban innovative elites. (Other ethnic minorities whose entrepreneurial roles might be studied include English Canadians in Quebec, Arabs in Zanzibar, Indians in Burma, East Africa, Trinidad, and the Guayanas, Greeks in Egypt, Slovenes in Yugoslavia, and French settlers in Algeria.)

In nearly every instance, urban ethnic minorities operate in a political environment that is intially controlled by an agrarian-based governing elite whose members belong to a different cultural, ethnic, or religious group. This situation is dramatically illustrated by data on East African cities. According to William and Judith Hanna, "In Kenya, 3 out of 100 residents are non-Africans, whereas in Nairobi the figure is 41 out of 100. Similarly, Uganda's population is just over 1 percent non-African, but for Kampala the percentage is 49. Comparable situations are found in Tanzania and Zambia."[30] And they continue: "With independence, some Africans moved to the top and, as a corollary, Asians and Middle Easterners have been left in a somewhat ambiguous position: subordinate to the new African elite, but on some measures superordinate to the African rank-and-file. The ambiguity arises because racial boundaries prevent Asians and Middle Easterners from entering a unilinear status hierarchy."[31] Many of these non-Africans were, in fact, born on the continent, but remain alien to the indigenous cultures.

Where innovative entrepreneurial elites are excluded from political power, a profound disjunction occurs between rural and urban development. Cities which have the largest concentration of innovative ethnic (cultural) minorites will experience the most rapid growth, while 'native' centers, tied to the rural economy in the periphery, are likely to stagnate. Under conditions of rural/urban disjunction or *economic dualism*,[32] urban-generated surpluses tend not to be used for developing the rural sector (which contains a majority of the total population), but are accumulated, in part to build up the modern commercial-industrial complex at the core and, in part, to be expatriated to the home country of the intruding elite. By the same token, innovations will be contained largely within the core because contact networks and investment resources will also tend to be ethnically (and culturally) controlled. As a result, the remainder of the country will supply the urban core with food, raw materials and labor and, in turn, provide a market outlet for certain core region products.

In situations of this sort, relations between innovative (urban-economic) and traditionalist (rural governing) elites will be variously characterized by patterns of coöptation, accommodation, and open hostility.

Under coöptation, the governing elite is placed in a client relation to the entrepreneurial elite. This is typically the case where the latter is of foreign extraction and unassimilated to the national society (Americans in Venezuela under Perez Jimenez, Japanese in occupied Korea, English in colonial Nigeria and Ghana, Russians in the former Baltic countries, Germans in Norway and France during World War II). For Spanish-speaking Latin America, it has been argued that foreign dependency and coöptation of national elites accounts for the extreme concentration of economic and political power in the national capital regions of countries such as Venezuela, Peru, Bolivia, Ecuador, and Chile.[33] Although this contention remains to be demonstrated, it is claimed that a more integrated form of spatial development will be achieved only if the governing elites regain a substantial measure of autonomy with respect to foreign entrepreneurial elites.[34] In South America, these claims have been advanced primarily by intellectuals, equally hostile to foreign and traditional (coöpted) elites and eager to assume a major governing role themselves. (In Peru, the military forces appear to have made these claims effective, though the results for development of the urban system remain unclear.)[35] It is noteworthy that the national 'counter-elite' of intellectuals is also the most receptive to modern technical and organizational innovation but sees its own aspirations for participation in governance thwarted by foreign powers and their national 'lackeys'.

An interesting case is that of Brazil, where the revolution which brought the military into absolute control of the country's governmental machinery may be interpreted, paradoxically, as the successful coöptation of the military—many of whose leading figures have strong provincial backgrounds by birth, education, and professional experience—by a national entrepreneurial establishment. Because unassimilated foreign elements constitute a relatively minor part of entrepreneurial groups in São Paulo and Rio de Janeiro, the military government has been able to pursue more nationalistic policies than would normally be expected under conditions of coöptation. These policies, however, have been directed more at problem areas that do not directly conflict with the central interests of the Brazilian business community, such as the building of trans-Brazilian highways and the colonization of new regions. Nationalistic efforts of this sort, as well as the absence of politics in the usual sense, have opened the door to the active collaboration of tecnicos and intellectuals with the government and have all but destroyed potential counter-elites in the country. The long-term spatial effects of these new policies are likely to be spectacular.[36] They will contribute to the spatial integration of the Brazilian territory under conditions of internal dependency to the major core regions of the country.[37] But they will also uncover new possibilities for resources development, shift the gravitational field of the country's economic development away from coastal areas to the western frontier, and stimulate new urbanization along the major routes of interior penetration.

Under *accommodation,* a spheres of influence agreement of mutual non-interference may be tacitly reached according to which the management of the rural sector is left in the hands of the traditional governing elite, while the urban sector is 'turned over' to the innovative minorities to develop as they see fit, essentially as an enclave within the larger national territory. Enclaves of this sort are likely to be related more to the international economy (i.e., to the international urban system) than to the rural areas within the country. In some cases, such as Singapore, urban enclaves may be politically separated as well.[38]

This process of accommodation has been analyzed by Marcos Mamalakis in his theory of sectoral clashes.[39] Although Mamalakis' theory is expressed primarily in terms of major economic sectors (industrial vs. agricultural) it is easily translatable into spatial (regional) terms as well. In pre-Allende Chile, where the theory of sectoral clashes appears to be most strongly supported by the empirical evidence—though supporting data also come from Mexico and Argentina—the urban elites contained a large proportion of national minority groups of Germans, English, Yugoslavs, Jews, and Levantines (in addition to foreign, predominantly American, nationals), whereas the governing elite (the rurally-based 'oligarchy') was primarily of Spanish and Basque origin. Sectoral conflicts, reflected in the formation of political parties, had therefore certain ethnic-cultural overtones as well.

Finally, under conditions of *open hostility* events occur that lead to the disruption of existing relations of coöptation and/or accommodation. Conflict may assume a variety of forms, including *campaigns of national liberation* (Algeria), *the nationalization of foreign enterprise* (Cuba, Peru, Argentina, and Chile) the *elimination of ethnic minorities by either their physical destruction* (Jews in German-dominated Europe, Chinese in Indonesia) or *expulsion* (Indians from Kenya, French *colons* from Algeria), *economic pressure* (Chinese in Malaysia), *civil war* (Ibo in Nigeria), and *peaceful secession* (Singapore).

In some instances, the conclusion of hostilities has resulted in a renewed interest in rural development (involving the forcible transfer of resources from the core), with a consequent decline of growth in core areas and the concomitant renascence of small to medium-sized provincial centers as base points for agricultural development.[40] Cuba provides perhaps the most clearcut evidence on this point, though a similar shift in allocation has also been reported for Malaysia.[41]

All of the situations discussed above relate to countries in which powerful innovative minorities in urban areas are *culturally distinct* from governing elites. But in other situations, such a split has not occurred and economic and political power is exercised conjointly from a dominant core region over ethnically and culturally varied populations (Northern Ireland, Soviet Union, Yugoslavia, Indonesia, Pakistan prior to the liberation of Bangladesh, Rhodesia, South Africa).

Where this occurs, the dependent regions will often claim to be 'oppressed' and generate political pressures for greater 'national' (i.e., regional) autonomy, ranging from complete secession to a number of 'protectionist' and 'federalist' solutions, including demands for 'preferential treatment.'[42]

Each of these solutions holds different implications for the development of urban systems. Some of them involve the massive transfer of populations (as has happened, most recently, in East Pakistan). Others lead to the isolation of the 'protected' areas from the 'virus' of urbanization (South Africa).[43] Still others produce vigorous urban-regional competition among federated states (Yugoslavia, India) with a consequent multiplication and strengthening of subsidiary core regions.[44] Occasionally, the mere threat of national independence or annexation to a neighboring country with similar ethnic traits may be sufficient to obtain preferential status (Commonwealth of Puerto Rico, French Quebec, South Tyrol).

These outcomes for urban systems may also be viewed from a perspective of (spatial) integration. The following table may help to recall the major patterns in this context. (The Roman numerals in the right-hand column refer to quadrants in Fig. 6.1; arrows indicate the principal direction of dominance.)

Dependency in Core-Periphery Relations: The Case of Chile

In the first section of this paper, a basic distinction was drawn between the stock of potential power controlled by a person or an organization and the uses of this power in exchange relations with others. From the standpoint of empirical research, the latter is much easier to observe than the former. The process of exchange leaves visible traces and results in behavioral changes by at least one of the actors in the transaction. It is from a long series of such transactions that changes in the stock of power held by the participating actors may

Table 6.1

Elite relationships	Urban system	Spatial integration
1. coöptation	complete dominance of a passive periphery by the core: strong urban primacy; typical pattern of internal colonization, with strong linkages to international urban system	integration based on dependency relationships and the continued imbalance of major urbanization process (I→IV)
2. accommodation	spheres of influence agreement leading to regional dualism: small number of modern urban enclaves relatively independent of traditional rural areas and joined more closely to international urban system than to national territory	weak integration on basis of economic dependency: rural 'migrants belonging to national majority groups are prevented from reaching controlling positions in the urban economy occupied by innovative ethnic minority groups (I→III)
3. open hostility	if innovative urban minorities are effectively neutralized, the result may be a gradual transfer of resources from core to periphery, followed by accelerated rural development and the renascence of small and medium-size provincial centers; development of a 'complete' urban hierarchy and attenuation or primacy	greater functional interdependency among regions and reduction of imbalances in urbanization: integration based on growing interdependency of urban centers (I→III)
4. regional 'protectorates'	policy of exclusion of urbanism from 'protected' areas or rural enclaves: core region dominance	partial integration of urbanized (dominant) areas based on 'protected' labor pools in stagnant rural enclaves: economic dualism (I→IV)

| 5. federative solutions | preferential treatment and greater autonomy of 'associated states' and federal territories: competition among urban areas: emergence of subcores within each region | although frequently a fragile political arrangement, this 'solution' may eventually lead to a strong pattern of spatial integration based on urban-regional interdependency and the gradual attrition of peripheries: structured urban/regional competition (I↔II, I→III) |

Commodity Flows and the Spatial Structure of the Indian Economy (Department of Geography Research Paper No. 111, The University of Chicago, 1966).

be inferred. In urban and, more generally, in spatial systems, the inferred distribution of power tends to be unequal, reflecting a dominant and persisting pattern of non-reciprocal exchange relations among cities and regions. I have called this the autonomy-dependency pattern and have argued that it will have a major influence on the relative growth and decline of cities whose economic and political fortunes are conjoined.

Code words such as city, region, or nation are useful for summing up exchange relations among a set of interdependent individual and organizational actors. Their use is permissible insofar as each refers to a relatively stable system of spatial relationships. Although integration may be achieved on a basis of either equality or dependency, the more interesting form, particularly in the case of newly developing nations, is the latter.

Spatial patterns of autonomy-dependency must be studied with respect to particular and limited domains of life. The processes of control by which dependency is secured are made effective through institutional arrangements which ensure a certain consistency of outcome. It is the spatial organization of these arrangements that allows us to extend the concept of dependency into spatial analysis and to refer to control over particular domains of life in the periphery by organizational actors whose base of power is solidified within core regions.

In the following case study of dependency relations in Chile, I shall focus on those arrangements by which a core region centered upon the national capital assured its continued dominance over urban life in the rest of the country. Although the description is in the present tense, the reader should be aware that the facts cited pertain chiefly to the decade of the sixties. The new forces released by the Popular Unity Government since 1970 may bring about significant changes in the distribution of power and the spatial development pattern of Chile's economy.

Chile is an unusually good laboratory for the study of dependency relations. Its population is small and relatively homogeneous in ethnic origin, and cultural regionalism plays only a negligible role in national politics. Spatial integration, as measured by a shared historical past, a shared language and religion, a shared political system of great stability, and a well-articulated system of national transportation is exceptionally strong. At the same time, the overwhelming dominance of central power over even the minutiae of daily life is an acknowledged fact. For these reasons, Chile may stand as a classic instance of dependency relations in their purest form.

Five dimensions of the spatial organization of dependency will be described: municipal government, provincial administration, financial power, neighborhood power, and party organization. In the concluding section, some of the consequences of these patterns for the development of Chile's urban system will be considered.[45]

1. *Municipal Government.* The 277 muncipalities of Chile are the only units of territorial government that stand between the individual citizen (or, more accurately, the extensive networks of familistic relations that form the texture of Chilean society) and the central authorities in Santiago. Elections for councilmen *(regidores)* are held every four years. The mayor is selected from the body of *regiodores* by means of indirect elections, except that the mayors of Santiago, Valparaiso, and Viña del Mar are appointed directly by the President of the Republic.[46]

Municipal revenues, principally from the sale of licenses *(patentes)* for vehicles, dogs, moving picture theaters, mines, concessions, and horse racing, as well as business permits, are so low that most municipalities manage to do little more than pay their employees and monthly office bills. In 1967, the average municipal budget was only eight dollars *per capita,* but the amounts varied by size of municipality, from a low of three dollars for smaller units to nine dollars for municipalities with a population of over 100,000. Only the municipality of Santiago had a substantially larger budget, or nearly twenty-three dollars for each of its inhabitants.[47] A select number of municipalities receive additional income, as determined by national legislation, from local resource-using industries (wooden match manufacture, for instance) as well as from special taxes levied on ports, airports, and tourist facilities. But, in any event, the total amounts available for physical improvement and social welfare at the local level are insignificant. Local governments are responsible for the collection and incineration of garbage, for traffic control, street lighting, and public markets and gardens. As a practical matter, all other functions vital to the wellbeing of local inhabitants are directly managed out of national ministries in Santiago, including housing, public utilities, street paving, education, health care, social welfare, and public security.

This being so, municipal governments have little to do that is of any consequence. Having little to do, their employees are poorly paid. Being poorly paid, their professional quality is low. Restricted technical competence is then cited by central bureaucrats as the reason why local governments cannot be entrusted with greater responsibility.

It is generally agreed that the legal powers theoretically available to municipalities are not being fully exploited. One reason is that the national government consistently fails to transfer the full share of income taxes collected locally to which the municipalities are legally entitled.[48] Despite financial difficulties, a handful of municipalities has provided imaginative leadership in the provision of local services. But the institutional environment in Chile is inhospitable to displays of local ingenuity, and these exceptional experiences have not been imitated.

Local development is thus left almost entirely to the arbitrary judgment of Santiago officialdom. As a result, the fate of local populations is subject to all the vagaries of centralized state management, such as the limited attention span of key decision makers, their slow reaction time to new information, and the expediencies of national politics.

2. *Provincial Administration*. Following the French practice, provincial governors *(intendentes)* are appointed by the President of the Republic and report directly to the Minister of the Interior. Traditionally, the *intendente's* job has been to maintain 'law and order' in the provinces, provide political intelligence, and coordinate the work of the decentralized field offices of national ministries. Except for small emergency funds, *intendentes* have no development budgets of their own.

Since 1925, the Chilean constitution has included a provision for the election of provincial assemblies, but this has never been implemented. To regularize this anomalous situation, the formal powers of provincial assemblies to regulate municipal activities and control municipal expenditures were transferred to the *intendentes* in 1942. By this manoeuvre, the central government has been able to interject itself directly into issues of local governance. According to Peter S. Cleaves, this penetration has taken two forms.[49]

> . . . independent servicing of the demands of the people and the coordination of interventions by the Minister of Housing and Urban Affairs and the Interior into functions that are directly under the jurisdiction of the municipality. To illustrate a recent trend in this direction: since 1965, the *intendencia* has had funds available for community action while the municipality has continued to suffer from a lack of money . . . In recognition of the *intendencia's* capacity to take effective measures, *pobladores* (i.e., residents of poor quarters) and others have more and more bypassed the municipal structure to petition for direct government consideration of their problems.

In recent years, some efforts have been made to assign a greater developmental role to the *intendentes*. The National Planning Office (ODEPLAN) has divided the country's 25 provinces into ten development regions (plus a metropolitan district for Santiago) and has established small technical planning offices in the most important city of each region. These offices have done good work in recommending central budget allocations for their areas, but have not taken an active part in the implementation of specific projects or development programs. Exceptions to this are the provinces of Magallanes and Tarapaca, located at the extreme southern and northern ends of the country respectively, and far removed from the bureaucratic influence of Santiago. Because of Chile's interest in protecting these provinces against presumably covetous neighbors (Argentina, Bolivia, Peru), they have been given greater autonomy over their development than other regions. The city of Arica in Tarapacá, for instance, has been authorized to operate a municipal casino and to retain funds derived from its operation for local improvements. A technical staff, provided by the National Planning Office, has been assigned to work with the *Junta de Adelanto* of Arica (Arica's Development Junta) to steer the uses of these funds into growth-promoting investments. For Magallanes, a regional development corporation has been established with revenues from the extensive oil drilling operations in the province. The local branch of the National Planning Office is serving as a technical staff to the Corporation, and the local *intendente* has, in effect, become a regional development manager. Both these efforts appear to have been quite successful in stimulating local economic activity.[50]

Notwithstanding these regionally oriented planning activities, Chile's provinces remain politically and economically powerless, and their economic fortunes continue to be directed from Santiago. Al-

though the information on which decisions concerning regional investments are made is better now than it used to be, the visible political
pressures in Santiago (ministers can watch street demonstrations from
their office windows!) are generally more persuasive than the com-
plaints of delegations from the largely 'invisible' provinces of Chile's
periphery. During the 1960s, the major newspapers in Santiago typically buried provincial news on the inside pages. The periphery of the
country was not considered especially newsworthy.

The general neglect of the provinces has left most provincial urban
centers in the backwaters of the sprawling national metropolis.[51] Devoid of political power and without an economically prosperous hinterland, these cities have remained the passive objects of occasional
national munificence. Local investments by the national government
are therefore regarded as 'windfalls' and tend to generate only minis-
cule multipliers, since most of these are captured by Santiago. With 75
percent of all cities falling in the range of 5,000 to 40,000 inhabitants,
none of Chile's cities, except for Santiago, have moved into self-
sustaining growth. Unemployment in provincial centers has typically
been two to three times the rate reported for the nation's capital, and
it may be fairly assumed that most migrants arrive at provincial
capitals, not because they expect to find a job there, but because living
conditions in the nearby rural districts from which they come are even
worse than in the city. Many migrants eventually move to Santiago.

3. *Financial Power*. In the late 1960s, Chile's public sector accounted
for about three-fourths of all investments in the country. Development
capital was channelled through a series of national corporations of
which the most important was CORFO (Corporación de Fomento)
which, in turn, controlled either wholly or in part a series of subsidiary
enterprises. The headquarters of these and other national corporations
(in housing, urban renewal, agrarian reform) were inevitably located in
Santiago. Their capital was obtained partly from national revenues
(including large-scale resource transfers from copper-producing
regions) and partly from their own revenue-producing operations.
CORFO, in addition, coordinated all major foreign loans.

Although CORFO maintained several regional subsidiaries (the most
important of which was CONORTE serving the northern provinces of
Chile), these, too, were run from the center and had only a vestigial
presence in their respective regions.

The remaining 25 percent of national investment was channelled
through the private banking system. But even in the private sector (it
might be more accurate to say, *especially* in the private sector),

Santiago clearly dominated the scene. Provincial branch banks were tightly controlled by their parent banks in the capital and were permitted to make only very small loans on their own initiative. A number of so-called regional banks, such as the Banco de Talca, also operated out of Santiago. Carrying the name of their province, these banks were usually controlled by local landowners and provided a convenient channel for the transfer of funds to the center. The whole system worked to concentrate wealth, not only at the center, but also in the hands of the traditional 'oligarchy' whose principal families established their residence in Santiago.

This capacity of the private banking system to transfer capital resources from the periphery to the country's principal core region is a very common phenomenon. Unfortunately, it has received scant attention by students of regional development. Most of the funds collected through Chile's private banking system eventually found their way into Santiago real estate and into large commercial or industrial ventures, for the most part also located in Santiago. Private capital did not ordinarily seek out investment opportunities in the provinces. By tacit agreement, this job was left to CORFO.

4. *Neighborhood Power.* Chile's hypertrophied centralization was not unqualifiedly endorsed by everyone. Although most technicians relished it secretly, politicans of various political persuasions, but particularly Christian Democrats, mildly criticized the system for its cumbersome procedures, its lack of responsiveness to local needs, and its tendency to exclude from active participation in the national society the vast majority of the population. This phenomenon was labelled *marginalidad,* and it was partly in answer to this problem, that the reformist government of President Frei undertook to promote the regionalization of development policy.[52] The accelerated organization of *Juntas de Vecinos* (neighborhood councils) was a second strategy pursued.

Juntas de Vecinos have a long history in Chile. As a rule, they spring into existence in the poorer urban barrios to mobilize the support of neighbors for petitioning the authorities to resolve some pressing local issue, such as paving a street, putting in a sewer system, or building a school. Once the problem is resolved, however, the Junta subsides into a dormant state until the next crisis. The Christian Democrats, after attaining to power in 1964, decided to use this traditional system for pointing the country more strongly in the direction of development.

Their original hope was to establish a national hierarchy of Juntas: the neighborhood Juntas of a given city would associate at the municipal level, federate at the provincial level, and confederate at the national level. The confederation of Juntas de Vecinos would then tie in with a National Ministry of Popular Promotion (*Promocion Popular*) that would represent the 'people's voice' (as filtered through the hierarchy of Juntas) at the cabinet level. Juntas were to be given full participation in local planning efforts and authorized to undertake certain public works on their own initiative.

Clearly, a system such as this could lend itself to a variety of purposes. A large number of proposals were floated, but only a few of them passed into legislation. The ideological commitment of the Christian Democrats was to mobilize the people for national development and so to transform popular discontent into a responsible voice. Or, as President Frei put it in his Second State of the Nation Message:[53]

> My position in government has made me feel as never before *the necessity for the people to organize;* after the election, I was impressed by the fact that the centers of effective power, in many cases in the extreme minority, perpetuate a dead weight on the life of Chile which is unacceptable. For this reason, the silence of a disorganized people must transform itself into a *responsible voice.* And therefore, Promoción Popular is not just an idea or even an electoral platform for us; it is the profound necessity to *transform in an organic manner the basic structures of our society* [emphasis included].

But the political opposition saw matters in a different light. They suggested a devious manoeuvre by the party in power to consolidate its political bases in the local barrios. A National Council of Popular Promotion survived the determined legislative opposition and, temporarily attached to the President's Office, continued its organizing work among the Juntas and other popular organizations, such as Mothers' Centers and Sport Clubs. But the Council no longer held a monopoly over community action. The parties of the left (Communists and Socialists) pursued the work of organizing local Juntas with equal vigor. At the same time, high-level officials in several government ministries (especially Housing and Agriculture) promoted their own versions of 'maximum feasible participation'.

This attempt to mobilize neighborhood power and harness it to the goals of national development had no immediately visible effects on Chile's urban system. At one point, it had been the intention of the Christian Democrats to create in the *Juntas de Vecinos* a system of power paralleling that of municipal governments, evidently in hopes of ultimately replacing the latter. (Municipal Councils tended to be controlled by members of parties in opposition to the Christian Democrats.) This hope, however, was effectively torpedoed. Nor was the national distribution of power significantly affected by this effort to mobilize the population of local communities and, particularly, the poor. Control over even local investments remained centralized and relations in ownership and production were left untouched.

5. *Party Organization.* Political parties in Chile reflect sectoral and class interests more than interests that are purely regional or local. During the 19th century, a major split divided rural-based Conservatives from urban-based Liberals, with the former dominated by large land-holding families and the latter representing the new commercial-industrial elites of Santiago. With the further growth of the national core area, however, additional urban parties came into existence, each finding support among incipient social groups. White collar office workers and small shopkeepers became the mainstay of the Radical party (Chile's Grand Old Party), Communists entrenched themselves among organized workers (initially in the copper mining camps of the North, but eventually shifting the base of their operations to the major cities in the center). Socialists (a relatively elitist group in Chile) found special favor among intellectuals and managed to win additional support in Chile's frontier areas, principally Magallanes, while the Christian Democrats appealed primarily to the new class of *técnicos,* recently enfranchised women voters, and broad sections of the relatively small, well-to-do middle class.

In national elections, parties would typically nominate their most trusted militants to run for political office from one of the provincial districts. For a brief, intensive period thereafter, the candidate would present himself to his local electorate. Once voted into office, however, the new *diputado* or *senador* from Province X would rush back to Santiago (where, in any case, he resided) to throw himself into the battle of national politics which was aligned principally by loyalties to a political party and strong, personalistic leaders. They were in no way expected to 'represent' local interests in the American sense.

Despite outward appearances of contest, mutual accommodation succeeded for a long time in governing relations between rural and urban parties, in the sense that neither would seriously interfere in the interest spheres of the other. Agricultural policy was thus left to the Conservatives, while urban policy became the battle ground of a number of mutually antagonistic urban parties.

With progressive urbanization, however, the Conservative Party lost ground and eventually transformed itself into yet another urban party that would form frequent alliances with other political parties in a conservative coalition.

In their ascendancy to power, the Christian Democrats had to compete against an opposition of Radicals, Communists, and Socialists whose main strength was in Santiago and other large cities (Antofagasta, Concepcion). This left the Christian Democrats chiefly with the rural periphery of the country, traditionally dominated by the Conservatives. As a result, the Christian Democrats became the first Chilean party actively to solicit the support of regional populations. It was this regional orientation which subsequently led the Party to advocate a more vigorous agrarian reform program than the preceding government of Jorge Alessandri had done and to promote the regionalization of development programs generally. But the effort was only half-hearted. It failed to bring about a drastic change in the distribution of governmental and economic power, and the earlier tendencies toward continued concentration of economic activities and population in Santiago continued.

The foregoing description of the spatial element in national politics is, of course, a highly simplified one. Not only did Chile have minor regionalist parties from time to time, such as PADENA, but the North of the country, with its heavy concentration of employment in coppermining, often played a decisive role in determining the outcome of national elections. Similarly, regional concentrations of national minorities (Germans, Yugoslavs) have occasionally influenced voting behavior in certain parts of the country. Nevertheless, spatial considerations were definitely subordinate to ideological and personalistic issues. One did not customarily rise to national prominence from local office; indeed, as I have tried to suggest, neither municipalities nor provinces provided much scope for political talent. Anyone who wished to succeed politically, had to move to Santiago.

The absence of political regionalism in Chile helps account for the sense of strong national unity. National politicians in Santiago generally thought in national terms (as well as sectorially and long class lines). The system suffered from an excessive factionalism which at times was carried to an extreme of personal bitterness, but the formation of regional blocks, so common in other countries, was not part of the picture. An appearance of regionalism is given by the geographic distribution of major economic sectors: miners in the North, industrial workers and middle class in the cities of the center, large-scale agriculture in the central Valley of Chile, and *minifundos* (small-scale farming) in the South. Yet, to this day [1972], it is the *national* point of view that prevails. And, invariably, the national point of view is that of Santiago.

6. *Conclusion*. It was the intent of this section to describe some of the ways in which relations of dependency are organized in Chile's urban system. In the absence of a strong countervailing power having a regional territorial base, most of Chile's cities in the shadow of the Santiago metropolis have been reduced to penury. An incipient active periphery was observed at the two extremes of the national territory, where the relatively exposed border positions of both Magallanes and Tarapaca have led to modest increases in their autonomy to make development decisions. But elsewhere, local populations wait more or less passively for the decisions of superior authorities, though they will occasionally seek to influence these decisions through appropriate political means. Initiative is at low ebb, and those who wish to find more scope for their gifts of enterprise, eventually relocate in Santiago.

The resulting ascendancy of the national capital in Chile's urban system is best illustrated by the following table, showing the historical evolution of three indices of primacy (the ratio of Santiago's population to the next three lower-ranking cities in combinations of two, three and four). Regardless of which index is chosen, the relative weight of Santiago's population has been continuously increasing and, during recent decades, at an accelerating rate.[54]

Final Comments

The influences on the development of urban systems are multiple and reciprocal. Governmental and economic power make up only one set of such influences, though I will argue that it is probably the most important set. In practice, of course, these influences are difficult to isolate, and it is still more difficult to measure their effects within a cybernetic framework of analysis. The customary two-variable regression models, dear to economists and sociologists, fail to yield the insights one would want. This suggests that we may have to choose

Table 6.2
Chile: Index of Primacy, 1865–1960

	1865	1875	1885	1895	1907	1920	1930	1940	1950	1960
2-city index	1.64	1.31	1.72	1.92	1.76	2.33	2.94	3.45	4.44	5.18
3-city index	—	1.08	1.36	1.40	1.28	1.67	2.11	2.40	2.82	3.18
4-city index	—	—	1.16	1.18	1.11	1.42	1.82	2.13	2.50	2.77

between quantitative precision in research, leading to very restricted and possibly misleading insights, and a more comprehensive, qualitative approach which may have to sacrifice the elegance of mathematical formulations for a deeper historical and conceptual understanding. If we should opt for the second approach, formal models of the sort introduced at the start of this paper serve primarily a heuristic purpose. They fall short of theoretical constructs that purport to model complex causal relations in the development of urban systems. On the other hand, they focus the attention of researchers on critical variables and their interrelationships and help in posing questions that may eventually lead to significant insights into the workings of historical processes. They are preliminary to empirical research.

I have placed the emphasis in this paper on the spatial distribution of governmental and economic power. It could be argued, as William Alonso has done, that the degree to which all national policies have implications for urban growth, sectoral rather than spatial distributions of power are the critical variables.[55] Most probably, both viewpoints are correct and complement each other. Whatever the conclusion, however, the model I have proposed points to a series of fascinating questions about the effect of power relations on the structural growth of hierarchical systems. It is with a view to clarifying these questions and setting the state for a large-scale research effort that the present paper has been written.

Notes

This essay was prepared for the Work Group on Comparative Urbanization of the Social Science Research Council. The present version is based on a preliminary draft, dated January 1972, but has been completely rewritten. I wish to thank John Hanna, Allen Howard, Richard Morse, Francine Rabinovitz, Edward Soja, and Myron Weiner for their generous and critical discussion of the earlier version.

1. Little agreement exists on what constitutes spatial integration. The term has come into recent usage by geographers who tend to use it in the sense of connectivity and who are likely to measure integration by functional linkages or transactions between places. This usage has much in common with that of Karl Deutsch and his associates. Political scientists have had a more long-standing concern with integration, particularly at the level of international relations. Current research has been brought together in a book edited by Leon N. Lindberg and Stuart A. Scheingold, *Regional Integration. Theory and Research* (Cambridge: Harvard University Press, 1971). For present purposes, the chapters by Ernst B. Haas and Fred M. Hayward are especially useful.

2. See, for instance, Irving Louis Horowitz, "Electoral Politics, Urbanization, and Social Development in Latin America," *Urban Affairs Quarterly,*

II, 3 (March 1967), pp. 3–35, and John Friedmann, *Urbanization, Planning, and National Development* (Beverly Hills, Cal.: Sage Publications, 1973), chapter 5, "Hyperurbanization and National Development in Chile."

3. The theoretical foundation for this matrix is in part derived from Peter M Blau, *Exchange and Power in Social Life* (London: John Wiley, 1964).

4. The systems approach to the study of cities was first formalized by Brian J. L. Berry in a justly famous article, "Cities as Systems Within Systems of Cities," reprinted in John Friedmann and William Alonso (eds), *Regional Development and Planning. A Reader* (Cambridge: The MIT Press, 1964), chapter 6. The original article appeared in 1963.

5. The scientific bases for prescriptive policies of urban development are still weak. But even if they were stronger, it is unlikely that they would provide unambiguous conclusions for optimal courses of action. A brilliant review of the current state of knowledge in urban systems analysis, from a perspective of public policy, is Harry W. Richardson's, "Optimality in City Size, Systems of Cities in Urban Policy: A Sceptic's View" (Centre for Research in the Social Science, University of Kent at Canterbury, Reprint Series No. 18 (1), (1972).

6. Much controversy has raged over the issue of whether the size distributions of cities is anything but an empirical curiosity. A great deal has been written specifically about the form of rank-size distributions and whether these are in any way related to conditions of economic development and integration. In a recent piece, Brian J. L. Berry, who has been in the center of this controversy, has revised his earlier view that the evidence for a clear-cut relationship is inconclusive. Basing his argument on time-series data for change in size distributions (whereas earlier analysis had been restricted to comparative statics), he now maintains that urban systems typically evolve from a low level equilibrium distribution (many small, equally sized urban places) via urban primacy to a high-level equilibrium characterized by a lognormal distribution of city-sizes. See his "City Size and Economic Development: Conceptual Synthesis and Policy Problems, with Special Reference to South and Southeast Asia," in Leo Jacobson and Ved Prakash (eds), *Urbanization and National Development* (Beverly Hills, Cal.: Sage Publications, 1971), ch. 5.

7. Richard M. Morse, "Planning, History, Politics," in John Miler and Ralph A. Gakenheimer (eds), *Latin America Urban Policies and the Social Sciences* (Beverly Hills, Cal.: Sage Publications, 1971), p. 194.

8. Chauncey D. Harris, 'Urbanization and Population Growth in the Soviet Union, 1959–1970," *Ekistics*, 32, 192 (November 1971), p. 360.

9. J. Barry Riddell, *The Spatial Dynamics of Modernization of Sierra Leone* (Evanston: Northwestern University Press, 1970), pp. 90–93.

10. Success in bargaining may depend on the strength of a number of variables, including the size of region, the ethnic/cultural composition of the region's population compared to that of core elites, the relative location of the region in terms of distance from the core and proximity to international frontiers, the unitary or federal structure of the government, and political finesse.

11. The most impressive evidence comes from a Swedish study by Gunnar Törnqvist, *Contact Systems and Regional Development* (Lund Studies in

Geography, Ser. B. Human Geography No. 35. Lund: C. W. K. Gleerup, 1970). For the United States, a statistical study of non-production personnel in manufacturing similarly suggests that locational separation between managerial and production functions exists, and that the former tend to be found in the larger, more rapidly growing metropolitan areas. See Esther Emiko Uyehara, *Production and Non-Production Employment in Manufacturing. A Comparative Analysis of Metropolitan Areas* (Master's thesis, School of Architecture and Urban Planning, UCLA, 1972).

12. Empirical evidence supporting a concept of nodal city is found in Thomas M. Stanback, Jr., and Richard V. Knight, *The Metropolitan Economy* (New York: Columbia University Press, 1970), *passim.*

13. I am assuming a strong connection—still to be demonstrated mathematically between Brian Berry's model of the evolution of city size distributions and Jeffrey Williamson's model of the evolution of regional inequalities of income. Williamson argues that regional income diverges from the mean during the early stages of economic development (analogous to the emergence of urban primacy under the first impacts of development) but subsequently, if gradually, converges as development proceeds (analogous to Berry's approximation to a lognormal distribution of city sizes). An explicit spatial mapping of these two processes had not yet been acomplished, however. For Berry, see footnote 6. Williamson's model was published as "Regional Inequality and the Process of National Development," *Economic Development and Cultural Change,* Part II (July 1965), pp. 3–45.

14. For India, Brian Berry has found four core regions of approximately equal influence and through which India's space economy appears to be organized. They are based, respectively, on Bombay, Delhi, Calcutta, and Madras. See Fig. 3 in Berry, "City Size and Economic Development," *op. cit.*, p. 121.

15. The strongest case, both theoreticaly and empirically, for the stability of the spatial and size distributions of urban systems comes from J. R. Lasuén, "Multi-Regional Economic Development. As Open System Approach," in Torston Hägerstrand and Antoni R. Kuklinski (eds), *Information Systems for Regional Development* (Lund Studies in Geography, Ser. B. Human Geography, No. 37. Lund: C. W. K. Gleerup, 1971), pp. 169–211. His findings are supported for the People's Republic of China by Yuan-Li Wu, *The Spatial Economy of Communist China. A Study of Industrial Location and Transportation* (New York: Frederick A. Praeger, 1967).

16. The starting point for the study of the spatial diffusion of innovations is Torsten Hägerstrand, *Innovation Diffusion as a Spatial Process* (Chicago: The University of Chicago Press, 1967. Original in Swedish, 1953). A comprehensive annotated bibliography of spatial innovation diffusion studies through 1968 has been compiled by Lawrence A. Brown, *Diffusion Processes and Location. A Conceptual Framework and Bibliography* (Bibliography Series no.4. Regional Science Research Institute, Philadelphia, 1968). The relation of spatial diffusion processes to economic development is worked out by Allan R. Pred, *Behavior and Location. Foundations for a Geographic and Dynamic Location Theory,* Part II (Lund Studies in Geography, Ser. B. Human Geography, No. 28. Lund: C W.

K. Gleerup, 1969), chapter 4, and by John Friedmann, "A Generalized Theory of Polarized Development," in Niles Hansen (ed), *Growth Centers in Regional Economic Development* (New York: The Free Press, 1972). Lausén's study (see footnote 15) is also relevant here, as is Edgar S. Dunn's pathbreaking study, *Economic and Social Development. A Process of Social Learning* (Baltimore: The Johns Hopkins Press, 1971). The basic reference for innovation diffusion studies generally is Everett M. Rogers, *Communication and Innovations. A Cross-Cultural Approach* (Second Edition. New York: The Free Press, 1971).

17. Allan R. Pred, "Large-City Interdependence and the Preelectronic Diffusion of Innovations in the U.S.," *Geographical Analysis*, 3 (1971), pp. 165–81. The more complete formulation of this model is presented in an unpublished manuscript by the same author, "Interurban Information Circulation, Organizations and the Development Process of Systems of Cities" (Department of Geography, University of California, Berkeley, 1972).

18. Everett M. Rogers, *op. cit.*, p. 27.

19. To make this proposition true, population size must be standardized for education and possibly also for income.

20. Fascinating data in support of this hypothesis have been brought together by Toshio Sanuki, "The City in Informational Society," *Area Development in Japan*, 3 (1970), pp. 9–23. Sanuki's study is frustrating, however, because he does not reveal the basis of his calculations.

21. Everett M. Rogers, *op. cit.*, p. 178. See also Edgar S. Dunn, Jr., *op. cit.*, and Allan R. Pred, *op. cit.*

22. Everett M. Rogers, *op. cit.*, p. 196.

23. J. R. Lasuén, *op. cit.*, p. 191.

24. Brian J. L. Berry and Elaine Neils, "Location, Size, and Shape of Cities as Influenced by Environmental Factors: the Urban Environment Writ Large," in Harvey S. Perloff (ed), *The Quality of the Urban Environment. Resources for the Future* (Baltimore: The Johns Hopkins Press, 1969), ch. 8.

25. Antoni Kuklinski and Ricardo Petrella (eds), *Growth Poles and Regional Policies* (The Hague: Mouton, 1972); and Antoni Kuklinski (ed), *Growth Poles and Growth Centers in Regional Planning* (The Hague: Mouton, 1972).

26. T. G. McGee, "Têtes de ponts et enclaves. Le probleme urbain et le processus d'urbanisation dans l'Asie du Sud-Est depuis 1945," *Tiers Monde*, XII, 45 (1971), pp. 115–14; Clifford Geertz, *Peddlers and Princes, Social Change and Economic Modernization in Two Indonesian Towns* (Chicago: Chicago University Press, 1963); and Allen E. Goodman, "The Political Implications of Urban Development in Southeast Asia: The 'Fragment' Hypothesis," *Economic Development and Cultural Change*, 20, 1 (Oct. 1971), pp 117–30.

27. Robert A. Levine, *Dreams and Deeds: Achievement Motivation in Nigeria* (Chicago: University of Chicago Press, 1966).

28. Everett E. Hagen, *On the Theory of Social Change* (Homewood, Ill.: The Dorsey Press, 1962), ch. 15.

29. Seymour Martin Lipset, "Values and Enterpreneurship in the Americas," chapter 3 in *Revolution and Counter-Revolution* (Rev. ed., New York: Anchor Books, 1970).

30. William John Hanna and Judith Lynn Hanna, *Urban Dynamics in Black Africa* (Chicago: Aldine-Atherton, 1971), p. 109.
31. *Ibid.*, p. 111.
32. For an excellent recent discussion of dualism and its consequences for development, see Hans W. Singer, "A New Approach to the Problems of the Dual Society in Developing Countries," *International Social Development Review*, 3 (1971), pp. 23–31.
33. Aníbal Quijano, "The Urbanization of Society in Latin America," *Economic Bulletin for Latin America*. 13, 2 (1968), pp. 76–93. This article is not signed. However, it follows in general outline a paper by the same author, "Dependencia, Cambio Social, y Urbanización en Latinoamerica," *Cuadernos de Desarrollo Urbano-Regional*, 6 (March 1968), Santiago (CIDU, Universidad Catolica de Chile).
34. Jorge Hardoy, "Urban Land Policies and Land Use Control Measures in Cuba" (Report for the United Nations Centre for Housing, Building and Planning, 1970).
35. Eric J. Hobsbawm, "Peru: The Peculiar 'Revolution' ", *The New York Review of Books*, December 16, 1971, pp. 29ff
36. See, for example, the extremely detailed study of new colonization along the Belém-Brasília Highway by Orlando Valverde and Catharina Vergolino Dias, *A Rodovia Belém-Brasília* (Rio de Janeiro: Fundaçao IBGE, 1967).
37. For one of the most concise statements on the 'internal colonization' effects of the government's gigantic road building program, see Armando D. Mendes, "Um Projecto Para a Amazônia" (unpublished paper, Univ. Federal do Para, December 1971).
38. T. G. McGee, *op. cit.*
39. Marcos J. Mamalakis, "The Theory of Sectoral Clashes," *Latin American Research Review*, IV, 3 (1969), pp. 9–46. In the same issue, see articles on Mexico by Barraza and Argentina by Merkx.
40. E. A. J. Johnson, *The Organization of Space in Developing Countries* (Cambridge, Mass.: Harvard University Press, 1970).
41. James F. Guyot, "Creeping Urbanism in Malaysia," in Robert T. Dalaud (ed.), *Comparative Urban Research. The Administration and Politics of Cities* (Beverly Hills, Cal.: Sage Publications, 1969), ch. 4.
42. Ivo D. Duchacek, *Comparative Federalism. The Territorial Dimension of Politics* (New York: Holt, Rinehart, and Winston, 1970).
43. T. J. D. Fair, G. Murdoch, and H. M. Jones, *Development in Swaziland* (Johannesburg, Witwatersrand University Press, 1969). Also, L. P. Green and T. J. D. Fair, *Development in Africa. A Study in Regional Analysis with Special Reference to Southern Africa* (Johannesburg: Witwatersrand University Press, 1969).
44. For Yugoslavia, see Ivo Barbarovic, *Regional Development Policies in Socialist Yugoslavia* (Unpublished Master in Regional Planning Thesis, Department of City and Regional Planning, Harvard University, 1966). For India, the concept of regional competition emerges from a study by Brian J. L. Berry, *Essays on Commodity Flows and the Spatial Structure of the Indian Economy* (Department of Geography Research Paper No. 111, The University of Chicago, 1966).
45. For a descriptive account of the political system in Chile, see Federico G. Gil, *The Political System of Chile* (Boston: Houghton Mifflin Co., 1966),

and James Petras, *Politics and Social Forces in Chilean Development* (Berkeley: University of California Press, 1969). Of particular value for an analysis of subnational development is Peter S. Cleaves, *Development Processes in Chilean Local Government* (Institute of International Studies, University of California, Berkeley, Politics of Modernization Series, No. 6, 1969), and John Friedmann (ed.), *Contribuciónes a las Políticas Urbana, Regional, y Habitacional* (Santiago: Universidad Catolica de Chile, Centro Interdisciplinario de Desarrollo Urbano-Reginal, 1970, with contributions by Francis Earwaker, Rene Eyhéralde, Charles Frankenhoff, Ralph Gakenheimer, John Miller, Walter Stöhr, and Francisco Vázquez. For Marxist views of Chilean Development, see André Gunder Frank, *Capitalism and Underdevelopment in Latin America. Historical Studies of Chile and Brazil* (New York: Monthly Review Press, 1967), and Dale L. Johnson, "The National and Progressive Bourgeoisie in Chile," in James D. Cockroft, André Gunder Frank, and Dale L. Johnson (eds.), *Dependence and Underdevelopment. Latin America's Political Economy* (New York: Anchor books, 1972).

46. An ironic comment on the politics of local government in Chile comes from Peter S. Cleaves, *op. cit.*, pp. 13–14:

> According to the Constitution, *alcaldes* or mayors are elected by the regidors from among themselves, except in the case of cities of over 100,000 inhabitants, where the president appoints an alcade. There is no constitutional stipulation that the presidential appointee must be a member of the elected municipal body. In 1969, there were thirteen cities in Chile with populations of over 100,000. However, since the Chilean Congress has avoided updating reapportionment since the 1930 census, alcades are appointed in only three cities: Santiago, Valparaíso, and Viña del Mar. Despite the low population of Viña in 1930, it was added to the list to facilitate tax supervision of its lucrative gambling casino.

47. Cleaves, *op. cit.*, Table 4.
48. *Ibid.*, p. 25.
49. *Ibid.*, p. 31.
50. Mariano Valle, *Planning Regional Development in Chile, Achievements and Perspectives* (MIT, SPURS, unpublished MS, 1969), and *The Planning Process in Chile* (MIT, SPURS, unpublished MS, 1970).
51. Public investments in Santiago increased from an average of 21.5 percent in the period 1960–64 to 31.5 in 1965–69. In the all-important housing and education sectors, the Metropolitan Zone of Santiago received 40.1 and 53.6 percent of all public investments in 1969, for a population that represented little more than one-third of the national total. As a result of these policies, Santiago had accummulated nearly one-half of Chile's regional product by 1970, over an area comprising only 2 percent of the national territory. See Sergio Boisier, *Polos de Desarrollo: Hipotesis y Políticas. Estudio de Bolivia, Chile, y Peru* (United Nations Institute for Social Development, Geneva, Report No. 72.1, January 1972), Tables 9, 17, and 18.
52. The study of *la marginalidad* has occupied leading sociologists in Latin America for a number of years. The literature is surveyed by José Nun (Instituto Torcuato di Tella) in an article appearing in *Revista Latinoamericana de Sociología* (1969). The exact location of this reference is not available to me at present.

53. Cited from Cleaves, *op. cit.*, p. 43.
54. John Friedmann, *Urbanization, Planning, and National Development, Op. cit.*, chapter 5, table 3.
55. William Alonso, "Problems, Purposes, and Implicit Policies for a National Strategy of Urbanization" (Working Paper no. 158, Institute of Urban and Regional Development, University of California, Berkeley, August 1971).

7
Urban Bias in Regional Development

Masahiko Honjo, one of Japan's premier urban planners, had successfully led the United Nations Center for Regional Development (UNCRD) in Nagoya, Japan. Over the course of a decade he had helped to raise this modest research and training institute to a rank of worldwide renown. When he stepped down from his post as director in 1981, his many friends and colleagues decided to honor him with a Festschrift. This essay was included in the collection and is dedicated to Honjo's great humanitarian spirit.

Written ten years after the preceding paper on the spatial organization of power, this essay also marked a turning point for me. For several years I had worked as a consultant to UNCRD and, in connection with my work, had made a number of extensive trips throughout Asia, from South Korea to Iran. It was on these trips that I first grasped the fundamental reality of the region. Seventy-five percent of Asia's two billion people were rural, and their numbers were increasing. The continent's economic development had therefore to be understood as essentially a rural problem: how to improve productivity and well-being among the impoverished rural masses.

My paper was intended as a footnote to Michael Lipton's 1977 essay Why Poor People Stay Poor. *All my life, I had worked with analytical models of urban spatial systems. In Asia, and more specifically at UNCRD, I learned about village-centered agrarian systems.*

To help focus my rural investigations, I coined the term agropolitan, *a combined form of agriculture and polis (see chapters 8 and 9). As with so much of my work at the time,* agropolis *was both a spatial and a political concept, and reflected my preoccupations with territorial thinking. But to elevate politics over economics seemed strange to most of my colleagues, trained as they were in the dismal science. So strange, in fact, did the agropolitan concept appear to them that they unanimously labelled it utopian. For the majority, rural-development thinking continued to be guided by considerations of growth efficiency; agropolitan development, was dismissed as a chimera, the illusion of a misguided do-gooder. A successful development of agriculture, argued economists, would have to be based on Green Revolution technologies and large-scale capital investment in the form of irrigation, machinery, and transport.*

Urban-biased thinking focussed on manufacturing industry and its growth. But a rural development would have to center on people. It would have to be a development "as if people mattered." To many experts this appeared an uncongenial prospect.

Several years ago, Michael Lipton of Sussex University's Institute of Development Studies wrote a major critique of prevailing development ideology and practice. In *Why Poor People Stay Poor,*[1] he charged the makers of modern development doctrine with "urban bias." By this he meant that they had given systematic preference to urban over rural investments far beyond what was required by the logic of efficiency and equity.

To grasp the full meaning of this distorted preference, it will be helpful to distinguish between basic theories, prescriptions and actual policies of development. Clearly interrelated, each of these facets of development is the responsibility of different actors working under different conditions, with very different ends in view.

Development theories—the handiwork of professors—concern the question of how the real value of national production may be raised faster than the increase in population. This is the classic formulation, and it is the only one on which serious theoretical work has, in fact, been done.[2] The ongoing theoretical discourse involves a number of assumptions and measurements of structural change.[3] Thus, it is generally taken for granted that economic development involves a shift in production and employment from primary, chiefly agricultural, to manufacturing and construction activities which are said to be more "dynamic" and "productive."[4] In parallel, it is assumed that this sectoral shift will be accompanied by a change in ecological patterns, with the formation of an integrated "system of cities" and the rapid urbanization of the entire population. It is cities which are now identified as "dynamic, radiating, technical innovations and development impulses" to a countryside that, according to this version, remains forever passive.[5]

Policy prescriptions are the responsibility of planners. Necessarily based on theory, they must be adapted in practice to existing possibilities. Theory insists on capital accumulation as the central process of development, and this immediately raises a question about the potential sources of the investment surplus. Two domestic sources—in addition to foreign aid—are usually identified: agricultural production and export earnings. This perception leads to the inevitable conclusion that "it is only the imposition of compulsory levies on the agricultural sector itself which enlarges the supply of 'savings' in the required sense for economic development."[6]

International advisers on national planning have accordingly stressed the augmentation of investment and production in export-oriented sectors and, at the same time, encouraged heavy capital outlays (involving foreign exchange) for urban infrastructure, such as port and airport facilities, interurban highways, telephone systems, water and sewage facilities, industrial estates, urban hospitals, universities, etc. Proposals for rural areas have usually been limited to large-scale irrigation projects. Rural savings, on the other hand, were to be mobilized through a price structure favourable to urban consumers and a banking system that would capture any remaining surplus for lucrative urban deployment. In addition, there would be always the unceasing flow of peasants to the city which, from an economist's perspective, involved the urban transfer of so-called human capital.[7]

Finally, we have to look at actual policies. These tend to be influenced by (a) the political context, (b) the national leadership, and (c) the stock of ideas in good currency. We have already seen that none of the "ideas in good currency" advocate rural development as a priority in the allocation of state funds, and political pressures typically come from bourgeois interests with direct access to the decision centres of the state. Given this constellation of forces, national leadership inclines to take the path of least resistance, yielding to the multiple temptations of "urban bias."[8] As a result, in nearly all parts of the world, agricultural production and rural development absorb only a small fraction of the national investment.

According to Lipton, urban bias has had counterproductive results. It has led to the persistence of massive poverty:

> Poor countries could have raised income per person since 1945 much faster than they did, if allocative urban bias had been reduced. I shall show that many of the resources allocated by state action to city-dwellers would have earned a higher return in rural areas; that private individuals, furthermore, were indirectly induced by administrative decisons and price distortions to transfer from countryside to town their own resources, thereby reducing the social (but increasing the private) rate of return upon those as well; and that ultimately, inadequate inputs of rural resources substantially reduced even the efficient use of urban resources. But so what? Unprecedented growth in poor countries has proved unable to make a major impact on the conditions of the poor people who live there. A reduction of urban bias might speed growth even further; but

why should that help the poor any more than past accelerations of growth?

The reason is that allocations biased townwards with respect to the efficiency norm are almost certainly heavily biased . . . with respect to the equity norm. By reallocating capital, skills and administrative attention from city to countryside, we can hardly help reducing the inequality of incomes; countrymen start much poorer than townsmen, share their income somewhat more equally, and are likelier to owe their poverty to conditions curable by income from work.

By shifting from city to country, a poor nation almost certainly relieves poverty in the short term . . .[9]

Lipton's theoretical arguments are couched in the antiseptic jargon of economists and somehow manage not to look threatening. The real results of urban bias, however, present a much more dismal picture.

Growing food deficits.

Urban bias has created a situation where more and more countries, once self-sufficient in food, are obliged to import large and growing amounts of staple foods to prevent or at least ameliorate mass starvation. For instance, in 1976, food comprised 28 per cent of all merchandise imports in India (compared to 21 per cent in 1960). Sri Lanka's food imports soared to 36 per cent and Bangladesh's reached 42 per cent.[10]

More serious is the long-term outlook for the world. The best available estimates are shown in Table 7.1.[11]

The expected shortfalls in food supplies, when projected to the end of the century, are ominous, and nowhere more so than in Africa where demand is expected to triple with respect to 1970, in sharp contrast to only a doubling of production. Unless food production is

Table 7.1.
Median Growth Rates
(Percent per annum)

	Food Demand		Production
	1970–85	1985–2000	1961–73
Africa	3.8	4.0	2.5
Far East	3.4	3.3	2.4
Latin America	3.6	3.5	2.9
Near East	4.0	4.0	3.1
Developing Market Economies	3.6	3.6	2.6
Asian Centrally Planned Economies	3.1	2.7	2.6

dramatically stepped up, the world gap between annual grain demand and production in the developing market economies may well reach 171 million tons by the year 2000.[12] This would be equivalent to 44 per cent of the actual 1970 consumption!

Increasing external dependency

This is of a threefold nature. First, there is the direct dependency of the country's population on the variable fortunes of export receipts. Second, in view of the insufficiency of exports, there is the country's dependency on external loans. In some cases, these have risen to such a volume relative to productive capacity, that the country becomes virtually a ward of the international financial community. In 1977, for example, The World Bank reported twenty-five countries with an external debt greater than 35 percent of GNP, ranging from the Ivory Coast and the Sudan (35 percent) to Egypt (69 percent), Somalia (93 percent), and Mauritania (112 percent).[13] If food deficits should indeed get worse, as is expected, countries which have no substantial oil producing capacity will either have to starve, receive massive and continuing grants-in-aid of food, or see their fledgling industrial economy come to a standstill, as tragic choices are forced between GNP and human survival. Third, there is the political power which food surplus countries, such as the United States, are able to exercise over the destitute, enlisting their aid in the global ideological conflict that continues to escalate.

Growing urban problems

"Urban bias" translates into rural underdevelopment. Because the chances for survival seem somehow better in the city, mass emigration from rural areas becomes everywhere the norm. But this invasion of cities, unrelated to the number of available jobs, must somehow be accommodated, and it is in the "informal" sector that the majority of migrants manage to eke out a living. Huge urban investments are nevertheless required to maintain the population. Its physical concentration, visibility, and capacity for political action gives it a clear advantage over the more numerous but dispersed rural households left behind. Yet, additional state expenditures, say, to build housing or expand educational facilities, only reinforce "urban bias" and accelerate the number of migrants bound for the city.[14]

Growing inequalities and revolutionary potential

"Urban bias" implies greater inequalities in levels of living, not only between rural and urbanized regions, which is self-evident, but also in the social division of income. It is precisely the countries which have made the furthest progress in urban-based industrialization that display the greatest social inequities. In Venezuela and Mexico, for instance, 35 and 37 percent respectively of household incomes are held by the top ten percent of households; in Turkey and Malaysia, the corresponding fraction is 40 percent; and in Brazil it rises to more than 50 per cent.[15]

The combination of growing inequalities, mass starvation, the deterioration of urban social and physical environments, and destitution among the masses of rural and urban workers results in an explosive mixture that spells continuing trouble and unrest among the population. The state's response to this is nearly always more repression, the installation of military regimes, and the expenditure of huge sums for internal security.

The global outlook, then, is bleak. A few favoured countries may in the end pull through and accomplish an urban-based development, even though great poverty may continue to exist alongside the economy's successful incorporation into the international division of labour. But the bulk of the world's low-income population can almost certainly look forward to a future in which development in any meaningful sense will remain an elusive goal.[16]

Urban Bias in Regional Policy

Properly understood, Lipton's argument is a regional one. "Urban bias" favours city regions over rural peripheries, and the relevant criterion is the residence of populations.[17] It follows that we should be able to discover in the literature on regional development and planning a reflection of "urban bias."

The earliest regional planning literature in the "new style," following the Second World War, was a simple application of the nodal principle as a device for ordering regional space.[18] Known as the "growth-centre approach," it was further developed by the present author in his study of regional policy in Venezuela.[19] The idea was to use directed and carefully scaled urban investments for achieving a greater regional "balance" in the appropriate indicators of development. Except as a reflection of urban development, however, agriculture did not receive close attention. Ten years later, the second edition of the popular collection of readings, *Regional Development Policy*, failed to include any mention of rural development, a point which the authors regretted but did nothing to remove.[20] Nor is Harry Richardson's otherwise excellent text on regional economics an improvement.

"Agriculture" is referred to in only four out of 289 pages of text, and the word "rural" doesn't appear in the index at all.[21] Finally, if we look at Asian contributions, such as Koichi Mera's carefully constructed essay on basic human needs,[22] we discover an explicit rejection of rural development—a policy he regards as merely redistributive—in favour of a hard-nosed accelerated growth policy based on massive core region investments in infrastructure and modern industries.

A special case is the interesting volume by Rondinelli and Ruddle, *Urbanization and Rural Development*.[23] The authors go further than almost anyone in advocating a regional approach to rural development. In the end, however, theirs is like the rest, an approach which focuses on the urban hierarchy in promoting rural development. The only difference is that Rondinelli and Ruddle follow the hierarchy down to the village level where it interfaces with the farming economy. In this, they follow the general schema first proposed by E. A. J. Johnson,[24] an economic historian with years of experience in India, who was captivated by the geometry of central place theory in the geographical literature, adapting it to planning uses.[25]

Reviewing this experience, we may say that the history of regional planning doctrines is peculiarly devoid of rural consciousness. Its answer to the underdevelopment of rural peripheries is simply . . . more urbanization—scarcely a satisfactory solution.

An explanation of this lopsidedness must unquestionably be sought in the "urban bias" of the development doctrines we have already discussed (see Chart 6.1). But "bias" also obtains from within the field of regional studies, beginning with location theory. The works of Christaller,[26] Lösch[27] and Isard,[28] all concerned the location of urban-based activities. And the only modern studies of agricultural location,[29] were conveniently ignored by planners. The great discoveries of the 1960s concerned the structure and stability of urban systems and their relationship to economic growth.[30]

In all these cases, theory tended to prescribe the appropriate doctrine. The literature from which regional planners drew their principal inspiration was entirely devoted to the structure of space as defined by its urban nodes. This essentially functional view of space facilitated the construction of models that were on the whole consistent with the assumptions of marginal economics, allocative efficiency, and the spatial division of labour. These models assumed the free movement of capital and labour, though the latter was largely constrained to the national space. Equity questions were neatly separated from the overriding preoccupation with economic growth, and could be dealt with at some future date, when the economy had reached a certain level of abundance. Growth efficiency pre-empted both theory and policy advice.

To assist the reader through the maze of the dominant regional paradigm, brought into relation with the mainstream theory of capitalist development, the following model has been constructed.

A brief comment may be ventured. To the extent that regional policies consistent with the model have actually been carried out (e.g., Brazil; Venezuela; Mexico), they have failed to bring about regional "balance" even when they were successful in achieving the integration of national economic space on a basis of uneven development.[31] This critique has been generalized in an important paper by Walter Stöhr and Franz Tödtling.[32] Following an extensive literature review, the authors summarize their findings (references have been left out):

1. Spread-effects from growth centres were usually smaller than expected, or less than backwash effects and therefore had a negative net result on the hinterland. They were narrowly limited in geographical extent, usually restricted to the commuting area, often as a function of the size of the centre.
2. Increases in income of lower-order centres or rural areas create strong income multipliers in higher-order centres but not the other way around. They seem to move upward rather than downward within the urban hierarchy.
3. In the context of policies for broad spatial development it is difficult to justify growth-centre policies for lagging areas due to their lack of spread-effects down the urban hierarchy or from the growth centre outwards to a broader hinterland.[33]

In short, "if functional change is given priority over territorial integrity, outright integration will tend to increase initial spatial disparities."[34] For a little while, the end of growth efficiency may be served in this way; but in the longer term, the expected results are mass starvation, increased external dependency, economic and regional inequalities, urban discontent, and social revolution.

The Search for an Alternative Regional Policy

What is the alternative to "outright integration" from a regional perspective? The serious critique of development policy began over a decade ago. Probing studies sponsored by the International Labour Office led to new concepts, such as "redistribution with growth" and "basic needs." Another loosely grouped set of ideas, evolved under

Chart 6.1
The Actual Model of National Economic Development

Economic Development Theory	Corresponding Regional Strategies and Policies
1. *Development* Seen as a global historical process of industrialization and modernization	Incorporation of all the regions of a country in the general development process
2. *Unit of Analysis* The national state	The region as a subsystem of the national economy: administrative and planning regions
3. *Analytical-normative Criterion* Increase in the rate of GDP/cap (i.e., increase in GDP greater than the rate of increase in population). None of the development theories include as criteria of equal importance, full employment, more equal income distribution, the satisfaction of basic necessities, etc. It is assumed that these criteria can be satisfied once the economy has "matured"	Increase in regional product or income per capita, calculated in relation to the national average. Frequently, this criterion is supplemented by physical and social indicators. All indicators are related to population.
4. *Hegemonic Institution* The market economy (material incentives and private accumulation of surplus)	IDEM.
5. *Dominant System* The world economy; international division of labour: exports of raw materials and simple manufactured commodities having a light content of direct labour; importation of food products, oil, machinery, skilled (specialized) services, luxury goods, etc.	IDEM. Nevertheless, the regional economy tends to be analyzed as a subsystem of the *national* economy (interregional division of labour; comparative regional advantage); heavy investments in transport and communication; transport pricing policies favouring peripheral regions
6. *Role of the State* To maintain political stability and so permit the smooth functioning of the market economy; investment in economic infrastructure; investments in social infrastructure (reproduction of the labour force, according to the needs of capital); transfer payments to capital; protectionist policies designed to maximize profits from domestic production	Integration of the national territory through the development of interregional transport and communications systems; incorporation of the region into the national and international economies; reduction of existing interregional inequalities in accordance with formal development criteria (see 3 above). Institutionalization of regional planning as a device for the administration control of local developments
7. *Mechanics of the Development Process* Continuous pressure to increase the productivity of labour, land, and capital through the transfer of technologies, economics of scale, scientific management, and constant innovation in products and methods of production	Establishing decentralized scientific research institutions; establishing specialized courses (e.g., scientific management) in regional universities

8. *Basic Economic Process*
Accumulation of capital: increase in the rate of domestic savings from 5 to 25 per cent; net transfer of resources from rural to urban activities

Establishment of Regional Development Banks to capture savings and lend on productive activities in depressed regions

9. *Principal Actor*
Individual or institutional entrepreneurs assume the risks of innovation and investment, organize the "factors" of production, markets, etc.

Establishment of Regional Development Corporations (the State as entrepreneur); technical and financial assistance to small-scale manufacturing concerns and agro-industry, mobilization of provincial elites (commercial and industrial) into Committees of Regional Development

10. *Sectoral Changes*
From small-scale subsistence agriculture to agro-industry and light manufacturing to heavy industry and associated services

To accelerate industrialization through the development of basic resources (e.g., hydro-energy); state investments in key industries and urban infrastructure, including industrial estates; capital (location) subsidies

11. *Spatial Changes*
High rate of urbanization, expulsion of rural labour, population concentration in large cities; the movement of labour obeys the same principles as the remaining "factors of production": it is in search of profitable employment (maximizing expected life-time earnings)

Contradictory policies in relation to the urbanization process (acceleration, deceleration); spatial programming of regional growth poles and growth centres; intention to articulate a "complete" urban system; incorporate rural markets into the emerging urban economy through the development of transport links; comprehensive rural development in a few urban-based areas

12. *Psychosocial Changes*
Modernization: work ethic, achievement motivation, functional rather than ascriptive relations, shift to nuclear family, rational calculation, competition, etc.

IDEM. To facilitate the penetration of urban settlements by mass communication media, for the most part controlled by private interests

13. *Dynamics of the Process*
Dynamic equilibrium (leads and lags)

"Polarized" development: so-called spread-effects larger than backwash effects

14. *Happiness*
Increase in individual consumption; free economic choice

IDEM.

different sponsorship, focused on "eco-development," (Ignacy Sachs) and still more elusively on "another development" (Dag Hammarskjöld Foundation), and helped popularize such notions as appropriate technology, self-management, and integrated development. Alongside these attempted reformulations of orthodoxy, there was an outpouring of Marxist critiques centering on "uneven development" (Samir Amin), the role of transnational corporations in the formation of the global economy (Osvaldo Sunkel; Immanuel Wallerstein; Barnet and Müller; and Fröbel, Heinrichs and Kreye), Gunder Frank's paradoxical formulation of the "development of underdevelopment," "unequal exchange" (Arghiri Emmanuel), "neo-imperialism (Ranjit Sau), and "dependency theory" (Tamás Szentes; Susantha Goonatilake; and Colin Leyes).[35]

Much of this rethinking of basic development theory took place in the shadows of the cultural revolution in China, news of which had by this time begun to filter into the West. Of particular interest was Mao Tse-tung's 1956 speech "On the Ten Great Relationships," which first appeared in an English edition by Stuart Schram,[36] and subsequently in a slightly modified official version.[37] Mao's speech outlined his views on the Chinese road to development or, as Suzanne Paine put the matter, [38] "the means to industrialization with rising mass consumption." The text is of fundamental importance for an understanding of the Chinese road to development. For our purposes here, its significence derives from its explicit rejection of "urban bias."

> The emphasis in our country's construction (writes Mao) is on heavy industry. The production of the means of production must be given priority, that's settled. But it definitely does not follow that the production of the means of subsistence, especially grain, can be neglected. Without enough food and other daily necessities, it would be impossible to provide for the workers in the first place, and then what sense would it make to talk about developing heavy industry? Therefore, the relationship between heavy industry on the one hand and light industry and agriculture on the other must be properly handled . . .

> The problem now facing us is that of continuing to adjust properly the ratio between investment in heavy industry on the one hand and in agriculture and light industry on the other in order to bring about a greater development of the latter. Does this mean that heavy industry is no longer primary? No. It still is, it still claims the emphasis in our investment. But the proportion for agriculture and light industry must be somewhat increased.

> What will be the results of this increase? First, the daily needs of the people will be better satisfied, and, second, the accumulation of capital will be speeded up so that we can develop heavy industry with greater

and better results. Heavy industry can also accumulate capital, but, given our present economic condition, light industry and agriculture can accumulate more and faster . . .

There are now two possible approaches to our development of heavy industry: one is to develop agriculture and light industry less, and the other is to develop them more. In the long run, the first approach will lead to a smaller and slower development of heavy industry, or at lest will put it on a less solid foundation, and when the overall account is added up a few decades hence, it will not prove to have been paid. The second approach will lead to a greater and faster development of heavy industry and, since it ensures the livelihood of the people, it will lay a more solid foundation for the development of heavy industry.[39]

In the Western development community, new voices faintly echoed Mao's words of twenty years ago. Perhaps more emphasis should have been given to the development of rural areas, they said.[40] But how was this to be done? The central importance of land reform had long been admitted.[41] And even though skeptics remained,[42] comprehensiveness was heralded as the new salvation.[43] After the ambivalent experience with the "green revolution,"[44] new hopes were being raised about decentralized planning and poverty-focused development.[45] Of special interest in this connection was an extended essay by Wahidul Haque, Niranjan Melita, Anisur Rahman, and Poona Wignaraja.[46] After the careful study of a number of Asian cases, the authors introduce a modified version of the Maoist model of rural development as the most consistent with the requirements of Asian conditions. Significantly, they labelled their approach "a strategy of microlevel development."

Just as the "urban bias" model of development planning had come out of the experience with Latin American industrialization,[47] so comprehensive rural development drew on the Asian context where the rural question simply could not be ignored.[48] It is not surprising therefore that much of the new thinking about regional development should have been brought together in the United Nations Centre for Regional Development in Nagoya, Japan, which was in constant touch with the realities of development planning throughout the Asian and Pacific region. Under the visionary leadership of Masahiko Honjo, the Centre produced a large number of empirical studies that would begin the challenging task of reconstructing regional doctrine. Once again, and quite independently of the work by Haque and others, the idea of microlevel development imposed itself as the most suited to Asian conditions. The real problem was how to link microstrategies with national planning for development.[49]

Before new ground could be broken, ideas contributed had to be carefully scrutinized in practice. This was done over a period of years, involving researchers from many institutions throughout Asia and culminated in a conference on growth poles and regional development.[50] The major theoretical contribution to this conference was an essay by the editors of the proceedings which called for models of regional development tested against the Asian experience.[51]

Their essay was still within the framework of "urban bias," however. In the same volume, a first effort was also made to ask the question of how an accelerated programme of rural development might be organized.[52] The focus here was on so-called agropolitan districts (the microlevel once again) as the appropriate spatial unit, and it particularly stressed the political organization of these districts for a new kind of self-reliant development. Subsequent work by Lo, Salih, and Douglass[53] elaborated on this model, introducing selective regional closure as a strategy which challenged classical theories based on the interregional division of labour.[54] Selective closure, the authors believe, would allow historical regions to develop from within, based on their own understanding of the appropriate structure of economic relations. Although it was couched in the jargon of economists, it was essentially a *political* model. The hope was to articulate differences in regional structure and conceptions of the good life. "Closure" did not mean autarky, but would help protect weak, peripheral regions against their domination and ruthless exploitation by more powerful core region interests.

In a second paper on agropolitan development, Friedmann[55] elaborated on some of his earlier work, stressing the political dimensions of the concept.[56] (See Chapter 8)

Unfortunately, political approaches to development are not particularly welcome. Because they assume a different distribution of power, they challenge the existing structures. And since they are merely the writings of scholars, politicians can safely ignore them. Ralph Diaz put the matter in a nutshell. In regional planning, he said, "politics is taboo."[57]

Conclusion

Hard upon the heels of the badly tattered growth centre model, it is no doubt inappropriate to formulate yet another planning doctrine. Still, the process of critically thinking through the main alternatives has been instructive. We have discovered the importance of microlevel development; have reached a better appreciation of the critical relationships between cities and countryside; know about the inadequacies of the economists' approach that avoids the inherently political questions of power, access and participation; recognize the existence of historical regions, along with their right to political self-determination; have a better understanding of what is involved in joining top-down administrative to participatory local planning and the decisive role in this process of regional authorities. Compared to the compelling simplicities of the earlier theories and doctrines of development, the picture which emerges is more complex, elusive and less easily codifiable as doctrine.

Finally, we have come to realize that regional planning does not work independently of the global commitment to development. So long as "urban bias" continues to dominate national policy, microplanning in rural districts will remain a speculative abstraction. Only when national leadership decides to rectify the existing imbalance between rural and urban, and to give top priority to national self-sufficiency in food production and to the diminution of regional and social inequalities, will some of the recent ideas for regional rural development emerge from text books into practice. Here and there, some tentative beginnings are being made.[58]

Notes

1. M.Lipton, *Why Poor People Stay Poor: Urban Bias in World Development* (Cambridge, Mass.: Harvard University Press, 1977).
2. L. G. Reynolds, *Image and Reality in Economic Development* (New Haven: Yale University Press, 1977).
3. H. B. Chenery, *Structural Change and Development Policy* (World Bank Research Publication Series)(New York: Oxford University Press, 1980).
4. H. G. Chenery and M. Syrquin, *Patterns of Development, 1950–1970* (A World Bank Research Publiction)(New York: Oxford University Press, 1975).
5. In regard to these questions, the Soviet version of development theory is not very different from bourgeois economics. The emphasis is on industrialization, and the overall indicator of economic development—as in the West—is the gross national product. The major difference, perhaps, lies in the Soviet insistence on "proportionality" by which is meant a planned balance in production, including the balance between agriculture and industry. The overall thrust of the theory, however, concerns the structural transformation of agrarian into industrial economies. In this transformation, agriculture is seen as playing a distinctly secondary role; see, V. L. Tyagunnenko, ed., *Industrialization of Developing Countries* (Moscow: Progress Publishers, 1973); see also, J. Friedmann, "The Role of Cities in National Development" in *Urbanization, Planning, and National Development* (Beverly Hills, CA.: Sage Pub., 1973).
6. Nicolas Kaldor, cited in M. Lipton, *Why Poor People Stay Poor*, p. 64.
7. Since about 1975, there has been a renewal of interest in agricultural

primacy and rural development. This "new" doctrine has by no means been universally accepted, however, and least of all in practice; see B. F. Johnston and P. Kilby, *Agriculture and Structural Transformation: Economic Strategies in Late Developing Countries* (New York: Oxford University Press, 1975).

8. Another reason contributing to "urban bias" is the need of the political elites in the new states to centralize power and to use their hold on cities, as administrative centres, for controlling the peasant masses. This, of course, implies that cities will be favoured in the allocation process.

9. Lipton, *Why Poor People Stay Poor*, pp. 70–1.

10. World Bank, *World Development Report, 1979* (Washington, D.C., 1979), table 10.

11. P. R. Crosson and K. D. Frederick, *The World Food Situation* (Washington, D.C.: Resources for the Future, 1977), Table 5.

12. Ibid., p. 29.

13. World Bank, *World Development Report, 1979*, Table 15.

14. Ibid.

15. Ibid., Table 24.

16. This gloomy outlook is reinforced if one considers the likely course of events for the core countries of the global economy, with their slow rates of growth, high unemployment, and two-digit inflation.

17. Lipton, *Why Poor People Stay Poor*, pp. 60–3.

18. See L. Rodwin in J. Friedmann and W. Alonso, *Regional Development Planning: A Reader* (Cambridge, Mass.: M.I.T. Press, 1964).

19. J. Friedmann, *Regional Development Policy: A Case Study of Venezuela* (Cambridge, Mass.: M.I.T. Press, 1966).

20. J. Friedmann and W. Alonso, *Regional Policy: Readings in Theory and Applications* (Cambridge, Mass.: M.I.T. Press, 1975).

21. H.W. Richardson, *Regional Economics* (Urbana, Ill.: University of Illinois Press, 1979).

22. K. Mera, "Basic Human Needs Versus Economic Growth Approach for Coping with Rural Imbalances: An Evaluation Based on Relative Welfare," *Environment and Planning A* 11 (October 1979): 1129–46.

23. D.A. Rondinelli and K. Ruddle, *Urbanization and Rural Development: A Spatial Policy for Equitable Growth* (New York: Praeger, 1978).

24. E.A.J. Johnson, *The Organization of Space in Developing Countries* (Cambridge, Mass.: Harvard University Press, 1970).

25. For a recent application to India, see J. Singh, *Central Places and Spatial Organization in a Backward Economy: Gorakhpur Regions; A Study in Integrated Regional Development* (Gorakhpur: Uttar Bharat Bhoogol Parishad, 1979).

26. C.W. Baskin, "A Critique and Translation of Walter Christaller's 'Die Zentralen Oert in Süddeutschland' " (Ph.D. diss., University of Virginia, 1957).

27. A Lösch, *The Economics of Location* (New Haven: Yale Univesity Press, 1954).

28. W. Isard, *Location and Space Economy: A General Theory Relating to Industrial Location, Market Areas, Land Use, Trade and Urban Structures* (Boston: M.I.T. Press, 1956).

29. E.S. Dunn, *The Location of Agricultural Production* (Gainesville, Fla.:

University of Florida Press, 1954); and M. Chisholm, *Rural Settlement and Land Use* (London: Hutchinson University Library, 1962).

30. B.J.L. Berry, *Growth Centres in the American Urban System*, 2 vols. (Cambridge, Mass: Ballinger Pub. 1973); L.S. Bourne, *Urban Systems: Strategies for Regulation; A Comparison of Policies in Britain, Sweden, Australia and Canada* (London: Oxford University Press, 1975); L. S. Borne and J.W. Simmons, *Systems of Cities: Readings on Structure, Growth and Policy* (New York: Oxford University Press, 1978); and A. Pred, *City Systems in Advanced Economies: Past Growth, Present Processes, and Future Development Options* (New York: Wiley, 1977).

31. J. Friedmann, N. Gardels and A. Pennink, "The Politics of Space: Five Centuries of Regional Development in Mexico," *International Journal for Urban and Regional Research* (forthcoming).

32. W. Stöhr and F. Tödtling, "Spatial Equity: Some Antitheses to Current Regional Development Doctrine" in H. Folmer and J. Oosterhaven, eds., *Spatial Inequalities and Regional Development* (Boston: Martinus Nijhoff, 1979).

33. Ibid., p. 152.

34. Ibid.

35. J. Friedmann and C. Weaver, *Territory and Function: the Evolution of Regional Planning* (Berkeley: University of California Press, 1979), ch. 7.

36. S. Schram, ed., *Mao Tse-tung Unrehearsed* (London: Penguin, 1974).

37. T. Mao, "On the Ten Major Relationships" in *Selected Works of Mao Tse-tung* (Peking, Foreign Languages Press, 1977) 5: 284–307.

38. S. Paine, "Balanced Development: Maoist Conception and Chinese Practice," *World Development* 4 (No. 4, 1976): 278.

39. Ibid.: 285–6.

40. Johnston and Kilby, *Agriculture and Structural Transformation*.

41. D. Lehman, *Agrarian Reforms and Agrarian Reformism* (London: Faber and Faber, 1974); and World Bank, *Land Reform: Sector Policy Paper* (Washington, D.C., 1974).

42. V.W. Ruttan, "Integrated Rural Development Programmes: A Skeptical Perspective," *International Development Review* 17 (No. 4, 1975).

43. World Bank, *Rural Development: Sector Policy Paper* Washington, D.C., 1975); B. Higgins, "Welfare Economics and the Unified Approach to Development Planning" in A. Kuklinski, ed., *Social Issues in Regional Policy and Regional Planning* (The Hague: Mouton, 1977), pp. 91–114; A.T. Mosher, *Thinking About Rural Development*(New York: Argricultural Development Council, 1976); and R. Weitz, *Integrated Rural Development; the Rehovot Approach* (Publications on Regional Development; 28)(Rehovot, Israel: Rehovot Study Centre, 1979).

44. B. das Gupta, "India's Green Revolution," *Economic and Political Weekly* February 1977): 241–60; and K. Griffin, *The Political Economy of Agrarian Change: An Essay on the Green Revolution* (London: MacMillan, 1974).

45. D.G.R. Belshaw, "Decentralized Planning and Poverty Focused Rural Development: Intra-Regional Planning in Tanzania" (Reprint 81)(Norwich: School of Development Studies, University of East Anglia, 1979).

46. W. Hague, N. Mehta, A. Rahman and P. Wignaraja, "Toward a Theory of Rural Development," *Development Dialogue* (No. 2, 1977): 11–137

47. A. Hirschman, *The Strategy of Economic Development* (New Haven: Yale University Press, 1958); and Friedmann, *Regional Development Policy*.

48. African experiences are the basis for Uma Lele's important work on rural development; see U. Lele, *The Design of Rural Development: Lessons from Africa* (Baltimore: Johns Hopkins University Press, 1975).

49. M. Honjo, "Role of Government in Regional Development," *Regional Development Dialogue* (Spring 1980): 1–20.

50. Fu-chen Lo and Kamal Salih, eds., *Growth Pole Strategy and Regional Development: Asian Experiences and Alternative Approaches* (Oxford: Pergamon Press, 1978).

51. Fu-chen Lo and Kamal Salih, "Growth Poles and Regional Poles and Regional Policy in Open Dualistic Economies: Western Theory and Asian Reality" in their *Growth Pole Strategy and Regional Development*, pp. 243–70.

52. J. Friedmann and M. Douglass, "Agropolitan Development: Towards a New Strategy for Regional Planning in Asia" in Lo and Salih, eds., *Growth Pole Strategy and Regional Development*, pp. 163–92.

53. Fu-chen Lo, K. Salih and M. Douglass, *Uneven Development, Rural-Urban Transformation and Regional Development Alternatives in Asia* (Nagoya: UNCRD, 1978).

54. See also, Stöhr and Tödtling, "Spatial Equity," for employment of the same concept in their own prescriptive analysis.

55. J. Friedmann, "The Active Community: Towards a Political-Territorial Framework for Rural Development in Asia," *Regional Development Dialogue* 1 (Autumn 1980).

56. See also J. Friedmann, *Urban Communes, Self-Management, and the Reconstruction of the Local State* (Los Angeles: School of Architecture and Urban Planning, UCLA, 1980).

57. Independently of the work ongoing at UNCRD are the rural development studies produced at the Settlement Study Centre in Rehovot, Israel. See especially Weitz, *Integrated Rural Development;* and R. Diaz, "Comment," *Regional Development Dialogue* (Spring 1980); 17–8.

58. D. Ghai et al., eds., Overcoming Rural Underdevelopment. Proceedings of a Workshop on Alternative Agrarian systems and Rural Development, Arusha, Tanzania, 4–14 April 1979 (Geneva: ILO, 1979); K. Griffin, ed., "Capitalist and Socialist Agriculture in Asia," *World Development* Special Issue (April–May 1979); and Fu-chen Lo and Byung-Nak Song, *The Saemaul Undong Movement: The Korean Way of Rural Transformation* (Nagoya: UNCRD, 1979).

8
The Active Community:
Toward a Political-Territorial Framework
for Rural Development in Asia

*This essay is my most carefully argued statement of an alternative
approach to worldwide poverty. By the end of the 1970s, it had become
plain that mainstream developmental policies were not working. Latin
American economic growth had slowed to a crawl, and there was
massive capital flight from a number of Andean nations. The debt
crisis (accompanied by runaway inflation) had taken center stage in
the deliberations of politicians, policy analysts, and global financiers.
The African continent was going through its own turmoil of drought,
civil wars, anti-apartheid struggles, and political upheavals. Economically, most experts agreed, Africa had become a ward of the world.
In Asia, though there were a few bright spots, poor agrarian economies failed to accomplish the transition to a mass-consumption society
envisioned by Rostovian theorists. Iran, Afghanistan, Pakistan, Bangladesh, Sri Lanka, Indonesia, and the Philippines were all encounter-
ing major political difficulties, their economic growth blocked by
forces that seemed quite beyond their control.*

*This picture of almost unrelieved misery and pain, made worse by
relentless growth in the population, gave rise, primarily in Western
Europe, to an intellectual movement advocating an "alternative"
development emphasizing self-reliance, the satisfaction of basic
needs, mass participation of the population, and harmony with nature.
Although its proponents were not ignorant of the need for continued
capital accumulation, they rejected maximizing economic growth and
incorporation into the global division of labor as major policy objectives. These subversive ideas were sponsored and diffused by the
Swedish Dag Hammarskjöld Foundation and the Swiss-based International Foundation for Development Alternatives. Paradoxically,
while "the West" was seriously questioning the mainstream development paradigm for its failure to produce what was called meaningful
development, the Communist Party of China was seeking to overhaul
its own mainstream, i.e., Maoist, strategy for building socialism and*

to adopt a growth-maximizing modernization model in its place. Many of the European advocates of "another" development had been influenced by Mao Tse-tung thought. They now found their erstwhile paragon demoted from the imperial throne, and the government inviting capitalist firms to help with China's gigantic modernization effort.

My paper was part of the movement to reassess the meaning of development. Written in 1979–80, it appeared in that most mainstream of journals, Economic Development and Cultural Change, *published at the University of Chicago. At the time, I thought it still necessary to state the case for rural development and to define it carefully with reference to broad policy objectives. I knew that I would be severely criticized and took care to document my argument fully.*

My position was that of a policy planner. I was less interested in "explaining" the failures or successes of rural development than in discovering better ways to accelerate such development. Toward this end, I proposed a "political-territorial" framework consisting of two main elements: an option of integrated territorial development and a search for appropriate forms of local governance. A state devoted to rural development would, I thought, engage in a dialectical process that would articulate central policy objectives with locally determined needs.

Opposition to an agropolitan approach in which the masses rather than the most efficient producers would benefit, in which rural capital accumulation would cut into urban capital accumulation, and where the planning process would be inherently political in nature came from two sources: theoretical economists, who argued the case for efficiency in the use of investment resources, and bureaucratic planners, who refused to part with the idea that decision-making processes were essentially a one-way street: from the top down. My critics had a field day attacking the many different facets of my model. The territorial approach was attacked from the alternative perspective of economic space; collective self-empowerment was seen as a danger by people who preferred to exercise bureaucratic controls over a passive population; giving priority to rural development was seen as an abandonment of growth through industrialization; self-reliance was opposed by those who favored national integration with the global division of labor; my emphasis on politics was seen as a capitulation to irrational forces.

The ensuing debate is not yet over. A few years later, I attempted to answer some of my critics (chapter 9). Soon I would find myself undertaking a study of territorial development at the neighborhood

*level in Latin American cities (chapter 5). Thus, the struggle for an
alternative continues.*

Introduction

This paper is an attempt to answer a specific problem in development
policy. How may rural development in the agrarian market economies
of Asia be accelerated in ways that will meet the following three
criteria: (1) rural development should be responsive to the needs of
rural people; (2) rural development should be compatible with local
conditions in the physical environment as well as with the long-term
future of communities whose livelihood depends on the sustained-yield
management of the land, water, and energy resources in their environment; (3) rural development should ensure an even spread of benefits
among the people.

The hypothesis to be pursued is that an answer to this problem
involves designing an appropriate territorial framework for rural planning and development. This focus on the territorial dimension implies
two things: first, an option in favor of a territorially integrated process
of development, and, second, a search for appropriate forms of territorial governance through which an integrated rural development may
be articulated.[2]

Integrated rural development is a planning concept which stresses
the coordination, within given regions, of programs intended to benefit
the majority of the population.[3] It is meant to involve (a) the preparation of a territorial plan which would formulate appropriate development objectives; (b) an organization capable of designing such a plan
and of harmonizing it with the plans of both higher and lower levels of
program integration; (c) an organizational structure for coordinating
program and service delivery; and (d) a political structure capable of
responsibly articulating a sense of local priorities, identifying projects,
and mobilizing resources for development.[4]

Local governance, which is the second major facet of a territorial
approach, is described by Uphoff and Esman as a "process of decision
making at many levels, including the farm level, and is affected by
decisions within public as well as private organizations. The process
entails allocation as well as regulation, mobilization and conflict resolution, orienting efforts toward production goals that are widely
shared. With respect to rural development, local governance includes
the provision of services needed for agricultural production and en-
hancement of rural welfare."[5] In this comprehensive sense of gover-

nance, public and private are merged as are residentiary and productive functions. It is a concept that greatly exceeds the received idea of a liberal state.

Why Rural Development

The recent, growing interest in rural development is largely the result of new perceptions and insights, among them the following: (1) The corporate (modern) production sectors are providing insufficient employment to absorb the growing numbers of nonproductive rural laborers.[6] (2) At present and foreseeable future rates of cityward migration, there continues to be a positive rate of increase in the rural population and labor force.[7] (3) Despite increases in agricultural production, physical living conditions for a very large number, possibly a majority, of rural people are deteriorating from levels which are already close to or below subsistence.[8] (4) The technical solution to the problem of food production, involving the so-called new seed-fertilizer-irrigation package, is limited in application to certain favored regions; future productivity gains, by physical extension of the green revolution to new areas and by intensification of existing areas, are going to come more slowly and more costly than in the past.[9] (5) Increases in agricultural production occur preponderately on larger farm holdings (defined as those lying above subsistence), leaving small farmers, who comprise the greatest majority, with a proportionately smaller share of the product.[10] (6) In many countries of Asia, the number of rural people with either no landholding or with landholdings so small as to be inadequate for the sustenance of life are forced to work for wages in rural areas; but in many regions, real rural wages appear to be constant or actually declining.[11] (7) The increase in rural population is substantially greater than the increase in cultivated land area, leading to a long-term and persisting decline in the ratio of population to land and to the absolute necessity of increasing the productivity of land.[12] (8) The index of inequality in landholdings is rising as a result of greater initial advantage on the part of large farmers in the adoption of new technology which enables them to acquire more land, especially from small farmers who are forced to sell, and continuing parcellization of small holdings under the relentless pressure of growing population.[13]

It is these pervasive conditions and trends that have led many development specialists to advocate rural strategies that are primarily oriented toward the needs of the small farmer and the millions of landless and near-landless families.[14] These strategies include a critical component for increasing production and productivity, but they are not limited to a simple sectoral, or agricultural, approach. For the most part, they are multisectoral as well as territorial strategies in the sense described in the preceding section. But precisely how to proceed in this remains a problem. The purpose of this paper is to propose some ways in which rural development in Asia might be designed and carried out.

Objectives of Rural Development

Our initial problem formulation listed three criteria which were intended to constrain the search for an answer to the question of accelerating rural development. These criteria require further specification. By stating broad objectives for rural development and discussing their wider implications, it will be easier to specify an organizational design that is compatible with them.

Objective 1: Creating Conditions for the Long-Term Economic, Social, and Political Viability of Rural "Communities" Whose Existence Is Based on a Principle of Self-Reliance

The term "community" needs to be clarified in this context. Because of the existing class (and sometimes caste) structure in rural areas, and because of different degrees to which rural people are integrated into the market economy, it would be quite incorrect to suppose that intimate solidarity relations exist even at the level of the traditional village. The extent to which solidarity relations exist is an empirical question that need not further detain us. Community will be used here in a political-territorial sense, referring to those institutions through which a legitimate political will may be formulated. In many countries, such a community exists only at the national level, with vestiges of political community remaining at the level of the village. In addressing the question of community viability in rural areas, however, the intent is not merely to strengthen forms of governance in villages but also at "higher" territorial levels. In any organized sense, political communities may not presently exist at these levels; they will have to be created. Communities arise from practice. Political communities arise from the practice of political choice.

Political communities require a strong economic foundation and a sustaining physical environment. These requirements are addressed in objectives 2 and 3 below. In addition, however, the viability objective 1 is constrained by a requirement for self-reliance in meeting the developmental needs of the community. It is important to be clear about this requirement.

In the first place, self-reliance does not mean territorial autarky. This is explicitly recognized in objective 5 below. It does mean that the "local community" (and higher intermediate levels, such as the region) should be empowered to carry out those programs and investments which are primarily of local benefit. This point is recognized in the current Draft Five-Year Plan for India:

> Some major investments which have regional implications, like large-scale irrigation, power and transport must necessarily remain outside the scope of planning for limited areas. But the bulk of investments on agriculture, minor irrigation, animal husbandry, fishing, foresty, marketing or processing, cottage and small industries, and local infrastructure and social services including water supply, housing, health, education, sanitation, local transport, etc., are clearly amenable to planning at the local level. Whether the appropriate planning level is the District, Taluka, Development Block, or a cluster of villages requires further consideration; it is possible that there should be a hierarchy on planning decisions at the different levels. The most appropriate unit for employment planning, with emphasis on agricultural productivity, would be the Development Block.[15]

The term self-reliance suggests a second meaning equally implicit in the notion of community. Although we recognized that solidarity relations may not exist among the people inhabiting a given area, the assumption was made that they would have at least a common interest in building political institutions for reconciling their differences and for articulating a political will with respect to the "development" of the territorial economy. In referring to self-reliance, therefore, the intention is to stress self-generated efforts in carrying out a political will in whose formation people take an active part. This presupposes a certain equality of access to the bases for accumulating social power, or at least steady and continuing progress toward a more equal access.

This formulation has been carefully considered. The "bases of social power" include at least the following: productive assets (good physical health, as well as land, water, and machinery); financial resources (principally production credit); markets (particularly outside the local area); social and political organizations (such as farmers' associations, cooperatives, political parties); social contact networks; useful information; and relevant knowledge and skills (such as irrigation farming and double-entry bookkeeping). Putting the emphasis on "equalizing access" to those bases of social power suggests, first, a continuing process of equalization (which is actually a ceaseless struggle for greater access by those whose access is relatively low) and, second, that the relevant criterion is not equality of outcome but equality of access to the bases of social power. A person or household might have easy access to certain lines of credit, and yet may choose not to use them. Similarly, information may be available to all, but not everyone will want to exploit it. The assumption is made that in any given period, anywhere, access to the bases of social power can be made more equal. Equalizing access is therefore not a prerequisite of effective rural development; it must be a continuing and central concern.[16]

Objective 2: Expanding Opportunities for Productive Work in Rural Areas, Especially for Young People and for Women, including in Extractive and Processing Industries and in Services

Although labor, seasonally, may be in critical supply, particularly where double-cropping is being practiced, it is accepted as axiomatic that the rural labor force in Asia is grossly underemployed, whether this is measured in terms of the time actually available for other work, or potentially available but subject to the reorganization of existing work, or in terms of the extemely low productivity of present work determined by economic and/or social schemes of valuation. One result of extensive rural underemployment is poverty sharing, that is, the common practice of providing food and shelter to those whose contribution to the social product is less than the amount they actually consume.[17]

The other result is out-migration to either a dynamic urban economy or a "rural growth pole," that is, a rural development area—such as Chainat in Thailand's central plan—which is the object of an intensive, government-sponsored development program involving land consolidation, irrigation, and the introduction of high-yielding varieties of rice and farm machinery. Whereas out-migration may be a solution to an individual problem, or even a solution for a single household, it is questionable whether such migration can be considered a "solution" from a social standpoint.

Because rural migrants remain in the city, on balance, for at least a major part of their active life, economists sometimes argue that they must also be content with their lot and therefore "better off" than in the countryside. That may be so in the arithmetic of misery, if by better off we mean expanded opportunities for material improvement either for oneself or for one's children. But what is good for one may not hold true for the community. It is relatively easy for us to equate development with urban-based development. But urban markets have not productively absorbed the major fraction of the expanding labor force, and continued heavy investments in urban growth poles only succeed in maintaining a dual labor market in which the majority of the incoming work force piles up in the so-called informal sector where, largely deprived of access to the major bases of social power, it is integrated into the corporate economy on a basis of inequality and dependency at living levels close to and even below subsistence.

Agriculture, of course, remains the basic production sector of the rural economy. Because of the importance of its food component, strengthening agricultural production is discussed under objective 4 in relation to the provision for basic needs. This may lead to increased opportunities for productive work, as may improving the conditions of the physical environment (objective 3). Here, however, the emphasis is on the diversification of the rural economy, particularly through industrial development. The intention is to increase rural incomes (and consequently assist in the process of capital accumulation) by expanding opportunities for productive employment in nonagricultural sectors. This is a particularly important consideration for young people, especially women, for whom employment opportunities both in the city and in rural areas are limited.

Rural industries are not a well-defined category. Usually, the concept refers to extractive and processing industries, though it may also include handicrafts and cottage industries of various kinds. Still other typically rural industries manufacture agricultural tools and implements and, indeed, may be devoted to any type of production which is conveniently located in rural areas (e.g., a cement plant may be called "rural" simply because of its location in the countryside) as well as industries producing primarily for the rural consumer market (e.g., candles, flashlights, bicycles).

The large-scale development of rural industries requires ancillary investments in electric energy, water supply systems, all-weather roads, telecommunications, postal service, and the like. Thus, the industrialization of rural areas can bring with it a major physical transformation. In China, industries have played a major role in rural transformation, and the employment in rural industries has been estimated at about 50% of total employment in manufacturing and mining or at 5% of the economically active population.[18] A similar contribution could, in principle, be obtained in other Asian countries.

Objective 3: Continued Upgrading and Improvement of the Natural Environment of Rural Communities

Even more so than in cities, which are largely artificial creations, life in rural communities depends for its inherent quality and long-term viability on conditions in the natural environment. Here, then, is a call for appropriate environmental management at the point of most immediate impact: the rural community in the sense in which this term was defined in objective 1 above. Four types of environmental management may be distinguished: (a) basic ecological conditions, including the management of renewable (flow) resources, such as forests and ground water supplies, the protection of watersheds from erosion, and the conservation of common pasture lands; (b) agricultural technology, including the construction and maintenance of small-scale irrigation systems and appropriate land preparation, such as terracing, land consolidation, etc.; (c) energy supply, including the sustained-yield management of existing forests and the reforestation of denuded areas, but also the construction of small hydroelectric installations and the installation of solar energy packages; (d) human environment, a comprehensive term that includes environmental sanitation, pest control, flood control, but also potable water supply and drainage systems, housing, community facilities (assembly hall, sport fields, nurseries for small children, etc.), and physical access facilities (roads, radio, and telecommunications).

A list such as this serves primarily for illustration; it is not an agenda for action. Which investments must be made, with what resources, and in what sequence remains to be determined locally by the appropriate institutions for this purpose. It is evident that careful judgments will have to be made concerning priorities, because, on the one hand, there are important interdependencies (between groundwater management and irrigation, for example) and, on the other hand, obvious and very restrictive capability limitations: not everything can be done at the same time. Implied in this list is therefore the existence of a planning and decision process through which a serious commitment of resources can be made. This refers back to the notion of a political community and the institutions of territorial governance which were discussed above under objective 1. It also implies a considerable degree of self-reliance and, therefore, a continuing struggle for equalizing access to the bases of social power.

This last point is extremely important in connection with questions of environmental management. For it may be taken as axiomatic that rural political communities will be prepared to make substantial efforts in the upgrading of the physical conditions in rural areas only if the resulting benefits can be distributed fairly and are not captured by a minority of well-to-do families. A style of "participatory" planning can help in raising people's awareness about the conditions of community viability, and what needs urgently to be done. But in order for this to happen, people must be able to relate the benefits of an investment (or a new set of management practices) to their own conditions of life instead of to a generalized other. Like other human beings, peasants are rational. Their struggle is for survival, and their calculations of costs and benefits are often razor sharp. Much of their so-called traditional, change-resistant behavior is, in fact, nothing more than a rational strategy for survival. If the benefits of environmental improvements are "captured" by someone else, the chances of obtaining voluntary contributions from the peasant masses are indeed slim.[19]

Objective 4: Providing for the Satisfaction of Locally Determined Basic Needs, with Respect to the Entire Population and as a Matter of Urgent Priority

Given conditions of rural existence in which one-half or more of the rural population in the agrarian market economies of Asia live at or below subsistence, an emphasis on "basic needs," as one of the objectives of rural development, is not surprising. But a closer look is necessary because, as it happens, the basic-needs concept is subject to various interpretations.

Introduced into recent discussions by the International Labor Organization (ILO), basic-needs strategies are still being debated.[20] For some, they signify an ordering of priorities by a technocratic elite which identifies certain poverty-stricken groups as "targets" and would help to raise their living levels above the poverty line (1) by the direct distribution of "basic" goods and services, or (2) by raising their real incomes to a level at which they could afford to meet their basic needs, or (3) by "investing in the poor."[21] In this interpretation, the basic-needs approach is seen as involving essentially a redistribution of income toward those living in destitution (usually defined as the lower 20%–40% of the income distribution), and as complementary to the mainline strategy of increasing production. In short, it is understood as a particular version of the well-known strategy of "redistribution from growth."[22]

An alternative approach would be to regard basic needs as a moral and reciprocal entitlement whose contents are to be decided in a public discourse in which needs are objectified and set in context by looking at them in relation to all the needs and wants of the relevant political community, the resources available for their production, the derived production needs, and the specific methods and forms of distribution.[23]

In objective 4, it is this second interpretation which has been chosen as defining the contents of rural development. The main themes of rural development are brought together here: its territorial base, its articulation through a political community, a planning process that is locally based and tied to political institutions, a planned equalization of access to the bases of social power, and self-reliance in economic management.

Again, it is important to point out that, even though the local setting for the satisfaction of basic needs is being stressed, it is not expected that they can be met entirely from local efforts. In many cases, some resource transfers will be necessary, and certainly there will be trade from one territorial community to another. But not to assume substantial self-reliance would be to treat rural people as social welfare cases and so to opt for "target group" and "redistribution from growth" approaches in which fundamental social relationships remain unchanged. Basic needs, as we have seen, refer to production as much as distribution, and therefore imply priority attention to the means for their satisfaction, especially in food production and other income-generating activities (see objective 2).

To treat basic needs in the context of production and a strategy of local self-reliance points to the necessity for encouraging a process of local capital accumulation. Given proper motivation, poor people can and, indeed, will save.[24] Where they do not save, it is generally because they do not see any benefits for themselves (their surplus production is expropriated by landlords, money lenders, and the like). The rural development approach which is being sketched would, in principle, provide substantial motivation for rural savings. In addition, of course, care would have to be taken to prevent the leakage of potential surplus out of the area through the well-known mechanisms of rent, export taxes, and unfavorable terms of trade between rural and urban production areas. By preventing the alienation of rural surplus, marginal capital accumulation in situ would be greatly enhanced, and very substantial rates of growth in rural production could be achieved. It is principally out of this production that basic needs will have to be met.

Objective 5: Achieving Balanced Rural-Urban Development

"Balanced development" is an elusive phrase. No rigid, mathematical balance is intended. What is meant instead is a sense of systematic interrelation between countryside and city in which their notorious differences in levels of living and opportunity will become progressively less pronounced.

The emphasis in this paper is on rural development, that is, development for the benefit of the 70% or 80% of the people who live in the rural areas of Asia. Such emphasis calls for a national commitment. To make such a commitment effective, different planning and action levels must be identified which will work in concert with each other: the locality, the region, and the nation. In addition, however, the existing functional system of cities must be considered, because it is this system which will help articulate rural developments spatially (just as the political system helps to articulate it territorially).[25] Given the enormous poverty in rural Asia, and further, given the undisputed fact that rural investments per person to achieve minimum basic-needs targets are only a fraction of the analogous investments that would be required in urban areas, we conclude the following: If objective 4 on basic needs is accepted, a national approach to development will—at least in the initial phases and until such time as destitution in rural areas has been virtually eliminated—be obliged to give priority attention to rural development, leaving urban-based industrialization and the concomitant investments in urban infrastructure to play a complementary and secondary role. A reversal of priorities can occur when the rural economy has grown sufficiently strong to provide the base in markets and resources to sustain a rapid urban industrialization process.

The functional value of rural development for urban-based industrialization has generally been ignored, even though it has been the way in which the "classical" development sequence occurred in Western Europe.[26] It is the argument made by Mao Tse-tung in his speech "On the Ten Great Relationships," in which he defended an agriculture-first policy in terms of its ultimate benefit for industrialization.[27] To follow a contrary model in which urban industrialization is pursued without first strengthening internal markets leads only to an externally dependent development in which the rural-urban gap becomes progressively larger and the urban economy lies at the mercy of international forces which are almost entirely beyond its control. Objective 5, therefore, is an attempt to state the thesis of an inward-directed development in which all externally oriented developments are carefully restrained to be subservient to the first.

A Linkage Hypothesis

In our search for a solution to the problem of accelerated rural development, we have identified the principal constraints to be observed. Before proceeding further, it may be useful to state a "linkage" hypothesis that will help to bridge the gap between the original problem statement and the proposed solution: Effective rural development which emphasizes improvement in the productivity and welfare of the majority of rural people significantly depends on the existence of a dense and multilevel network of public and private organizations and organizational linkages in which there is a good balance between upward and downward flows of information and a multiplicity of alternative and often redundant channels of communication.

This hypothesis summarizes the conclusions of the excellent empirical study by Uphoff and Esman on local organization for rural development in Asia.[28] By using a scoring system whose details need not detain us here, Uphoff and Esman were able to compare 18 countries according to the effective strength of organizational linkages in rural development and the relative importance of organizational (communication and control) channels. Although they caution the reader not to assume a simplistic cause-and-effect relationship between organization and rural development performance, their overall findings are both impressive and suggestive. Given the low overall scores of agrarian market economies in Asia, the prevalence in their organizational design of top-down bureaucratic control supplemented by an active private sector that has moved in to fill the organizational gap, and the relatively low status of local-level organizations for development (the almost complete absence from rural areas of political organizations should also be noted); and further, given the shockingly poor development performance of these countries, one may tentatively conclude that an improved organizational format, especially at the local level, will materially aid in the acceleration of rural development. As Uphoff and Esman assert at the beginning of their fascinating study, local organization is a necessary though not sufficient condition for such a development. Similar conclusions are also drawn from John Montgomery's study of 25 countries which finds that "arrangements for devolving administrative functions to local noncareer officials produced significantly better results for peasant welfare than arrangements using professional administrators, whether in a centralized or decentralized bureaucratic system."[29]

Toward a General Solution

Strict logic would require that a solution be traced, point for point, from the preceding criteria, objectives, and linkage hypothesis. We will forego this exercise, however, leaving it to the reader to make his/her own connections. And so we will jump directly into the proposed solution or "design" for policy. Following a statement and discussion of the general solution, further details will be provided. The solution will then be justified. Its theoretical advantages will be shown, and some indications will be given of how it might work in practice.

Rural development must be centrally guided but locally based.

Central guidance is only possible, however, if there are organizations capable of receiving and responding to guidance. As we have seen, the problem of many Asian countries is that they have inadequate forms of local organization for managing a rural development effort based on the principle of self-reliance. Therefore, a first and necessary step is to devolve substantial and effective power to a democratically constituted level of local governance that is concerned with the determination and implementation of rural development programs. In other words, it is to create a political authority capable of speaking for and acting on behalf of local people. Such an authority would provide a forum for the resolution of objective conflicts of interest and a technical organization in planning and administration capable of formulating development plans (in consultation with other governmental entities) and of carrying them into practice.

A second step, coincident with the first, involves the delimitation of a territory over which this newly constituted political authority will extend its rule. Generally speaking, the territory should be large enough to meet most of the basic needs of the population out of its own resources, including diversification of the local economy; on the other hand, it should be small enough so that the entire population of the area might have reasonable physical access to the center for political decision making, planning, and administration.

In a typically Asian situation, where rural densities are high, these conditions may be satisfied at the level of a "district" encompassing several dozen villages, with a total population of approximately 50,000. This size should not be taken as a fixed criterion, however. Smaller districts are conceivable (while still meeting the basic design criteria), and somewhat larger population sizes would not detract from the solution, so long as physical access to the "center" remained relatively convenient. Because they are self-governing districts in which agriculture is the principal occupation, we shall call them "agropolitan districts."

The district approach to rural development is not new to Asia. India has experimented with the development block; Pakistan has initiated an integrated rural development program which is centered upon the *markaz;* Bangladesh has just introduced a territorial, self-reliant approach to rural development (or *swainirwar*); the Republic of Korea is extending the territorial scope of its *saemaul undong* or village regeneration program; and China, of course, has had nearly 25 years of experience with the commune system of rural organization.[30] What is still relatively unheard of under Asian conditions (though certainly not entirely unknown) is the actual empowerment of elected district authorities to formulate and carry out rural development programs in the context of a system of national and regional priorities. All too often, the district is considered as merely an administrative convenience, as a means for rationalizing the location of field offices of national line agencies, and as a more or less arbitrarily defined unit for registering people's wants as they petition the government for early and favorable consideration of their requests. To avoid this identification of agropolitan district development with so-called field administration, a closer look at the constitution of district political authorities is necessary.

In what follows, the details are unimportant. They will in any event require adjustment to local circumstances and historical conditions. But the general form of the solution cannot so easily be put aside. Without it, the formation of agropolitan districts would have little meaning.

Accordingly, political authority is to be vested in an agropolitan district assembly. Members of the assembly, of which there will be several hundred, are elected as delegates from their respective electoral units. It is contemplated that there will be two kinds of delegates: those elected territorially by village neighborhoods and those elected by designated functional organizations such as farmers' associations, farm labor syndicates, women's groups, cooperatives, youth groups, etc. Village neighborhoods, representing the basic political unit under agropolitan development, would each elect one delegate, though in addition one or more alternates or deputies may be chosen to speak for the neighborhood in both the village council and/or the district assembly. It is assumed that neighborhoods would be designated based on clusters of up to 500 people. Delegates from organizations would, of course, speak for a larger group, say on a ratio basis of 1:2,000. In general, the intention would be to restrict territorial membership in the assembly to not more than two-thirds of all delegates, the remainder of the seats going to mass organizations.

A number of things would be achieved with the establishment of such a system. Most important, it would make control of the assembly by traditional landholding elites virtually impossible. In the second place, it would allow delegates to speak for political units (neighborhoods, organizations) which are based primarily on face-to-face relations. Delegates are strictly accountable to their electoral units and must maintain a close and active relationship with their political base. Through the system of alternates and through periodic elections, many people in the community would have a chance to serve as spokesperson or delegate in the village council and assembly. The political system is thus conceived as a massive learning process that will allow for a close and evolving relationship between, on the one hand, the basic production units together with the various service and interest organizations in the district and, on the other hand, the district's chief political authority.[31]

We may now turn to consider the powers of the assembly. Without getting into unnecessary detail, the assembly would have five major formal powers: (1) to raise revenues both in cash and in kind, including labor contributions for work of benefit to the entire community; (2) to draw up a long-range development plan for the district and to approve the annual program and budget; (3) approve projects and programs and to assist others, such as village councils and organizations, in carrying out projects of their own; (4) to approve all construction work and activities related to resources development and exploitation, by both public and private agencies, within the boundaries of the district; and (5) to contract with both public and private agencies for the performance of the required tasks.

These powers are fairly straightforward and need little interpretation. The raising of revenues (probably based on production) is an obvious requirement, though in an economy that is only partially monetized and which has a grossly underutilized labor force, some of the revenues could be rendered in the form of "work in lieu of taxes." Such work might, indeed, be made a general requirement (as is military service in some countries) in order that all might share in the experience of building up the resource base and social infrastructure of their communities.

The power to plan, and to draw up programs and budgets, is obviously a counterpart to the first empowerment and requires no specific comment. Neither does the power to implement action programs. If it seems strange to talk of rural districts in Asia as actually doing these things, it is merely a sign of how much distance must be covered before an adequate political framework for rural development can be brought into existence.

Next, the power to approve of project work done by others within the boundaries of the district is to enable the people of the district to develop a sense of pride in place and to protect their territorial interests and resources. Essentially, it is to give them veto power over any construction and resource-management activity within the district. Both psychologically and practically, this is an extremely important power to have and to use. In order to avoid that a district prevent the construction of facilities that are clearly in the interest of higher territorial units, such as the region or nation, special safeguards may be written into the organic law establishing these powers.

Finally, the contract power is to recognize the district assembly, for certain purposes, as a "legal person" able to enter into contractual agreements with others. This is especially important in working out the hierarchical relations between district, region, province, and nation, where contractual agreements may be used to implement critical facets of higher-order development plans. By the same token, the district may wish to contract with a private firm, for instance, to do certain construction work, or with other districts for the joint management of a common body of water.

The assembly is made up of its delegates. In order that it might function as any other government, it will need an executive and technical arm, here simply called the *secretariat*. The secretariat will be staffed by professionals and paraprofessionals, and will be in charge of the preparation of plans, programs, budgets, and the associated documentation, as well as of the administration of district development under the general guidance and supervision of the assembly. The chief executive officer is appointed by the assembly and is accountable to it. He or she may also serve as a member of the assembly ex officio, without voting power.

The agropolitan district is thus the lowest territorial unit into which the state is linked directly through its several institutions and agents.[32] It is a logical arrangement, but excessively decentralized. For the state would have to be directly present across the full spectrum of public activities in each and every one of dozens, possibly hundreds, and in the case of India, even thousands of districts. Being so widely dispersed, the institutions of the central government would need to be immensely strengthened to be effective at the local level. And this is contradictory, for the bureaucracy so strengthened would vitiate the attempt at decentralization and increased local autonomy.

A partial answer to this problem may be found by interposing a regional level of governance between the district and the central state (Fig. 8.1)[33] By building up an intermediate level of state organization—with corresponding autonomy in matters of economic, including rural, development—some of the potential independence of the district might, in fact, be taken away and recentralized at the regional levels, but development planning and action as a whole would gain.[34] In order for the regional level to exercise legitimate powers of coordination over districts, regional assemblies would have to be created, with membership drawn by indirect vote from district delegates. In addition, however, regions would have a more extensive bureaucratic apparatus at its center, as well as a larger urban nucleus.[35]

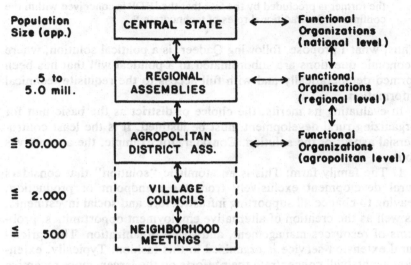

Figure 8.1
State-local relationships in agropolitan development

Evaluating the Solution

The agropolitan approach to development, incorporating the ideas of self-management and basic needs, is a political and therefore a territorial conception.[36] As such, the agropolitan approach is an attempt to respond to the stinging critique of Mohammad A. Qadeer that integrated rural development is "essentially technocratic in spirit and approach." It may be worthwhile quoting the entire paragraph in which this accusation, specifically directed at Pakistan's Integrated Rural Development Programme (IRDP), was made:

> The success of a rural development programme lies in generating a dynamic, prosperous and just rural society. Inequitable power structures and traditional economic organizations are the primary obstacles militating against the realization of these goals. *To remove these obstacles, bold political and social measures are needed.* The IRDP is essentially technocratic in spirit and approach. It is a gradualist's conception of rural development to be promoted through reformed existing institutions. Almost a quarter century of experience in promoting rural development indicates that incremental changes are appropriated by the traditionally powerful for their personal advantage and class benefit. The critical mass effect that the IRDP aspires to precipitate is seldom obtained through increased and concentrated inputs in conventional sectors. *The IRDP needs a political strategy* as much as a bureaucratic mechanism. And

the former is precluded by the fact that the IRDP is conceived within the confines of the traditional roles of technocrats.[37]

Thus, what I propose, following Qadeer, is a political solution, where economic questions are subordinated to a political will that has been formed democratically and with full access to the requisite technical information.

In evaluating its merits, the choice of district as the basic unit for organizing rural development must be justified. It is the least controversial aspect of the solution. Consider, for example, the alternatives to it:

1. The family farm: This is an atomistic "solution" that considers rural development exclusively from the standpoint of production, leaving to chance all supporting infrastructure and social investments, as well as the creation of alternative employment opportunities, problems of resources management, and social organization. The agricultural extension service is organized in this fashion. Typically, extension agents will concentrate their efforts on the larger, more receptive farmers in the hope that their example will spread or "trickle down" to smaller farmers. Problems of landless workers are not considered.

2. The village: This was the principal object during the early phase of the community-development program in India. It came to be replaced by the development block, but the concept of the village community sharing common interests apparently dies hard. A recent evaluation of *taluk* level administration of rural development in Karnataka State points out how taking the entire village "as the primary unit for both planning and organization" leads to ineffective program formulation and field action.[38] The reason given is "the conglomerate interest structure" of the village.

3. The growth center: This geo-economic concept has enjoyed a certain popularity, especially since its persuasive advocacy by E. A. J. Johnson.[39] It underlies much of the thinking around the *markaz* concept in Pakistan. According to Qadeer,

> a *markaz* is a field unit of the IRDP establishment. A village or a small town is chosen as the centre of the *markaz* area. The *markaz* centre is envisaged to provide a spatial focus for the area and is meant to perform an integrative role by bringing together not only the officials of the rural development department but also functionaries of other nation-building departments literally under one roof in a building called the *markaz* complex. The *markaz* centre has a key role in the development of a *markaz* area. It is meant to be a growth point which through commercial and industrial development would become a service town (Agroville) for the *markaz* area.[40]

The trouble with this concept is that expectations that these "points" or centers would "grow" and "spread their benefits" to the surrounding countryside have not been fulfilled. In Qadeer's evaluative study in the Punjab, "the *markaz* centre . . . did not show any tendencies to be a growth point and competing central places were . . . emerging in the area."[41] The growth-center concept again reveals the "urban bias" which has characterized so much of regional planning in the past. Innovations (and other presumably beneficial things) were always imagined to be diffused from centers. That anything interesting and new might happen first at dispersed locations in the countryside was rarely seriously considered. And yet, a little reflection will show that lower-order centers in an urban hierarchy are likely to be responsive to developments in agriculture more than they generate them of their own accord.

Farm, village, growth center: these are the major alternatives to the district concept. And they have not worked and cannot work, in principle, if the objectives of rural development are to be achieved. Furthermore, none of the three alternative focuses for rural development is conceived in political terms. Although the village might be considered a proto-political institution, its political relationships are heavily influenced by tradition, established client relationships, and socioeconomic class. Village government is typically a government of notables and elders. It is not, by itself, a government capable of dynamic, developmental action in the interest of the rural masses. Moreover, too many conditions are fixed in the village, so that there remains only minimal space for maneuver. The game being played is called "beggar thy neighbor," and where a large part of the village population lives at or below subsistence, any departure from existing arrangements will be seen as a direct threat to one's existence and will be fiercely resisted.

The matter is different with the proposed agropolitan district. Without attempting to claim too much for a simple territorial-political concept, we can say that: (1) The influence of entrenched power relations is minimized at this level because agropolitan districts have not existed in the past as areas significant for social or economic relations. (2) The size of a district, with a projected population of about 50,000 and extending over perhaps 20–30 villages, provides potential scope for recombining existing elements in innovative ways to further rural development objectives. (3) This size is also convenient from an economic standpoint, providing, as it would, a fair-sized local market, a reasonably large service population for a full range of rural services, and a sufficient resource base for establishing processing industries.

(4) Agropolitan districts are also of a convenient, if not to say classical, size for political management.[42] Up to the late eighteenth century, self-governing cities in Europe were, with very few exceptions, of a size less than 100,000, and the same appears to have been true for much of urban Asia (India, China, Japan). Thus, the vast majority of towns was of middling size. Even today, we find that the typical self-governing municipality wedged inside metropolitan regions has a population size of only several tens of thousands. Although size alone does not necessarily make for better government, small size makes for a more "intimate" government where the forces at work are more transparent and mismanagement is easily detected. (5) Agropolitan districts are a convenient level for the formation of a political will with extensive democratic participation and for interfacing local political processes with the state bureaucracy. The district may not always win, but at least it cannot be ignored. (6) The agropolitan district permits an approach to physical and economic planning that is reasonably attuned to local ecological conditions.

The district, then, can be provisionally accepted as an appropriate and perhaps even the optimum level for rural development. The more difficult, contentious part concerns its political dimension. A rather elaborate design was proposed, involving the formation of assemblies and a delegate system that, at first sight, must appear formidable indeed. As many as 150 delegates may serve in the district assembly, drawn from small village neighborhoods and functional organizations officially designated on the basis of their inclusiveness with respect to their membership and their national scope. In addition, assemblies were assigned substantial powers to work toward a self-reliant development. Above the districts, finally, an agropolitan region was interposed to mediate state efforts between the lower levels of neighborhood, village, district, and the center.

Lip service is often paid to the need for local self-governance, though perhaps not as often as the perennially popular notion of "participation"—a much looser and ambiguous term. In India and Nepal, for example, the *panchayat raj* has been refurbished, and in Pakistan there has been talk of turning the *markaz* into a unit of local self-governance. But in practice, throughout the Asian region, local political power has been largely a hollow concept. Where this is not the case, the state bureaucracy holds nearly all the trumps. As Uphoff-Esman have shown, downward linkages in Asian countries are generally two to three times as important as upward linkages. This finding is rendered more vivid by the case study reported by Amal Ray to which we have already referred. According to Ray, "the present system of communication seriously impedes field work (at the *taluk* level). Communication up the line is not encouraged. Both information and instruction flows are structured into a series of 'command channels.' The result is enormous delay in work. There is no effective mechanism for inter-sectoral coordination in development at the *taluk* level.''[43] And also this laconic statement: ''The existing rapport between the field administration and the rural people is not appropriate for securing mass mobilisation.''[44]

Even where the bureaucracy may have socially progressive ideas, the structure of power at the local level virtually guarantees that benefits will accrue to the few who are powerful. Qadeer's study of the IRDP in Pakistan comes to the tentative conclusion that ''the IRDP has attracted the same class of rural bourgeoisie *sofad posh* which normally appropriate any public development programme. In this case, the voluntary association with a co-operative group further reinforced cliquish tendencies. Co-operation societies were *ad hoc* functional groups which could seldom be credited with local representativeness. Whatever little benefits the IRDP confers, most likely these are being appropriated by the middle and upper classes.''[45]

In the one case, then, we have a self-regarding bureaucracy, in the other case, a self-regarding elite. Effective self-government is found in neither instance. Unless this problem can be surmounted, it makes no sense to speak of a decentralized rural development, or of agropolitan districts, or the empowerment of assemblies for greater self-reliance. In that event, we cannot go beyond the experience of either India or Pakistan, whose rural programs have bogged down even in relatively prosperous areas such as the Punjab.

It would appear, then, that there are only two options for overcoming the problem of unequal power in rural areas. The first is to smash the power of the landlords and large peasants through a radical land reform. The experience of China comes to mind, where land reform was carried on the wings of a powerful revolutionary movement and resulted from a political struggle which lasted many decades.[46] The other major land reforms in Asia (outside the socialist countries) were carried out with the backing of a foreign power. In Japan, Korea, and Taiwan, it was U.S. influence which made possible a peaceful but nonetheless drastic redistribution of lands. But neither the one nor the other method may be considered true ''options'' in the sense of involving deliberate choice.

The other possibility is the one that is being proposed in this essay. It is to balance the power of the rich by greatly enlarging the local political assembly and to ensure that their base among the people is sufficiently diverse to allow for the expression and reconciliation of a variety of class and functional interests. While it may not at first be possible to ensure that the least organized groups and small peasants and landless workers will have a voice in the assembly, neither would they be, in principle, excluded. On the contrary, it should be possible, given time, to organize these groups and encourage their full participation in political deliberation. Indeed, the political parties (where they exist) might wish to make it their urgent business to advance with all deliberate speed toward an active, organized community in which all parts of the population will have access to organizations that can articulate their interests and through which they can, in turn, gain access to the principal political forums in the country.

In this connection, one objection must be faced. Doubts are frequently expressed, mainly by government functionaries and professional types, that the illiterate peasant masses are incapable of self-government. To turn over the reins of government to them is to invite gross mismanagement, anarchy, and chaos. Given the social and economic conditions in most rural districts, this charge of incompetence, leveled at potential peasant leadership by the existing elites, has a hollow ring. Incompetence for what? Neither peasants nor bureaucrats are angels. Both have something to give, something to learn. To dismiss the possibilities of self-government in rural areas because of what might happen is nothing but self-serving prattle. Let us listen to Edgardo M. Virina, national executive vice-president of the Federation of Free Farmers in the Philippines.

> Generally, peasant leaders are educated people or degree holders. Often, a college degree is more of a hindrance rather than an asset in leading and uniting the peasantry. This is so because the system of education has isolated these people from the peasants culturally, socially, psychologically, and even linguistically. They cannot understand the peasants in so many ways and the peasants likewise do not understand them. Many tend, in fact, to look down on the barefoot, dirty, slow-thinking and "lazy" peasants. If and when they start to work with the peasants, their attitude and approach is paternalistic or messianic.

> Moreover, the educated leaders presume that they know the problems of peasants—they are going to tell the peasants how to solve their problems. They are like birds in the air trying to teach the fish in the sea. The birds want the fish to move this way and that way, but without success because the birds do not go down to the water and see the problems of the fish as the fish see them.

> But going down to the water does not merely mean a change of position in space, just as incarnation does not merely mean to put on flesh. It

means "emptying oneself." The teacher learns from the person he wants to lead, the leader follows the person he wants to lead.[47]

The problems of mass leadership are real. But without letting the masses gain experience in governing their own destiny, how will they learn, how will they improve their skills? Opportunities for local leadership must be created. So long as peasants are kept in a serflike, dependent status, they will confirm the worst imaginings of the elites. But once the chains of their dependency are broken and they are responsible for their own freedom, who can say to what heights they might not aspire?

This design of a political-territorial framework is, on the whole, consistent with the linkage hypothesis which made effective rural development dependent on the structure of organizations. It is also consistent with the specific recommendations of Uphoff and Esman in their study of rural governance in Asia.[48] The authors made seven recommendations in all. They are reproduced here, followed by a brief comment, to show how and to what extent agropolitan development conforms with them.

1. "Local institutions should have more than one level of organization." In agropolitan development, the levels include the village neighborhood, the village, the district, and the region. There is as well a political basis in recognized functional organizations that are inclusive in their membership and national in scope.

2. "Local communities should be linked to higher-level decision centers by multiple channels both to achieve the benefits of specialization in communication and to enjoy alternative avenues of influence." In agropolitan development, a key role would be assigned to functional organizations which, in addition to operating through the assembly structure, would have their own vertical and horizontal communications linkages conforming to the nature of their specific interests.

3. "As a rule, local institutions should be vested each with several functions to insure their viability and capacity to integrate diverse services." In agropolitan development, district assemblies would have broad powers and responsibilities for action in achieving the multiple purposes of rural development within their territorial realm.

4. "The more successful cases had engaged much more extensively in decentralization of operating decisions as well as local-level planning." In agropolitan development, local and regional assemblies exist not merely to petition the higher authorities, but to act dynamically and aggressively on their own behalf. They are self-managing institutions engaged in planning, programming, and action.

5. "Politics—the competition and conflict among groups for influence and resources—must be accepted as unavoidable and legitimate in rural local organization." In agropolitan development, politics is "in command."

6. "Leadership is perhaps the most critical variable for establishing and maintaining local organizations." In agropolitan development, this principle is recognized. Local leadership among the peasantry will emerge in response to the challenges of self-government. It cannot be expected to materialize in advance of this challenge. Leadership involves a process of social learning.

7. Distribution of assets and income: "a more equitable distribution appears to be a necessary if not sufficient condition for extensive rural development." Specifically, the authors declare: "We found no successful case of rural development in the absence of both effective local organization and reasonably widespread distribution of the ownership of assets." In agropolitan development, a priori redistribution of assets, especially of land, is not required. But the struggle for greater equality of access to the bases of social power forms an important part of the whole strategy. To prevent the domination of agropolitan development by landed interests and therefore a minority of traditionally oriented "notables," membership in the assembly was greatly expanded, and a delegate system rooted in local community structures and in functional organizations was suggested.

We turn now to the final question with which this assessment of the proposed solution must be concerned. If the design for a political-territorial framework is consistent, in the main, with the requirements and specifications for integrated rural development, can we be sure that it will also accomplish the basic purpose with which we began this investigation? Will rural development be accelerated to conform with the criteria of need responsiveness, environmental stability, and equity in distribution?

Those who look for simple answers will be disappointed. Though necessary, the agropolitan framework does not, by itself, ensure results for accelerated rural development. A framework provides the context within which development occurs; it is not itself that development. The framework, of course, should be facilitative, and it should direct the stream of development activities in the desired direction. But how well it does its work will depend on other circumstances, not least on the commitment of the central government to the goal of agropolitan development.

Initiating action, leadership, and guidance must come from the state. It cannot and will not originate with the new structures for rural governance; indeed, these structures will never come into existence without the full support of the state. Action must be locally based and motivated, but the state must prepare the right environment for action.

Agropolitan Development: A Synopsis

I have argued that an agropolitan approach must start with organizing for development, and that this organization has political as well as territorial dimensions. It is pleasant to think that one might somehow ignore these difficult and fuzzy topics and concentrate instead on the specific project, for instance, the control of rodents, or the opening of new forest land to settlers. Thus, Hunter and Jiggins from Britain's Overseas Development Institute (ODI), insist on functional tasks, specificity, the identification of concrete opportunities for investment, and on the ultimate arbitration among alternatives according to the universal standard of efficiency.[49] As foreign experts, they are frankly skeptical of "political" approaches in an era which they describe as "highly technical, planning-conscious, and centralizing." Condescendingly, they conclude that "the freely elected three-tier democratic local government experiments do not seem to have much future in LDCS."[50] Finally, they point to Pakistan's *markaz* organization and to farmer service societies as possible models.

But we have already seen that the bureaucratically dominated *markaz* scheme is not "developmentally efficient" (to use a favorite expression of Hunter and Jiggins), and even though the careful benefit-cost accounting methods of the World Bank may be project wise, they are development foolish. In deciding which approach to use, the true demographic and physical dimensions of rural development in Asia must be constantly held in view: 60%, 80%, even 90% of the population is rural, spread out over the physically settled expanse of the country-side, measured in millions of square kilometers, and it is in close symbiosis with nature that a livelihood is produced for the masses of people. In the near future, rural development means simply a better livelihood for these people. And so the question becomes, How is this to be done?

It is not a matter of reaching 50,000 or 100,000 peasant farmers with an impressively financed program in irrigation, where the construction work is supervised by Dutch, Taiwanese, or Israeli engineers. This approach never leads to anything other than a showpiece. If the rural masses are to see a substantial improvement in their lives, it is they themselves who will have to do the work, who will have to organize themselves, and, rising from below, transform the social and physical conditions of their existence. In such a development—which is rooted in the household economy, the village, and the agropolitan district—central government must act to inspire, to empower, to guide, to facilitate, to promote, to assist, and to support. It must not plan, command, administer, or implement projects of its own unless in support of the entire effort and therefore beyond local capacity.

It used to be thought that political organization, territorialism, and local self-governance were merely ideological issues, questions in political philosophy that could be debated at leisure. This point of view is now in dispute. In opposition, I would maintain that rural development—meaning a mass-based and egalitarian development—cannot be accomplished in any other way. Rural development requires the empowerment of the people.

Notes

I should like to thank Dr. Masahiko Honjo, director of the United Nations Centre for Regional Development, for the opportunity he afforded me to learn about development in Asia and for his unstinting support during the preparation of this paper. The center's coordinator for policy research programs, Dr. Fu-chen Lo, was especially helpful and, in the course of many hours of discussion, helped to shape the ideas that are here expressed. Among the center's research staff, I am indebted to Mike Douglass, now at the University of Hawaii, who shared in the formulation of some of the original thoughts about an agropolitan development and with whom I have been having a running discussion of the related issues of basic needs, self-reliance, and territorial planning. Many thanks are also due to Om Mathur for his many perceptive comments, criticisms, and observations. As is customary, all my mentors are in advance absolved of guilt by association. They should, however, share in whatever merit this paper might be found to have. Special thanks go to Susan Ehrhart, a doctoral student of urban planning at UCLA, for her extensive editorial work in preparing the present version of this essay, which was first presented in the seminar on "Rural-Urban Transformation and Regional Development Planning" held at UNCRD, Nagoya, October 31-November 10, 1978.

1. My earlier attempts to tackle this same topic include: John Friedmann, "A Spatial Framework for Rural Development: Problems of Organization and Implementation," *Economie appliquée* 28, nos. 2–3 (1975): 519–44; John Friedman and Mike Douglass, "Agropolitan Development: Towards a New Strategy for Regional Planning in Asia," in *Growth Pole Strategy and Regional Development Policy: Asian Experiences and Alternative Approaches*, ed. Fu-chen Lo and Kamal Salih (New York: Pergamon Press, 1978); and John Friedmann and Clyde Weaver, *Territory and Function: The Evolution of Regional Planning* (Berkeley: University of California Press, 1979), chaps. 7 and 8.
2. For an excellent discussion of the necessity for expanded political participation, particularly local governance, to achieve integrated rural develop-

ment, see Dennis A. Rondinelli, "Administration of Integrated Rural Development Policy: The Politics of Agrarian Reform in Developing Countries," *World Politics* 31, no. 3 (April 1979): 389–416.

3. A useful classification of rural development activities is found in A. T. Mosher, *Thinking About Rural Development* (New York: Agricultural Development Council, 1976).

4. These same points are developed somewhat differently in the World Bank sector policy paper, *Rural Development* (Washington, D.C.: World Bank, Feburary 1975), pp. 33–34. The ability to devise an appropriate framework for integrated rural development and to make it work successfully has been questioned by many people, most notably Vernon W. Ruttan in "Integrated Rural Development Programs: A Skeptical Perspective," *International Development Review* 17, no. 4 (1975): 9–16.

5. Norman T. Uphoff and Milton J. Esman, *Local Organization for Rural Development: Analysis of Asian Experience* (Ithaca, N.Y.: Cornell University, Center for International Studies, Rural Development Committee, November 1974), p. 3.

6. Time-series data on corporate-sector expansion do not exist and are difficult to construct. Nevertheless, this broad statement is not generally disputed so long as it is restricted to the agrarian mixed-market economies of Asia which, for the purpose of the present essay, include nine countries: Bangladesh, India, Indonesia, Malaysia, Nepal, Pakistan, the Philippines, Sri Lanka, and Thailand. In the proportion of the economically active population assigned to agriculture, they range from close to 50% (Malaysia, Sri Lanka) to over 80% (Bangladesh, Nepal). The proportion of the total population living in rural areas would be considerably higher (data taken from Asian Development Bank, *Key Indicators of Developing Member Countries of ADB* [Manila: Asian Development Bank, April 1977]).

7. For actual data, see the World Bank paper, *Rural Enterprise and Non-Farm Employment* (Washington, D.C.: World Bank, January 1978), annex 1, which, for the period between 1950 and 1970, shows an increase of about 80 million in the rural labor force of East and South Asia as compared to only 30 million in the urban labor force.

8. There is a growing body of literature which paints a dismal picture of rural living conditions in Asia. The figures indicate that one-half or more of the rural population in agrarian market economies in Asia live at or below subsistence, even in areas which have been the target of major development policies such as the green revolution. Moreover, the trends depicted are structural and not greatly subject to short-term fluctuations. Thus, with each passing year, the situation, already desperate in many regions of Asia, is likely to get worse (see International Labour Organisation [ILO], *Poverty and Landlessness in Rural Asia* [Geneva: ILO, 1977]). As for agricultural production, the recent picture for agrarian Asia may be summarized as follows (data are for the period 1970–75 and are taken from the United Nations Economic and Social Council for Asia and the Pacific [ESCAP] *Economic and Social Survey of Asia and the Pacific* [Bangkok: ESCAP, 1975], pt. 2, table 6): production increases roughly equal to population growth: India, Indonesia, Thailand; production increases less than population growth: Bangladesh, Nepal, Pakistan, Sri Lanka; production increases more than population growth: Malaysia, Philippines. In

interpreting these data, the reader should remember that even in countries with so-called surplus production, malnutrition affects probably a majority of the rural population. See ILO and ESCP for details.

9. See, e.g., Vernon W. Ruttan, "The Green Revolution: Seven Generalizations," *International Development Review* 19, no. 4 (1977): 16–23. Annual statistics on the extent of acreage covered by HYV rice and wheat are published by ESCAP.

10. For data showing the importance of the small-farm sector in selected countries of Asia and the degree of inequality in landholdings, see ESCAP, table 2. The question of the impact of the new seed-fertilizer-irrigation technology on farm size has been hotly disputed in the literature. Macrostudies have shown that small farmers in green-revolution areas adopt the technology, but at a point later in time than large farmers (Ruttan, "The Green Revolution: Seven Generalizations," fig. 2). The real issue, however, is not adoption of the new technology but how the technology affects the process of capital accumulation. Because of differential access to financial resources as well as the bases of social and economic power—such as contact networks, education, and information—large farmers generally seem to be able to accumulate capital more rapidly than smaller farmers. This is one of the important lessons of the green revolution. See, for example, G. S. Bhalla, "Income Distribution among Cultivators in Harayana: Impact of the Green Revolution," in *The Indian Economy: Performance and Prospects*, ed. J. C. Sandesarg, Papers and Proceedings of the Golden Jubilee Seminar of the Department of Economics (Bombay: University of Bombay, 1974), pp. 133–36.

11. According to an estimate by the World Bank, landless workers in India, Pakistan, and Indonesia totaled some 60 million in the late 1960s, or 30% of the active population in agriculture (World Bank Sector Policy Paper, *Land Reform* [Washington, D.C.: World Bank, May 1975], annex).

12. Despite the continuing expansion of land, this Malthusian hypothesis generally appears to hold true for Asia (see Asian Development Bank [n. 6 above], table 10) for data on the average annual rate of change in area harvested under paddy between 1967 and 1976. If change in land area is compared to population growth, it becomes immediately apparent that just to maintain per capita production of paddy, land productivity will have to be raised quite considerably, year in, year out. And rice-deficit countries will either have to import growing quantities of basic foods (assuming there is a worldwide surplus, and that the prices are affordable) and find a way to distribute this food to the masses of the destitute poor (e.g., in Bangladesh, the Philippines, and Java), or else redouble their efforts to raise production on existing lands in ways that will allow the destitute poor (who comprise between 40% and 50% of the rural population) to share in this increase on an equitable basis. Most countries in the region have been trying to avoid the dilemma posed by this choice. But in the longer view, there is no way to escape it.

13. For Punjab data, see Indira Rajaraman, "Growth and Poverty in the Rural Areas of the Indian State of Punjab, 1960–61 to 1970–71," in ILO, *Poverty and Landlessness in Rural Asia*, fig. 6. See also the concluding paragraphs of Sheila Bhalla's "New Relations of Production in Harayana Agriculture" (*Economic and Political Weekly* [March 27, 1976], pp. A23–A30), where

there is a brief discussion of land fragmentation. Also see the Gini coefficients for land distribution in T. Onchan and L. Paulino, *Rural Poverty, Income Distribution, and Employment in Developing Asian Countries; Review of Past Decades* (Bangkok: Basetsart University, Department of Agricultural Economics, January 1977), table 3. The data suggest increases in asset inequality in Bangladesh, India, Malaysia, and Sri Lanka and probably in Pakistan as well, and very modest declines in Indonesia, Philippines, and Thailand. The trustworthiness of these data remains an open question. Large shifts in Gini coefficients, however, may probably be accepted as indicating at least the direction of change (Bangladesh, Malaysia, Sri Lanka).

14. See, e.g., ECAP (n. 8 above), which is devoted to a study of the small farmer in Asia.

15. Excerpts from India, Planning Commission, *Draft Five Year Plan 1978–83* (New Delhi, March 1978), 1:16–17 (prepared for the National Conference on Development Goals and Strategies for India: The Next Decade).

16. See John Friedmann, "Urban Poverty in Latin America," *Development Dialogue* 1 (1979): 98–114.

17. The term "shared poverty" was originally applied by Clifford Geertz to certain social institutions in Java. Ingrid Palmer, in her study of rural poverty in Java, suggests that Java may be coming to the end of the period of "involution" and poverty sharing (Ingrid Palmer, "Rural Poverty in Indonesia, with Special Reference to Java," in ILO, *Poverty and Landlessness in Rural Asia,* p. 226).

18. Jon Sigurdson, "Rural Industrialization in China: Approaches and Results," in *Growth Pole Strategy and Regional Development Policy: Asian Experience and Alternative Approaches,* ed. Fu-chen Lo and Kamal Salih (New York: Pergamon Press, 1978), chap. 6. For a more extended treatment, see the American Rural Small-Scale Industry Delegation, *Rural Small-Scale Industry in the People's Republic of China* (Berkeley: University of California Press, 1977).

19. J. Greenwood, *The Political Economy of Peasant Farming: Some Anthropological Perspectives on Rationality and Adaptation* (Ithaca, N.Y.: Cornell University, Rural Development Committee, 1973); also James Scott, *The Moral Economy of the Peasant* (New Haven, Conn.: Yale University Press, 1977).

20. ILO, *Meeting Basic Needs: Strategies for Eradicating Mass Poverty and Unemployment* (Geneva: ILO, 1977).

21. See, e.g., Paul Streeten, "The Distinctive Features of a Basic Needs Approach to Development," *International Development Review* 19, no. 3 (1977): 8–16.

22. For a critique of this strategy which is being advocated by, among others, the World Bank and Sussex University's Institute of Development Studies, see John Friedmann; "The Crisis of Transition: A Critique of Strategies of Crisis Management," *Development and Change* 10, no. 1 (January 1979): 125–76.

23. This concept is spelled out more completely in John Friedmann, "Basic Needs, Agropolitan Development, and Planning from Below: The Constitution of Political Communities" (paper presented at the International Symposium of Regional Development [New Dimensions of Spatial Development], Seoul National University, July 9, 1978).

24. The evidence on the savings potential of small farmers is summarized by Michael Lipton, *Why Poor People Stay Poor: Urban Bias in World Development* (Cambridge, Mass.: Harvard University Press, 1976), pp. 246–48. Lipton's figures, by the way, do not include estimates for nonmonetary capital formation through labor contributions. This could indeed become a major source of capital formation in rural areas, especially in relation to the physical environment (objective 3).

25. The distinction between spatial and territorial is the same as that indicated by M. K. Bandman, who writes: "In Soviet scientific literature on regional research, the term 'Territorial Production Complex' is used more often than 'Spatial Production Complex,' in order to emphasize that a specific territory (rather than an abstract space) is meant" ("Scheme and Composition Models of Optimization Models of Forming Spatial Production Complexes," in *Regional Development Planning: International Perspectives*, ed. A. R. Kuklinski [Leyden: Sijthoff, 1975], p. 201n.). See also Freidmann and Weaver (n. 1 above).

26. This is argued by Lipton.

27. Mao Tse-tung, "On the Ten Great Relationships," in *Collected Works* (Peking: Foreign Languages Press, 1977), vol. 5.

28. Uphoff and Esman (see n. 5 above).

29. John D. Montgomery, "Allocation of Authority in Land Reform Programs: A Comparative Study of Administrative Processes and Outputs," *Administrative Science Quarterly* 17 (March 1972): 62–75.

30. China's experience with institutions of rural governance is assessed in Benedict Stavis, *People's Communes and Rural Development in China* (Ithaca, N.Y.: Cornell University, Rural Development Committee, November 1974).

31. The general form of this constitution follows the Yugoslav model of political-territorial organizations (see Susana Mendaro, "Structure and Process in Yugoslav Self-Management Planning" [unpublished paper, Urban Planning Program, University of California, Los Angeles, May 1977]).

32. It is therefore the basic unit of governance in rural areas. Most districts will contain one or more small to medium-sized cities or towns. These form part of the district, however, and will not have an independent government. Larger cities, on the other hand, may require a different treatment. A special problem arises in the urban "shadow" region which is again predominantly rural or "agropolitan." Because of the close functional linkages between shadow region and metropolitan core, a mixed system of governance may be necessary in this case.

33. We have excluded consideration of a provincial level of governance in order to avoid the inevitable red tape as more and more levels of decision and coordination are created. Provinces already exist, as do provincial governments. Most of their functions, however, would be preempted by the new forms of agropolitan governance.

34. For interesting corroboration of this thesis, see Dorothy J. Salinger, *Regional Government and Political Integration in Southwest China, 1949–1954: A Case Study* (Berkeley: University of California Press, 1977), chap. 8.

35. I am specifically avoiding use of the term "growth pole" in this connection. The preferred term would be regional or territorial "production

complex" (following Soviet practice) which is simple and straightforward and avoids much of the metaphysics which has crept into Western growth pole literature (see n. 25 above).

36. Every political organization has a territorial counterpart in which its legitimacy is acknowledged and over which its authority extends. Territory and politics are therefore inseparable. (There is an organizational "politics" as well, which may be dissociated from territory, but this refers to a different process than the one by which human communities govern themselves.) The recognition of the fundamental relationship between rural development and politics also informs the work of Wahidul Haque, Niranjan Mehta, Anisur Rahman, and Ponna Wignaraja, "Towards a Theory of Rural Development," *Development Dialogue* 2 (1977): 11–137.

37. M. A. Qadeer, *An Evaluation of the Integrated Rural Development Programme,* in *Monographs in the Economics of Development,* no. 19 (Islamabad: Pakistan Institute of Development Economics, 1977), p. 4 (emphasis added).

38. Amal Ray, *Organizational Aspect of Rural Development: Taluk-Level Administration in an Indian State* (Calcutta: World Press Private, 1976), p. 73.

39. E. A. J. Johnson, *The Organization of Space in Developing Countries* (Cambridge, Mass.: Harvard University Press, 1970.

40. Qadeer, p. 7.

41. Ibid., p. 39.

42. Robert A. Dahl and Edward R. Tufte, *Size and Democracy* (Stanford, Calif.: Stanford University Press, 1973).

43. Ray, p. 73.

44. Ibid.

45. Quadeer, p. 72.

46. Geoffrey Shillinglaw, "Land Reform and Peasant Mobilization in Southern China, 1947–1950," in *Agrarian Reform and Agrarian Reformism,* ed. David Lehman (London: Faber & Faber, 1974).

47. E. M. Virina, "Internal Problems," in *Organization of Peasants in Asia,* Regional Experts Workshop organized by Friedrich-Ebert-Stiftung in cooperation with the Food and Agriculture Organization of the United Nations and the International Labour Organisation, October 28–November 2, 1974 (Bangkok, 1974), pp. 263–64.

48. Uphoff and Esman (n. 5 above), pp. xviii–xx.

49. Guy Hunter and Janice Jiggins, "Farmer and Community Groups," in *Rural Development Technology: An Integrated Approach,* ed. Asian Institute of Technology (Bangkok: ADI 1977), p. 465.

50. Ibid., p. 463.

9

Political and Technical Moments in Planning: Agropolitan Development Revisited

In August 1982, I presented a final defense of the agropolitan approach to rural development. The occasion was a geographers' congress in Belo Horizonte, Brazil. The paper that follows, published three years after the event, is the result. In rereading it for the present edition, I am struck by my attempt to dress what most of my critics thought to be a utopian notion in the respectable clothing of social science. There are forty references and fifteen footnotes. The language is technocratic: "multi-centric, multi-level system of societal guidance," "structured competition," "conflict management model," and so forth. I was evidently trying to persuade my peers and not, say, the minister of agriculture in Sri Lanka or Sierra Leone. I had constructed a normative model.

Now models have their uses in the academy, but they are next to worthless in political discourse. Because in political discourse you always deal with the specificity of a situation. You have to weigh the political impact of arguments, and you must always think in terms of implementation. In short, your advice has to be practical.

Does the model then bear no relationship to the practical? It does, indeed. But not in any mechanical sense. The components of a model and their relationships must be thoroughly internalized in order to be successfully applied in practice. Models serve primarily as a learning device: hence their abstract quality. They are a teaching tool for planners. Unfortunately, the critics of models rarely understand their limited utility in this sense. They attack models on grounds that are, more often than not, irrelevant, such as that a given model is "unrealistic." But, of course, all models are unrealistic; that is the nature of models. It is a pity that most planning academics fail to understand the meaning and intent of modelling, including normative models.

Over the past several years, I have tried to introduce to the literature on socioeconomic development a model of territorial planning which I

236

called agropolitan development (Friedmann, 1975; 1980; 1981b; 1982a; Friedmann and Douglass, 1978; Friedmann and Weaver, 1979). Its principal provisions are these (see also chapter 8)[1]:

1. As a concept in *socioeconomic change,* agropolitan development refers to a selfreliant development which aims at a substantial increase in the productive forces of rural populations and the betterment of rural life. Through the extension of basic services, such as electric power, clean water, modern communications, primary education, and health clinics, agropolitan development looks to the 'urbanization of the countryside'. Along with the provision of these services, a social guarantee of 'basic needs' to rural households is suggested in the model. Last, a strategy is proposed that relies heavily on the peasantry's capacity for social learning.

2. As a *geographical* concept, agropolitan development refers to a bounded space, a territory, which defines an area for common decision and action. Lying at the intersection of political, economic, and cultural spaces, this territory constitutes the immediate habitat of the rural population. Agropolitan districts are operationally defined as containing at least one small urban center and a population of between 40,000 and 60,000 who live no further than a day's return travelling distance from this center by nonmechanized means of conveyance.

3. As a *political* concept, agropolitan development refers to the entire district population as a political community to which is ascribed a capacity for self-determination in matters of common concern. The community regulates access to land and water, and it may call on its members to contribute with their time and energy to public works. The community, defined by an agropolitan district and operating through its political assemblies, becomes the principal recipient of state assistance and the major agent, above the level of household, of comprehensive rural development.

Preconditions for this model include a strong commitment by the national government to rural development and an egalitarian (postreform) agrarian structure.

Originally, I had developed this model with reference to rural areas in Asia, particularly in Southeast Asia, with their predominant village culture and high demographic densities. Subsequently, I suggested that it might also be applicable to parts of Africa where very different conditions prevail. I now think that as a generalized approach to a territorially based development, it is applicable as well to the more urbanized regions of the Americas and Western Europe.

For a number of reasons, the agropolitan concept has aroused strong emotions. Some critics thought I had embraced the trendy philosophy of 'small is beautiful', others that I was proposing a strategy that would leave the countries of the world periphery forever mired in rural backwardness. I had deserted (these critics asserted) the proven strategies of forced industrialization and accelerated urbanization. But the majority of critics attacked what they thought was my failure to come to grips with 'political and economic realities'. Contemptuously, they dismissed the agropolitan strategy as "utopian" (Boisier, 1982, page 92). Some regional planners, such as Mathur, thought I liked "to dream and romanticize" with my head in the clouds (1980, page 93), and the director of regional planning in India, Sundaram, thought that the agropolitan concept displayed "an astonishing degree of superficiality, if not naivity [sic]" (1980, page 99).

There was, in addition, a neo-Marxist critique. The agropolitan strategy was an attempt to reconcile the contraditions between social and economic forces that together compose a 'unity of opposites'. In this dialectic, forces rooted in the political order and organized on a territorial basis, were said to stand both in need of and in opposition to forces which, like the transnational corporation, are organized according to functional principles. For Soja (1982, page 16), however, this abstract opposition "mystifies" actual relations of power: "To oppose territory and function is . . . entirely misleading. . . . To assert an eternal meaning to territoriality or to put it against an anti-territoriality in some grand schema is . . . pure mystification". In Marxist philosophy, neither the political order nor its politics play a decisive role in history: in the last instance, both are 'determined' by the class relations of society. Whatever its 'conjunctural' importance may be, territorial organization is epiphenomenal. And to the extent that it divides working-class interests, it is dysfunctional for social progress[2].

I should like to take this occasion to answer my critics by generalizing the concept of a territorially based development, grounded in wheat is largely an argument from political theory. In so doing, I also hope to provide a fuller rationale for a decentered system of societal guidance.

It is clear that the question of development 'from above or from below' is very much the topic of the day, as regional planners search for a new framework that will help them define their tasks and practices. As many have noted including Boisier (1979) and Stöhr and Taylor (1981), regional planning doctrine is in crisis, even as the world economy is in critical transition. Ideas that were valid twenty years ago are no longer useful. Within the rich traditions of regionalism, we must initiate a search for new approaches that are consistent with the actually prevailing socioeconomic and political conditions.

In the remainder of this essay, I shall propose the following arguments.

1. As commonly understood, socioeconomic development occurs at different territorial levels of organization, ranging from village and neighborhood community to national international levels. Focused on nation and region, development theory recognizes, though there is a failure to state this premise, the primacy of territorial life and the conditions of the natural environment on which the historical continuity of this life depends.

2. Development is generally understood as a set of territorially based processes of valued social, economic, and environmental change. Decisions affecting these processes of restructuring are essentially political in nature, that is, they are ultimately accountable to the pertinent political community.

3. To ensure effective societal guidance, the relative autonomy of territorial centers over a range of issues affecting their development must be secured at all the relevant levels of territorial organization: locality, region, and nation[3].

4. Because of the present tendency towards a hypertrophic centralism in the practice of societal guidance, with its accompanying phenomena of technification, bureaucratization, and political repression, 'development from below *and from within*' needs to be strengthened. In practice, this calls for the advocacy of a multicentered multilevel system of societal guidance.

5. The case for a dramatic devolution of power in the system of societal guidance involves political, ecological, as well as technical arguments. Each set yields a sufficient reason for a radically decentralized democratized system of societal guidance; taken together, they appear to be compelling in their logic.

6. In the context of these general considerations, a strategy of agropolitan development is shown to be a special case of a territorially based development adapted to prevailing conditions in the agrarian societies of the Third World.

Life space and political community

Before launching upon my central theme, I will introduce two relatively unfamiliar concepts: life space and political community.

People's life spaces may be viewed as the theater of their everyday activity (Friedmann, 1983). Defined by spatial patterns of social interaction and shared concerns, they are formed because historical patterns of settlement and migration tend to persist[4]. (see Chapter 4.)

As a territorial concept, life spaces are physically centered in the household and its activities. From this origin, they can be built up into an imperfectly and loosely structured hierarchy of partially overlapping and interdependent spaces. One such hierarchy includes one's home, street, neighborhood, city, metropolis, region, country, multi-country region, and the world[5]. There are other ways of arranging and naming it, but some such hierarchy, representing the territorial basis of social life, is a universal phenomenon[6].

People tend to identify with their life spaces which become, as it were, an extension of themselves. Where do you live? Where do you come from? These are familiar questions. And usually people are proud to answer, I'm from Vienna or Los Angeles, I'm Egyptian, I'm a 'carioca' from Rio de Janeiro, I come from the Bronx. And if your interlocutor is knowledgeable, you might be pushed a little further: in what part of town do you live? Such information places you; it rounds out the contours of your being-in-the-world. For life spaces have not only names (Westview Towers, North LaCienega Boulevard, West Hollywood, etc), but a history which implies a future that is viewed as a continuation of the past. The people who share your life space also have a shared concern with the emergence of this future and the particular form that it will take. We do not, of course, identify with all our life spaces with the same intensity of feeling (am I a Californian who is also American, or an American who happens to live in California?). And 'cosmopolitan types' may escape territorial identification altogether, claiming to have greater affinity with essentially functional forms of social organization and to be placeless. Nevertheless, most people have strong and abiding affections for the life spaces they inhabit. They wish to protect their integrity. As well, they wish to be secure, autonomous, and free within them.

Political community, my second concept, is one of several divisions—the others being civil society, the economy, and the state—that together constitute what we may call the *public domain* or space for public action. Specifically, it is the political face of civil society and emerges from an implicit compact among individuals and households jointly to address their shared concerns which result from living together within given territorial confines. As a means for managing their common affairs, political communities may bring a state into existence. And even though it has a substantial autonomy of action, the state, based in the bureaucracy, is held to be accountable to the political community, which is the sovereign body of the people organized for a common life[7].

The organized political community takes its concrete form as political parties, social movements, and other groups of citizens mobilized for a political purpose, *to the extent that they are independent of the state*. In some cases, organized political activity exists merely as a claim against the powers that preempt the political rights of the people[8]. In other cases, it is an expression of an autonomously functioning community.

The concepts of political community and life space are intimately connected with each other: for every life space there exists, at least potentially, a political community[9]. This follows from the fact that all life-sustaining activities are centered in a space where they require, for their normal development, a political ordering of social relations.

In the Western World, political communities are typically organized at the level of city, province, and the nation-state. They are less frequently found at the microlevels of street, neighborhood, and district, although social movements are increasingly being organized also at these scales (Castells, 1983). Some activists have even argued for the concept of a contractual community at the level of the household as a means to break the hegemony of patriarchal rule at its source.

An important normative criterion attaches to the concept of political community: it is claimed, and the claim is generally sustained, that sovereign powers reside inherently within it. From this claim, a number of corollary propositions may be derived:

1. Political community makes sense only insofar as it remains free from state interference and manipulation by capital.

2. The sovereignty of a political community extends only to the territorial limits (legal, social, and historical) of its life space. Beyond these limits, it comes up against the equal claims of other communities, and its authority either ceases or needs to be shared. Political community is a territorial form of organization.

3. The claim to territorial sovereignty which is frequently asserted by the state is, in fact, asserted in the name of the sovereign people.

4. Every existing sovereignty is constrained by (a) all other sovereignties within the complex of life spaces of which it forms a part and (b) the ability of the community successfully to assert its claims to sovereignty against potential challengers.

Consequently, within a given life space, the pertinent political community can and often does assert a claim to an autonomous development 'from within'. And this leads us to the central argument of this paper, which is the rationale for a system of societal guidance decentralized to the relevant life spaces of a national society[10].

Arguments for a radical devolution of powers

Political, ecological, and technical reasons support arguments for a radical devolution of powers in development decisions to the lowest orders of territorial organization[11]. I shall take up each line of argument in turn.

Political self-determination

Regardless of its relative position in the hierarchy, each life space has at least a potential claim to an autonomous, if externally constrained, development. Insofar as they are posed by the entire complex of life spaces, some of these constraints must be articulated through a comprehensive system of political order.

The claim to an autonomous development means essentially to have adequate powers to do four things: (a) defining what is (and is not) a matter of public concern (that is, a question in the public domain), (b) ordering the priorities for public action, (c) choosing an appropriate set of implementing devices whenever alternatives for implementing public priorities exist, and (d) marshalling resources necessary for carrying the proposed action into practice. Fundamentally political, these powers more closely define the meaning of sovereignty. Moreover, they are powers that cannot be preempted by planners whose claim to authority rests primarily on their specialized technical knowledge.

Politics, of course, is about conflicting interests and their resolution. Here the state itself appears as a major contestant having interests of its own at stake, particularly in the sphere of production. But its role is far from being exhausted by these interests. The state may also be regarded as a 'terrain' for the waging of the political struggle (Offe, 1975). Useful to the extent that it creates an expectation of indeterminacy with regard to the outcome of struggle, the spatial metaphor is grievously misleading where it suggests a merely passive and indifferent state. In the last analysis, the state is aligned with the dominant class in the society and will use all of its powers to safeguard the basic interests of this class.

Before we leave the argument of political self-determination, it might be well to ask what would happen if such arguments were brushed aside. In the absence of a considerable measure of self-determination, or in the presence of heteronomous power, the sense of a public domain would atrophy. More precisely, to the extent that state power is arbitrarily imposed upon the political community, the community itself is reduced to irrelevance. Under these conditions, development becomes in some considerable measure a dependent development that is no longer in the interest of the population. In the worst-case scenario, the very idea of an autonomous life disappears, as people retreat into their private spaces, struggling to survive alone in a brutish world (Banfield and Banfield, 1958; Turnbull, 1974).

I should like to emphasize that the foregoing argument for self-determination is valid throughout the hierarchy of life spaces, which is to say, for all levels of territorial organization, beginning with the household. Although the question of ordering the totality of this system remains, this much can be asserted: the system will be loosely structured, with a good deal of autonomy remaining at very local levels of territorial life.

Ecological balance and the quality of the built environment

Political communities have continuity in time. The implicit compact which establishes the community is of indefinite duration.

This dimension of durability has significant implications. Political communities require an environment capable of sustaining life in perpetuity; more specifically, they require a built environment that both facilitates and expresses life activities (Lynch, 1981). This condition can be met only through a process of development and planning that is decentralized down to the smallest life spaces of home, street, neighborhood, and village.

The sustaining of social life requires, above all, a balanced natural environment. Yet, without making ecological balance a public concern, communities face the danger of vanishing water supplies, salination of soils, deforestation, erosion, and other forms of resource deterioration. Disaster areas can be found in all parts of the globe, from the northern plains of China to the Ecuadorean highlands. Such disasters can be averted or even reversed through actions that take into account the enormous variety of local ecological conditions and the specific stresses to which they are subject, one village at a time, and even household by household. Larger ecosystems are built up from smaller ones. Their dynamic equilibrium can be maintained only if an overall ecological balance is achieved at the microscale[12].

In many parts of the world, the problem is how to achieve greater resource productivity, even as the sustained use of land and water resources is maintained. More than merely technical skills are involved. Whole new farming systems may have to be introduced to specific peasant populations to meet both their immediate needs and the longer-term needs of the political community for a sustainable and productive physical base.

The question of the built environment is even more obviously a local matter, being intimately related to social life activities (Alexander, 1977). Here, as much as in matters even closer to livelihood and survival, the political moment of societal guidance—defining what is socially significant, establishing priorities, selecting the appropriate means, and marshalling the necessary resources—is of paramount importance. Arranging the built environment is only in small measure a technical question. And the political decisionmaking that is required is, at least in the first instance, a local responsibility. Ultimately, of course, the necessary mix of regulations may include pertinent interests at higher levels as well. Conserving the core of such ancient urban centers as Mexico City is obviously a national more than a local interest that will require intervention by the state. But this need not always be the case, and the more painstaking the social analysis, the more are local issues likely to move into the foreground (Tabuenca et al., undated).

Technical considerations: social learning and the management of information

Is central planning sustainable on purely technical grounds? In attempting to answer this question, I will set aside matters already discussed, such as the likelihood of a diverging ordering of life-space objectives, or the fine grain at which ecological balancing must be attempted. Instead I will focus on the management of information.

Effective guidance activities must conform to a model of social learning (Friedmann, 1981a). This model, in turn, requires complex feedback loops between actions and their consequences. And the tighter the feedback loops (that is, the shorter the time elapsed between knowledge of the results and specific actions), the more accurate will tend to be the guidance of these actions in the public domain. Three additional conditions must be satisfied if this statement is to be accepted as valid. First, the information must be disaggregated to the extent made necessary by the contemplated action. Second, the information must be reasonably accurate. And third, it must be correctly interpreted.

In general, central planning systems are unable to meet these criteria except for their own level of policy intervention. This is the reason why the so-called systems approach to planning is so spectacularly unsuccessful. Nationally, for instance, effective planning for fiscal and monetary policy, sectoral resource allocation, and the design and implementation of major projects is, in principle, possible. But where lower-order life spaces are concerned, central planners typically operate with models that are too highly aggregated, whose policy instruments are confined to those available to the state, whose feedback loops are excessively long, and whose information contains unknown biases and errors. The evidence on this is overwhelming (Morgenstern, 1963; Wilensky, 1967; Caiden and Wildavsky, 1974; Berlinski, 1976; Lindblom, 1977; Ellman, 1979; Wildavsky, 1979). For the most part, central planners are ignorant about the technical conditions for appropriate guidance in all life spaces below the central level itself.

But planners are not usually inclined to admit their ignorance in public. They are more likely to claim omniscience. As a result, centrally planned systems are beset with many forms of pathological behavior, as planners try to cover up for what they do not know, imposing layer upon layer of bureaucratic controls (Bahro, 1979). And when bureaucratic artifice fails, planners fall back on the mailed fist, quieting dissert and enforcing central rules even when the results are plainly counterproductive.

And so, the technical superiority of central planning is not by any means self-evident. This conclusion is reinforced when we consider the virtual impossibility of successfully coordinating actions at the requisite levels within a single planning framework. Nowhere does this become more evident than in rural development where the actions of millions of peasants must be 'coordinated' within the national plan (Hyden, 1980). Even an administered system of agricultural and input prices can serve as a coordinating mechanism for only the small number of farmers who have already adopted commercial practices. And for this limited group, the system will often work in unexpected ways, for example, by encouraging a black market in exportable commodities. It is small wonder, then, that central planners are tempted to resort to radical simplifications, concentrating on large-scale projects and preferring to work with agribusiness interests who have learned to speak their language. From a social point of view, such policies, for instance, in Brazil or in the Philippines, have had disastrous consequences, creating massive rural poverty, resource destruction, and vast urban slums.

Summary

We are now ready to summarize our findings. Decentralizing societal guidance activities down to local neighborhood, district, and village— leaving aside the question of the role of households as producers— appears necessary for three reasons: (a) the need for self-determination on the part of political communities that are embedded in a loose imperfect hierarchy of life spaces, (b) the need for a fine-grained planning of ecological balances and the built environment, and (c) the need to base development planning on tight feedback loops, accurate disaggregated information, and appropriate methods of coordination. Each of these reasons by itself would be sufficient to sustain an argument for decentralization. Together, they would seem to clinch the case in its favor.

Implementation of decentralized guidance

Devolving the authority and means for effective decisionmaking power to the politically organized life spaces of the international system is not to suggest the dismemberment of the system into its smallest units. The interdependency of life spaces across all levels of organization is an established fact. Although the specific terms of integration with the international system may be subject to unilateral action, functional interdependence in system guidance is a basic condition for the successful formulation of territorial policies. To close off, say, a region from the rest of the world is in the long run to condemn it to economic and social backwardness.

Although the case for a territorially decentralized development has been stated, serious problems remain, as we pass from philosophical questions to more practical matters. The implementation of a decentralized guidance system requires political changes that will be far from simple to bring about[13].

Toward a multicentered, multilevel system of societal guidance

A basic premise of this essay is that a loose hierarchy of overlapping life spaces (and correlative political communities) can be identified. The invocation of hierarchy, however, is not intended to convey the notion that the higher will always dominate the lower levels. Instead, a two-way process of influence is implied without which a genuine politics cannot exist. It follows that the effective autonomy of all lower-ranking communities must be protected in the law. In short, a hierarchy of interdependent political communities suggests a form of societal guidance so articulated that no territorial unit may consistently dominate decisions for the system as a whole.

Given, then, the need to ensure the substantial autonomy of political communities in each of the interdependent life spaces of the global hierarchy, the totality of the guidance system must be devised so as to include many centers (one for each life space) at different levels in the hierarchy. Particularly the populations in the lower-order communities (for example, in agropolitan districts), must be able to deal forthrightly with development issues as they appear to them. But to be so empowered, means to have substantial access to knowledge, organization, and basic economic resources. Without such power, political autonomy remains an empty phrase.

Suppose now that these admittedly difficult conditions have been met, there would still remain the critical problem of coordination. For in a well-functioning system of societal guidance, both the vertical (multilevel) and horizontal coordination of actions is required. Most proposals for decentralization fall apart over this issue. It appears that planners tend to think of coordination in excessively mechanistic terms. In fact, three models of coordination must be considered:

(a) *The market model.* Coordination occurs as mutual adjustment to information about the recent and prospective actions of all the players in the game (Lindblom, 1965).

(b) *The conflict-management model.* Coordination occurs as a result of negotiation or bargaining over specific issues among two or more actors whose interest, though in conflict, converge over a limited range. Coordination through bargaining typically results in written agreements, such as compact, treaty, or contract (Wildavsky, 1979).

(c) *The bureaucratic model.* Coordination occurs by hierarchy as actors in superior positions coordinate the actions of lower-placed actors by the authority at their command (Ellman, 1979).

All three models depend on sanctions to obtain compliance: business failure in markets, the power of the courts in contractual agreements, and under command planning, administrative punishments 'from above'. Generally, all three models are used in successful guidance endeavors, though the particular mix of coordinative strategies will vary with both the issue at hand and political style. The French 'indicative' planning of the late 1960s, for example, used models (a), (b), and (c) in roughly that order of importance, but gave critical attention to investment plans (a) and industry-wide agreements (b) (Cohen, 1969). Soviet-style planning reverses this order, relying more heavily on command forms of coordination (c) but making extensive use as well of bargaining techniques (b), and even markets (a) (Ellman, 1979). Systems of societal guidance that rely exclusively on a single model of coordination (for example, Thatcherism in England with its faith in markets combined with moral exhortation) are unlikely to be very effective.

A multicentered, multilevel guidance system will therefore need all three models of system articulation. Clearly, however, the command model (c) should be used rather sparingly and then only in conjunction with the model of conflict management (b), involving all affected parties. In general, where each participating territorial unit is to preserve a substantial measure of autonomy, models (a) and (b) appear to be vastly superior forms of coordination.

Societal guidance as structured competition among territorially organized social formations: the role of regions

The foregoing understanding involving the idea of both autonomous centers and an interdependent hierarchy of centers, views societal guidance as essentially a political process. Technical planning contributes with its specialized skills to this process. Planners sharpen problem definitions, they provide specific analyses that may help reduce the area of ignorance, they may suggest problem solutions, they carry out evaluations, and they provide for a continuous flow of information about ongoing actions and their consequences. These are among the typical things planners do, and they are linked into the system of societal guidance at all the pertinent decision points. Planning does not eliminate politics; it tries rather to strengthen it.

Expressed as a conflict over the proper direction of public actions and the allocation of resources in the public domain, politics takes place primarily among territorially organized political actors. (There are other forms of political life and they are discussed further below.) Given the vast number of actors whose interests must potentially be accommodated (households, neighborhoods or villages, cities), some grand simplifying strategy is needed if the 'directive in history' is not to terminate in a massive stalemate. One aspect of this strategy is to reserve certain powers to each hierarchical level of decisionmaking that can be wielded autonomously without having to refer to higher authorities (though all lower levels would need to be consulted). The second aspect concerns the territorial scale of decisionmaking. Here, special importance attaches to the region.

Conceived territorially, regions appear as a distinctive category of life space and thus as a political community which perforce coexists with other political communities both above it and below it[14]. To enable regions defined as territorial entities to assume a role which mediates between the life spaces of locality and nation, the guidance system of society must be structured in ways that will allow for conflicts over the direction of development to be resolved at their specific level. Where powerful regional governments exist, as in the US system, national decisionmaking needs chiefly to consider the potential conflicts among regionally initiated programs as well as questions of regional equity and social justice. Thus, regions should be construed as a level of political community that in most matters is hierarchically superior to its constituent members and exceeded in only a few key areas by the nation as a whole and by such supranational communities as may exist.

The formal description of these relationships may seem a bit forced. It is intended to point to the principle of federation which is the only method so far devised by which autonomous units may join into a larger entity without losing their autonomy in critical decision areas. Historically, the application of the so-called federal principle has taken many forms, and no single construct would do justice to its actual variety. It does involve a formal allocation of spheres of autonomy among territorial actors and an emphasis on rules that encourage political discussion, bargaining, and negotiation among the federated units (Hoffman, 1959; Elazar, 1972; Proudhon, 1979; Weaver, 1982).

The formal division of powers, of course, is only a start. More important is the cumulative impact of the political process on this division. In US history, a seesaw struggle has traditionally been waged between the States of the Union and the federal government. To judge from this experience, it is improbable that any federal system would reflect in its actual behavior the purely formal territorial division of powers. The continuing tensions between local, regional, and national interests are likely to have quite different outcomes.

The role of class and other forms of social struggle

A decentered multilevel system of societal guidance implies an intensification of territorial and especially regional struggles for autonomy. In many parts of the world such struggles are actually ongoing and are often interrelated with other emancipatory movements. A self-reliant territorial development is often informed by socialist ideals of equity, reciprocity, participation, and self-management. There is no necessary contradiction, then, between emancipatory struggles based on class, gender, or ethnicity, on one hand, and territorial struggles, on the other. Indeed, and this is often forgotten by those who question the validity of territorial struggles or grant them only an epiphenomenal character, a territorially organized politics may be regarded as an essential condition for political struggle. Political life is always constrained by territorially articulated patterns of authority. The object of political struggle may actually be to overturn this pattern, but this would not, in itself, deny the primacy of territorial forms of political organization. The first thing that a successful revolutionary movement must do is to reestablish a political order within the territory it controls. And where the issue is, as it is in most places most of the time, the *reform* of particular social institutions, political actions are focused on only limited aspects of the political order. Of necessity and, indeed, by choice, the rest is assumed to be given (Wildavsky, 1979).

Conclusion

In conclusion, I should like to return to the original question. I have argued that the strategy of agropolitan development—a strategy specifically proposed as a solution to problems of rural underdevelopment in the more densely populated regions of Asia and subsequently adapted to peasant mobilization in East Africa—is a special case of territorial development. And territorial development, I insisted, calls for a system of social guidance that is decentralized and simultaneously active at different territorial levels.

The agropolitan concept was originally proposed as a practical measure to achieve the transformation of peasant societies—their self-transformation, to be more precise—under conditions where the total number of rural people is increasing over a limited land base, and where industrialization is insufficient to provide productive jobs to all but a minority of urban workers.

The countries in Asia and Africa for which I intended this strategy had, it seemed to me, little choice in the matter. With relatively limited prospects for export, and in the face of dwindling external assistance, they had not only to devise new ways of feeding their people but to create an expanding domestic market. In relation to the resources at their command, they faced enormous economic difficulties. Their rural policies, for instance, had to address more than merely the question of agricultural productivity. In many regions, the number of landless peasants was already in excess of 40%. Rural poverty and unemployment were assuming massive proportions.

Given this situation, it seemed reasonable to suggest the integration of rural households on a district basis, to encourage their self-development, and to stimulate the interaction between town and countryside. From the beginning, agropolitan development was modelled as a learning process in which the learners were to be the peasants themselves who would initiate their own development with the assistance of the state. The concept assumed that for several decades at least, official policy would be explicitly biased in favor of the peasantry (as opposed to the traditional urban slant), and that priority in resource allocation would be given to the development of productive capacity and infrastructure in agropolitan districts.

Central to the agropolitan strategy, particularly in its later versions (compare Friedmann, 1981b), was the idea of self-management.

Whereas in urban areas, municipal officials are basically concerned with the provision of services and social infrastructure—what Castells has called the collective consumption of a city—their rural counterparts must deal with questions of production and distribution as well. Rural development involves the total organization of life. Community resources—especially its time and energy resources—must be mobilized, reciprocity relations must be furthered, and the satisfaction of basic needs must be collectively guaranteed. The central government may provide the leadership as well as material assistance in this effort. It can hardly expect to replace self-management with the machinery of central planning and administration[15].

Agropolitan development represents a special case of a territorial approach that involves the mobilization of political communities primarily for their own benefit. It is a proposal to push political autonomy down to household, village, and district levels in countries where development still tends to be identified with forced industrialization, and where elitist bias resists the strategy of the people. Nevertheless, the gap between the rhetoric of modernization and its practice must be closed. To modernize an economy requires, as a first step, a strengthened rural base. All other strategies are bound to fail.

Notes

I wish to thank Deryke Belshaw, Margaret FitzSimmons, and Goetz Wolff for many helpful comments, queries, and suggestions.

1. Over the years, my understanding of the agropolitan strategy has changed, though not in any fundamental sense. What follows is a current attempt at synthesis.
2. Marxists are by no means of one mind on the question of territorial development, particularly when it comes to matters of strategy. For instance, one of the best theoretical defenses of a territorial approach to development (albeit at the national level only) is by Senghaas (1978) who very clearly works within a Marxist tradition of scholarship. He calls it *autozentrierte Entwicklung* (self-reliant development) and the associated strategy *Dissoziation* (selective closure).
3. Societal guidance refers to a process of decisionmaking and its consequences for socioeconomic and physical developments, involving both state and private sector at the level of territorially organized social formations.
4. This definition explicitly rejects the older geopolitical concept of *Lebensraum* and the expansionary doctrines based on it, including the American doctrine of 'manifest destiny'.
5. Although very few people have everyday social interactions on a global scale, the world is taken here to be the ultimate life space; Boulding called it 'spaceship Earth'. It is the habitat of the human race, and we all depend on its survival.

6. Most migratory movements take place over short distances within life spaces that are relatively familiar. Migration becomes traumatic and turns into 'emigration' when people move to a life space with which they had no previous acquaintance and whose social patterns are very different from the ones they left behind. This is especially true where migrants are forced to adopt a different language and other cultural practices. Migrants often cope with this problem by reestablishing a replica of their former life space in their new environment: witness the China Towns, Little Italys, and other immigrant quarters in major cities throughout the world.

7. This formulation is generally consistent with the conceptions of the so-called contract theorists in political philosophy, such as that discussed by Montesquieu, Locke, Madison, and Rousseau, in which polity and state are separately defined and which has given rise to the ringing phrase with which the Constitution of the United States of America begins: "We the people . . .". Although it is a peculiarly Western conception, it has become the basis for legitimizing revolutionary states around the globe, including those that declare themselves to be People's Democracies. Indeed, without some belief in a political community, no revolutionary action from below could ever be regarded as legitimate.

8. Another way to look at political community is to say that it is the public face of civil society which rests within the structures of family and other civil institutions.

9. This relationship and its historical derivation are more fully treated elsewhere (Friedmann, 1982b).

10. For the sake of the present argument, I will bypass possible supranational life spaces and their potential organization as political communities.

11. For the household as a form of territorial organization, see Friedmann and Ehrhart (1982).

12. This way of putting the matter may be too simplistic. Ecosystems are interdependent, and the balance within a smaller system will often be affected by conditions in the encompassing systems of which it forms a part. Still, the microscale in ecomanagement cannot be overemphasized, especially in regions where the way individual farmers husband their land (within given institutional constraints) is critical for the overall condition of environmental and resources quality.

13. Just because the implied changes may be difficult, the proposal to make them cannot be dismissed as 'utopian'. When a patient refuses to submit to surgery (and subsequently dies), the survivors cannot blame the surgeon for his 'utopian' treatment. The only valid argument, then, would be a course of action that is more acceptable, or an altogether different diagnosis. Unfortunately, we can never know in advance which recipe is the right one. Only practice can tell us that, but the conditions are severe: one course of action at a time, and the experiment cannot be repeated.

14. I use 'region' loosely here to signify an intermediate level of societal guidance between locality and nation.

15. A successful experience with an agropolitan strategy, although it made no reference to the concept, and indeed was conceived earlier and independently, was in connection with the Chilean land-reform movement between 1964 and 1973. This has recently been written up in language that brings out the affinity to the agropolitan model (see Chonchol de Ferreira, 1982).

References

Alexander C, 1977. *A Pattern Language: Towns, Buildings, Construction* (Oxford University Press, New York)

Banfield E C, Banfield L F, 1958. *The Moral Basis of a Backward Society* (Free Press, New York)

Bahro R, 1979. *The Alternative in Eastern Europe* (New Left Books, London)

Berlinski D, 1976. *On Systems Analysis* (MIT Press, Cambridge, MA)

Boisier S, 1979. "Regional planning: what can we do before midnight strikes?" *CEPAL Review* 7 133–166

Boisier S, 1982. *Cuardernos ILPES, 29. Politica Económica, Organización Social y Desarrollo Regional* (Papers of the Latin American Institute for Economic and Social Planning, 29. Economic Policy, Social Organization, and Regional Development), Instituto Latinoamericano de Planificación Económica y Social, Santiago, Chile

Caiden N, Wildavsky A, 1974. *Planning and Budgeting in Poor Countries* (John Wiley, New York)

Castells M, 1983. *The City and the Grassroots: A Cross-cultural Theory of Urban Social Change* (Edward Arnold, London)

Chonchol de Ferreira E, 1982, "Planificación del desarrollo local: un enfoque de pedagogía social" *Revista de la Sociedad Interamericana de Planificación* (Journal of the Interamerican Planning Society) 16 (62) June issue, 74–99

Cohen S, 1969. *Modern Capitalist Planning: The French Model* (Harvard University Press, Cambridge, MA)

Elazar D J, 1972. *American Federalism: A View from the States* 2nd edition (T Y Crowell, New York)

Ellman M, 1979. *Socialist Planning* (Cambridge University Press, Cambridge)

Friedmann J, 1975, "A spatial framework for rural development: problems of organization and implementation" *Economie appliquée* 28 519–544

Friedmann J, 1980, "The territorial approach to rural development in the People's Republic of Mozambique: six discussion papers" *International Journal of Urban and Regional Research* 4 97–115

Friedmann J, 1981a. *Retracking America* reissue, with a new preface (Rodale Press, Emmaus, PA)

Friedmann J, 1981b, "The active community: toward a political-territorial framework for rural development in Asia" *Economic Development and Cultural Change* 29 236–261; an earlier version appeared in *Regional Development Dialogue* (UN Centre for Regional Development, Nagoya, Japan) 1 (2) Autumn 1980 issue, 38–101, with critical comments by J Hillhorst, O P Mathur, B S Booshan, K V Sundaram

Friedmann J, 1982a, "Regional planning for rural mobilization in Africa" *Rural Africana* numbers 12–13, Winter-Spring issue, 3–20

Friedmann J, 1982b, "Urban communes, self-management, and the reconstruction of the local state" *Journal of Education and Research in Planning* 2 37–53

Friedmann J, 1983, "Life space and economic space: contradictions in regional development" in *Regional Problems on the Periphery of Europe* Eds D Seers, K Oström (Macmillan, London) pp 148–162

Friedmann J, Douglass M, 1978, "Agropolitan development: towards a new strategy for regional planning in Asia" in *Growth Pole Strategy and Regional Development Policy: Asian Experiences and Alternative Approaches* Eds F Lo, K Salih (Pergamon Press, Oxford) pp 163–192

Friedmann J, Ehrhart S, 1982, "The household economy: beyond consumption and reproduction" paper presented at the 10th World Congress of Sociology, Mexico City, August; DP 159, Graduate School of Architecture and Urban Planning, University of California, Los Angeles, CA 90024

Friedmann J, Weaver C. 1979. *Territory and Function: The Evolution of Regional Planning* (University of California Press, Berkeley, CA)

Hoffman S, 1959, "The areal division of powers in the writings of French political thinkers" in *Area and Power: A Theory of Local Government* Ed. A Maass (The Free Press, Glencoe, IL) pp 113–149

Hyden G. 1980. *Beyond Ujamaa in Tanzania: Underdevelopment and an Uncaptured Peasantry* (University of California Press, Berkeley, CA)

Lindblom C E, 1965. *The Intelligence of Democracy* (Free Press, New York)

Lindblom C E, 1977 *Plan and Markets: The World's Political-Economic Systems* (Basic Books, New York)

Lynch K, 1981. *A Theory of Good City Form* (MIT Press, Cambridge, M)

Mathur O, 1980, "Comment" *Regional Development Dialogue* 1 (2) autumn issue. 90–93 (UN Centre for Regional Development, Nagoya, Japan)

Morgernstern O, 1963. *On the Accuracy of Economic Observations* 2nd edition (Princeton University Press, Princeton, NJ)

Offe C, 1975, "The theory of the capitalist state and the problem of policy formation" in *Stress and Contradiction in Modern Capitalism: Public Policy and the Theory of the State* Eds L N Lindberg, R Alford, C Crouch, C Offe (Lexington Books, Lexington, MA) pp 125–144

Proudhon P-J, 1979. *The Principle of Federation* (University of Toronto Press, Toronto)

Senghaas D, 1978. *Weltwirtschaftsordnung and Entwicklungspolitik: Plädoyer für Dissoziation* (Suhrkamp, Frankfurt)

Soja E W, 1982, "Spatiality, politics, and the role of the state" paper presented at the Latin American Congress of International Geographical Union, Rio De Janeiro, August; copy obtainable from the author at Graduate School of Architecture and Urban Planning, University of California, Los Angeles, CA 90024

Stöhr W B, Taylor D R F, 1982. *Development from Above or Below? The Dialectics of Regional Development in Developing Countries* (John Wiley, Chichester, Sussex)

Sundaram K V, 1980, "Comment" *Regional Development Dialogue* 1 (2) autumn issue, 98–101 (UN Centre for Regional Development, Nagoya, Japan)

Tabuenca A García, Cabíria M, Tuñón P, undated *El Espacio de la Fiesta y la Subversion: Analysis Socioeconómico del Casco Viejo de Pamplona* (Horago, Pamplona)

Turnbull C, 1974. *The Mountain People* (Pan Books, London)

Weaver C, 1982, "From drought assistance to megaprojects: fifty years of regional theory and policy in Canada" *The Canadian Journal of Regional Science* 5 5–37

Wildavsky A, 1979. *Speaking Truth to Power: The Art and Craft of Policy Analysis* (Little, Brown, Boston, MA)

Wilensky H, 1967. *Organizational Intelligence* (Basic Books, New York)

10
Planning in Latin America: From Technocratic Illusion to Open Democracy

This paper is constructed like a classical drama. It speaks of origins and history, delineates the present crisis, and points toward possible starting points for reconstruction. The crisis of planning is not specific to the Latin American continent. Rather, it must be ascribed to the undue attention given to the functional model, to the point where its territorial counterpart was in danger of dissolution. Reconstruction, naturally, was portrayed as the slow recovery of politico-territorial community on the terrain of economic space. In essence, the paper pits a political solution against the increasingly obvious failures of neoclassical economics. Neither side, of course, can win this contest, because together they form a "unity of opposites." The current objective is to rebalance the system; it is not a matter of winning. I presented the paper in September 1986 at the twentieth anniversary of the Central Planning Institute in Brasília. And an apposite time it was to state the case for "open democracy" in planning. Brazil had just won back its liberty, and the Plan Cruzado (or currency reform) had brought a respite to the economy. On the other hand, it must be acknowledged that the decentralized, open-ended approach to planning does not sit well with the political culture of Brazil. Bureaucratic management by the state, coupled with an irresponsible private sector, are not the optimal combination for development.

What the future will bring is anybody's guess. Of one thing only can we be sure: planning in whatever form won't go away. Both state and people need planning, more so now than ever, not in the sense of a central directive, but in the sense of technical judgment coupled to a political will. Planning supplements politics; it does not replace it. Indeed, I am tempted to suggest that planning and politics form yet another unity of opposites. The politics is a democratic politics, where the marketplace is filled with what Benjamin Barber calls the strong talk of citizens. In our complex world, however, strong talk is not enough, but needs to be interlocked with the technical calculus of planning. On the other hand, a technical calculus without "strong talk" soon slips into error, and from error crashes into disaster. That

255

is the moral both of this essay and of all the essays in this book. Planners started with a technocratic approach to the guidance of developmental change. We must now experiment with suitably democratic forms. And every form of democratic politics requires a territorial base.

The modern idea of planning reaches back to the beginnings of the nineteenth century, when Henri Saint-Simon, inspired by young engineers from the new Ecole Polytechnique in Paris, envisioned a new and humane society, freed from the shackles of agrarian feudalism (Hayek 1955). This society would be blueprinted by visionaries like himself and built, according to a plan, much as children construct dream-castles with erector sets. Saint-Simon's secretary, Auguste Comte, carried the dream forward, linking planning to the inevitabilities of Progress and the Stages of History. Scientific reason would guide the human enterprise. It would discover the "laws" according to which history was moving ineluctably from its primitive mythological beginnings to its final mastery by human reason. Having discovered the laws of historical movement, planners, whom he conceived to be a kind of social engineer, would organize the efficient means by which Progress might be attained.

The Comtean idea reverberated throughout the entire century, linking up with the philosophies of positivism and utilitarianism, those twin legacies of the Enlightenment, to burst forth into actual practice in the early decades of the present century. Even Marx was not exempt from what passed as the "modern spirit." He, too, was a scientific rationalist; he, too, believed in historical "laws of motion" that led ever upward, albeit dialectically, to a greater and more encompassing mastery of history by human reason. And when the first revolution conducted in his name turned out to be successful, the construction of the new society would be directed by a series of overlapping five-year plans. The role of the state in planning proved to be crucial. Comte had addressed countless epistles to the great rulers of nations offering his services as planning consultant. His letters went unanswered. But when planning was finally tried, it was to be planning by the state for the national economy. Thus, a hierarchical relationship was established. The state planned in the interest of the whole (*raison d'état*, the national interest understood collectively), and the rest of the country subordinated itself to the specific functional commands that emanated from the state. It was very much an engineering vision. Comte thought it would be "good," because the plan was merely a translation of historical inevitabilities into programmatic terms: to defy the plan was no more possible than to set aside the law of gravity. Marx added a class dimension to this belief in the scientificity of planning. As the carrier of the next stage of history, the proletariat would plan for the general welfare, which, by definition, could not be in opposition to itself. Lenin, finally, entrusted the tasks of planning to the vanguard party that would speak in the name of the proletariat, or to the state, *tout court,* which presumably was not in working-class hands.

This thumbnail sketch of the historical roots of planning is intended to remind us that nineteenth-century ideas are still with us, albeit in somewhat modified form, a curious instance of a historical "lag." The modern equivalent of Progress is the idea of Development. Belief in scientific and objective reason has been narrowed to a faith in economic rationality. The state still plans, even in so-called mixed economies, where a good part of the system operates according to market principles. The interest of the state is still presumed to be identical with that of all the people. The principle of hierarchy remains intact.

But plans, in fact, are far from being all-powerful, and the course of historical change does not necessarily follow from the target calculations of planners. Contemporary consciousness is no longer in the mould of the Enlightenment. Belief in Development—one thinks here of Rostow's "stages of growth" and popular modernization theories—lies in shambles as all the talk is about "global crisis." The positivistic faith in science has yielded to postempirical philosophies of knowledge, such as hermeneutics (Bernstein 1985). Classical hierarchies have been replaced by social networks and learning structures as organizations adapt to "turbulent environments" (Lawrence and Lorsch 1967). The limits of state power have come to be recognized, as the legitimacy of state authority has increasingly been called into question and the international financial system holds more and more countries for ransom. Civil society, for so long consigned to play a passive role in the reproduction of social relationships, has suddenly emerged as an active force in social movements, claiming new rights of autonomous action and demanding that both states and corporations be held accountable in the exercise of their powers (Offe 1985; Bowles and Gintis 1986).

None of this implies that planning in the sense of linking knowledge to action in the public domain should be abandoned. It does mean that we have to reconceive planning, to fit it to our new understandings of what is knowledge and who are the genuine actors struggling with the common problems that face national societies in a world of close interdependencies and uneven relations of power. The theory of this new planning has not yet been written, but much of the critical work has been done (Ulrich 1983; Friedmann 1987). The task of reconstruction is at hand.

In this paper, I should like to examine the present crisis of planning, specifically in light of Latin American experience. The continent has had its own history of planning and, related to that, its own history of "development." Unless we are aware of the specificity of this background, we cannot hope to make meaningful prescriptions. The remainder of this essay is consequently organized as follows. In the next section, I will highlight some of the critical events in the evolution of planning practice in Latin America. This is followed by a brief critique of that experience and of the hopes and beliefs that undergirded it. A review of what is by now a universally acknowledged crisis follows in order to characterize it as either conjunctural or structural, and economic or political. The argument will be made that the crisis is indeed rooted in structural relations and will therefore not yield easily to, say, some clever scheme for postponing Latin America's international indebtedness. Further, while the crisis has important economic dimensions, its solution hinges primarily on political questions, such as the massive incorporation of working people into an ongoing democratic process of decision making and self-empowerment. Open democracy is therefore proposed as the new object of planning, linked to appropriate economic policies, as will be shown. A concluding section summarizes the argument.

Planning in Latin America

The story of national (and regional) planning in Latin America begins, oddly enough, with the imperial history of the United States. During World War II, Franklin Delano Roosevelt appointed Rexford Tugwell as governor of Puerto Rico. Tugwell, a former professor at Columbia University, had been one of Roosevelt's closest associates during the early phases of the New Deal. A strong advocate of central planning in the Comtean tradition, he believed that planners should devise comprehensive designs that would express a general, public interest, and that such plans, once they were approved by the legislature, could indeed provide a directive in history. Henceforth, a nation would no longer be tossed about by the blind forces of the market. Nor would it be governed by powerful business interests in a political system that invariably favored the few over the many. Rather, it would be designed according to the best insights of experts, who, removed from politics, would fashion their plans according to what served the interests of the nation best (Tugwell 1940; 1975). Tugwell had been bitterly attacked for his views both during his years with the Roosevelt administration and subsequently as President of the New York City Planning Commission. But he found a receptive climate in Puerto Rico. He got basic planning legislation approved (though not quite in the form in which he had intended) and made converts to planning among the political and technical elites, especially Muñoz Marín, who would succeed Tugwell as the first elected governor of the Commonwealth (Goodsell 1965).

Planning in Puerto Rico "took off" in the late 1940s, its specific policies guided by studies that had been initiated under Tugwell by one of his proteges, Harvey S. Perloff, a young Harvard economist, and subsequently chairman of an innovative planning program at the University of Chicago. Perloff's studies were among the very first to link planning with the question of economic growth and, specifically, with industrialization in a capitalist country (Perloff 1950). Years later, Perloff would reappear among the Nine Wise Men of the Alliance for Progress to become one of the principal advocates of national economic planning in the region.

Concurrent with these events, three developments would set the stage for the rapid diffusion of planning ideas during the 1960s. The first was the Marshall Plan (1947–1952), which successfully disbursed $12 billion for European reconstruction on the basis of concrete planning proposals. The second was the establishment in the early 1950s of the French Comissariat du Plan, whose aims dovetailed with those of the Marshall Plan (industrialization, modernization of infrastructure). The Comissariat pioneered a form of "indicative" planning that, the French claimed, represented a major institutional innovation in adapting state planning to the realities of large-scale national capital (Cohen 1969). The third development was the invention by the United Nations Economic Commission for Latin America (ECLA) of its own investment programming techniques (1953; 1955), which it would teach to dozens of young development economists throughout the region. As conceived by ECLA, investment programming was holy simplicity itself. Economic growth was equated to national development, which, in turn, called for an accelerated industrialization process based on protected markets. As envisioned at the time, industrialization would be "planned" through the use primarily of the capital/output ratio, which would translate sectoral requirements into macroeconomic targets. ECLA's practice was heavily influenced by the work of the Dutch econometrician Jan Tinbergen, who was subsequently rewarded with the Nobel Prize for his path-breaking work on economic policy (Tinbergen 1953; 1964).

Venezuela was among the first countries in South America to undertake national planning seriously. (There had been earlier efforts, in Brazil, for example, to meet the requirements of the Alliance for Progress for macroeconomic balances and investment priorities.) Acción Democrática had come to power with Rómulo Betancourt in 1958, replacing an old-fashioned, corrupt dictatorship, and in December of that year legislation was passed establishing a national planning office. CORDIPLAN (as it was called) brought together two important sets of influences. The chief architects of Venezuela's planning system, Enrique Tejera Paris and José Antonio Mayobre, had spent considerable time in ECLA's Santiago offices, absorbing much of that organization's developmentalist philosophy. Betancourt himself had lived in Puerto Rican exile between 1954 and 1956. There he had befriended Governor Marín, becoming persuaded of the political utility of democratic planning for development. Another close associate of his, Luis Lander, was at the time serving as a consultant to the Puerto Rican government, having just completed a course in city and regional planning at Harvard University. Lander, who later rose to the presidency of the Interamerican Society of Planning (SIAP), lost no opportunities to impress upon the future president of Venezuela the importance of planning, and collected for him basic information on Puerto Rico's experience with Operation Bootstrap (Friedmann 1965, ch. 2).

In 1961/62, the Alliance for Progress was established on the initiative of President Kennedy. Based on the positive experience of the Marshall Plan a decade earlier, the stress was placed on national planning as a condition for large-scale economic aid. Various aid packages would be coordinated in Washington on the basis of these plans. Among the Committee of Nine established to review national development plans were Harvey S. Perloff and Raúl Saez, a Chilean engineer who had served many years as head of the Chilean Development Corporation (CORFO). In a jointly authored article, the two men expressed the hope that, just as the Marshall Plan had given rise to the Organization for European Economic Cooperation, so the Alliance would be a "beginning for multinational planning" (Perloff and Saez 1962, 155).

Although the Alliance soon hit rocky bottom, the idea of planning, institutionalized during the early 1960s, persisted. In 1964, the Christian Democrats were getting close to capturing national elections in Chile. Chief economic advisor to Eduardo Frei, the Christian Democrats' candidate for president, was Jorge Ahumada, then director of the Center for Development Studies (CENDES) at the National University in Caracas. Ahumada had been connected with ECLA and had seen the work and achievements of Venezuela's CORDIPLAN at close range. He helped Frei to draft legislation that would establish a Chilean version of CORDIPLAN as soon as the Christian Democrats came to power. But Ahumada died unexpectedly, and his Oficina de Planificación (ODEPLAN) never achieved the prominence of its Venezuelan model. Short-run budgetary and fiscal planning took over, while ODEPLAN concerned itself primarily with national accounting and regional planning. Nevertheless, the tradition of planning took hold in Chile, and continues to this day (Boeninger 1984).

Critique

By the end of the 1960s, a certain disenchantment with planning had begun to set in. The fruits of development were supposed to have been harvested with the new technology, but now seemed further away than a decade earlier, when hopes were still high and the first "development" decade was announced with great fanfare. The very meaning of development was now being called into question (Seers 1969), and the methods of planning were coming under critical scrutiny (Faber and Seers 1972). The greatest concern was with the failure of "trickledown" mechanisms, as the number of the world's "poor" was dramatically increasing and becoming more visible, especially in urban areas. At about this time, the ILO's World Employment Program was begun under Louis Emerij, sponsoring "employment missions" to different countries in an effort to change the balance of policies in favor of the un- and underemployed sectors of the population. Then, in 1972, the so-called informal sector was "discovered" (ILO 1972), and a few years later a new concern with "basic needs" was put on the international agenda (ILO 1977). Under the leadership of Robert McNamara, the World Bank initiated new policies meant to address the needs of the poor with programs in self-help urban housing and rural development (Ayres 1984). On the side of "hard" investments, a new doctrine of industrial export promotion was coming to replace the bankrupt "import-substitution" strategy. It reflected, on the one hand, the apparently successful development in the Four Little Dragons of the Pacific Rim—South Korea, Hong Kong, Taiwan, and Singapore—and, on the other, the growing awareness of a new international division of labor, with its origins in the currently ongoing processes of industrial restructuring and recapitalization in the older industrial areas of Western Europe and the United States (Paauw and Fei 1985; Friedmann

1979; Bluestone and Harrison 1982). Clearly, a new and unprecedented situation was beginning to develop and played havoc with the older faith in the linearity of progress and rational planning. The 1970s saw the beginnings of huge corporate mergers, the rise of transnational corporations and their web of global finance and global markets, the rapid spread of new information technologies, a marked slowing down in the rates of economic growth throughout the world, and, in the industrialized countries, the first rumblings of a withdrawal from the traditional free-trade doctrine in face of long-term rising rates of unemployment. All this was happening against a background of the 1973 oil shock, accelerating national indebtedness, the growing influence of the international Monetary Fund in the management of national financial systems, and mounting problems of decapitalization, impoverishment, and hyperinflation. In many Third World countries real wages declined, income was transferred to the rich, food shortages became endemic, and external dependency relations became more severe.

Set against these events, technical planners were helpless. If, as some had said, there had been a "crisis of planning" in 1969, planning found itself in total disarray a decade later.

Planners need a relatively stable environment in which to project their targets and calculate the optimal trajectories of growth and structural change. But in the 1970s, the global environment was anything but stable. This was a time for new experiments and a deep assessment of experiences to date. Some of the experiments were in the direction of neoliberal policies, Friedman-style monetarism, and deregulation. The results of these experiments, as shown by events in Chile, Argentina, Uruguay, and Brazil, were disastrous. On the other hand, taking stock of three decades of planning and development experience was leading to some firm conclusions (Gross 1967; Boeninger and Sunkel 1972; Lindblom 1977; Revista Interamericana de Planificacion 1974; Friedmann 1987), to wit:

1. Planning cannot be separated from politics. The belief in an "objectively neutral" planning practice resting on scientific methodologies is an illusion. Planning and development are therefore not one and the same. The goals of development must be fought over but are not independent of the actual constraints under which countries labor or of the range of options that national policy makers can exercise.

2. The state is only one among several major actors on the national plane. It is neither wholly autonomous nor wholly an instrument of class domination. Its actions are, in any event, constrained. By the same token, the state is not a naturally benign or morally neutral actor

but has certain interests of its own to advance, which it pursues relentlessly, often in opposition to the interests of other potential actors in the field, such as civil society (Poulantzas 1980).

3. The implementation of policies is a major problem that must be addressed simultaneously with the setting of objectives and targets. It involves competition among several possible actors, who may have stakes in the outcome of specific policies, and needs to consider new forms of organization, participation, incentives, and regulation, all of which are highly problematical in themselves (Grindle 1980).

4. Comprehensive, or synoptic, planning is a virtual impossibility, because the actions of multiple actors both inside and outside the bureaucracy cannot be fully coordinated (Lindblom 1977). Comprehensive plans are therefore little more than statements of good intentions that assume stability in the conjunctural conditions over which the state has no significant measure of control. It is thus a doubly fruitless exercise.

5. The Tugwellian belief in planning as a "directive" in history, which in Latin America had led planners to identify development with planning, making the two terms almost synonymous, has turned out to be a fantasy. Few national plans, in fact, represent serious commitments to policies and sectoral allocations. Most of them are drawn up at the request of international agencies that are looking for criteria to solve their own resource-allocation problem.

6. The long- and medium-term planning horizon consecrated in the literature appears more like an exercise in academic speculation than a serious effort at "forecasting" the future. The long term seems almost always driven out by short-term crisis coping and what Albert Hirschman has called reform-mongering (Hirschman 1963). There is always a certain improvisational aspect of policy making that may subsequently be rationalized in formal statements and documentation but which, in fact, represents a necessary adaptation to a constantly changing internal and external environment.

I do not wish to draw what to some readers may seem like an obvious conclusion from this critique, which is based on several decades of experience. A "design for planning" must take account of the broad conditions of development, the current global crisis, and possible political responses to this crisis. Anything less will lead to an empty exercise in abstract reasoning. This much is clear. As we move toward the end of the century, a totally new situation confronts us compared with that of thirty or forty years ago. The Rostovian model of economic growth that undergirded so many dreams of "making it" has lost its powers of persuasion. Modernization theory fares little better, except in China, where it has become the basis of current state policies. Virtually all countries of the semi-periphery are in deep crisis, confronting internal violence, war, loss of fiscal autonomy, decapitalization, and other harsh conditions. The "miracle countries" of the Far East are the major exception to this generalization, but a country such as the Philippines that, until only a few short years ago, was portrayed as a model of enlightened development policy has gone into a downward spin of increasing entropy and dissolution. A quick look at this crisis and possible responses to it must therefore precede any serious effort at reconstructing planning practice.

Crisis

The current crisis has been much analyzed, and it is not my intention to add to the rapidly proliferating literature with my own interpretations (Sunkel 1985; CEPAL Review 1985). But for the completeness of my argument, certain conclusions must be presented. It is commonplace by now to speak of *world interdependency*—markets, division of labor, state systems, and even urban systems. Although crisis conditions have their specific national profiles, the condition of crisis is a general one. A crisis exists when customary ways of acting are no longer possible without making things worse, when traditional solutions are no longer viable and innovative responses are called for. Crises, then, are opportunities, but the opportunities must be seized, and not every country is equally capable of doing that. Those that do may eventually pull out of crisis; those that do not will ultimately be overwhelmed by internal disorder and/or external aggression.

What, then, are the conditions that we have called the global crisis?

1. It is generally agreed that the conditions of super-rapid economic growth that characterized the 1950s and 1960s are not likely to return. There is some speculation about long cycles of economic growth and innovation, but even assuming that we are now at the beginning of a new long cycle of expansion, it is extremely unlikely that sustained growth rates of 6 or more percent a year can be achieved. Part of the reason for this pessimistic conclusion is the rising ratio of investment to output, as new technologies come ever more dearly and require greater and greater savings efforts. But there are other reasons, too, including the finite limits imposed by the environment, negative externalities, and the failure of the new investments to generate sufficient employment productivity to absorb the new additions to the urban labor force coming on line.

2. Unlimited accumulation in a finite environment creates negative

spillover effects that must be counted as a cost of economic growth. The question, then, is whether further growth in given environments will lead to positive or negative rates of growth when these are adjusted to reflect the true costs of economic "progress" (Friedmann 1983; Seers 1976; Scitovsky 1976). The Club of Rome has made some highly contentious pronouncements on the subject (Mesarovic and Petel 1974), but even if we discount a large part of their gloomy vision, we are still left with the realities of such undoubted facts as the progressive destruction of tropical rain forests, desertification, growing nuclear scares, acid rain, increasing social tensions, etc. These costs would logically have to be deducted from any increases in GNP by the conventional measure in order to obtain a true picture of growth in terms of human well-being. It is no longer clear then whether (and to what degree) the modest growth rates that are actually being measured signify a genuine development in the sense of human progress. In any event, given the economic growth model that still represents the conventional wisdom of today, further growth and accumulation are likely to increase "spillovers" and thus the relative social costs of future economic growth.

3. Given the need for national economies to remain competitive on a world scale, the prospect is for a type of economy in which the modern sector fails to generate sufficient momentum to achieve anything like full employment under the traditional definition (Handy 1984; Offe 1985). Typical unemployment rates in developed countries stand above 7 percent, ranging to 12 percent and more in certain instances; in the developing countries, such as in Latin America, urban unemployment is substantially higher, up to 20 percent (García and Tokman 1984). Open unemployment, however, is not the only relevant measure. In addition, account must be taken of the behavior of average (and sectoral) wage rates (which have shown a steady decrease in Latin America over the last ten years), and the rate of underemployment (formation of the so-called informal sector) which, in Latin America, ranges from 25 to 35 percent of urban employment. In practical terms, then, conditions of livelihood have become increasingly harsh for more than half the urban labor force. The prospects for young people to find productive work have grown correspondingly dim, even as expectations are aroused by popular images of the good life. Some sectors of the urban middle class have begun to share in this downward spiral of realistic expectations. The observed results has been a rise in hooliganism, drug addiction, and other psychosocial disorders that result from a pervasive loss of meaning (anomie). These, too, are social costs that would need to be deducted from a comprehensive social accounting to

obtain an undistorted picture of the relation of growth to social well-being.

4. The rise of the super-corporation has, of course, been observed and amply commented upon. Less attention has been given to the political consequences of this trend, where corporations whose global revenues often exceed the national incomes of all but the most powerful state systems are no longer in any significant sense politically accountable. Even more serious is what Bowles and Gintis (1986) call capital strike, i.e., the ability of capital to pull out of existing commitments in repsonse to conditions that it regards as unacceptable. The result is the well-known phenomenon of disinvestment. According to Sergio Bitar (1985), "the net movement of capital less interest payments and dividends has left a deficit, for Latin America, of U.S.$18.4 billion in 1982, 30.1 billion in 1983, and 26.7 billion in 1984, i.e., U.S.$75.2 billion in the last three years" (162). These figures fail to describe the further consequences of disinvestment in the form of lower and even negative growth rates, rising urban unemployment, and the physical deterioration of capital stock.

5. Third World countries can be roughly (and usefully) classified into semi-peripheral countries and what I should like to call the peasant periphery. The former are already heavily urbanized, have a sizeable industrial sector, and per capita incomes that, according to World Bank statistics, have reached (or are about to reach) the middle range. Peasant peripheries are still predominantly rural societies. Examples of semi-peripheral countries abound in Latin America; African countries (other than South Africa) constitute a typical set of peasant peripheries. Both types of national economy are experiencing severe crises, though for different reasons. Semi-peripheries appear to be struggling to overcome a series of "transitional" crises (in addition to the global crisis already described), involving demographic, sectoral, and urban growth. Where these crises are aggravated by other (for example, political or international) considerations, the situation so deteriorates that it becomes virtually unmanageable. Iran, Lebanon, South Africa, and Chile are examples of countries that seem to have gotten more deeply mired in their national crises without the prospects of an early recovery. The Philippines, Egypt, Mexico, Peru, Argentina, and Uruguay seem in various ways headed in the same direction. These countries would seem to have very few cards left to play. The peasant periphery, on the other hand, with the notable exception of the two national giants, India and China, is suffering even more serious consequences. Their state systems are typically very weak, and their national economies have become almost entirely dependent on interna-

tional handouts. Countries of the peasant periphery are typically unable to feed themselves. In Central America, popular revolt against traditional dictatorships have met with U.S. intransigence, and the entire region has become embroiled in both overt and covert warfare.

In sum, we are living in very difficult times. There are no quick and easy solutions to the problems I have sketched. But neither is the present a time for despair. Planning is not merely a kind of prospective decision making in the form of national plans; it is also an attempt to make our best current understandings of the world effective in charting new courses of action. There are those who seek a cure through economic policies, others who propose political solutions. For reasons that will become clear, I hold with this second view, believing that the primary task of planning in Latin America today is to create the conditions for an effectively working democracy that consists of strong representative institutions and the collective empowerment of ordinary citizens in their own communities, an *evenly balanced, participatory, open system that is prepared to engage in major social experimentation.*

Planning for Open Democracy

This normative direction is not arbitrarily selected. The conditions for it already exist. In recent years, most countries in Latin America, rejecting a military rule that has become discredited, have returned civilians to power. The resulting democracies are still quite weak and unstable, but they offer tremendous opportunities for overcoming the conditions of structural crisis that they confront. The second event of truly historical significance is the mobilization of civil society, particularly its popular sectors. In the old scheme of things, a powerful national bourgeoisie controlled the state apparatus (or at least exerted a major influence upon it), and state and economy divided whatever power there was between them. Now a new actor has appeared on the stage. A change in language is significant here. The anonymous masses used to be called the "marginal" population, because they were thought to be excluded from the mainstream of society (Sabatini 1986). But now, greatly swelled in numbers, this same population is no longer an amorphous mass but an increasingly self-conscious sector of the population with a high degree of self-organization and capacity for action (Jacobi 1985; Max-Neef 1985; Friedmann and Salguero 1986). Given their presence, the question of planning relates, in the first instance, to state action and, in the second, to the new popular sectors that are self-organizing and self-managing. A third relation concerns planning for the relationship between the two.

To correctly grasp the implications of this triple relationship, we need to consider the broad question of national development. In the past, state planning concerned itself primarily with planning for the modern, capital-intensive sector of the economy. A large percentage of the population was excluded from this planning. In the 1950s and 1960s, the "marginal" sectors numbered perhaps 20 to 30 percent of the urban population. During recent years, however, their numbers have doubled in relative size. As a result, the problem of "marginality" can no longer be treated as if it were of secondary importance relative to the question of economic growth. And the "marginal" population, with growing self-confidence, now speaks and acts for itself. It has become "civil society," and thus part of the sovereign in a democratic polity.

To address the question of the popular sectors whose basic livelihood is at stake, the state will need to adopt a dual-track strategy that extends the scope of planning equally to both the modern and popular sectors of the economy. To speak with Sergio Bitar, advances must be made, on the one hand, "in industrialization, in the strengthening of technology and human resources, in closer internal linkage between industry and agriculture, in import substitution, and in Latin American integration" (1985, 162). On the other hand, civil society itself must be strengthened (ibid., 163). And that implies specific actions that will lead to the collective self-empowerment of the popular sectors, beginning in their own communities.

The planning/power relationships are sketched in Figure 10.1.

Four urban employment sectors are shown. Traditional planning, especially during the 1950s and 1960s, was addressed primarily to the state and corporate capitalist sectors (AB). It was a highly centralized planning, with no direct participation of the people. During the following decade, many planning controls were lifted, but because of its inconveniently growing numbers and the ILO's aggressive World Employment Program, the informal sector (B1) was coming increasingly to be noted. Research showed it to be not only productive but sometimes even preferred it over work in the formal sector (Moser 1984). Planners exhorted governments to cease their opposition to informal-sector activities and to take positive measures in support of this sector. Now, during the 1980s, we find that not only has the informal sector itself expanded still further (to roughly 30 percent), but a new sector, the communal economy (C), has become visible (Lomnitz 1977; Hardy 1984; Friedmann and Salguero 1986). This sector includes work per-

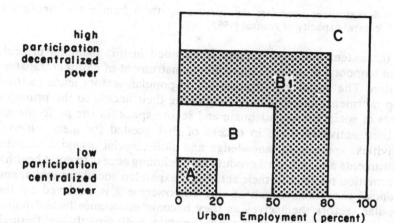

URBAN EMPLOYMENT AND DIRECT PRODUCTION SECTORS

A   state and state capitalist (20%)
B   private capitalist: corporate (formal) (30%)
B₁ private capitalist: small - scale (informal) (30%)
C   cooperative and household: communal economy (20%)

Figure 10.1

formed within the household and in community-based cooperatives, as well as the performance of critical services, housing construction, and even the production of commodities for sale. Together with the informal sector, it constitutes the base of the *survival economy* of urban Latin America.

A dual-track strategy of development such as I am proposing would encourage and support both the informal and communal sectors of the survival economy. In practical terms, this would mean support for the collective self-empowerment of civil society as well. The matrix for this is the local state and the barrio economy as a combined housing/production/living unit involving new relationships of power. This view coincides again with Sergio Bitar, who writes:

> The return to democracy should rely more and more on local governments, with regional and sectoral decentralization; there should be a drive to promote cooperatives and medium-sized and small enterprises. This line of action gives scope for social energies and local initiatives and eases the burden on the State, allowing the public apparatus to concentrate effectively on strategic problems. At the same time, it

decentralizes conflicts, thus preventing them from overwhelming the central capacity of control (1985, 163).

To the extent that civil society is included in this planning project, open democracy becomes an essential instrument of national transformation. The social mobilization of the popular sectors leads to their empowerment, specifically by improving their access to the principal bases of social power: adequate and secure space for the performance of their activities, time in excess of that needed for mere survival activities, appropriate knowledge and skills, social organization, the instruments and means of production (including access to good health), information relevant to their activities, expanded social networks, and financial resources. Much of this empowerment is achieved by the popular sectors themselves as they become economically and politically active. But at the same time, the state, both directly and through the agency of the local state, can facilitate and assist their quest for increased social power. Decentralization and high participation will tend to transform the political system as we have known it up to now, turning it into a more open, responsive, and stable system. And once civil society has been empowered in its local bases of strength, it may well become active as well at regional and national levels through its own political organizations: associations of cooperatives and community groups, and political parties.

An open political system is something unprecedented in Latin America (Veliz 1980). Rather than weakening and destabilizing the state, it will strengthen it in its dealings with the transnational system of power, the giant corporations, the IMF, and North American political pressure. It will enable it to control inflation, because this will no longer be done at the expense of the popular sectors. And it will encourage it to seek solutions within the system of Latin American states for the closer integration of regional economies.

Conclusions

In their present form, the national planning systems of Latin America have outlived their usefulness. They have become instances of a historical lag that no longer corresponds to the complex realities of today's world. For the same reason, traditional development strategies have become empty and futile exercises in rhetoric. To continue with them as if nothing had changed is to court disaster. A dual-track strategy has been proposed that would shift planning from an exclusive concern with state and corporate sectors to an equal concern with the survival sectors of the informal and communal economy that, together, comprise in excess of 50 percent of the urban population. To do this, new democratic institutions must be devised that will address the problems of economic survival of civil society. A dual-track strategy implies planning for an open, participatory democracy. Six specific actions by the state are involved:

1. to promote and protect open political discourse;
2. to encourage and facilitate the social and political mobilization of the popular sectors of civil society around their primary concerns of economic survival and political participation;
3. to facilitate the collective self-empowerment of the popular sectors by helping them gain greater access to the bases of social power;
4. to devolve formal powers to local and regional authorities that will enable them to deal more effectively with questions of development as they concern the popular sectors;
5. to increase the productive potential of the popular sectors (their informal and communal economies) and increasingly to incorporate them into a dual-track strategy of national development; and
6. to establish a guaranteed floor of consumption and collective services for popular-sector households as an explicit policy of income redistribution.

Notes

1. This story could be told in other ways, emphasizing the economic role of the state as early as the 1930s. Chile's Development Corporation (CORFO), for example, which was to play an important role in the country's industrialization and agricultural modernization, was established in 1939. But as a set of coordinated target setting and as a method for economic policy formation, national planning spread rapidly only in the 1950s. Regional planning became popular during the same period (Stöhr 1975). In Brazil, the first training course in regional planning was conducted in 1955 (Friedmann 1960).
2. Earlier Keynesian planning had been designed for anticyclical government action. Though it presupposed an interventionist state, it did not address the question of savings, investments, and economic growth.

Bibliography

Robert L. Ayers (1984) *Banking on the Poor: The World Bank and World Poverty*. Cambridge, Mass.: MIT Press.
Richard J. Bernstein (1985) *Beyond Objectivism and Relativism: Science, Hermeneutics and Praxis*. Philadelphia: University of Pennsylvania Press.

Sergio Bitar (1985) "The Nature of the Latin American Crisis," in *CEPAL Review*, 27, (December), 159–164.

Barry Bluestone and Bennett Harrison (1982) *The Deindustrialization of America: Plant Closings, Community Abandonment, and the Dismantling of Basic Industry*. New York: Basic Books.

Edgardo Boeninger (1984) *"Planificación en el Cono Sur: el Nuevo Papel del Estado,"* Revista Interamericana de Planificación, 18, 72 (December), 127–147.

Edgardo Boeninger and Osvaldo Sunkel (1972) *"Structural Changes, Development Strategies and the Planning Experience in Chile: 1938–69,"* in Faber and Seers, op. cit., Vol. 2.

Samuel Bowles and Herbert Gintis (1986) *Democracy and Capitalism: Property, Community, and the Contradictions of Modern Social Thought*. New York: Basic Books.

CEPAL Review (1985) *"A Selection of Addresses Delivered at the Expert Meeting on Crisis and Development in Latin America and the Caribbean* (Santiago, Chile, 29 April to 3 May 1985) 27 (December), 153–183.

Stephen Cohen (1969) *Modern Capitalist Planning: The French Model*. Cambridge, Mass.: Harvard University Press.

Mike Faber and Dudley Seers (1972) *The Crisis in Planning*. 2 vols. London: Chatto & Windus for Sussex University Press.

John Friedmann (1960) *Introducao Ao Planejamento Regional*. Cadernos de Administracao Pública No. 51. EBAP/FGV. Rio de Janeiro: Fundacão Getúlio Vargas.

John Friedmann (1965) *Venezuela: From Doctrine to Dialogue*. National Planning Series, No. 1. With a Foreword by Bertram M. Gross. Syracuse, N.Y.: Syracuse University Press.

John Friedmann (1979) *"The Crisis of Transition: A Critique of Strategies of Crisis Management,"* Development and Change, 10, 1 (January), 125–176. With comments by Martin Bronfenbrenner, Gustav Ranis, Hans Singer, and a Rejoinder by the Author. (See chapter 2).

John Friedmann (1983) *"Life Space and Economic Space: Contradictions in Regional Development,"* in Dudley Seers and Kjell Ostrom, eds., *The Crises of European Regions*. London: Macmillan. (See chapter 4).

John Friedmann (1987) *Planning in the Public Domain: From Knowledge to Action*. Princeton, N.J.: Princeton University Press.

John Friedmann and Mauricio Salguero (1986) *"The Political Economy of Survival and Collective Self-Empowerment in Latin America: A Framework and Agenda for Research,"* UCLA Graduate School of Architecture and Urban Planning. MS. (See chapter 5).

Charles T. Goodsell (1965) *Administration of a Revolution: Executive Reform in Puerto Rico Under Governor Tugwell, 1941–46*. Cambridge, Mass.: Harvard University Press.

Norberto García and Victor Tokman (1984) *"Transformación Ocupacional y Crisis,"* Revista de la Cepal, 24, 103–116.

Merilee S. Grindle, ed. (1980) *Politics and Police Implementation in the Third World*. Princeton, N.J.: Princeton University Press.

Bertram M. Gross, ed. (1967) *Action Under Planning: The Guidance of Economic Development*. New York: McGraw-Hill.

Charles Handy (1984) *The Future of Work*. London: Basil Blackwell.

Clarisa Hardy (1984) *Los Talleres Artesanales de Conchalí*. Santiago (Chile): Academia de Humanismo Christiano.

F. A. Hayek (1955) *The Counterrevolution of Science: Studies on the Abuse of Reason*. New York: Free Press.

Albert O. Hirschman (1963) "Models of Reform-mongering," *The Ouarterly Journal of Economics*, 77 (May), 236–257.

International Labour Office (1972) *Employment, Incomes, and Equality: A Strategy for Increasing Productive Employment in Kenya*. Geneva: ILO.

International Labour Office (1977) *Meeting Basic Needs: Strategies for Eradicating Mass Poverty and Unemployment*. Geneva: ILO.

Pedro Jacobi (1985) "Movimentos sociais urbanos e a crise: da explosão social a participaçâo popular," *Política e Administraçâo*, 1, 1 (July-Sept.), 223–238.

Charles Lindblom (1977) *Politics and Markets: The World's Political-Economic Systems*. New York: Basic Books.

Paul R. Lawrence and Jay W. Lorsch (1967) *Organization and Environment: Managing Differentiation and Integration*. Boston: Graduate School of Business Administration, Harvard University.

Larissa Adler Lomnitz (1977) *Networks and Marginality: LIfe in a Mexican Shantytown*. New York: Academic Press.

Manfred Max-Neef (1985) *"Another Development Under Repressive Rule," Development Dialogue* (Uppsala), No. 1, 30–55.

Mihajlo Mesarovic and Eduard Pestel (1974) *Mankind at the Turning Point*. New York: Dutton.

Caroline O. N. Moser (1984) *"The Informal Sector Reworked: Viability and Vulnerability in Urban Development," Regional Development Dialogue*, 5, 2 (Autumn), 135–183.

Claus Offe (1985) *Disorganized Capitalism: Contemporary Transformation of Work and Politics*. Ed. John Kean. Cambridge, Mass.: MIT Press.

D. Paauw and J. Fei (1975) *The Transition in Open Dualistic Economies: Theory and Southeast Asian Experience*. New Haven, Conn.: Yale University Press.

Harvey S. Perloff (1950) *Puerto Rico's Economic Future*. Chicago: University of Chicago Press.

Harvey S. Perloff and Raúl Saez (1985) *"National Planning and Multinational Planning under the Alliance for Progress,"* in Leland S. Burns and John Friedmann, eds., *The Art of Planning: Selected Essays of Harvey S. Perloff*. New York: Plenum Press.

Nicos Poulantzas (1980) *State, Power, Socialism*. London: Verso.

Revista Interamericana de Planificación (1984) "Condicionantes Políticos de la Planificación en los Países del Cono Sur," (December).

Francisco Sabatini (1986) *"Knowledge for Planning: Marginality Theories in Latin America,"* UCLA Graduate School of Architecture and Urban Planning. MS.

Tibor Scitovsky (1976) *The Joyless Economy*. New York: Oxford University Press.

Dudley Seers (1969) *"The Meaning of Development," International Development Review*, 2, 6 (December).

Dudley Seers (1976) *"The Political Economy of National Accounting,"* in A. Cairncross and M. Puri, eds., *Employment, Income Distribution and*

Development Theory: Problems of the Developing Countries. Essays in Honour of H. W. Singer. London: Macmillan.

Walter Stöhr (1975) *Regional Development: Experiences and Prospects in Latin America.* The Hague: Mouton.

Osvaldo Sunkel (1985) *America Latina y la Crisis Económica Internacional: Ocho Tesis y Una Propuesta.* Buenos Aires: GEL. Colleción Cuardernos del RIAL.

Jan Tinbergen (1952) *On the Theory of Economic Policy.* Amsterdam: North Holland.

Jan Tinbergen (1964) *Economic Policy: Principles and Design.* Amsterdam: North Holland.

Rexford G. Tugwell (1940) *"The Superpolitical," Journal of Social Philosophy,* 5, 2 (January), 97–114.

Rexford G. Tugwell (1975) *"The Fourth Power,"* in Ed. Salvador M. Padilla, *Tugwell's Thoughts on Planning.* San Juan: University of Puerto Rico Press.

Werner Ulrich (1983) *Critical Heuristics of Social Planning: A New Approach to Practical Philosophy.* Bern: Verlag Paul Haput.

United Nations Economic Commission for Latin America (1953) *"Preliminary Study of the Technique of Programming Economic Development,"* Santiago (Chile), Document E/CN.12/292.

United Nations, Department of Economic and Social Affairs (1955) *Analysis and Projections of Economic Development, I. An Introduction to the Technique of Programming.* New York: UNO.

Claudio Veliz (1980) *The Centralist Tradition of Latin America.* Princeton, N.J.: Princeton University Press.

Part III
EPILOGUE

11
The Crisis of Belief

In the spring of 1985, I helped to organize a UNESCO-sponsored conference that we called World in Transition: The Search for Alternatives. *For a week we met high in the mountains of Switzerland in a free, unstructured search for practical utopian visions in different domains of civic action: work, women, social movements, world order, agriculture, education, science, and technology. Toward the end of the week, in the course of one evening's discussion, we thought we should call ourselves citizen pilgrims, secular pilgrims in search of a future for humankind beyond the destructive forces that we had identified as dominating the present.*

The starting point for our discussions, as indeed it must be for any search for future direction, was a critical dissection of our own place and time. Any "solution" would have to be grounded in a thorough understanding of what was wrong in our collective life and why. What were the sources of our troubles? My contribution was the paper that I offer here as both epilogue and introduction to the essays collected in this volume. I conclude with a series of open-ended questions. My answer to them, partial as it may be, is also the thread that links these essays into a single story. What is of greatest importance in the transition through which we are living is the recovery of a territorial politics on a broad democratic foundation and its ascendence over the primacy of capital, in which all principles are melted down into the single principle of profit. Though it is certainly not a definitive answer, it seems to me that it can serve us well as a basis for the task of ideological renewal, as we are entering upon a new millennium of human history.

The Vienna I knew as a child seemed to me to be an immense city; it was, as we learned to say in school, a *Millionenstadt*. And what a splendid city it was, filled with palaces and parks, ancient cathedrals and stately mansions. As a boy, I experienced the city as if it had always been there, splendid even in its origins on the perimeter of the Roman Empire. I was still spared the terrible awareness of historicity, the fleeting nature of human existence. Only eight years before my birth, Austria had been reduced to a tiny Alpine republic, and many of

277

the older generation had seen their life plans shattered at Versailles. Mourning their lost Empire of the East, they kept a sorrowful company with fading memories of *Felix Austria*.

My political initiation came when I was only seven years old. One early morning in February 1934, I woke to the boom of cannon fire, aimed, Father told me, at a group of armed workers who had barricaded themselves inside the Karl Marx Hof, the most famous of Vienna's many housing projects. Some of Father's closest friends had been implicated in the workers' uprising against the fascist state. When he visited them in a *Konzentrationslager* surrounded by barbed wire on the outskirts of Vienna, I went along and stared at these familiar friends who had visited our apartment so often and who were now in prison for a crime I did not comprehend.

That same summer, I experienced another shock: Nazi assassins had shot the Austrian chancellor Dollfuss in cold blood. The attempted coup failed. But the diminutive Dollfuss was a martyr only to some. Father's friends remembered him as a fledgling dictator whose private army of storm troopers had massacred Viennese workers only a few months earlier. In 1934, life for a seven-year-old was already very complex.

Four years later, German soldiers goose-stepped into Austria. I had become an ardent nationalist by then (and a socialist to boot, even though I was not quite sure of what that was), and in the weeks preceding the *Anschluss* my schoolmates and I threw our little hearts into the struggle for an independent Austria. But it was useless. Countries, we learned, could crumble like dry English biscuits. Hitler annexed Austria without firing a shot. When the so-called plebiscite was held, something like 98 percent of the people voted in favor of joining the Third Reich. With that vote, the Austrian Republic was demoted to the rank of a mere province. A German proconsul arrived from Berlin, and hallowed Österreich became the German Ostmark. My school atlas was duly issued in a new edition to reflect the change.

In September 1938, all Austrian Jews were rounded up by Hitler's bullies, Jewish stores were looted, synagogues desecrated. The code name for this tightly coordinated operation—*Kristallnacht*—has remained forever etched in memory. Father, too, was arrested. Leather-jacketed toughs with swastika arm bands hauled him out of bed at 5 in the morning. They ransacked our apartment looking for any incriminating evidence. In the wake of this terrible night, many Jews would be sent to concentration camps in Germany on their way eventually to the gas ovens of Theresienstadt, Belsen, and Auschwitz. But Father was lucky. He returned, ashen-faced, after two weeks. A few months later, he was gone, on a roundabout journey that would take him to the United States. The rest of the family followed him there in due course on one of the last ships to leave Genoa before Italy's entry into the war.

The world of my youth had gone up in flames. Those of Father's relatives who had remained would perish. But I was a boy of only fourteen at the time, and it wasn't long before I learned to speak English and became, by stages, an American.

Franklin Delano Roosevelt was still president when I became a citizen in 1944. We were now a nation at war, and new dreams were being formed. To think of a better, happier future *after* the war became itself a legitimate wartime activity. The propagandists in Washington thought it would give us something worthwhile to fight for. Democracy, of course, would be victorious. There would be an economy of full employment in which everyone would have enough to eat. Former colonial territories would achieve independent nationhood. We hailed the Four Freedoms, including the revolutionary freedoms from fear and from want, and set our high hopes upon the United Nations and the farther shores of One World.

With the end of the war, these dreams would surely come true, we believed. We would make them come true. It was this dreaming that gave meaning and direction to our lives. There was a more somber side, too, of course. The atomic bombs that had obliterated Hiroshima and Nagasaki cast a deathly pall over the world, and atomic scientists, terrified at the horrible powers they had unleashed, set the clock at five minutes to midnight.

But overall, in our youthful enthusiasm, we held on to our faith that the world's problems would be made to yield, if only we persisted, to an enlightened reason. Properly applied, scientific and technical knowledge, we thought, would help to bring about a world of peace, justice, and plenty. For a short while, it seemed as though we might almost succeed.

In the following pages, I want to set down some of the beliefs of my generation, beliefs that would eventually come undone under the impact of historical events. I want to show what happened to our beliefs, and why. The thoroughness with which they were destroyed for some of us may be hard to grasp in its full significance. It was something altogether different from shedding the ''illusions'' of one's youth. The image of the world we had built up in the mind and that sustained us in the very real sense as the substance from which we lived was being swallowed up by events, much as had the world of my youth. With little more than the clothes on my back I was cast out from that world. Now we are all of us outcasts, refugees from a world lying in shambles. And we have no country to which, in our need, we can turn, no safe and promised land of exile, except for that which we shall dream for ourselves.

That is the reason why it isn't enough to say what the world looks like once it is stripped of all beliefs and hopes and fond illusions. The circumstances of our lives compel us to articulate as best we can another world toward which we would wish to find our way.

Belief in Unlimited Growth

There was a time when we believed that economic growth would go on forever. Showering its blessings upon us all, it would eradicate poverty throughout the world and provide a more dignified human existence for everyone. A new measure of economic growth had been devised—the national economic accounts—and the aim of public policy was to make the gross national product rise steadily from year to year. So long as there was growth, we believed, the resulting increments of income would make it easier to attain the goals of social justice. The wheels of progress would be oiled. Inequalities would be reduced. And as material needs were satisfied, higher needs could be attended to. Growth would lead to a new Renaissance.

These certainties were to be shattered. The first Club of Rome report in 1970, *Limits to Growth,* sent up a warning signal: ecologists and systems analysts expressed fundamental doubts about rising resource and pollution costs. The sudden jump in the price of petroleum after 1973 dramatized the finite nature of the most fundamental of energy resources. The resurgence of worldwide hunger despite increases in the productivity of agriculture reinforced widening concerns about the compatibility between capitalist methods of production and human welfare. "Trickle down" did not work; or, where it had worked, it required a special political climate that, by the 1980s, had vanished even in the industrialized countries. That climate had never materialized in the Third World.

There were technical questions, too, about the very measure that served as the bellwether of economic progress. Did the GNP accounts furnish an adequate measure of net social benefit? Fundamental doubt was expressed on this score. Existing social accounts failed to measure the production that took place outside the exchange economy, primarily in the household, and that accounted for between one-third and one-half of GNP in the advanced economies. They showed as net gains in production a rising quantum of goods and services that had actually come to be required in the course of production itself and should therefore have been excluded as a cost, such as internal security, the services of industrial psychologists, legal services, anti-pollution equipment, and social welfare. Moreover, high and rising unemployment, disinvestment in land, housing, and public infrastructure, the destruction of forests from acid rain and of coastal fisheries from chemical wastes, the devastation of old industrial areas from economic restructuring—all these costs and more, borne by the community at large, failed to show up in the accounts at all. If the appropriate corrections were to be made, it is more than likely that what now appear to be modest yearly gains in the national product would turn into negative rates of growth. That such is actually the case may be surmised from the sense of dissolution, unease, and generalized apprehension that has become pervasive among urban dwellers in both Western Europe and North America.

To be sure, through certain political and military measures, the most powerful of the industrialized countries might succeed in assuring for themselves a livelihood at the expense of weaker and more vulnerable societies. But global exploitation had not been part of the original dream, which held that sustained economic growth was not to benefit the few but the many.

Today, as we look toward the future, we see military expenditures on the rise, the costs of extracting raw materials and energy resources climbing steadily upward, giant corporations determining the way we live, the quality of life diminishing even as the quantity of things produced continues to increase. So here, then, is a contradiction with which we had not reckoned. How might quantity and quality in economic growth be brought into a new relation so that the quality of life might be improved for everyone?

Belief in Universal Development

The postwar era saw the awakening of what would come to be called the Third World. It was an impoverished world harboring 80 percent of the global population who, for the most part, followed agricultural pursuits and whose means for self-development were few. But economists reassured us that success was within the reach of virtually every country, however backward and remote. The key word was industrialization. All that was needed to become industrialized, they said, was to increase the rate of internal savings to something like 20 percent and to accept temporary assistance to supply the pertinent know-how and skill.

The most popular development treatise of the time was by W. W. Rostow, an American economic historian, whose *Stages of Economic Growth*, published in 1960, became the ideological rallying point for Western experts. Rostow hypothesized a long period during which certain preconditions would have to emerge within a country that was readying itself for the "take-off" into rapid, cumulative growth. Once the take-off had been accomplished, several decades would follow during which the transition to the final stage of mass consumption would be completed. This period would be characterized by a series of structural "transitions," including the well-described demographic, sectoral, and urban transitions. As they occurred, they would inevitably give rise to social inequalities, but inequalities would be reduced as the stage of high mass consumption was being reached.

The suggestive power of this model was enormous. Critics might point to the possibility of "breakdown" along the path toward "modernity," they might question the implicit policy prescriptions contained in the model (such as the primacy given to industrialization), they might speak of structural impediments to the achievement of cumulative growth, but the model held firm. Its promise was that, given the right combination of policies, every country had a chance to "catch up" with the West. The United Nations declared the 1960s and 1970s as the Development Decades.

Today, as we look back over forty years of development planning, the results are far from encouraging. A few miracle countries have indeed been brought into the exclusive club of the industrialized nations. They include the ambiguous cases of Japan, whose modernization efforts date back to the middle of the nineteenth century, and tiny Israel, whose modernization was helped by massive infusions of capital from West Germany and the United States. In addition, there are the "newly developing nations" of South Korea, Taiwan, and Singapore, with their separate and rather special histories. But arrayed against these stars in the capitalist heaven, there is the vast tragedy of Africa, with its rising population and shrinking food supplies; the staggering indebtedness incurred by the middle-income countries of Latin America, which has made them prisoners of the world's banking system; the tide of violence that has engulfed Central America, South Africa, and the Middle East; and the collapse of a number of modernizing regimes, most notably in Iran. Many parts of the Third World have become an armed camp supported by the United States, brutal dictatorships flourish, and the number of people living below subsistence is both massive and rising. The two largest countries in the world, China and India, are also among the poorest, with annual incomes of less than $500 per capita.

The picture that emerges is not a pretty one. One thinks of starving refugees from the Sahel in western Africa, of massive transmigrations from Java to Indonesia's outlying islands, of similar migrations from the highlands of Peru, Ecuador, and Nepal that redistribute poverty from one intolerable situation to another. In the cities, sociologists note the swelling numbers of semi-employed, low-productivity workers in the so-called informal sector, while enormous squatter areas surround the villas of the rich, who protect themselves against this sea of misery with barbed-wire fences and private security guards. In the mountains and tropical forest lands of countries such as El Salvador, Guatemala, the Philippines, Kampuchea, and Afghanistan, tenacious guerilla wars are being waged in the name of people's liberation.

In 1985, then, the prospects for universal development seem remote. The multinational corporations and their bankers that dominate the global marketplace operate according to a logic that has little to do with the specific interests of poor countries. The hopes of some countries, such as China, to catch up with Western economies within a lifetime are likely to be vitiated by the probability that the world cannot sustain an unlimited expansion of productive forces. The economic determinism contained in the prevailing models of national development has led to false expectations, as deeper needs find expression in social movements for self-determination, liberation, religious revival, and cultural self-expression.

But if a universal development is no longer on the agenda of world history, what then? Human needs must be fulfilled in some fashion. Among them are the need to live peacefully, productively, and in intercourse with others. The eradication of dire poverty is among these fundamental human needs. But in an interdependent world, how shall we respond to human need when the universal model of development has lost its credibility?

Belief in the Great Consensus

In the first two decades of the postwar era, the United States was governed by the Great Consensus. Forgotten were the soup kitchens and bread lines of the Depression, as rising GNP and full employment filled people's pocketbooks and created an affluence without historical precedent. More than 60 percent of American households would come to own their own homes. Looking out from their picture windows in suburbia, they felt comfortable and reasonably secure. Their life was bought on credit, but so long as the paychecks kept coming and there were hefty increases from year to year, what need was there to worry?

Unlike Western Europe, class politics had, for the most part, been absent from the U.S. scene. Labor unions liked to stick close to workplace issues and battle the "bosses." But few workers begrudged their bosses six-digit incomes when their own annual take-home pay climbed to nearly $23,000. Just about everyone was agreed on the good life. As the sociologist Daniel Bell argued in his much-discussed book *The End of Ideology* (1960), U.S. society had finally outgrown European class-politics and ideological posturing. A Great Consensus held the Republic together, as rich and poor converged upon the mainstream of the middle class.

It wasn't long after this confident analysis that President Kennedy was shocked to "rediscover" poverty in the United States and decided to launch his famous "war" against it. At the time he took office, almost a third of all Americans were living below a poverty income of $3,716 for a family of four. A quarter of them were black or belonged to other oppressed minorities. Many were single mothers. But when the decade erupted into one of the most turbulent eras in U.S. history, it marked the beginnings of a new segmented politics that was carried forward not by political parties but by social movements that cut across class lines: blacks, Hispanics, antiwar activists, environmentalists, women, and gays, to mention only some. Although they did not, for the most part, engage in a revolutionary politics—revolutionaries occupied only the fringes—they succeeded in breaking the prevailing belief in the Great Consensus. Life in the United States was no longer a matter of small technical adjustments, or "fine tuning," as many of us had believed. The adjustments now called for were structural: End poverty! Dismantle the military-industrial complex! End racism! Abolish patriarchy! Stop despoiling the environment!

It was a contentious politics. The 1970s and 1980s led to further fragmentation. Unemployment rose to nearly 10 percent, and though it subsequently declined somewhat, the high rates reflected the severe readjustments that were taking place in the economy. From the mid-1970s onward, the number of people in poverty started to rise again, reaching one-fifth of the total population in 1983, with a much higher ratio for black and other minority groups. At the same time, median incomes began to fall. Organized labor lost ground as well and was forced into fighting desperate rearguard actions, for the most part unsuccessfully. For the first time, there was talk of a permanent underclass in the United States.

In an increasingly divided polity, the traditional parties found it more and more difficult to put together winning coalitions. Americans talked an increasingly virulent language and showed little inclination to compromise on issues as they saw them. The main thing for activists was to gain access to the media. But for the great mass of the people there was no genuine rallying point. Personal charisma was sold over TV like toothpaste, and news was turned into prime-time entertainment. A genuine politics was denied to them, however.

As we approach the end of the century, U.S. society seems to have lost its center. The Great Consensus has broken up. People are turning to their private affairs, to entertainment. The poor are disempowered. And the energy for a revitalized politics seems to be missing. How, we might well ask, under these conditions, can people be enticed back into active citizenship?

Belief in the Welfare State

With the Great Depression, a new kind of state made its appearance in North America. The Roosevelt administration launched a series of far-reaching reforms "from above" that, although designed to save capitalism from itself, claimed state responsibility for the overall direction of economic life.

Following the war, many of these reforms were consolidated and expanded into the welfare state, which became the dominant form of state system in Western Europe and North America. Taken as a whole, the reforms helped to define a clear public interest in such matters as old-age security, unemployment, housing, urban transportation, education, health, the quality of the environment, distressed regions, natural resources, and the development of science and technology. This comprehensive welfare system did not result from unilateral state action. Rather, it evolved as a pragmatic patchwork of state responses to an increasingly aggressive national politics of claims. The American people, it appeared, were prepared to tax themselves for services which, acting individually, they were unwilling or incapable of providing for themselves.

In devising welfare policies, from the early 1930s to the late 1960s, the state performed two major civilian functions. The first was countercyclical, whereby it would finance public works and social programs during periods of economic downturn. (The other phase of Keynesian policy, retiring the public debt during periods of recovery, was never effectively implemented). The second role was redistributive.

But by the beginning of the 1970s, the whole philosophy of welfare came under severe attack. In the end, belief not only in the welfare state but in the state's civilian functions overall was all but obliterated. Two developments contributed to this assault on the ideology of a socially benign state.

First, in parallel with the welfare state, emerged a *warfare state* of gigantic proportions. Beginning in World War II, the military-industrial complex played an increasingly determining role in U.S. life. Successive high points were reached with the Cold War, the arms race, the hot wars in Korea and Vietnam, the space program, and, most recently, the Strategic Defense Initiative, or "Star Wars." The militarization of the United States led to an inevitable clash between military and civilian expenditures. The first attempt to deal with this conflict was, in effect, to bypass it through large-scale deficit finance. This was President Johnson's strategy during the Vietnam era, and it led to spiralling inflation. A second strategy was subsequently tried (without, however, reducing the budget deficit): the cutback of nonessential civilian expenditures by the state. What turned out to be nonessential, however, was virtually the entire panoply of welfare measures, except for Social Security, which the politics of claims had succeeded in institutionalizing during the preceding generation. The abrupt dismantling of the welfare state left the warfare state intact. In fact, under Ronald Reagan, the warfare state would flourish as it had never done before in peaceful times.

The second development undermining belief in the civilian functions of the state was a growing conviction in the United States that the large, bureaucratic state was unproductive, inefficient, heavy-handed, and inept. Contributing to this image were studies by social scientists who typically would rush into action whenever a new government program was launched to "evaluate" its results. They would race to publish definitive findings before the next presidential election two or three years down the line. Not surprisingly, virtually all these studies found government programs to have "failed." Some, more dramatically, would argue that government intervention, instead of solving problems, only made them worse.

This condemnation of the civilian state by the experts went hand-in-hand with a populist political rhetoric that would praise the virtues of old-fashioned individualism and accept as axiomatic the productive efficiency of corporate (private) capital.

With the decline of the economy, rising unemployment, and the resurgence of poverty in the late 1970s, the state was forced to refocus public attention on the question of economic growth. In line with the general disparagement of the welfare state that had found widespread public assent, the government itself would argue now that its own maze of regulations and involvements was holding back a business-led economic recovery. In order to re-energize America, the story went, capital would have to be unfettered, taxes on business would have to be drastically reduced, the economy would have to be decontrolled. At the same time, a stepped-up anti-Soviet rhetoric and an artificially induced anticommunist hysteria allowed government to increase the national debt to beyond a trillion dollars. Most of the increment was channelled in the direction of the Pentagon and its civilian suppliers.

The answer from the political Left was ambiguous. One can understand why the majority of Americans would buy an argument that promised national strength, lower taxes, and the debureaucratization of national life. But one might have thought the Left would have had a different response. Such was not to be the case, however. The warfare state, of course, was vehemently attacked, but the state's civilian role was not enthusiastically defended. While Marxists withdrew into their esoteric journals to "retheorize" the state, the New Left joined in the chorus against Leviathan. As activists they threw themselves into a politics of localism and social movements. *Think globally, act locally* became a slogan of the times.

Significant though it is, the new localism is quite unable to cope with the big issues of transition. It lacks not only an economic vision, but a clear sense of the public interest. Instead, it concentrates on certain trendy issues that, though in themselves important, are incapable of levering fundamental changes in society. What is lacking is a new conceptualization of the state. For neither Left nor Right has any other understanding of the state than the already discredited ones of social reform, welfare, and national defense.

How might a new policy then be defined? Given a capitalism reaching for global control and which, by virtue of this control, is posing an increasing threat to the legitimacy of the state, what new forms of the state will need to be evolved to deal effectively with the multiple crises of the current transition?

Belief in Salvation by Science

In the decades following World War Two the practical optimism of Americans raised science and its applications to new heights of social veneration. Scientists had "unlocked the secrets of Nature" and helped turn them to profitable use. Science also meant power: it made the United States invincible. Scientists and engineers became the culture heroes of the age.

Social and behavioral scientists perceived their disciplines to be lagging behind the natural sciences, but they harbored similar aspirations: to unlock the secrets of human individual and social behavior and to use this knowledge in helping humanity achieve its age-long dream of perfect happiness. New fields of professional practice sprouted in the postwar period: economic and social planning, policy analysis, operations research, systems analysis, organization development, futurology, and more. In one way or another, planners believed that societal problems would yield to scientific understanding and the manipulations of technical experts. The dominant approach was mechanical. If there were too many people in the world, give them the pill. If they were hungry, give them the "green revolution" of genetically modified varieties of grains. If resources became scarce from overuse, replace them with technical substitutes or develop new technologies for lifting minerals from the bottom of the sea. If people were unhappy, a little behavior modification might do a lot of good. And so it went.

Public acclaim of the social/behavioral scientist was never very great, and the profession had some problems "selling itself" to its potential sponsors. Still, it can be said that in its tougher-minded, esoteric forms, which involved mathematical modelling, long-term forecasting, simulations, and the like, it shared in some of the reflected glory of the scientific enterprise.

But the worm of doubt was at work from the very beginning, and it would grow larger and larger as the decades wore on. The story of this doubt has many facets and can be told from many different perspectives. Here are some of them.

One of the dramatic achievements of "the scientific enterprise" was the controlled chain reaction of atomic fission. But the energy released during this first successful experiment in 1942 was applied to the physical annihilation of 200,000 civilian victims in the bombings of Japan. Thus, what was to be the most spectacular application of science to a human use proved in the first instance to be an act of horrifying destruction.

A different doubt about the beneficent effects of science came from a more philosophical quarter. Natural science proceeds through a structure of research that is atomistic, highly compartmentalized, and hyperspecialized. In this process, the view of the whole, the dense connectedness of things, is inevitably lost.

Social and behavioral scientists adopted much the same procedure. And they, too, lost sight of the whole. More specifically, they lost a sense of history and place; access to humanistic knowledge; and the ability, as scientists, to make both ethical and political judgments. The knowledge they gathered was not about living men and women in particular social settings, but about lifeless abstractions unrelated to a larger problematic. Conclusions based on such knowledge might have some meaning in the theories of social science, but the import of these theories for practice was open to doubt. Planners might indeed be inventive, in seeking applications for their science, but the results were generally disappointing. Not all the blame can be laid at planners' feet, but a good part of the trouble derives from methodologies grounded in the positivism of the social and behavioral sciences on which they have come to rely.

The most important doubt, however, arose with the question of who would apply the knowledge generated in the course of scientific work. In the case of the natural sciences the answer was self-evident. The principal users were the state and the corporations that had paid to obtain it. The former exploited the sciences chiefly for military ends, the latter for commercial purposes. In a business civilization, the ultimate payoff was profits and the military strength to defend the right to their private appropriation.

But the case of the social and behavioral sciences is not very different. The state wants access to this knowledge to control its subjects more effectively, and corporations want it to improve their sales. Clearly, neither form of application is liberating in any real sense.

But if knowledge is not liberating, if it does not set us free, what transcendental purpose does it serve? How can there be a rational belief in "salvation by science" when the results of scientific work are used primarily to destroy, control, and manipulate people?

There are those who argue that it is not scientists who invent these uses of oppression, but social institutions. Apart from the facts that science is also a social institution and scarcely exists apart from its setting, and that science and technology must be seen increasingly as having fused into a single operation, there remains the larger question of a scientific understanding that is atomistic, compartmentalized, and hyperspecialized.

Science was not always this way, nor need it remain what it has become. Still, it is clear that many people, including practitioners of science and those who stand in line of application, have begun seriously to question the scientific enterprise as it exists. They ask about new ways of thinking about the world in both its natural and human aspects. They seek to rejoin the many fragments of knowledge into a holistic and ethical vision, no longer divorced from history and place and ethics. Above all, they search for a knowledge that will be accessible to people in the process of their quest for self-empowerment and liberation.

Concluding Questions

I have argued that our time is characterized by a general collapse of meaning. The home truths of yesterday, still clung to in some parts, are no longer tenable in light of the experience of the past forty years. Economic growth is no longer thought of as the panacea that will shower its material blessings upon all of us for ever and ever. The dream of a universal model of development has been exploded by the realities of the Third World. In place of universal development, more and more people are living in dire need, and the semi-industrialized world is mired in the contradictions of a lopsided development and growing violence. The Great Consensus built around the mythology of an ever-expanding middle class has broken down, and the political community is more polarized than it has ever been. But because political leadership is missing, discontent is manifesting itself as a retreat into privatism for the majority and, as dedication to chiefly local action for those who remain politically engaged. The civilian state, in its specific form of the welfare state, has become discredited in the minds of many, and there has been surprisingly little opposition to its dismantling by its enemies. Private business—capital—is reasserting its strength over territorial communities, and the state is increasingly attending to its military functions. The warfare state has replaced the welfare state. Finally, we have lost faith in the powers of science to provide us with a way out of the present historical impasse. As an instrument in the hands of the state and the corporations, science has contributed to destruction, control, and manipulation for the sake of shoring up the powers of the powerful. It has not delivered on its promise to liberate humanity from the ensnarements of its persisting ignorance.

The hegemonic ideology thus lies in shambles, and no alternative is in sight. The situation is serious. People need to believe. Not believing, they turn into cynics and nihilists. They are frozen into inaction and will seek alternative means of release in sheer violence, privatism, other worldly cults, the rigid verities of fundamentalist religion. They become ready to follow any leader whose rhetoric can reach the atavistic energies that lie dormant in the deepest recesses of their psyches.

The danger signals are there for all to see. Residual hopes that the spectre of crisis will somehow resolve itself, and that we will return to a world of stable progress and ever-encompassing humanity, are not going to be fulfilled. There are no ready solutions lying about. Nor will salvation come by way of science. What is needed is a new set of rational beliefs that will express new sets of power relations. Such a counterhegemony, as Antonio Gramsci called it, must necessarily arise from outside the existing structures of domination. It cannot be merely invented, but must arise from the everyday practices of ordinary people as they struggle to carve out a small niche for themselves in the incipient chaos.

So, in ending, I have no answers, only questions. And my questions, which I take to be beacon lights in the progress of humanity, are these:

- How might quantity and quality in economic growth be brought into a new relation so that the quality of life might be improved for everyone?
- In an interdependent world, how shall we respond to human need when the universal model of development has lost its credibility?
- Where the poor are disempowered, and the energy for a revitalized politics is missing, how can people be enticed back into active citizenship?
- Given a capitalism that is reaching for global control and which, by virtue of this control, is posing an increasing threat to the legitimacy of the state, what new forms of the state will need to be evolved to deal effectively with the multiple crises of the current transition?
- What new ways of thinking about the world will help us to achieve a unified approach to science that, while open to surprise, is yet informed by ethical and political commitments and that will be accessible to people generally in their quest for self-empowerment and liberation?

Appendix to Chapter Two
"THE CRISIS OF TRANSITION":
AN EXCHANGE

A.
Mr. Friedmann's Development Nightmare

If anything can go wrong it will (Murphy's Law)

Martin Bronfenbrenner
Kenan Professor of Economics and Lecturer in History at Duke University (Durham, North Carolina, USA).

Mr. John Friedmann, a planner rather than an economist by background, provides a 1984-type horror story of the worst possible outcomes of two currently-favoured 'Western' development strategies. He also considers them the most probable outcomes, and herein lies the basis for my disagreement.

One cannot, alas, rule out in advance Friedmann's dystopian outcome of continued or even worsened poverty and underdevelopment. But it is not legitimate to depict such an outcome as either the Freudian wish of Western development economists or the necessary implication of any Western strategy.

Let us consider Friedmann's two strategies in turn, together with his expectations of their consequences.

I

Strategy 1 Friedmann calls 'export substitution'; the conventional term is 'export promotion'. It is the *expansion* or *proliferation* of a country's menu of exports beyond agricultural and mineral raw materials to comprise labour-intensive light-industrial products—and perhaps eventually heavier industrial products as well. (Japan is an historical example of development along this line; South Korea and Taiwan are contemporary ones.) In addition to raising a country's measured growth rate, export expansion is expected to reduce the extent of poverty, especially rural poverty, and possibly even to equalize the personal income distribution, as workers are attracted from subsistence agriculture to urban labour by the various attractions of city life,

295

including higher real incomes. Initial urban wage rates indeed remain low, even below 'poverty' standards, by Western ways of thinking, but eventually there will come a 'turning point' marked by urban labour shortages, after which wage rates rise toward developed-country levels. But these last steps are dependent on preventing the rise of labour aristocracies of organized urban workers, which raise wage rates prematurely for the first migrants, and condemn later migrants to long periods of urban unemployment in over-crowded labour markets.

Ah, but (says Friedmann), what if something like an enclosure movement, a Green Revolution, or a cotton-picker drives workers off the land into the city slums even as wages below the predevelopment subsistence level? And what if 'population explosion' postpones the turning point indefinitely by providing a continuous flow of rural-urban migrants? Herein lies the major Friedmann nightmare.

Can these things happen? Indeed they can; we can be faulted for insufficient frankness in admitting that they can. But does any development economist want them to happen? Certainly not; proponents of export promotion are decided anti-natalists. Does any capitalist of standing, whether native or multinational, any twentieth century Gradgrind or Bounderby, want them to happen? If so, he keeps his secret well guarded. Are these things likely to happen anyway? This is the real problem. The answer, alas, varies from country to country and from time to time. Generalizations and abstractions are, I think, premature and misleading.

With a heterogeneous and/or a trainable labour force, by the way, there may be no single turning point anywhere in the development process. What we may see is rather a rising proportion of skilled and semi-skilled labour, well before the wage of the unskilled rises significantly. Friedmann equates this process of increasing productivity with the Marxian concepts of speed-up and longer working day (increasing relative and absolute exploitation rates, respectively). I suspect this may have been atypical even in the days of Marx and Engels. It is more atypical today. Increasing productivity means primarily on-the-job training or, if you prefer, learning by doing.

We turn now to the day after the turning point. Once labour costs begin to rise for unskilled labour, will not the wicked multinationals (who, Friedmann believes, provide the bulk of urban employment) then close their plants or move them, and throw their workers on to the street? This is what Friedmann anticipates; such cases cannot, once again, be ruled out ex ante. But let us inquire about the forces which have pushed wages up in the first place. If, as we suppose, these include a general labour scarcity as traditional wage rates, the disemployed can surely be absorbed with minimal difficulty, assuming only a monetary-fiscal policy short of 'savage deflation'.

II

Friedmann also takes a nightmare view of a Strategy 2, centering upon the IBRD-Sussex study of *Redistribution with Growth*, which he calls simply 'RwG'. This strategy features the development and financing of 'appropriate technologies'—more properly, in my own view, appropriate *output mixes*—to combine acceptable though usually not maximum rates of measured growth with fuller employment and higher incomes for the lower 60 percent of the population.[1] If my understanding is correct, this approach is more nearly *alternative* to the export-led expansion of the modern sector than an aspect or accompaniment of Strategy I.

This is indeed, as Friedmann complains, a difficult strategy to define or 'pin down' as to specifics. The difficulty arises not because proponents are in any way 'slippery' (Friedmann's term), but from the highly pragmatic nature of the specifics. They may be quite different in Gambia from what they are in Zambia, and the results may also be quite different.

There are pitfalls aplenty in 'RwG' strategy, as none have denied. Friedmann expects the temptation to 'creaming' to be irresistible.[2] The visiting expert, the international development-sponsoring agency, or the domestic development planners, are also tempted to rest content with showpiece pilot projects, Potemkin villages, or 'duodecimo editions of the New Jerusalem'. Nor should we overlook the corresponding temptation for financial authorities to limit participation to the minimum required to maintain aid, and to plead inability to expand or even continue the strategy after the aid expires. But admitting all this, we need not go all the way with Friedmann's wholesale damnation of 'RwG' strategy in advance for failing to revolutionize the society's underlying structure, or for being somehow linked with 'export substitution'.

A good government will indeed be required to administer 'RwG' effectively. Strategy 2 is not for Idi Amin's Uganda or Bokassa I's Central African Empire. But a good government, with or without foreign advisors, need not be a body of Supermen, either in administrative skills or ideological purity, to make the strategy work satisfactorily-though-imperfectly.

III

In conclusion, I shall try to summarize under three heads the reasons I fear Freidmann goes too far in substituting nightmare for analysis; this even though I too am long-term-dubious about 'export substitution' in a world of developed-country protectionism and about 'RwG' for some of the reasons sketched immediately above.

1. Friedmann is insufficiently empirical in either the historical or the statistical senses. A hard look at either Meiji Japan or post-1945 Japan would have done him a world of good. This is not to deny that generalization and abstraction have their places, but simply to urge relation of their results to whatever evidence is available.

2. Friedmann sees 'export substitution' and 'RwG' as two aspects of grand Western strategy to avoid development crises where, to quote the late George Papandreou, 'the figures prosper but the people suffer'. In fact, the two approaches are to a great extent rivals, the first stressing exports and the second domestic production, although mixtures are not to be ruled out.

3. Friedmann is not a 'well-poisoner' in the grand Stalinist manner. He does, however, appear inclined to assume the worst for capitalist institutions, and to assume likewise that capitalists themselves, multinationals particularly, conspire the worst for their host countries. He therefore concludes, or perhaps assumes at starting, that nothing short of restructuring of society (including complete overthrow of capitalism) can bring off successful development—or permit the shaping of reasonable development theory.

Notes

1. In terms of the Harrod development identity: Let G be the measured growth rate, s the society's saving ratio, and C the incremental capital-output ratio. Then Harrod shows $GC = s$ or $G = s/C$. In 'appropriate-technology' language, we are searching (but may not always find) sets of inputs and outputs which will, by lowering C, permit co-existence of a high G and the low s which can be expected under an egalitarian income distribution even when supplemented by foreign assistance.

2. To 'cream' means in this context to concentrate redistributive efforts on the most able, appreciative, co-operative, and efficient members of the lower n per cent who form one's 'target group'. Such folk are apt to be clustered at the group's statistical upper bound, and to omit 'the poorest of the poor'.

B.
Mr. Friedmann's 'Crisis':
A Reluctant Rebuttal

Gustav Ranis
Professor of Economics at Yale University

In my view Mr. Friedmann's piece suffers both from a faulty grasp of the intellectual history in the field of development and from the absence of analytical spectacles through which to judge current LDC transition strategies. But these are both properly the subject for scientific debate, and I am perfectly prepared to respond and then let the reader judge the merits of the case. There is, however, another dimension to Friedmann's comments which places them quite beyond the pale—namely, the effort to claim for himself the high moral ground, cast doubt on the real motives of those he disagrees with—and then proceed to use the time-tested (by other zealots) tools of partial quotes and guilt-by-association to establish his case. I will attempt mainly to deal with the substantive issues and thus try to avoid a total descent to the same level of discourse.[1]

Turning first to Mr. Friedmann's characterization of development theory during the past quarter century, he places Rostovian stages theory, Kuznets's transition to modern economic growth, and Chenery's patterns of development in the same analytical bed. He awards neo-classical labels to both Arthur Lewis and Paul Streeten and he completely disregards the important prior work of Martin, Nurkse and Rosenstein-Rodan on the importance of mobilizing rural labour, and of Kuznets on the importance of not neglecting equity in the course of growth. Schumpeter is interpreted as advocating the flow of resources to a select few in restricted markets rather than describing the process by which occasional swarms of entrepreneurs are followed by even larger hordes of imitators until the profit rate is driven down to zero. Perhaps this is enough to establish Friedmann's credentials in the history of thought.

It is, of course, true that most economists paid much less attention to the distributive aspects of growth in the 1950s and 1960s than they do today; but this is equally true for politicians and policy makers and

299

in both the South and the North—at least in terms of the voices that could or can be heard. It is also true that overall actual LDC performance during both periods continues generally satisfactory with respect to growth and unsatisfactory with respect to equity; but it is equally true that some of the fastest growing countries also exhibited the most equitable distribution of income. Consequently, per capita income growth is not an evil indicator which needs to be 'dethroned' because it is inevitably associated with what Friedmann calls the 'model of uneven development'; rather, as Japan earlier, and a small subset of contemporary LDCs including Taiwan have shown, choosing an alternative way in which output is generated can both enhance per capita income growth and render the path more equitable. What Friedmann calls 'strategies of crisis management' are nothing more than efforts to better understand the possibilities of achieving such complementarity among development objectives and of moving perhaps more typical LDC situations—such as that of the Philippines—in similar directions.

What the ILO Philippine Mission, in fact, recommended is *not* a strategy of export substitution—as Friedmann contends—but a two-pronged strategy of rural mobilization plus export substitution within which balanced rural growth is clearly given priority. The Report states (pp. 35–36) that 'the first prong of our strategy is directed towards the mobilization of the rural sector of the Philippine economy . . . Without substantive progress on this front, no matter what happens in the relatively small urban industrial sector can make much of a difference'. What indeed could be clearer? The misunderstanding here can only be called intentional with the Report going to great lengths to emphasize the detailed merits of decentralized, internally oriented development.

Instead of reading the Report, Mr. Friedmann has chosen to continuously associate it with out-of-context quotes from another, unrelated source, the Paauw/Fei volume which he asserts to be the *locus classicus* of the underlying analysis. While the Philippine Mission is certainly ready to acknowledge its intellectual debt to some of the earlier work by Paauw and Fei and by Fei and Ranis, it has its own conceptual as well as policy moorings, and should in all fairness be appraised on its own bottoms. Friedmann, after admitting that the Philippine Report contains 'additional features—important to note' chooses to virtually ignore the key role accorded these in both the analysis and the policy recommendations.

Mr. Friedmann moreover misunderstands or purposely misinterprets the export substitution prong of the proposed development strategy for the labour surplus developing economy. If the (prior) import substitution sub-phase favoured large-scale foreign (and domestic) industrialists, to cite one example, it is the very policy changes (i.e. liberalization of various markets) suggested by the Mission which are intended to give the domestic medium and small-scale entrepreneurs their access and chance to participate in the export substitution process.[2]

It is not suggested, to cite again, that real wages be 'allowed to fall below subsistence needs'. Rather, wages cannot be expected to rise much as long as the labour surplus overhangs the market; neither the ILO Mission, nor presumably Mr. Friedmann, knows a way to legislate against the endowment—and to make it stick. Although the Philippine Report is replete with references to the importance of realizing that *wage rate* restraint will favour *wage incomes* as long as the labour surplus persists, Mr. Friedmann chooses to ignore it and play to (rapidly emptying) galleries. To call the maintenance of the relatively low wages of the already employed labour force elite 'exploitation', rather than (as we do) the rising unemployment of the unorganized rural workers, which would surely follow from his call for increased union pressure, is nothing short of cynical. Since the Mission was at pains to point out that the struggle between wages and profits in the organized sectors of the typical LDC really represents a 'settlement' among bilateral monopolists, leaving the basic social problem of effective labour absorption to one side, we can only surmise that Friedmann did not wish to understand.

A final illustration of Friedmann's 'methodology' is provided by his effort to misuse the conveniently emotive issue of the foreign investor. The Report is explicitly accused of trying to facilitate the exploitation of Philippine workers by the multinational corporation. In fact, the Report urges more systematic screening and 'additional measures . . . to discourage the notion of "making hay while the sun shines".' Friedmann, moreover, denigrates the role of the foreigner who, having helped the developing country reach unskilled labour shortage (the so-called turning point) via a labour intensive export drive, is then forced to turn to other activities. He is admittedly interested in profits—and nobody ever claimed otherwise—and he will admittedly have to adjust to the new circumstances—either by moving to another more labour surplus country (and what is wrong with that?) or by adjusting his output mix in a more skilled labour and technology intensive direction (e.g. in Taiwan after 1968 when labour shortage was reached foreign investment more than doubled). Empirically foreign firms, in fact, do some of both, as one would expect. Again, what is wrong with that—as long as the policy environment does not give special favours to the foreigner? Even socialist countries recognize the validity of taking advantage of the international product cycle or, if you will, forever changing rules of dynamic comparative advantage; but Friedmann marches on, alone, claiming that once the 'labour advantage has disappeared . . . no other advantage exists'.

We could go on—but we won't. Exchanges of this kind usually involve alternative explicit or implicit models of how the real world operates and alternative interpretations of the empirical record. But this one is different. We are accused of 'approving of population growth' and recommending 'mechanization in agriculture' presumably so that sufficient workers can be 'forced into industry at starvation wages'—in spite of suggesting methods of improved access to family planning programmes and in spite of a major attack on tractorization which invoked the ire of a lot of vested interests. We are accused of devoting 'exactly 15 lines in a text of 16 pages of recommendations' to land reform—a comment which ignores an entire Chapter and the statement that we consider such reform 'one of the major contributions to a more equitable distribution of income in the Philippines'. We are accused of wanting to 'move people off the farm as quickly as possible and into the cities, where they will join the lumpenproletariat . . . whose function is to hold wages down'—in the face of our consistent elevation of the rural mobilization/balanced growth strategy to get 'the rural sector to "hold" its people in productive employment'. We are accused of subscribing to some automatic 'universal harmony of interests' when we spend the entire last chapter (Ch. 12) summarizing the need to form social consensus coalitions of interest groups to effect the necessary changes in policy. Mr. Friedmann apparently knows what the 'real intentions' behind our 'clever strategy' were, presumably to do the devil's or the multinationals' dirty-work. On p. 45 the low point is reached: 'the text is specifically devised to give an incorrect impression of what are the real intentions . . .'. I can only wonder about Mr. Friedmann's—and urge the reader to draw his own conclusions.

Notes

1. Had *Development and Change* not actively sought this comment, I am frank to admit I would have been happy to let Mr. Friedmann's diatribe speak for itself.
2. He has, moreover conveniently distorted the facts (in context on p. 283 of the Report) concerning the relative role of foreign investors in the base period. US investors held 76 per cent of total foreign equity investment, not of 'total equity', and foreign investment accounted for 33.5 per cent of the total assets of respondent firms, all large-scale, rather than of 'all industry'.

C.
The Crisis of Transition: A Brief Rejoinder

Hans Singer
*Professor Emeritus and Professorial Fellow of the Institute of
Development Studies at the University of Sussex.*

John Friedmann's paper is certainly provocative. He reminds me of a wild shooter who sprays his bullets widely at what he imagines to be his main targets. In the process he possibly scores one or two hits and some interesting near-misses. (For instance, I agree with Friedmann that there can be no confidence in the idea of a 'turning point' towards greater equality once you engage in a strategy of growth through inequality—and have myself argued this in several places.) But many of his shots are wide of the mark and, irresponsibly, also hit some innocent bystanders. (I am thinking, for instance, of his comment on Schumpeter.) However, in this rejoinder I shall limit myself to the last few pages of his paper, in which he directly comments on the Kenya Report and its underlying ideas. I realise that the Kenya Report, and its associated ideas of Redistribution from Growth (RfG) and Redistribution with Growth (RwG), are only secondary targets. His primary target is the Philippines Report and export substitution; I understand that Gus Ranis will also comment, and he can be expected to take care of that part of John Friedmann's criticisms. I would, however, point out that, contrary to the impression which John Friedmann seems to have, the two approaches seem to me birds of very different feathers.

Just one other broad comment: John Friedmann describes the Kenya/RfG/RwG approach as 'slippery'. Leaving aside the disagreeable insinuations of that word, I can only assume he wants to say that he found it difficult or impossible to get to grips with these ideas. Has it occurred to him to ask himself whether this inability could lie in the limitations of his own thinking rather than in the limitations of the concepts which he criticizes?

One illustration of this would be his description of the RwG strategy as 'reform-mongering'. What does he include as reform-mongering? He lists five items: 'accelerating GNP growth through raising savings;

allocating resources more efficiently, with benefits to all groups in the society; redistribution of existing assets; assets redistribution by redirecting new investment into the creation of assets generating income for the poorest; and transfer of income in support of consumption of the poorest'. If that is reform-mongering, what is missing? Is anything left, beyond the redistribution of existing assets, income transfer, and redirection of new investment? The only thing that seems to me missing is the element of violence and revolution. Does John Friedmann believe, like Frantz Fanon, that violence and revolution are good, 'cleansing' in themselves? Unless he answers that question in the affirmative, I fail to see how anybody, including John Friedmann, can fail to be a 'reform-monger'.

In any case, to base the Kenya Report on the assumption of a situation ripe for violent and revolutionary change would have been absurd. I may add that personally I do not believe that either theoretical or empirical evidence leads us to the conclusion that the inclusion of revolutionary violence is likely to bring us any nearer to the set aim of reduction of poverty and satisfaction of basic needs, including political and human rights.

In this connection let me quickly dispose of another accusation, i.e. that the Kenya Report (as well as its associated philosophies) fails to warn against the reduction in urban wages down to and below starvation level by a process of inflation. In the first place, at the time the Kenya Report was written (1972) there was no inflation in Kenya, nor was there any great balance of payments crisis. Does John Friedmann criticize us for not foreseeing the OPEC action and the subsequent oil and balance of payments crisis for Kenya, beginning in late 1973? Moreover, urban wages in the modern sector were a high multiple of rural incomes—nor were the multinational corporations conspicuous by wage-cutting or laying workers off or preventing trade union organization—quite on the contrary, they saw their interests in different directions. Applied to the Kenyan situation, the John Friedmann approach would have been utterly unrealistic.

I might also comment on John Friedmann's criticism of RwG and the basic needs approach in relation to the need to define a 'target population'. If he wishes to make nonsense of this concept or to read sinister implications into it, there is nothing to prevent him from doing so. But it should be quite clear that the concept refers to the definition of a group of poor beneficiaries[1] for suggested 'reform-mongering' policies. To serve this purpose the 'target' must obviously be defined as a reasonable and manageable proportion of the total population— say, the poorest 20 or 30 percent. Admittedly, the words 'reasonable' and 'manageable' are somewhat vague and arbitrary or—if John Friedmann prefers that word, 'slippery'—but in that quality they simply reflect life. A target of 100 percent of the total population is clearly nonsense, as John Friedmann rightly points out. But the confusion is his mixing up the idea of a target population with a concept of absolute poverty.

I agree with Friedmann that 'only policies that *place growth incentives where the people are* and that are capable of producing a true merger of growth with distribution, efficiency with equity, have any hopes for long-term success'. I believe that is exactly what we have done in the Kenya Report. Several of our recommendations cannot be more specific in 'placing growth incentives where people are'—I refer particularly to our recommendations concerning decentralization of investments funds (Chapter 19) and our recommendations concerning the informal sector (Chapter 13). I further agree with him that this approach requires definition of the poor 'in terms of their relative lack of access to social power (and not their level of consumption)'. But if I look at John Friedmann's footnote 9 describing five aspects of 'multi-faceted' social power, I once again find that the Kenya Report very clearly and explicitly tries to cover all the five facets which Friedmann mentions: productive wealth in land and tools; information and knowledge; education for adaptive action and for further learning; financial resources; contact networks.

I conclude this rejoinder by expressing a sense of deja-vu. Much of the discussion has already been anticipated by Colin Leys' and the exchanges which followed his book—of which John Friedmann was clearly unaware when he first wrote his article—and nobody who reads the brief chapter on 'The Cost of Inaction' (Chapter 20) in the Kenya Report can believe that the authors of that Report, or those pursuing associated ideas of RwG, were as politically naive as John Friedmann seems to think.

Notes

1. Perhaps the term 'beneficiaries' has even more sinister implications than the term 'target'?

D.
A Rejoinder to Bronfenbrenner, Singer, and Ranis

John Friedmann

What are we discussing here, what is the nature of the problem, and how should it be addressed?

What are we discussing?

A scientific theory of how economic growth and development came to be realized in Japan, the Republic of Korea, and Taiwan? And perhaps for comparison's sake, also in England, the United States, and the Soviet Union? And thus, perhaps, a theory of history? Or a political model of how one variable, for instance GNP, responds under given assumptions to different policy settings? Or a prescriptive the ory—a doctrine—of how the currently 'less developed countries' should act in order to achieve high economic growth with equity and full employment?

I take it to be the last of these questions. And where doctrine is concerned, moral and political questions cannot be 'bracketed'; they must be directly addressed. It is illusory to think that we can discuss prescriptive theory without explicitly introducing an ideological dimension. I will go further to assert that the issues we address are too important to be left to 'experts'. We must engender a public debate about them, and this enjoins us to use language to which 'non-experts' can respond. In such a context, a purely scientific discourse, such as Gustav Ranis would be prepared to join, is clearly out-of-place.

What is the nature of the problem?

We do not seem to be completely in agreement. I might phrase it as follows: is there a crisis to which we should respond, or isn't there? And if there is a crisis, what is its nature? Martin Bronfenbrenner thinks I am 'substituting nightmare for analysis', and Gustav Ranis finds that though there is indeed a problem of income distribution, a crisis is nowhere in sight.

In light of these doubts, consider the following snapshots.

India. Population 621 million. 'According to a recent estimate using norms of calorie consumption, the percentage of population below the poverty line in 1977–78 may be projected at 48 percent in rural areas and 41 percent in urban areas. The number of the poor so defined would be about 290 million.[1]

Pakistan. Population 72 million. 'We conclude, therefore, that more than 58 percent of all farms in West Pakistan are below subsistence level. The total number of rural *households* below the subsistence line might be greater, not only because many farms are jointly cultivated by more than one household, but also because we must include in that category landless labourers who contributed about 11 percent of the civilian labour force in agriculture in 1961 . . .[2]

Bangladesh. Population 76 million. 'The living standards of the vast majority of the rural population . . . declined in absolute terms during recent decades. The real wages of agricultural labourers fell [from TK. 2.27 in 1961 to TK. 1.28 in 1975]. These phenomena have been particularly pronounced in recent years. Comparing the decline in recent years with the already dreadful poverty in the benchmark year, it is clear that the vast majority of the rural population today must be suffering from severe undernutrition and starvation in various degrees. It seems highly likely that mortality rates have increased and that the expectation of life has declined from the already unfavourable levels mentioned earlier'.[3]

Java. Population 85 million. 'Unfortunately the figure for the absolutely landless in 1970 is not available, but according to the 1963 agricultural census they amounted to 21 percent of all rural households. Combining the 1963 and 1970 survey, it can be said that in 1970 at least 41 percent of rural households had no land or less than 0.1 hectare . . . By 1973, almost half of Java's rural households were, or were virtually, landless. This number does not include those unknown numbers of tenants and their families operating farms more than 0.1 hectare, but who have been reduced to de facto landless labourers through the modernization of rice production'.[4]

Philippines. Population 44 million. 'Our results show that for the country as a whole, families with either expenditure or income less than the food threshold of poverty have been increasing both in proportionate and absolute values during the past years . . .'

'The food threshold is the lower limit of the matrix of minimum needs. The minimum is defined only in terms of physical survival . . .

And yet, even then, nearly 41 percent of our families are unable to meet this standard. [The ratio rises to 48 percent in rural areas]. In 1971, nearly 3 million families were unable to feed themselves adequately . . .'

'The total threshold is perhaps more remarkable for what it omits than for what it includes . . . It merely states the barest minimum by which subsistence can be theoretically achieved. Yet, our results indicate that nearly ½ of our urban population and ¾ of our rural families are impoverished'.[5]

These data are for 1971. At that time, the absolute number of rural people living in poverty was estimated at more than 20 million. Urban areas added another 6.3 million, for a total poverty population of 26.5 million. These estimates are based on expenditure data. Income data would raise the number of the rural poor to 83 percent or 21.2 million people.

Thailand. Population 43 million. Between 1968/69 and 1972/73, it is likely that the number of people who would have to borrow money to maintain minimum food consumption levels in the Central Region about doubled from 21 to 40 percent. The principal reason for this was accelerated inflation during this period as well as worsening income distribution.[6]

The foregoing quotations are not especially selected with an eye to shocking the reader. They are matter-of-fact reports, repeated time and again in the literature, of present-day 'nightmares' and could easily be replicated for much of the agrarian world outside of China. The indicators suggest a general worsening of conditions, with no relief in sight. Are 'export promotion' and 'redistribution with or from growth' likely to improve the conditions described within a reasonable period? The answer seems doubtful at best. And if 300 million people in India go to bed hungry, is it a 'crisis' or not?

There are indeed some notable exceptions. Professor Bronfenbrenner thinks I should have done more reading on the economic history of Japan, and there are the usual oblique hints at the 'miracles' of South Korea, Taiwan, and Singapore. These countries have successfully joined the world economy by exploiting their comparative advantage in manufacturing and are beginning to be treated as 'junior partners'. It might be more accurate to say it is their national business elites that have been elevated to junior partnership, and that the countries themselves are invited into the club only by virtue of their political stability. But, do these countries provide the rest of the poverty-stricken world with appropriate models of how they *ought* to proceed in managing their national affairs? And what, after all, ought the objectives to be?

The very notion of 'development' is currently in contention. The Swedish Dag Hammarskjöld Foundation is pursuing 'another development', and Dudley Seers has recently proposed that we consider 'self-reliance' as the appropriate goal.[7] The problem for a given country may not simply be to move increasing numbers of the poor across an arbitrary income threshold, but to consider what social and political relations should be fostered as it steers its shaky course from an irredeemable past into the future. To be sure, this question has an economic dimension, but this is subordinate to more broadly conceived considerations of political thought.

I may not be able to persuade my critics that there is indeed a 'crisis' which manifests itself in sub-human conditions throughout much of the world and on a scale that far exceeds even Mr. McNamara's famous 40 percent. Professor Singer doubts that a 'target population' of 100 percent makes sense. I am not so sure. Where would he draw the line in Bangladesh, or Java? My point is this: the problems of survival are so pervasive that only structural solutions have the remotest chance of coming to grips with them. This does not necessarily mean revolution. But it means something more than incremental change.

How should the problem be addressed?

Or more precisely, should we speak the language of positive economics or political economy? In the first tradition, the question of efficiency in production is separated from that of equity in distribution, with the former pre-empted as the realm of science, while the latter is left to politics.[8] This formulation allows for the construction of the well-known trade-off models which are usually phrased so that a gain in equity must be paid off out of gains in production and therefore future income. Such is the thinking which underlies both of our 'crisis' doctrines. If wages are allowed to rise, export industry must be sacrificed; if the 'informal' sector is to grow, there will be a decline of investment in the 'formal' sector. In either case, social justice will lead to loss of GNP.

In political economy, such separation is inconceivable. Social purposes underlie both the overall pattern of resource allocation *and* the distribution of the product. The market is also a chosen instrument of allocation. It is not a 'natural' phenomenon. In political economy, therefore, we are dealing with a total way of life, in which 'fact' and 'value' are not hermetically sealed off from each other, and where the substance of economics is, in the last analysis, political.

As his comment makes clear, Hans Singer joins me in the belief that the relevant language is that of political economy. But with both of my other critics, the political dimension of economics is reduced to vestigial proportions. Professor Bronfenbrenner introduces it obliquely when he mentions the need for 'good government' to effectively administer a RwG strategy (though 'good' in this connection apparently means nothing more than 'reasonably competent'), while Gustav Ranis subsumes the political element of economic theory under the curious phrase 'social consensus coalitions'. Those familiar with Philippine politics over the last twelve years can form a fairly accurate picture of how this social consensus was obtained and whose interests were 'coalesced'. One thing is clear: peasants and workers, comprising 90 percent of the population, lack both voice and presence in the political life of the country as they do indeed throughout most of the world periphery.

I should now like to pass on to more specific comments. Martin Bronfenbrenner thinks that the two policy doctrines under discussion are 'to a great extent rivals, the first stressing exports, the second domestic production'. But that is because he is able to detect in redistribution with growth a central and powerful idea: appropriate technology or 'output mixes'. If that is indeeed the case, it has escaped me. My interpretation of how the RwG doctrine is being interpreted in practice is that *growth* is to be produced by the usual route of modern but labour-intensive investments in a 'formal' sector which, lacking domestic markets, is increasingly turning towards exports, while *redistribution* is to be effected by channelling some surplus from growth primarily towards medium and small-scale farming and general rural development, though the amounts are insufficient to make a noticeable difference. The World Bank, in particular, is helping to finance some expensive rural projects that succeed in raising production and improving the incomes of a small number of successful peasants (as well as generating 'multipliers', though most of them tend to be captured by the major cities). What does not seem to be realized is that these capital-intensive projects suck in the bulk of rural investments, both national and foreign.[9] The rural 'growth pole' of Chainat in Thailand's rice bowl is a striking example. Here is a ten-year project to benefit 100,000 families. But as national energies are pumped into Chainat, the 3.5 million families in Thailand's poverty-stricken Northeast are perforce left to their own devices. Where efficiency and equity are divided, it is efficiency that usually wins all the arguments.

I should like to assure Professor Bronfenbrenner that I am neither a Stalinist well-poisoner nor a conspiracy theorist. I am simply asking whether the relatively easy ES and RwG doctrines, if conscientiously applied, could be expected to produce a major change in the conditions of powerlessness to which a billion people in the world periphery are still condemned. As we move into the twenty-first century, shall we continue to hear stories of landless Indian peasants who mortgage members of their family to work as indentured servants in the household of their money-lender? A look at what is actually happening in India and elsewhere is, to say the least, not reassuring on this point.

With Hans Singer, my quarrels seem to be mainly semantic. I object to the term target population for two reasons: first, because it betrays a technocratic cast of mind and second, because where the great majority are poor, something more is needed than client-specific policies carefully stitched together into a programme acceptable to the ruling elites. No, I do not advocate revolution for the same reasons, I think, that Mr. Singer doesn't. But isn't there something more that could be demanded than a politics of muddling through? Surgery may be necessary for a patient suffering from cancer (though the patient has the right of refusal) and radical or structural reforms may be necessary for social formations half of whose population live below a poverty level defined by survival. Countries, too, have the right of refusal, but it is the physician's responsibility to advocate the course of action he/she believes is essential to the patient's recovery.

I turn now to Gustav Ranis's 'reluctant' rebuttal. He begins by faulting me for ignorance and proceeds by accusing me of malice. On the first charge, I shall enter a plea of *nolo contendere*. I admit that my language in the lead-in paragraphs, because extremely condensed, is open to some misinterpretation. Specifically, however, I did *not* say that Joseph Schumpeter advocated channelling the social surplus to a minority of entrepreneurs. That argument was made by Arthur Lewis and W. W. Rostow to justify their advocacy of transitional growth with inequality. Equity in distribution would come at a later point in time, when the economy had gained maturity.[10]

On the second charge, I want to assure Professor Ranis that I have no intention of impugning his motives. My comments were directed at published documents, and at the meanings they conveyed to me. I tried to be fair in my quotations (though I admit to the inaccuracy reported in Professor Ranis's footnote on the importance of foreign capital in the Philippine economy). As I pointed out, the bulk of my quotations are from the Paauw-Fei volume's summary pages 115 to 117, from which they are taken without a break; they are, in fact, an

I should like to assure Professor Bronfenbrenner that I am neither a Stalinist well-poisoner nor a conspiracy theorist. I am simply asking whether the relatively easy ES and RwG doctrines, if conscientiously applied, could be expected to produce a major change in the conditions of powerlessness to which a billion people in the world periphery are still condemned. As we move into the twenty-first century, shall we continue to hear stories of landless Indian peasants who mortgage members of their family to work as indentured servants in the household of their money-lender? A look at what is actually happening in India and elsewhere is, to say the least, not reassuring on this point.

With Hans Singer, my quarrels seem to be mainly semantic. I object to the term target population for two reasons: first, because it betrays a technocratic cast of mind and second, because where the great majority are poor, something more is needed than client-specific policies carefully stitched together into a programme acceptable to the ruling elites. No, I do not advocate revolution for the same reasons, I think, that Mr. Singer doesn't. But isn't there something more that could be demanded than a politics of muddling through? Surgery may be necessary for a patient suffering from cancer (though the patient has the right of refusal) and radical or structural reforms may be necessary for social formations half of whose population live below a poverty level defined by survival. Countries, too, have the right of refusal, but it is the physician's responsibility to advocate the course of action he/she believes is essential to the patient's recovery.

I turn now to Gustav Ranis's 'reluctant' rebuttal. He begins by faulting me for ignorance and proceeds by accusing me of malice. On the first charge, I shall enter a plea of *nolo contendere*. I admit that my language in the lead-in paragraphs, because extremely condensed, is open to some misinterpretation. Specifically, however, I did *not* say that Joseph Schumpeter advocated channelling the social surplus to a minority of entrepreneurs. That argument was made by Arthur Lewis and W. W. Rostow to justify their advocacy of transitional growth with inequality. Equity in distribution would come at a later point in time, when the economy had gained maturity.[10]

On the second charge, I want to assure Professor Ranis that I have no intention of impugning his motives. My comments were directed at published documents, and at the meanings they conveyed to me. I tried to be fair in my quotations (though I admit to the inaccuracy reported in Professor Ranis's footnote on the importance of foreign capital in the Philippine economy). As I pointed out, the bulk of my quotations are from the Paauw-Fei volume's summary pages 115 to 117, from which they are taken without a break; they are, in fact, an the quality of social relations, human dignity, and democratic partici-pation become the true indicators of national progress. But this re-quires a political solution.

Notes

I wish to thank the United Nations Centre for Regional Development in Nagoya, Japan, for staff assistance in preparing this reply.

1. India, Planning Commission, Draft Five Year Plan 1978–83, Vol. 1 (Docu-ment prepared for National Conference on Development Goals and Strat-egies for India: the Next Decade, New Delhi, 28–31 Marhch 1978), 10.
2. Hamza Alavi, 'The Rural Elite and Agricultural Development in Pakistan', in Robert Stevens, Hamza Alavi, and Peter Bertocci (eds.), Rural Devel-opment in Bangladesh and Pakistan (Honolulu: The University Press of Hawaii, 1976), 336.
3. A. R. Khan, 'Poverty and Inequality in Rural Bangladesh', in ILO, Poverty and Landlessness in Rural Asia (Geneva: ILO, 1977), 153.
4. Ingrid Palmer, 'Rural Poverty in Indonesia with Special Reference to Java', in ILO, Poverty and Landlessness in Rural Asia, 211.
5. Ma. Alcestis S. Abrera, 'Philippine Poverty Thresholds', in Mahar Man-ganas (ed.), Measuring Philippine Development (Manila: The Development Academy of the Philippines, 1976), 243–44.
6. M. Krongkaew and C. Choensiri, 'Determination of the Poverty Band in Thailand', Warasarn Thammasat, 5: 1 (June-Sept. 1518), 48–69, and Na-tional Statistical Office, Thailand, Report on Socio-economic Survey 1968/69 and 1971/73 (Bangkok, n.d.).
7. Dudley Seers, 'The New Meaning of Development', International devel-opment Review, XIX, 3 (1977), 2–7.
8. Paul Streeten writes: 'In the thirties and forties of this century, just as in the discussions of the last century, one school of rehabilitators [of welfare economics] attempted to separate production (including exchange) from distribution, and thus "efficiency" from "equity" or "justice", and to render pronouncements on "efficiency" (= or the sphere of production) non-controversial (= subject to interest harmony). The critics again em-phasized that "efficiency" and "justice" cannot be separated conceptually and that interest conflicts cannot be sidestepped by such devices'. 'Appen-dix: Recent Controversies', in G. Myrdal, The Political Element in the Development of Economic Theory (Cambridge, Mass.: Harvard Univer-sity Press, 1955. Original German version, 1932).
9. Typical World Bank projects in rural development cost from $1,200 to $68,000 per beneficiary family, and the number of families involved is rarely more than 100,000. See Agricultural Land Settlement (A World Bank Issues Paper. January 1978), Annexes 1 and 2.
10. Thus, W. Arthur Lewis: '. . . it is certainly true that a developing economy needs large profits if it is to have an adequate level of savings . . .' And: 'For the essential change is rather the emergence of a new class in society—the profit-making entrepreneur—which is more thrifty than all the other classes (the landlords, the wage earners, the peasants, the salaried middle classes), and whose share of national income increases

relatively to that of others'. And: 'Finally, economic growth may be deplored insofar as it depends on inequality in income. That this dependence exists cannot be denied since growth would be small or negative if differential awards were not available for hard work, for conscientious work, for skill, for responsibility and for initiative. It is arguable in any given situation whether the existing differentials are too great or too small, in the restricted sense of being greater or less than is required to achieve the desired rate of economic growth. But it is not arguable . . . that significant economic growth could be achieved even if there were no differentials at all . . .' *The Theory of Economic Growth* (Homewood, Ill.: Richard D. Irwin, 1955), 101; 226; and 428–9).

This traditional case for meritorious inequality is echoed by W. W. Rostow: 'The notion of economic development occurring as a result of income shifts from those who will spend (hoard of lend) less productively to those who will spend (or lend) more productively is one of the oldest and most fundamental notions in economics. It is basic, for example, to the *Wealth of Nations'*. *The Stages of Economic Growth*. A Non-Communist Maniffesto (Cambridge: University Press, 1961), 47. But all that ends, ends well. 'As societies achieved maturity in the twentieth century two things happened: real income per head rose to a point where a large number of persons gained a command over consumption which transcended basic food, shelter, and clothing; and the structure of the working force changed in ways which increased not only the proportion of urban to total population, but also the proportion of the population working in offices or in skilled factory jobs—aware of and anxious to acquire the consumption fruits of a mature economy . . . It is in this post-maturity stage . . . that, through the political process, Western societies have chosen to allocate increased resources to social welfare and security. The emergence of the welfare state is one manifestation of a society's moving beyond technical maturity. . . .' (Ibid, 10–11).

11. ILO, Yearbook of Labour Statistics (1976).
12. FAO, Production Yearbook (1976).

Index

Printed in the United States
by Baker & Taylor Publisher Services

Printed in the United States
by Baker & Taylor Publisher Services